1,001
Old-Time
Garden
Tips

1,001 Old-Time Garden Tips

Timeless Bits of Wisdom on How to Grow Everything Organically, from the Good Old Days When Everyone Did

Roger Yepsen
Editor

RODALE

Library of Congress Cataloging-in-Publication Data

1001 old-time garden tips : timeless bits of wisdom on
     how to grow everything organically, from the good old days
     when everyone did / Roger Yepsen, editor.
          p.   cm.
     Includes bibliographical references and index.
     ISBN 0–87596–766–3 hardcover
     ISBN 0–87596–917–8 paperback
     1. Organic gardening—Miscellanea.   2. Gardening—
Miscellanea.   I. Yepsen, Roger B.   II. Title: One thousand
one old-time garden tips.   III. Title: One thousand and one
old-time garden tips.
SB453.5.A15   1997
635'.0484—dc21   97–4681

Distributed to the book trade by St. Martin's Press

     4   6   8   10   9   7   5   hardcover
2   4   6   8   10   9   7   5   3   1   paperback

We're always happy to hear from you. For questions or comments concerning the editorial content of this book, please write to:

Rodale Book Readers' Service
33 East Minor Street
Emmaus, PA 18098

Look for other Rodale books wherever books are sold. Or call us at (800) 848-4735.

For more information about Rodale Organic Living magazines and books, visit our Web site at:
     www.organicgardening.com

Project Editor: Joan Benjamin
Interior Book Designer: Karen Coughlin
Interior Illustrators: Julia S. Child, pages 3, 4, 11, 12, 13, 15, 18, 20, 26, 27, 35, 36, 42, 43, 44, 47, 49, 53, 54, 55, 62, 77, 78, 96, 109, 110, 120, 123, 129, 130, 132, 134, 143, 146, 148, 155, 162, 163, 164, 169, 179, 185, 195, 196, 197, 204, 205, 206, 207, 209, 215, 222, 225, 227, 229, 244, 254, 258, 264, 272, 277, 278, 281, 282, 284, 295, 297, 298, 300, 301, 304, 305, 309; Jen Miller, pages 24, 28, 29, 38, 39, 71, 79, 116, 125, 173, 175, 269, 274, 281, 299, 300, 309, 310, 311, 312, 314, 315; Gwendolyn Wong, pages x, 1, 16, 17, 30, 31, 82, 83, 114, 115, 166, 167, 192, 193, 230, 231, 240, 241, 266, 267, 292, 293, 306, 307
Cover Designers: Karen Coughlin (hardcover); Patricia Field (paperback)
Cover Illustrator: Gwendolyn Wong
Technical Artists: Karen Lomax, Dale Mack
Senior Research Associate: Heidi A. Stonehill
Copy Editors: Sara Cox, Mary Ellen Raposa
Manufacturing Coordinator: Melinda Rizzo
Indexer: Lina Burton
Editorial Assistance: Rebecca S. McElheny, Susan L. Nickol, Jodi Rehl, Lori Schaffer

Rodale Organic Living Books

Executive Editor: Margot Schupf
Art Director: Patricia Field
Content Assembly Manager: Robert V. Anderson Jr.
Copy Manager: Nancy N. Bailey
Editorial Assistant: Sara Sellar

The publishers have generously given permission to use quotations from the following copyrighted works. Reprinted with permission of Macmillan USA, a Simon & Schuster Macmillan Company, from *The Fragrant Path* by Louise Beebe Wilder (New York: Macmillan, 1932). From *The English Flower Garden*, by William Robinson, reprint of the 15th edition, 1933 orig. Sagaponack, NY: Sagapress 1995.

Acknowledgments

I'd like to thank the librarians who generously gave their time to help me search out the historic sources used in this book. I'd also like to thank the organizations that opened their library doors for me: Longwood Gardens, the Pennsylvania Horticultural Society, Rodale Inc., and the Schwenkfelder Library.

Contents

About This Book

Gardeners are always full of questions. How can I stretch the growing season to get more vegetables? What are the best plants for dry shade? Are there good shrubs for late-summer color? And, invariably, do you know a good recipe for green tomatoes? Fortunately, other gardeners are always ready to offer advice. It's been that way for centuries, judging by the number of how-to garden books and magazines published from the seventeenth through the early twentieth centuries.

What You'll Find

In *1,001 Old-Time Garden Tips* I've gathered together the best wisdom from these past generations of gardeners. Like you, the authors of these hints were always looking for better ways to deal with weather, pests, and plant diseases. They found lots of great solutions that worked for them and that will work for you, too. How can that be? Take a look. You'll quickly discover that though garden styles may change from year to year, the challenges and pleasures stay the same.

After some tips, I've added an editor's note with a word of explanation about a technique or plant. In other notes, I've referred you to mail-order sources for the plants these old-time garden writers were so enthusiastic about—heirloom vegetables, fruits, and flowers in an incredible range of colors, flavors, and scents. By growing these plants, your garden becomes something of a time

machine. You'll feel a kinship with gardeners of past centuries. The same sun warmed their backs, after all, and they enjoyed plants with tastes and colors you can still enjoy today.

This book is arranged by topic, with chapters such as Vegetables, Herbs and Home Remedies, and Flowers designed to help you find the information you need. Multiple entries within a topic are listed alphabetically. Most of the tips

are practical, but just for fun, I've included a scattering of impractical advice under the heading "Strange But True." Look for the "Old-Time Wisdom" headings if you want to find classic gardening advice from famous and not-so-famous gardeners, and be sure to sample the tasty old-time recipes that appear throughout the book.

You'll find the addresses and phone numbers for mail-order nurseries that offer hard-to-find heirloom plants and tools in the "Sources" list at the back of the book. The "Recommended Reading" list that follows "Sources" includes all of the publications used to compile this book.

Please note that I abridged some of the quoted material and modernized some of the spelling and grammar to make the tips easier to read—early garden writers tended to be long-winded.

Some Things Never Change

If your ancestors could visit your home, the sight of your high-tech appliances and utilities would send them into instant future shock. But as you led them into your yard, they would feel immediately at ease. In spite of hybridizing and genetic manipulation, your plants aren't so different from those grown a century or two ago.

Today, gardeners are busy growing mesclun salad greens and switching annual flower beds into gardens of perennials. These are old, tested ideas; more than a century ago, garden writers were busy explaining the advantages of both. Even our current gardening styles are largely recycled. For example, publications of the mid-1800s were big on natural landscaping, much as we are today. And as early as 1712, when most of North America was wilderness, British garden writers were explaining how to create a "natural wilderness" in the yard.

Every several decades, it seems, gardeners get tired of jumbled, busy designs, and look to the simpler gardens of the past for inspiration. On these pages, you'll find tips on using wildflowers, single blossoms (rather than fancy double blooms), subtle colors, and foliage plants as cures for a yard that looks a little frantic.

Long before commuter flights and cellular phones came along, gardeners were using their green spaces as refuges from stress. Gardening magazines of the late 1800s ran statistics to show that only ministers had longer average life spans than flower lovers. This confirmed the centuries-old belief that plants have special powers to relieve ills of the body and mind. It wasn't even necessary to make a tea or special potion to enjoy this cure; you could simply wear a garland of an aromatic plant, or lie down in the garden and inhale.

Family Gardening

Back in the days of simpler amusements, the garden was often the center of family life. People of all ages worked and relaxed there, raising plants for food and drink, as well as for handicrafts, home decorations, and gifts. Trellises and arbors were cloaked with vines to make outdoor rooms with natural air conditioning. A sundial was as much a fixture of the garden as a coffee table is to our living rooms. Birdwatching and nature study were popular pastimes.

But young people, then as now, were eager to look elsewhere for excitement. Garden writers suggested to parents that the home would be more inviting to children if there were curious flowers, plentiful berries, hidden nooks among the hedges, and wildlife all about. Several of these notions are included in this book. And you'll find ideas on gardening as a community activity, too.

May This Book Inspire You!

I've compiled the tips in this book in the hope that you will be inspired to make more and better use of your yard. The ideas that follow are reminders of the many roles a garden can play—as a source of food and flowers, of course, and also as a sanctuary, a nature preserve, and a place for the family to be together.

Roger Yepsen
Editor

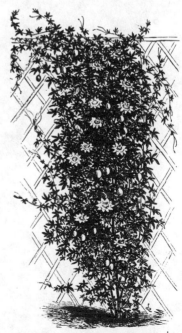

Planning Your Yard and Garden

What do you need to create beautiful flower beds and lush lawns? Proven design tricks! Let old-time gardeners supply the solutions, whether you want to make your yard look bigger or smaller, hide eyesores, or win praise from neighbors.

Planning Your Yard and Garden

Design Ideas That Work

Lay Out a Larger Yard

If a ready-made house has not been purchased, the owner of the plot will find it worth his while to build either close to the street or close to the rear boundary of his domain. This will leave the full extent of un-occupied ground with which to work. Let the house not be set in the middle of the plot.

Amelia Leavitt Hill
Garden Portraits, 1923

Simple Is Better

In planning, strive to get simple broad effects instead of startling ones. The novelty, in time, passes away by the latter method and a more restful, homelike, and less expensive result is secured by the former plan.

Herbert J. Kellaway
How to Lay Out Suburban Home Grounds, 1915

Less Looks like More

It may be laid down as a general rule that much elaboration makes the small place seem smaller; while the man or woman who can keep the small place simple and tasteful has, in such very forbearance, an aid to beauty by means of which wonders can be done.

Amelia Leavitt Hill
Garden Portraits, 1923

Plan Before You Plant

Go into the woods and fields and find out for yourself what manner of plants thrive in your locality. Visit nearby nurseries—nurserymen don't mind in the least you coming, whether you buy or not; in this way, you can make a personal acquaintance with the plants at their season for receiving visitors. Take a large piece of brown paper and put a plan of your place on it, tack it up somewhere, then as you see a shrub or plant you like, mark each name down on your plan just where you think you would like to put it.

Frances Duncan
The Joyous Art of Gardening, 1917

Editor's Note: Getting to know plants before you add them to your landscape saves lots of time and trouble. If you see how trees, shrubs, and flowers look before you plant, you'll know which areas of your yard they'll look best in. Visit public gardens and arboretums in addition to nurseries so you can become acquainted with a wide variety of plants.

Make a plan using pictures you've cut out of seed and nursery catalogs so you can tell at a glance how plant sizes, colors, and shapes go together.

Dark Paint Hides a Treeless House

In proportion as a house is exposed to view, let its hue be darker, and where it is much concealed by foliage, a very light shade of color is to be preferred.

Andrew Jackson Downing
The Architecture of Country Houses, 1850

Editor's Note: Downing's writings on landscape gardening made him the foremost American tastemaker of the Victorian era.

Dense foliage, light-colored paint

Sparse foliage, dark-colored paint

The denser the foliage around the house, the lighter the wall color should be. Pale siding will do a better job of showing off thickly planted trees and shrubs.

In the Yard, Avoid Extremes

Mankind generally runs to extremes. Landscape gardening confirms this. The old system of squaring all walks, carrying them at right angles, shearing and clipping every tree, was so very absurd that in the revulsion of ideas that followed, a *line* in any way became an unpardonable offense against the new creed. Let it be the work of our generation to make extremes meet. Utility is the basis on which all ornament in nature rests.

Thomas Meehan
The Horticulturist, 1852

Combine Utility and Beauty

The double purpose of a garden—for use and pleasure—has been forgotten in landscape gardening. You either get a kitchen garden useful but ugly, or a pleasure garden not useful, and only redeemed from ugliness by the flowers themselves. The charm of the older garden is in the combination of the two.

Harry Roberts
The Book of Old-Fashioned Flowers, 1904

Editor's Note: You can make a vegetable garden beautiful and a flower garden useful. Try mixing edible flowers in with your vegetables and planting a border of red-leaved lettuce or herbs around a flower bed.

Don't Dot Your Lawn Trees

The dotting system consists in placing a number of objects in nearly equidistant positions, without reference to their intrinsic or relative importance. On the lawns of many gardens this paltry and tasteless system has been carried out to the greatest perfection. In short, *grouping* is everywhere productive of interest and beauty; *dotting*, of insipid monotony and languor.

Charles H. J. Smith
Parks and Pleasure Grounds,
1852

There's No Need to Plant beneath Trees

Gardeners have a quite unnecessary panic if the bole (trunk) of a tree is not hidden by shrubbery, and if nothing whatever is planted beneath, and yet half of a tree's beauty is in the outline of stem and branches balanced by the quiet stretch of greensward beneath. If grass will not grow, the trees when left to themselves will usually provide a very charming carpet of brown dead leaves and little hardy ferns, but to attempt flower beds underneath them is a mistake—both trees and plants will be unhappy, and the trees will do their best to prevent you. But you can plant lilies-of-the-valley, and tuck into the ground any quantity of early-flowering

bulbs which will come up year after year.

Frances Duncan
The Joyous Art of Gardening,
1917

Create Suspense in Your Landscape

Many objects on the place may be partially concealed by planting all with the view of exciting the curiosity to know how much more is beyond.

The Gardener's Monthly, 1874

Editor's Note: In other words, use gently curving walks that invite you to see what's around the corner, and stagger plantings to give an impression of depth. Try diagramming your yard and plotting the sight lines—how far a person can see from certain windows of the house, from the patio, from the street. By interrupting some of these sight lines with trees, shrubs, and structures, you can increase visitors' curiosity about what lies on the other side.

Grow a Cool Landscape

In laying out and designing country places, one of the chief studies should be how to make a place agreeable even in the hottest weather. It is somewhat remarkable that with the great love of shady spots, which our climate excites in all of us, more attention is not given to making bowers of living trees. There is nothing better than the weeping ash (*Fraxinus excelsior* 'Pendula'). The branches can be trained over wires, and thus we can make the room beneath the tree as extensive as we could wish. For very large spots, a half dozen or so trees can be used. Set in one circle, and the trees about twenty feet apart. Such an arrangement would make a delightful place for parties and picnics—entirely in the shade, yet with an abundance of room and air all around.

The Gardener's Monthly, 1872

Editor's Note: Homeowners of the 1800s were intrigued with training trees. For other projects, see "Tree 'Houses'" on page 200.

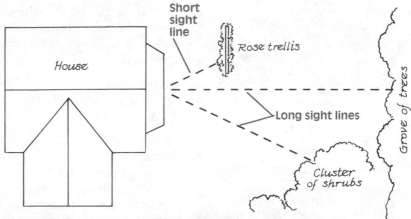

A combination of long and short lines of sight creates more interest in your yard than a single view.

Gardening under a Crabapple

Here is a full-flowered crabapple tree, *Malus ioensis* (Bechtel's double-flowering crab), like a great bouquet against the gray garden wall. Beneath the spread of its wreathed branches are groups of May iris—the old purple flag and the French gray florentina (*Iris florentina*); and scattered all about are pink and cherry-colored tulips—all Darwins. At the other side of the garden is another crabapple spreading its branches above a group of delicately flushed tulips that rise from a waving sea of forget-me-nots.

Louise Beebe Wilder
Colour in My Garden, 1918

Editor's Note: Bechtel's double-flowering crab (*Malus ioensis* 'Plena') is a variety of a native species. It continues to be a popular ornamental tree for American yards even though it's very susceptible to diseases like rust. Try a more disease-resistant variety like *M. ioensis* 'Klehm's' for a similar effect with less maintenance.

Enjoy a Patterned Lawn

The study of tree shadows upon a well-kept lawn has never received the consideration which it deserves, but charming effects are produced thereby.

Amelia Leavitt Hill
Garden Portraits, 1923

OLD-TIME WISDOM

On handling criticism. Don't be cast down by adverse criticism unless your judgment tells you it is deserved. The person who "knows it all" is never so much at home as in someone else's flower garden, where the principal labor may be done with the tongue.

Ida D. Bennett
The Flower Garden, 1904

Living Lawn Ornaments

Cattle, sheep, and deer, grazing or else reclining in the shade, contribute an effect to scenes that without them would be tame.

Elias A. Long
Ornamental Gardening for Americans, 1884

You may not want "lawn ornaments" that are quite this lively, but you can certainly add the cutout or statuary versions to create a pleasant scene.

Spare the Axe, Spoil the Yard

When a fine tree interferes with the beauty of something else, then their rival claims should be carefully weighed, and if the tree prove the lighter in the balance, it should be sacrificed as willingly as one would scrape a second-rate painting off a wall if Michelangelo's hand were waiting to cover it afresh. Our attitude toward trees today is not rationally artistic; it is purely sentimental. Not once in twenty times does an owner recognize the fact when his pleasure grounds need to be relieved of a tree. A bleeding stump may almost make a heart bleed for the moment, but the wound will be quickly healed by the increased beauty of the trees which remain.

Mariana Van Rensselaer
Art Out-of-Doors, 1893

Know Thy Lot

On a place of any size it is of inestimable benefit to have lived there for a time or to know it thoroughly before selecting the site for the garden.

Julia H. Cummins
My Garden Comes of Age, 1926

Editor's Note: So, what do you do in the meantime? You can try interesting effects with annuals. Or place perennials and shrubs with an experimental attitude, knowing you'll want to shift some around within a couple of years.

Set Your Sights from a Height

The ridiculous idea occurred to me to have the garden as a picture to be looked at from the house alone. The result was nothing but an ugly muddle—indescribably so when one happened to be in the midst of the garden itself. For two or three years I bore with this unhappy condition of things; when, chancing to look down upon the garden from an upper window, the real state of things suddenly revealed itself, and from that day I set about to plan and plant in a totally different fashion. I have come to see that balanced planting throughout is the only planting for a garden that has any design worth the name.

Louisa King
The Well-Considered Garden, 1915

Take a High View

One of the easiest ways for the amateur to determine and decide on his outlines for gardens is to mark out the proposed beds with white tape, or the like, then go to an upper window and look down on it. He can tell at a glance whether the paths are too wide or too narrow or if the beds are in the right relation, and it is a simple matter to have these tentative boundaries shifted until it "looks right."

Frances Duncan
The Joyous Art of Gardening, 1917

OLD-TIME WISDOM

Enjoy your mistakes! For my part, I like to go my own wild way in my garden, and do things wrong, and find out my mistakes by myself. Nature and Robinson, alone, will furnish all the instruction any one can ask for.

Rose Fay Thomas
Our Mountain Garden, 1904

Editor's Note: And who is this Robinson? Through his best-selling *The English Flower Garden* and other books, William Robinson (1838–1935) introduced thousands of gardeners to an informal style of gardening, based on large drifts of perennials and wildflowers.

Don't Break Up the Lawn with Beds

In the North, from October until June—eight months in the year—island beds are brown, unsightly objects. The same flowers planted near the house, against a background of vines, or in border beds with shrubs behind them, are infinitely more at home.

Frances Duncan
The Joyous Art of Gardening, 1917

Editor's Note: Island beds are plantings surrounded by lawn. They have their place, especially when you want to screen off a view or create privacy. If you plant island beds only with annual and perennial flowers, you'll end up with the brown look Duncan despises. Add evergreen shrubs to your island beds to have color all year long.

Strange But True

In London, England, if a man improves his lot and his next door neighbor does not, the improver gets a reduction on his tax, and the non-improver a rise. This is rather a good idea, and when carried out, must tend to greatly improve the appearance of towns and villages.

The Household, 1879

Editor's Note: If only it were still true! Of course, then there'd be the problem of getting everyone to agree on what was an improvement or wasn't.

Keep the Lawn Clear

Place your flower beds along the walks, at the house, or along the lot lines, but do not clutter the center of your lawn with them. An open grass plot adds apparent size and dignity to any place.

W. C. Egan
Making a Garden of Perennials, 1912

Take a Tip from Nature

In designing the planting it is a good idea to study nature. Walk along the roadside or in the fields, and observe how masses are formed by the intermingling of the various trees and shrubs. These have character and grouping that is often artistically perfect.

Herbert J. Kellaway
How to Lay Out Suburban Home Grounds, 1915

Editor's Note: While you're out for your stroll, bring along a little notebook for jotting down nature observations.

A Little Bit of Everything

I have several acres about my house, which I call my garden, and which a skillful gardener would not know what to call. It is a confusion of kitchen and parterre, orchard and flower garden, which lie so mixed and interwoven with one another that if a foreigner who had seen nothing of our country should be conveyed into my garden at his first landing, he would look upon it as a natural wilderness.

Joseph Addison
Spectator, 1712

Editor's Note: A parterre is a collection of beds and paths laid out in a geometric pattern.

Don't Forget the Roadside

Let me introduce you to a new kind of gardening which will cost nothing, which you can begin right now, and which, I guarantee, will yield you more pleasure, for the time and effort expended, than anything you have ever done before. The name of this new type of floriculture is roadside wild gardening.

Spend the equivalent of one day's time in beautifying one portion of the roadway that you use daily. The best vines for roadsides are Virginia creeper for its brilliant autumn foliage, wild grape for its fragrant blossoms and pretty small berries, trumpet creeper for its large orange blossoms which attract the hummingbirds, wild honeysuckle for fragrance, wild clematis for its clouds of white flowers and silky seeds, and bittersweet for its red berries that last all winter.

The following shrubs will furnish flowers from March to September in the order named: spicebush, redbud, sheep or mountain laurel (*Kalmia angustifolia*), red elderberry, blue false indigo (*Baptisia australis*), sumac, Hercules club (*Aralia spinosa*), and witch hazel.

The following perennials are easily obtained because they multiply so fast in gardens that everybody has some to give away: Boltonia (*Boltonia asteroides*), beebalm, sneezeweed (*Helenium* spp.), New England aster, perennial sunflower, spiderwort (*Tradescantia* spp.), sweet rocket (*Hesperis matronalis*), mint, and thyme.

Thomas McAdam
The Garden Magazine, 1908

The trumpet creeper is an excellent roadside plant, needing no attention from you, but attracting admirers and hummingbirds with its large orange and scarlet, trumpet-shaped blooms. The roadside may be the best place for this vigorous clinging vine. It can grow to 40 feet tall and thrives in all types of soil.

Give Wild Woodies a Home of Their Own

One little rule may be found valuable. It is best to segregate wild or native material from the purely gardenesque (ornamental plants). The various native viburnums and cornels, *Pyrus arbutifolia* (red chokeberry), and native thorns will assemble into well-unified enclosures, for instance, while such gardenesque plants as snowballs and lilacs, mock-oranges and deutzias and spireas, get along nicely together.

Elsa Rehman
Garden-Making, 1926

Editor's Note: Cornels refers to the *Cornus* spp., which include dogwoods and bunchberry.

A Garden to Relax in

Space ought to be allotted as a reserve garden, a place where escape can be obtained both mentally and morally, from the ambition of producing the largest fruit or striking varieties.

Thomas H. Mawson
The Art and Craft of Garden Making, 1907

Not All Nice Effects Are Planned

Passing an unoccupied house with its little twenty-by-twenty-foot grass plot in front, with no tender fingers to weed the garden, we saw a burdock had possession of the center.

The yellow celandine, some stray branches of honeysuckle, and other homely things had grown among and over the leaves. It was a charming sight.

Meehans' Monthly, 1895

For an Old-Time Garden, Relax

A bit of real untidiness may be justified at times. Our gardens are apt to look too well swept. A rosy pool of fallen crabapple petals or a snowy field of fallen plum blossoms may be welcome. Our gardens are apt to be too trim. Let the grass grow between the broken stone of the walks and let it be vernal grass (*Anthoxanthum odoratum*) so that you may crush it into fragrance underfoot. Let a hundred little rock plants and trailers grow between the stones and let edging plants grow in tangled masses over the edges of the walks. For there is real charm in blurring the edges of a garden. It is these things that make a garden appear as if it had always been there.

Elsa Rehman
Garden-Making, 1926

What to Plant?

Grow no plant which does not strike you as either beautiful or interesting.

Harry Roberts
The Book of Old-Fashioned Flowers, 1904

What *Not* to Plant in an Old-Time Garden

First to avoid are these: highly colored maples, variegated evergreens, trees such as the weeping mulberry, crimson rambler roses, *Hydrangea paniculata* var. *grandiflora*, and cannas. These would spoil the atmosphere of an old-fashioned garden as conclusively as a gas range would spoil the effect of a Colonial kitchen.

Frances Duncan
The Joyous Art of Gardening, 1917

Editor's Note: The weeping mulberry that Duncan prefers to keep in modern gardens is actually not a mulberry at all but a catalpa, *Catalpa bignonioides* 'Nana'. This dwarf, bushy form of the southern catalpa is usually grafted on a straight trunk to form a tree with an umbrella-like head. It makes an interesting novelty but doesn't produce the spotted flowers and long, bean-like seed capsules of the species.

If at First You Don't Succeed...

It is a good plan, when a plant supposedly easy to grow fails to materialize, to try it in another part of your own garden, and if it does not do well there, discard and forget it—the world is full of good things.

W. C. Egan
Making a Garden of Perennials, 1912

Rural Plants May Not Make It in the City

The city gardener lays stress on what the horticulturists call "habit," that excellence of form and character which is to a plant what good manners are in the social equipment of a person. Some of the plants most brilliant in their time of flowering are not good to look at in the off season, and there is no way of making them retire from the stage. This narrowly limited space of the town garden demands a certain finish, a correctness of demeanor; a loose, careless growth wholly charming on a country roadside is here out of place.

Frances Duncan
The Joyous Art of Gardening, 1917

Sixteenth-Century Raised Beds

The author of *The Gardener's Labyrinth* (1577) advises that beds should be kept to such a size as that "the weeder's hands may well reach into the middest of the bed"; twelve feet by six is given as the size. Each bed was to be raised about one foot above the ground. The edges were to be cased in with stout planks framed into square posts with finials (decorative pieces) at the angles, with intermediate supports.

Reginald Blomfield and
F. Inigo Thomas
The Formal Garden in England, 1892

Inspired Gardening

If you would inspire your own children, then draw about you such an array of beauty as no one but the cultivator of the soil can collect. When building the fence, let it be beautiful as well as substantial. While arranging your vegetable gardens and orchards, do not overlook geometrical regularity. Do not, on any account, omit the planting of flowers and the various kinds of fruit trees.

Anonymous
Ten Acres Enough, 1864

Editor's Note: This book is the ancestor of today's gardening books but was criticized at the time for making gardening sound like a weekend hobby. *American Agriculturist* magazine complained, "The horticultural novels of a few years ago, of which *Ten Acres Enough* was the forerunner, have done a world of harm, by conveying the idea that one, brought up to a city life, can with great ease drop into the cultivation of fruits, vegetables, or flowers and at once reap large profits."

The Enabling Garden

In all families there are invalids at some time or other, and a great object is to render the garden an alleviation to their sufferings. The designer ought to contrive gently inclined planes instead of steps or stairs, and to avoid all corners in walks and paths.

J. C. Loudon
An Encyclopedia of Gardening, 1850

Tall Bellflowers for Containers

All those whose houses are surrounded by terraces will find great interest in growing a succession of plants in pots for decoration; half a dozen pots of a kind would be sufficient unless the terrace is very large. The tall-growing chimney bellflower (*Campanula pyramidalis*) is especially beautiful. Large, strong plants, one year old in May, if potted and fed often, will be six feet high by the second week in August, and remain covered with either white or blue blossoms for a month.

Helena Rutherfurd Ely
The Practical Flower Garden, 1911

Many bellflowers grow only ½ to 1 foot tall, but you can create dramatic effects with varieties that grow to 4 feet and higher. In addition to the chimney bellflower, try milky bellflower (*Campanula lactiflora*), which reaches 3 to 4 feet in height, and the great bellflower (*C. latifolia*), which is 2 to 5 feet tall when fully grown.

9

Guard against Propagation Mania

It is always a temptation, when seeds sprout, and runners put forth from precious shrubs, to save the healthy little treasures by enlarging old beds, or adding new ones. But it is very easy to ruin one's effects instead of heightening them by too much decoration. It is like fussy trimming on a dress. If one has nobody to give the little plants to, then one must ruthlessly dig them up and throw them away.

Rose Fay Thomas
Our Mountain Garden, 1904

OLD-TIME WISDOM

The basic law of how-to. Finish one job before you begin another. This advice is trite, but it is of great importance; and there are few cases where it cannot be attended to.

J. C. Loudon
An Encyclopedia of Gardening, 1850

Why Not a Winter Garden?

I have often wondered that those who are like myself, and love to live in gardens, have never thought of contriving a winter garden, which would consist of such trees only as never cast their leaves. We have very often little snatches of sunshine and fair weather in the most uncomfortable parts of the year; and have frequently several days in November and January that are as agreeable as any in the finest months. At such times, therefore, I think there could not be a greater pleasure than to walk in such a winter garden as I have proposed. I have set aside a whole acre of ground. The walls are covered with ivy instead of deciduous vines. The laurel, the horn beam, and the holly, with many other trees and plants of the same nature, grow so thick in it that you cannot imagine a more lively scene.

Joseph Addison
Spectator, 1712

Great Garden Drainage

Excellent garden drains may be made by partially filling the ditch with stones, particularly if flat stones are to be had so that a conduit (channel) can be laid in the bottom. Such drains not only give the advantage of under-drainage, but also afford a means of disposing of superfluous stone.

L. H. Bailey
The Principles of Vegetable Gardening, 1901

Editor's Note: This drainage scheme works just as well in a flower garden. For a more ornamental look, plant the ditch edges with water-loving plants.

Visual Tricks

Crops Cut View of Neighbors

If your lot is directly against your neighbor's, with not even a fence between, screen it by planting rows of corn with the tall and rather coarse white of the tobacco plant (*Nictotiana*) in front of it, and blue cornflowers (*Centaurea cyanus*); this would give you a pleasing combination.

Frances Duncan
The Joyous Art of Gardening, 1917

Expand Your Property with Optical Illusions

It is possible by slightly converging the boundary lines of a garden, perhaps by making paths somewhat smaller at a distance than they are near at hand, to give an exaggerated appearance of length to a garden through its apparently great diminution in perspective. A similar exaggeration may be brought about by using trees in the distance which, while apparently full grown, are really smaller than might be expected.

Henry Vincent Hubbard and Theodora Kimball
An Introduction to the Study of Landscape Design, 1929

Strange But True

Green turns blue with distance. A good way of showing this is to tear a roundish hole in any large bright green leaf, such as a burdock, and to hold it at half-arm's length so that a part of a distant landscape is seen through the hole, and the eye sees also the whole surface of the leaf.

Gertrude Jekyll
Home and Garden, 1900

How to Make a Boulder Disappear

Where there are but few boulders and these not more than three or four feet in diameter, the quickest way to dispose of them is by burying them. Excavate a trench for a heavy stick or fence post, two feet longer than the stone is wide. With the supporting timber in place, a proper excavation may be made and the stone undermined to half its width at least. There will be no danger of its falling as long as the ends of the stick are firmly embedded in the banks as they should be. When the hole is of the proper depth to sink the boulder, the stick is removed by prying up one end.

American Agriculturist, 1894

Editor's Note: There's an easier solution to dealing with boulders: Turn them into garden features. Choose perennial plants that thrive in your soil and light conditions, and use them to set off the rocks. It's a simple way to create a natural-looking rock garden.

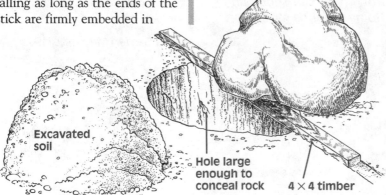

Excavated soil

Hole large enough to conceal rock

4 × 4 timber

Instead of hauling heavy boulders away from your garden, bury them. Dig out just enough soil to slip a fence post under the rock for support. Then dig a hole under the rock, pull out the timber, and presto—the rock drops out of sight.

Help for Small Plots

Much may be done for a small plot by making the surface irregular. A dead level, or a regular plane, looks smaller than it really is.

The Gardener's Monthly, 1874

Dark Looks Deeper

The depth of a recess or glade in the woods is much increased by planting trees and shrubs of a full green or dark green color at the point where the effect is desired.

Charles H. J. Smith
Parks and Pleasure Grounds, 1852

Use Color to Open Up Your Yard

Color may be used to give the more distant foliage a still greater effect of distance. For this result, plants of a warmer green would be placed nearer the observer, through various tones to distant foliage of a light and bluish hue.

Henry Vincent Hubbard and Theodora Kimball
An Introduction to the Study of Landscape Design, 1929

Editor's Note: Landscape painters use blue shades to create the illusion of depth on a flat canvas. To prove this effect for yourself, see the "Strange But True" tip on this page.

Bright Flowers by the House

Where the lawn approaches the house, beds of bright flowers may be introduced, but broken colors at the far end detract from the length. At that end shrub beds should generally be placed.

Henry Vincent Hubbard and Theodora Kimball
An Introduction to the Study of Landscape Design, 1929

Editor's Note: This visual trick works because the eye interprets areas of great contrast as being close up. Shrubs, with a quieter effect than mixed beds, look farther away.

Clematis to the Rescue

Plant the scented clematis against the pigsty.

J. C. Loudon
An Encyclopedia of Gardening, 1850

Editor's Note: Don't have a pigsty? Clematis can also create a fragrant screen for garbage cans or a shed. Train the vine up a lattice formed by nailing ready-made wooden sections to 4 × 4 posts sunk in the ground.

Plant "Distractions" Help Hide Views

Plants having strikingly unusual characters of growth or coloration of their foliage have a distinct place in landscape planting. Judiciously placed, these trees and shrubs render an important service in leading the line of sight away from undesirable objects that cannot well be hidden.

The Garden Magazine, 1905

Editor's Note: Trees and shrubs with twisted forms and unusual coloring have the power to distract viewers from features you'd rather not have them focus on. The corkscrew willow (*Salix matsudana* 'Tortuosa') and Harry Lauder's walkingstick (*Corylus avellana* 'Contorta') are two plants with unusually twisted branches that can easily capture viewers' attention.

Sizing a Screen

If the groups of plants are planted near the house, trees or shrubs of small size will often cut off objectionable views which would require much larger specimens if planted at greater distance, as shown.

Herbert J. Kellaway
How to Lay Out Suburban Home Grounds, 1915

Best Perennial Screen

The best hardy perennial for a screen is the plume poppy (*Macleaya cordata*) and it does equally well in the shade and in the full sun. The leaves are light green above and a silvery white underneath. The creamy white flowers are borne in plumelike spikes which need not be removed after the blooming period, as the seed vessels are also pretty. The plume poppy grows six to eight feet high; will grow in any soil; and when once established its suckers are hard to eradicate—therefore, it belongs to the wilder parts of a garden.

W. P. Longland
The Garden Magazine, 1907

Editor's Note: You can also try *Macleaya cordata* 'Plum Tassle', with smoky purple blossoms.

A Birch Illusion

The cut-leaved birch (*Betula pendula* 'Dalecarlica'), placed at the distant point of a long narrow border, adds light and gives the impression of distance.

The Garden Magazine, 1905

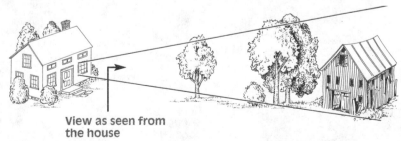

View as seen from the house

The closer you are to a tree, the more of the view it will block. Keep that in mind when you decide on plantings to screen a part of the landscape you don't care to look at.

Place Rocks Tastefully

The judicious distribution of stones may greatly heighten wildness and picturesque beauty.

J. C. Loudon
An Encyclopedia of Gardening, 1850

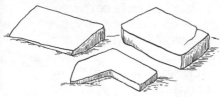

Avoid placing garden rocks at random on the ground's surface.

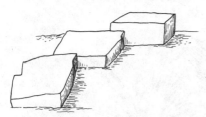

Don't link rocks like a string of railroad cars either.

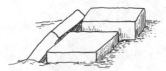

The more natural the arrangement is, the better.

In nature, stones often touch each other and are piled together almost haphazardly.

Partially concealed rocks look the most natural and are best in plantings.

Advice for Lush Lawns

Fragrant Grass Mix

In our lawn grass we always put a little sweet vernal grass (*Anthoxanthum odoratum*), on account of its delightful fragrance.

Vick's Illustrated Catalogue and Floral Guide, 1872

Editor's Note: Sweet vernal grass is a pasture grass that carries the scent of coumarin, a compound we associate with new-mown hay. It grows in Zones 5 to 10 and prefers full sun, except in very hot climates, where it needs partial shade.

Make Lawns Look Bigger

An irregularity of outline to the lawn gives an idea of size.

Peter Henderson
Henderson's Handbook of Plants, 1890

Editor's Note: Regular geometric shapes such as squares and rectangles make lawns look smaller. Add some gentle curves to your turf area to make it look larger. Easy curves have another benefit, too: They're easier to mow than sharp curves.

How to Grass a Bank

For each square rod (about 270 square feet) to be planted, take half a pound of lawn grass seed and mix it intimately and thoroughly with six cubic feet of earth and loam. This should be placed in a tub, and liquid manure diluted with about two thirds of water added and well stirred in, so as to bring the whole to the consistency of mortar.

The slope must be cleansed and made perfectly smooth, and then well watered, after which the paste just mentioned should be applied with a trowel and made as even and thin as possible. Should it crack from exposure to the air, it must again be watered and smoothed up day by day until the grass makes its appearance, which will be in from eight to fourteen days, when the whole declivity will soon be covered with a close carpet of green.

Boston Globe, 1903

Editor's Note: There are easier ways to plant a grassy bank, though they don't have the "hands in the dirt" appeal of this tip. You can cover newly seeded slopes with straw mulch to hold seeds in place. For extra-steep slopes, lay coarse, untreated burlap over the planting and pin it in place with wire. The grass seeds will poke through the fabric, which will eventually disintegrate. You can buy large rolls of burlap through garden-supply catalogs.

Bank On These Plants

Here are some good ground-covers for steep banks where it is difficult to maintain good turf: wichuraiana rose, Hall's honeysuckle, trailing euonymus, myrtle (vinca), bittersweet, and English ivy. Plant as soon as frost is out of the ground.

Loring Underwood
A Garden Diary and Country Home Guide, 1908

Editor's Note: Most of Underwood's plant choices are good ones, but beware of Hall's honeysuckle (*Lonicera japonica* 'Halliana'). This vine is so aggressive that it will smother any other plants in its path—it's a noxious weed in many parts of the eastern United States.

A No-Mow Strip for Easy Maintenance

A foot-wide strip of sod between the fence and the cement sidewalk was hard to keep looking presentable. It was impossible to cut that grass with a lawnmower, and hand-clipping 120 feet of frontage is something of a task. The sod was turned under, and a row of portulacca, mignonette, and sweet alyssum seed planted. The second season, enough self-sown "volunteers" appeared to make reseeding unnecessary. One of the greatest pleasures of this idea is that it is being copied by others in this town.

H. R. Mosnat
The Garden Magazine, 1906

Color Your Lawn with Crocuses

None of us expects to see any flowers out of doors in November amid a desolate landscape. Yet you can have dozens of them springing up in your lawn. It amazes beginners that these bulbs should bloom *within three or four weeks* after planting. That we can enjoy them *every day for two months after a killing frost* seems too good to be true. You can cause your friends more surprise and delight with a dozen autumn-blooming crocuses for thirty cents than if you spent ten times that sum on spring-blooming crocuses!

Wilhelm Miller
The Garden Magazine, 1907

Editor's Note: Prices have gone up a bit since 1907, but the idea remains a good one. Add a selection of fall-blooming crocuses to your yard for a colorful carpet of white, lilac, and blue flowers. Plant in groups or drifts for the showiest effect.

Fall-blooming crocuses appear when you least expect them and when you need them most—from September into December.

Keep Pine Needles off the Lawn

Do not allow pine needles to remain on growing grass; they pack so tightly that they kill out anything that is underneath them. Rake off the needles each spring, if not oftener.

The Garden Magazine, 1908

Editor's Note: The same quality that makes pine needles death to lawns makes them a great weed-smothering mulch under trees and shrubs. Pine needle mulch packs so tightly that it keeps out light, and no light means no weeds.

The Grass Is Greener with Good Winter Lawn Care

It is a very good practice to cover lawns with manure at this season. Two good results flow from this course; the frost is prevented from penetrating so deeply, and the ground, being warmed much sooner in spring, is green and cheerful sometime before unprotected lawns.

The Gardener's Monthly, 1871

Editor's Note: Make sure you use well-composted manure if you decide to try this project. Fresh manure can burn your grass. Use 100 to 200 pounds of manure per 1,000 square feet of lawn.

Watch Your Grades

One excellent hint I would give to all owners of small lawns that must slope. In grading such lawns, see to it that your grade is in a dipping, or concave, line, and the effect, though a subconscious one on the beholder, is totally different from that created by the convex grade on a slope. Also, it is far more agreeable.

Louisa King
The Little Garden, 1921

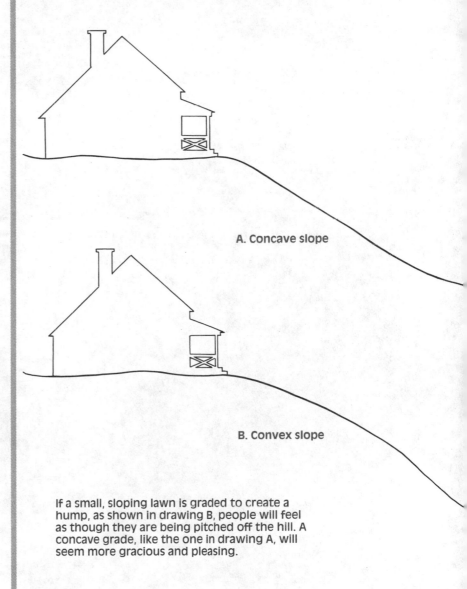

A. Concave slope

B. Convex slope

If a small, sloping lawn is graded to create a hump, as shown in drawing B, people will feel as though they are being pitched off the hill. A concave grade, like the one in drawing A, will seem more gracious and pleasing.

Planting and Caring for Gardens

Get your garden off to a healthy start with time-tested soil- and plant-care advice. Early gardeners had to get it right since they depended on their crops instead of grocery stores. Their know-how will help you grow a very green thumb—and a bountiful harvest!

Planting and Caring for Gardens

Keeping Track of Plants

Key to Success: A Garden Scrapbook

I have found a carefully indexed scrapbook and record of gardening to be a great help. One division of the book contains accurate copies of orders, with dates, prices, and names of nurserymen. Near the front of the book are pasted magazine articles giving instruction on soils, plant enemies, and agricultural formulae. A third division contains the dates of bloom for all flowers in the garden, making an interesting study over several years and helping greatly in planning new beds. Finally, the largest part contains experience—the index points to many a record of failure, followed by success as lessons are learned.

Mary R. G. Williams
The Garden Magazine, 1908

Plant Labels Don't Last

Each year's experience shows that the only trustworthy plant label is *none at all*. That is, every tree, vine, or permanent plant should be so recorded by its position, that though labels may be lost, though the memory may fail, and though our place may come into the hands of another, the names of each tree or plant should be so recorded that one can readily refer to it himself and another will have no difficulty. For safety, the record may be transferred to a small book to be carried in the pocket. Ours runs something thus: "First row south, beginning east end of row, 2 'Buerre 'd Anjou', 5 'Duchesse d' Anjouleme'," and so on.

American Agriculturist, 1885

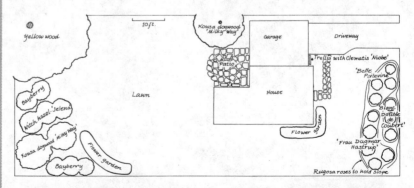

A written record of your plants is handy for on-the-spot garden planning. Transfer that information to a map for an overview of your entire yard. Use circles or other shapes to represent plants, and draw your map on graph paper so it's easy to show accurate spacing.

OLD-TIME WISDOM

Books as brain fertilizer? "Manuring with brains," like most proverbs, conveys an important truth. We look upon books as quite as essential implements as spades, rakes, or other garden tools. Winter is the time for study and reading.

American Agriculturist, 1878

Stake Out Slow Pokes

Some plants are late in appearing aboveground in the spring, platycodons (balloon-flowers) for instance, and there is danger of their being dug up by impatient amateurs who have either forgotten their presence or imagined they were dead and the ground vacant. It is well, therefore, to place in the fall some cane stakes at each plant or in a row around a group to indicate their presence.

W. C. Egan
Making a Garden of Perennials, 1912

Don't Sweat the Labels

Do not pay much attention to labelling; if a plant is not worth knowing, it is not worth growing.

William Robinson
The English Flower Garden, 1883

September Is Label Month

Go over your grounds and examine all your labels, lest the storms which are approaching should destroy them.

Henry Ward Beecher
Fruits, Flowers and Farming, 1859

Long-Lasting Labels

Let zinc labels oxidize a little by dipping them in water for a day or two before using, and then write with a common lead pencil. We have seen labels in use for twelve years so written, as "black as ink" and with all the appearance of lasting for half a century.

The Gardener's Monthly, 1872

Sensible Soil Care

Hold Your Horses

Dig garden ground only when the soil is warm and dry. Do not be in a hurry, or you may get behind. When a clot of earth will crush to powder when you tread on it, it is time to dig—not before.

The Gardener's Monthly, 1876

Editor's Note: Procrastinating can even save you time. Digging wet soil turns it into hard clods that may keep you out of your garden for weeks.

Food for the Soil (and Soul)

Green manure crops are very nice to see. The rye, sowed last fall just ahead of a freeze-up, has given us a bright green lawn to look at whenever the snow is off. The vetch that now covers another patch with a thick mat of its prostrate stems is also persistently green, and will bloom in purple glory if I do not get it turned under very early this spring. It is better than the rye, the soil-sharps tell us, because it gathers from the air the expensive and essential nitrogen, storing it in little nodules along the roots. As the whole plant is to be turned under, I get this nitrogen to work, and also the humus resulting from the buried herbage.

J. Horace McFarland
My Growing Garden, 1915

The vetches, like all legumes, are excellent nitrogen fixers. They can convert nitrogen from the air into a form plants can use. Sow hairy vetch in late summer and till it into the ground early the next spring before making your garden.

A General-Purpose Fertilizer

A mixture of stable dung, seaweed, lime, and vegetable mold (compost), which has lain in a heap for three or four months, and has been two or three times turned during that period, will make an excellent manure for most kinds of garden land.

J. C. Loudon
An Encyclopedia of Gardening, 1850

Treat a Jaundiced Garden with Leaves

If the garden earth looks gray or yellow, rotten leaves—quite rotten leaves—will improve it.

The Gardener's Monthly, 1876

Editor's Note: Adding rotted or composted leaves to your garden is a great way to build up soil that's low in organic matter. Spread two to four inches of leaves, or one inch of compost, on your garden each year, and eventually your soil will develop a healthy, rich black color.

"Water" with Your Hoe and Rake

Too much attention is given to watering and too little to cultivating. Do your watering with hoe or rake, and you will raise better plants. By scratching up the surface of the soil, moisture is retained, and the capillary attraction of moisture is broken, and the evaporation of water from soil to air is checked.

Loring Underwood
A Garden Diary and Country Home Guide, 1908

How Much Manure?

In ordering manure for the garden, bear in mind that most good garden soil needs as much as six cords to an acre. An acre contains 43,560 square feet, which is equal to a piece of land about 208 feet square.

Loring Underwood
A Garden Diary and Country Home Guide, 1908

Editor's Note: How much manure does *your* garden need? According to Underwood's figures, you'll need one cubic foot of manure per 56 square feet of garden. An easier solution is to let the manure compost for a year. Then spread one inch of the stuff over your garden.

Watch Out for Weedy Manure

Any manure that has been piled up for a year or more in a weed-infested corner and used on your grounds, especially on your lawn, is the best promoter of exercise I know of and can keep you busy all summer dislodging the weeds that spring from the seed its bosom protected.

W. C. Egan
Making a Garden of Perennials, 1912

A Green Screen for the Manure Pile

A friend of mine once worked out a very pleasing idea. He had to have the manure for the garden dumped right in the corner of it. So he placed pea brush around the manure and then planted cucumbers underneath. He not only saved garden space, but entirely shut from view the manure pile.

William C. McCollom
Vines and How to Grow Them, 1911

It's simple to hide a manure pile or a compost heap behind a wall of vegetables. Grow cucumbers, squash, gourds, or even tomatoes up pea brush or a trellis for a pretty, productive screen.

Sink Your Compost Heap

There is one eyesore which is of prime interest to the enthusiastic gardener—the compost heap. A pit may be dug for it, and fitted with a top of weathered boards.

Amelia Leavitt Hill
Garden Portraits, 1923

"Warm" Soil Works Wonders

A good loam—that is a mixture of clay and sand with a proportion of such decayed matter as leaves and the fibrous roots of grasses—is the best garden soil, being what is termed "warm and early." A preponderance of clay makes what is known as "cold" soil.

Ida D. Bennett
The Flower Garden, 1904

Keep Your Heap Weed-Free

Keep weeds from your compost heaps, as they exhaust the soil, and bear seeds for future browsweatings.

The Gardener's Monthly, 1871

A Recipe for Potting Soil

In making soil for potting plants, get some from the woods, some from the pasture, and some from the garden; add a liberal amount of sand.

Meehans' Monthly, 1898

Break Down Sod with Spuds

In order to transform grassland into good garden soil, it is best to cultivate it the first season by sowing some crop, like potatoes. By this method the old sod becomes thoroughly disintegrated and decays, and all weeds are killed by the process of cultivation.

Loring Underwood
A Garden Diary and Country Home Guide, 1908

A New Twist for Soil Care

In making beds that have been worked before and need no enriching, excellent results may be secured by pushing a long spade into the ground the whole length of its blade and twisting it around. This breaks up and mellows the ground more effectually than turning it over, while it leaves the good soil on top where the young plant roots can get it. Young plants must have mellow, nourishing soil from the start.

Ida D. Bennett
The Flower Garden, 1904

Prevent Cruelty to Plants: Mulch!

There ought to be a Society for the Prevention of Cruelty to Plants. Watering without mulching afterward is not even half a kindness, for the soil is sure to bake unless you stir it the morning after.

The Garden Magazine, 1908

Strange But True

A blind man was once laughed at for going to select a farm. On being helped out of the vehicle, he asked that the horse might be led to a bunch of thistles. He was told there were none. Then he remarked that docks would do as well. This request they were able to gratify. He subsequently bought the farm. When asked the reason for his "cranky" desires, he replied that thistles grew on poor land, docks only on rich soil.

Meehans' Monthly, 1893

Ferns Show Friable Soil

The old country people who have always lived on the same poor land say, "Where the fern grows tall anything will grow"; but that only means that there the ground is somewhat better and capable of cultivation, as its presence is a sure indication of a sandy soil.

Gertrude Jekyll
Wood and Garden, 1904

Ferns prefer moist, well-drained soil. If you have a patch growing on your property, build a flower garden around them with other moisture-loving plants such as irises, astilbes, and cardinal flowers.

Keep Mulch in Its Place

Leaves are nature's own mulch, and answer admirably. If there is danger of their being blown away, brush laid over them, or even a little earth sprinkled on them, will keep them in place.

Peter Henderson
Henderson's Handbook of Plants, 1890

A Key to High-Acid Soils

Canada mayflower (*Maianthemum canadense*)

Star grass (*Hypoxis hirsuta*)

Wood anemone (*Anemone quinquefolia*)

Frostweed (*Helianthemum canadense*)

Pinxter flower (*Rhododendron periclymenoides*)

Black huckleberry or lowbush blueberry (*Gaylussacia baccata*)

Late blueberry (*Vaccinium angustifolium*)

Four-leafed loosestrife (*Lysimachia quadrifolia*)

Cow wheat (*Malampyrum lineare*)

Dockmackie or mapleleaf viburnum (*Viburnum acerifolium*)

While most of these plants are more or less frequent all over the place, locations in which they are notably abundant and dominant always show the higher degree of acidity.

Herbert Durand
Wild Flowers and Ferns, 1925

A Key to Low-Acid Soils

Lady fern (*Athyrium filix-femina*)

Jack-in-the-pulpit (*Arisaema triphyllum*)

Bloodroot (*Sanguinaria canadensis*)

Wild geranium (*Geranium maculatum*)

Poison ivy (*Toxicodendron toxicarium*)

Enchanter's nightshade (*Circaea quadrisulcata*)

Figwort (*Scrophularia marilandica*)

Sweet cicely (*Myrrhis odorata*)

Goosegrass or catchweed bedstraw (*Galium aparine*)

Goldenrods (*Solidago* spp.)

These species spread only sparingly into the more acid soil and their dominance of any locality is a reliable indication that the soil there has a low acid content.

Herbert Durand
Wild Flowers and Ferns, 1925

Not All Leaves Are Equal as Mulch

Oak and chestnut leaves do not decompose so quickly as leaves of soft-wooded trees, but they contain more plant food. The hardwood leaves are best for protecting plants in winter as a mulch.

Loring Underwood
A Garden Diary and Country Home Guide, 1908

Editor's Note: To speed up the breakdown of hardwood leaves, shred them with a lawn mower before using them as mulch. Decomposed leaves make an excellent soil amendment, and they provide food and moist shelter for worms.

Planting Time

Wait, and Visit Nurseries Late

It is the fashionable thing now to visit nurseries after the spring rush is over. The nurseryman has nothing to do then and is glad enough to have visitors. And hardy plants can be had from pots any day during the summer.

Henry Maxwel
The Garden Magazine, 1908

Telling Good Seeds from Bad

Every purchaser should examine seed carefully before sowing, in order to ascertain whether they are good or not. With a common pocket lens in hand, no one could fail to be satisfied whether the seed was in germinating condition or not—imperfect seeds being yellowish; while sound seeds, usually, being of ivory white.

Meehans' Monthly, 1893

Care Is a Gardener's Best Tool

One can with success plant anything at any time, *if he takes trouble enough.*

J. Horace McFarland
My Growing Garden, 1915

A Seedbed for Slow Starters

Seed sowing, like all other planting, requires a great deal of thought and consideration. One seed bed is required that can be left entirely alone for (say) two years, except for just breaking with a handfork and weeding, as some seeds germinate very slowly.

Marie Theresa Villiers Earle
More Pot-Pourri from a Surrey Garden, 1899

OLD-TIME WISDOM

Try this gardener's breakfast beauty tip. Wearing gloves at night after soaking the hands in wet oatmeal is supposed to make them white.

American Agriculturist, 1895

A Simple Summer Seedbed

Make a seedbed outdoors in June and sow vegetables and flowers for fall and winter use. Put brush on the bed to keep off cats, dogs, and chickens. Lay newspapers over the brush and sprinkle carefully every day until the plants are up.

The Garden Magazine, 1908

Seed Depth Maxim

Someone has given as a rule that seeds should be covered twice the depth of their own diameter; that is, that a seed $1/16$ inch through should be covered $1/8$ of an inch. Perhaps that is as near correct as any general rule can be.

Vick's Illustrated Catalogue and Floral Guide, 1872

Sowing Seeds for Sports

A seedling contains all the elements of chance. The seedling grown in the garden may develop entirely different traits from its parent. Cultivation aids the sporting varieties to play the wildest freaks. A notable instance of this is a seedling from an obnoxious ragweed that crept into the garden. This young ragweed was a sport from the beginning. The parent plant had coarsely cut leaves. The seedling showed leaves minutely cut and crinkled like parsley. This characteristic was shown in every leaf until the plant stood nearly four feet high, when it was as beautiful a rich green foliage plant as one could wish for in the center of a bed.

Flora Lewis Marble
The Garden Magazine, 1908

Editor's Note: Let vegetables and flowers go to seed in your garden if you'd like to experiment with new plants—but be prepared for more weeding.

Beneficial Soil Bake

If you bake the soil in which fine flower seeds are to be planted, you will not be troubled so much with weeds.

Farm Journal, 1905

Editor's Note: You can kill weed seeds by sterilizing your soil mix. Place the soil and a potato in a shallow pan, and bake them in a 200°F oven. When the potato is done, so is the soil.

Sow Seeds Thinly

There is one great rule to be borne in mind in sowing all kinds of seed, and that rule, printed in largest type, should be placed wherever gardeners are to be found: SOW THINLY. At no stage of its career should a young plant be pressed upon by its neighbor.

Harry Roberts
The Book of Old-Fashioned Flowers, 1904

Let There Be Space

It taxes our faith sorely to believe that a seed as large as the point of a needle will give a plant which will be a foot in diameter. Let each have room to develop its full proportions, and to show the foliage, which is often quite as beautiful as the flower, to advantage.

Edward Sprague Rand
Seventy-Five Popular Flowers and How to Cultivate Them, 1872

Strange But True

A gentleman, anxious to ascertain the effect of transplanting at night instead of by day, made an experiment with the following result: he transplanted ten cherry trees while in bloom, commencing at four o'clock in the afternoon. Those transplanted during the daylight shed their blossoms, producing little or no fruit; while those transplanted in the dark maintained their condition fully.

The Household, 1883

Bottled Seeds Sow Best

A very simple contrivance for sowing small, smooth seeds is shown herewith. It is a bottle with a cork and a large quill in the cork. In order to sow with greater regularity, an ounce of seed may be evenly mixed with a half pint of sand.

Farm Journal, 1887

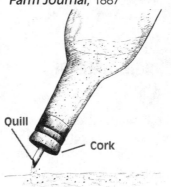

Quill

Cork

For fumble-fingered gardeners who just can't spread seed evenly, this bottle will help. Instead of a quill, you can use a section of a plastic drinking straw to regulate how many seeds come out.

Be Cruel to Be Kind

The kindest gardener is the one who thins vegetable and flower seedlings most cruelly.

The Garden Magazine, 1908

Transplant into a Puddle

There is one infallible method of transplanting known to most "flower fans." It consists merely in the filling of the hole, which is prepared for the reception of the plant, with water, and setting the plant in. By this method, plants do not wilt down, but remain fresh and crisp, even in warm weather.

Amelia Leavitt Hill
Garden Portraits, 1923

Editor's Note: When you fill the planting hole with soil, you'll create a muddy puddle that holds your plant steady and keeps the roots from drying out.

A Trial Bed for New Plants

I find it a distinct advantage putting new things in one place, as then one sees how they do, and what spreads and flourishes and what is only a dry stick and a label the following year.

Marie Theresa Villiers Earle
More Pot-Pourri from a Surrey Garden, 1899

Soaked Seeds Mean Speedy Seedlings

My way of "first-aiding" seeds is to tie them loosely in a wisp of fine cheesecloth or muslin, leaving a length of string for a handle (as tea is sometimes prepared for the pot by those who do not like mussy tea leaves). Dip the bag in hot (not boiling) water, and leave it there at least an hour, oftentimes all night. In this way the seed is softened and germination awakened.

Barbara
The Garden, You, and I, 1910

Editor's Note: A homemade "tea bag" makes it easy to soak and drain seeds before planting them outside. If you're starting seeds indoors, you can soak them after planting them. Sow seeds in cell packs or a seed flat with drainage holes, then set the container in a shallow pan of water overnight. The soil will take up the water slowly and soak even fine seeds without washing them away.

Perfect Plant Propagating

Watch for Happy Accidents

If a new variety springs up in the seed patch, it ought to be kept from the other plants—its seed gathered separately, and propagated by itself. There are many points for experimenting: height (dwarfs and giants), form of petals, different colors, fasciations (cockscomb), etc. Causes which produce albinism and other changes of color are little known. Cultivating in an impoverished soil, flowering in the shade, injuries to the seed germs, seeds of different ages, changes in the size of the seeds, etc., may aid in producing accidental variations.

Meehans' Monthly, 1897

The Propagator's Rule

It may be laid down as a general axiom, that nature requires always three years in which to perfect anything. During the first year she devotes herself chiefly to the roots, in the second she develops the stalks and leaves, and by the third she is ready for flowers.

Rose Fay Thomas
Our Mountain Garden, 1904

A Snap Test for Good Cuttings

With exceptions so few that it is hardly worth while to allude to them, cuttings of all kinds root freely from slips taken from the *young wood*, that is, the succulent growth, before it gets hardened, and when in the condition indicated by the "snapping test" as it is called.

Peter Henderson
Henderson's Handbook of Plants, 1890

Editor's Note: Cuttings taken from the succulent spring growth of woody plants such as azaleas and magnolias are called softwood cuttings. You can collect softwood cuttings from April through June, when the plant's new leaves are fully open but the stems are still soft. When the young twigs are mature enough to snap if you bend them, they're ready to be used as cuttings.

Tips for Taking Wild Cuttings

Cut wildflowers with scissors or pocketknife; never pull them. Never strip a plant of all its flowers; leave enough to perfect (form) seed. Cut, cleanly and sparingly, branches of flowering or fruiting shrubs and trees. Never break or tear them off.

Herbert Durand
Wild Flowers and Ferns, 1925

The Saucer System for Successful Cuttings

It is the safest of all methods in inexperienced hands. Common saucers or plates are used to hold the sand in which the cuttings are placed. This sand is put in to the depth of an inch or so, and the cuttings inserted in it close enough to touch each other. The sand is then watered until it becomes in the condition of mud, and placed on the windowsill of the sitting room or parlor, fully exposed to the sun and never shaded. *The sand must be kept continuously saturated, and kept in the condition of mud.* When the cuttings are rooted, they should be potted in small pots, and treated carefully by shading and watering for a few days.

Peter Henderson
Henderson's Handbook of Plants, 1890

Editor's Note: The one-inch depth is our clue that the "saucers" referred to here are plant pot saucers, not china saucers. Here's one time when the plastic version should come in really handy—no stains on the windowsills!

Homemade Pegs for Layering

This simple method of propagation is principally adopted in the case of low-growing or slender plants which cannot readily or conveniently be multiplied either by division, cuttings, or seed. A branch or stem of the plant or tree is bent down, and pegged or otherwise fastened or held below the soil, with its growing extremity above the ground.

F. W. Burbidge
Cultivated Plants: Their Propagation and Improvement, 1877

Editor's Note: Layering is an easy way to propagate many of the shrubs, trees, and perennials in your yard. Grapes, native azaleas, magnolias, raspberries, rosemary, and verbena are all good candidates for layering.

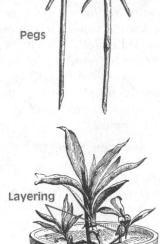

Pegs

Layering

A simple peg (*top*), cut from a forked branch, or a piece of wire will hold supple young branches in the soil for layering. Cover stems with soil where they touch the ground but leave the stem tips uncovered (*bottom*).

Propagating Pot 1

Take a two-inch clay pot and plug the hole at the bottom with a cork. Then take a six-inch pot, put a layer of drainage in the bottom, and set the little pot in the middle so that its rim is level with that of its six-inch associate. The space between the two pots is filled with sand, and here the cuttings are placed. The inner pot is filled with water. This affair is very professional looking, and is also very easy to manage.

Frances Duncan
The Joyous Art of Gardening, 1917

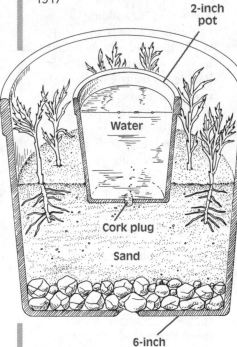

2-inch pot

Water

Cork plug

Sand

6-inch pot

Here's a variation on Duncan's pot-within-a-pot arrangement. Use it for cuttings that need extra humidity. Pour water in the small center pot to saturate the surrounding sand and place a piece of glass over the top.

Propagating Pot 2

Procure a large flower pot, and lay at the bottom of it large loose pieces of brick just so high that a small flower pot placed inside upon them may have its rim on the same level as the rim of the large pot. Fill in the interval between the pots with perfectly dry sand or earth. Fill the inner pot with pure sand, and insert the cuttings. Take another pot just of the size that, when turned upside down, it may fit in on the earth between the rims of the large and small pots. Break out its bottom, and lay over it a piece of window glass. Water the cuttings as they require it with tepid water, allowing none to fall on the earth between the pots. When condensation takes place upon the pane of glass, merely turn it over.

Thomas Firminger
Firminger's Manual of Gardening for India, 1918

Be a Weather-Wise Gardener

You're Surrounded by Storm Indicators

The coming of a rain or electric storm may often be detected by the drooping attitude of many plants and tree leaves; they are one of nature's many warnings of "coming events": wild oxalis, Canada or wood violet, wild vines, parsley, vetches, and the *Dicentras* (bleeding hearts).

John Hugh Ross
Meehans' Monthly, 1902

Editor's Note: Plants aren't the only storm indicators. You may also notice extra-busy ants, huddled cows, or silent birds.

Shelter from the Sun

Many suffer a severe headache, and a restless night after an exhausting day's work. The sun beats down upon the head and neck with great force. The head should be protected in such cases by wearing a straw hat, with a broad brim, and by placing a leaf of cabbage or lettuce, or a wetted cambric handkerchief in the crown of it. The very sensitive back of the head and neck is best protected by means of a white handkerchief fastened by one border to the hat band.

American Agriculturist, 1876

Red Sky at Night...

When it is evening, ye say, It will be fair weather: for the sky is red. And in the morning, It will be foul weather today: for the sky is red and lowering.

The Holy Bible (Matt., 16:2–3)

Birds as Barometers

Birds fly high in fair weather and low in foul weather. The explanation is that in fair weather the barometer is usually high, the air heavier and denser, and capable of sustaining a given weight at a greater elevation than when less dense during the passage of a storm.

L. H. Bailey
Farm and Garden Rule-Book, 1911

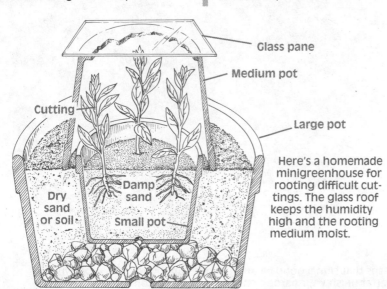

Glass pane

Medium pot

Cutting

Large pot

Dry sand or soil

Damp sand

Small pot

Here's a homemade minigreenhouse for rooting difficult cuttings. The glass roof keeps the humidity high and the rooting medium moist.

Forecasting Weather

1. The wind never blows unless rain or snow is falling within one thousand miles of you.

2. When cirrus clouds are rapidly moving from the North or Northeast, there will be rain inside of twenty-four hours.

3. Cumulus clouds always move from a region of fair weather to a region where a storm is forming; cirrus clouds always move from a region where a storm is in progress to a region of fair weather.

4. The wind always blows from a region of fair weather toward a region where a storm is forming.

5. When the temperature suddenly falls, there is a storm forming south of you; when the temperature suddenly rises, there is a storm forming north of you.

C. H. Adams
Farmer's Club of the American Institute Farm Journal, 1906

Forgo February Fever

Don't get the garden fever in February and uncover things on the first fine day. More damage is done to all plants during March than at any other time of the year. Plants that have been protected all winter are not able to stand severe changes and they will surely suffer from the late frosts if uncovered too early.

W. C. McCollom
The Garden Magazine, 1908

Editor's Note: When February fever strikes, it's hard to resist working in your garden. Instead of uncovering tender plants, cool your fever with more suitable garden chores. A mild February day is a good time to prune dormant trees, start seeds indoors, clean the bird feeders, build a new compost bin, or work on your landscape plan.

Shadows Predict Frost

When the sunshine is very hot and the shade very cold and the shadows very deep, there is frost in the air, because the air is very dry and radiation of heat little checked.

L. H. Bailey
The Horticulturist's Rule-Book, 1895

Cirrus

Cumulus

Cirrus clouds (*top*) are high white wisps that signal good weather, while cumulus clouds (*bottom*) are puffy masses that mean you'd better finish your garden chores—a storm is coming.

Strange But True

Dr. Franklin's advice when you see lightening approaching is to sit in the middle of a room on one chair and laying the feet on another. It is still better, he says, to bring two or three mattresses or beds into the middle of the room and, folding them double, to place the chairs upon them, for they are not so good conductors as the walls.

J. C. Loudon
An Encyclopedia of Gardening, 1850

the moon. Plant everthing that goes to root (like potatoes, beets, turnips, carrots, etc.) in the dark of the moon. I do not mean to say that so doing will *insure* your crops; seed and soil conditions must likewise be right and seasonable.

Samuel Campbell
Farm Journal, 1906

Not in Tune with Planting by the Moon

The long-continued and repeated observations of practical farmers and scientific men have demonstrated that the assumed influence of the moon is a fable. We advise all our farming friends to remember that their business is with the Earth, and that planting or farming in the moon is one of the poorest of speculations.

Genesee Farmer, 1838

Editor's Note: Advances in science don't necessarily mean the death of old folk wisdom. Gardeners still depend on the moon for planting clues. See the tip that follows for moon planting advice.

Ignore the Moon at Your Peril

If the moon has such an effect upon the great oceans, why shouldn't it affect the land? To get the best results, sow or plant all grain in the light of the moon; plant all vegetables and fruits that produce their fruits above ground, in the light of

If you'd like to try planting by the moon, consult an almanac and plant underground crops during the time of the full moon to the new moon, and grains and aboveground crops during the time of the new moon to the full moon.

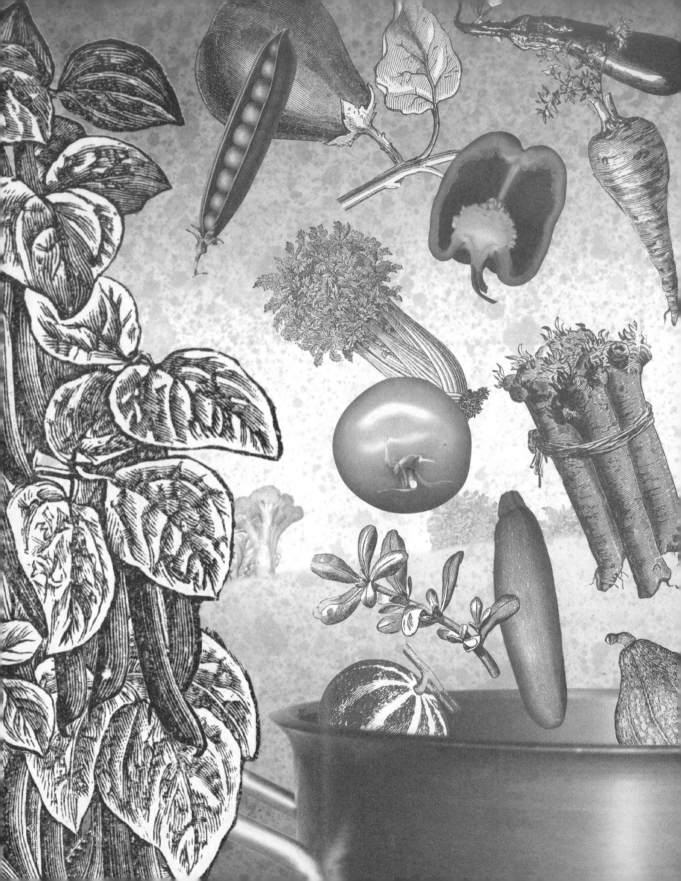

vege**ta**bles

Get ready for growing tips and plant recommendations galore. Old-time gardeners were nothing if not creative. So expand your garden plot and prepare your tastebuds for treats like tomato honey, pickled peppers, squash biscuits, and parsnip curry!

Vegetables
Plan before Planting

What's Your Garden Worth?

Aside from the pleasure of raising your own vegetables, make a test to see if it is economical for you to raise them. This can be done easily by keeping an expense account, and by recording the market value of the vegetables you raise.

Loring Underwood
A Garden Diary and Country Home Guide, 1908

See Garden Sights in September

Go around and visit neighboring gardens this month, making notes of their size and also of the manner in which they are laid out. Ask the successful gardeners what varieties they use in certain crops that are particularly fine, and make a note of it.

E. L. D. Seymour
Garden Profits, 1911

Southern Exposure

The exposure should be towards the south and the aspect at some point between south-east and southwest, the ground sloping to these points in an easy manner.

J. C. Loudon
An Encyclopedia of Gardening, 1850

A Good Reason to Visit Your Neighbor

What one can do may be accomplished by another—that is the tonic of seeing other gardens than one's own.

Barbara
The Garden, You, and I, 1910

Editor's Note: Who is this Barbara? A gardener who chose to remain anonymous but who gave good advice.

Segregate Perennial Vegetables

Plan the vegetable garden so that permanent plants shall be at one part of the garden where they may not be interfered with when the rest of the garden is plowed in spring. Rhubarb, asparagus, globe artichoke, mint, chives, and strawberries should occupy such a location.

Loring Underwood
A Garden Diary and Country Home Guide, 1908

Editor's Note: Another way to handle perennial vegetables is to tuck them into perennial flower beds. Rhubarb, globe artichokes, and herbs make outstanding ornamental plants.

You can find solutions to garden problems and inspiration for new projects at your neighbors' gardens and at public gardens and arboretums. Make sure you visit other gardens often to see how plants and plantings change throughout the seasons.

Where to Plant Corn and Potatoes

Corn grows so much taller than anything else cultivated that it should, if possible, be placed in the rear. In front of it the few hills of early potatoes which it is possible to grow on a city lot may be planted, as they are the least ornamental of vegetables.

Ida D. Bennett
The Vegetable Garden, 1908

Soils, Heavy and Light

A safe rule for preparation of vegetable garden soil in spring is to plow or fork heavy soil as deep as possible, and light soil shallow. A heavy soil in which there is clay is mellowed by this process, and a light soil will retain moisture better if not broken up more than eight or ten inches in depth.

Loring Underwood
A Garden Diary and Country Home Guide, 1908

A Neighborly Crop Exchange

We and our next-door neighbor agreed to divide our energies, so that each should produce a different crop, and exchange products. It was a capital idea, and might be more often carried out. It was my business to grow garden fruits, and his to grow vegeta-bles. I acknowledge I grew lima beans, which I did not quite trust to my neighbor.

E. P. Powell
The Orchard and Fruit Garden, 1914

Lima beans are very cold sensitive, so you might want to grow your own crop and trade less touchy vegetables with neighbors.

Secret for Early Planting Success

There is a way to get one's land into condition for early planting that is practiced by some gardeners, but is unthought of by many, and that is to plow the garden into ridges late in the fall, after the manner shown here. One can plant in the spring along the tops of these ridges very much earlier than he could had the land have been left flat.

American Agriculturist, 1895

Follow Crops with Clover

Get a pound or two of crimson clover seed now. Just as soon as one row of vegetables is past, out with it and put in crimson clover to fertilize your soil. It is a beautiful plant and makes nitrogen cheaper than you can buy it.

The Garden Magazine, 1908

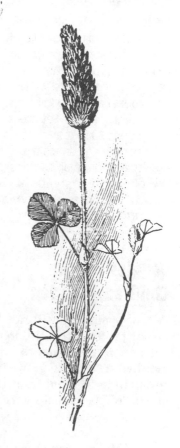

Crimson clover is an annual legume. It converts nitrogen from the air into the form plants use. Chop the clover and turn it under before it blooms to add nitrogen to your soil. Wait several days before planting a new crop to give the clover a chance to decompose.

Stretch the Season with a Windbreak

A well-grown windbreak of evergreens on the north side of the vegetable garden will give you vegetables a fortnight earlier in the spring and will prolong the season in the fall.

Loring Underwood
A Garden Diary and Country Home Guide, 1908

Editor's Note: If you have a large garden, a row or two of evergreens such as white pines (*Pinus strobus*) or Norway spruces *(Picea abies)* will protect your spring and fall crops from blasts of cold. Set the evergreens 20 feet away from your garden and space them 6 feet apart. For small gardens, a row of evergreen shrubs like dwarf mugo pines (*Pinus mugo* var. *mugo*) will do the trick.

Veggies for the Children's Garden

A few vegetables will not be out of place in the children's garden. Beets, carrots, and radishes are easy to grow, and the pulling of them from the ground is a perennial source of pleasure. And if Mother will "put up" a glass or two of carrot marmalade, the garden will be doubly remembered during the winter and looked forward to with renewed anticipation the succeeding spring.

Amelia Leavitt Hill
Garden Portraits, 1923

OLD-TIME WISDOM

Necessity is the mother of big gardens. A piece of ground 100 feet square should supply a family of six with vegetables the entire summer.

Loring Underwood
A Garden Diary and Country Home Guide, 1908

Editor's Note: That's not 100 square feet (a little 10-by-10 footer), but 100 feet on a side, or 10,000 square feet—nearly a quarter-acre. Most vegetable gardens of a century ago were run like small farms. Families grew as much of their own food as possible and would tally their savings in cash at the end of each season.

A Tale of Two Vegetable Gardens

In the squares designed for the use of the kitchen, I have avoided putting anything disagreeable either to sight or smell, having another garden below for cabbage, onions, garlic, etc.

Lady Mary Wortley Montague (in a letter, 1748)
Walter Howe
The Garden, 1890

Editor's Note: Compare this hint with the following gardener's rule, written 100 years later.

Combine the Beautiful with the Practical

To unite the agreeable with the useful is an object common to all the departments of gardening.

J. C. Loudon
An Encyclopedia of Gardening, 1850

Editor's Note: Combining ornamental plants with useful ones is both challenging and rewarding. Border a flower bed with parsley to see how well the two can mix.

Seeds and Seedlings

Give Yourself Planting Deadlines

It is an excellent plan to mark the date when seeds should be sown on all the packets, so that by looking over the seed drawers once a month nothing escapes notice.

F. W. Burbidge
Cultivated Plants: Their Propagation and Improvement, 1877

Editor's Note: Although planting dates are printed on most seed packets, they're easy to miss at planting time. Rewrite the date on each package in large letters, with a thick marker, and you won't miss any sowing seasons.

Speed Seed Sprouting with a Soak

I have noticed nearly a week's difference between the germination of soaked and unsoaked seeds—and anyone who has practiced this will doubtless tell you the same story.

E. L. D. Seymour
Garden Profits, 1911

Brick Trick for Seed Flats

The growth of seeds may be greatly hastened by placing a hot brick under the seedling box night and morning.

The Household,
1882

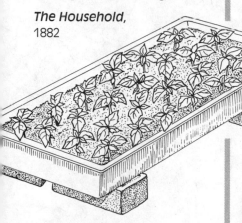

If you don't have an electric heating cable or mat for seedlings, try using bricks to supply bottom heat. Warm the bricks on top of the furnace or a wood stove, or slip them in the oven when you're baking or broiling. Old-time gardeners used wooden seed flats to start plants, but you can use the plastic flats that are widely available today.

Get Those Seed Orders in the Mail

Whoever starts well ahead of the season will be likely to keep ahead of it. The market gardeners, when they would speak of one who is slack, and always just a little behind his work, say, "He lets his pussley get ahead of him."

American Agriculturist, 1878

Editor's Note: "Pussley" is an old term for purslane, the succulent garden weed.

Wood Ashes Give Seeds a Strong Start

Carrot and beet seed, soaked twenty-four hours and rolled in wood ashes, come up stronger, and of a finer color than without the application.

The People's Journal, 1854

How to Handle Furrows for Seeds

The handle of a rake, placed so that the teeth stand up from the ground, makes a good furrow.

The Garden Magazine, 1909

Editor's Note: A hoe or rake handle will work, as long as you return your tool to a safe position once you're done with it.

Order Seeds Conservatively...

"Few and good" should be the amateur's motto in ordering seeds. Calculate what will be required, and confine your orders to old or well-tried kinds rather than to novelties of which the quality is unknown to you.

F. W. Burbidge
Cultivated Plants: Their Propagation and Improvement, 1877

Editor's Note: How do you know what's required? Check books like *Rodale's Garden Answers* that list the number of vegetables to grow per person.

...And Plant Conservatively

Remember there is a July as well as an April; and lay out in April as you can hold out in July and August. By reference to a garden journal we find that we planted in 1840 sixteen kinds of peas; seventeen kinds of beans; seven kinds of corn; six kinds of squash; eight kinds of cabbage; seven kinds of lettuce; eight sorts of cucumber, and seven of turnips—seventy-six varieties of only eight vegetables! Although we worked faithfully, early and late, through the whole season, the weeds beat us fairly.

Henry Ward Beecher
Fruits, Flowers and Farming, 1859

OLD-TIME WISDOM

Bigger is not necessarily better. All who have to do with gardeners and seedsmen should fight against the deterioration of some of our best vegetables through their mania for size. A change in size, by adding to the watery tissue and fibrous framework of the plant, may entirely destroy the quality we enjoy in it.

Mme. Vilmorin-Andrieux
The Vegetable Garden, 1885

Settle Seeds in Dry Soil

The tramping down of the seed should never be omitted when the ground is in a dry condition. Planted in loose soil, the seed may lie in a space between two particles of soil, very tiny, but to the little hairlike roots a veritable cavern, through which they will grope in vain for food and moisture.

Ida D. Bennett
The Vegetable Garden, 1908

Planting Dates Are Meant to Be Bent

In any garden, plant a little earlier and a little later than is recommended—general directions have to be merely averages, which successive seasons often are not.

E. L. D. Seymour
Garden Profits, 1911

Room to Grow

In thinning close crops, as onions, carrots, turnips, etc., be sure that they are not left too near; for, instead of reaping a greater produce by so doing, there would be a loss. When they stand too close, they will make tall and large tops, but are prevented from swelling in their roots: it is better to err on the wide side, for, though there are fewer plants, they will be finer and better flavored.

Rev. Charles Marshall
An introduction to the Knowledge and Practice of Gardening, 1796

Hotbed Results— Without a Hotbed

A simple means of hurrying crops is to grow them in flat boxes, in the kitchen or in any sunny window of the house, where the temperature will not go below 60°F. I have the record of a corn lover who obtained ripe ears on June 20 by planting seed in boxes indoors on April 20, and transplanting to ground that had been well enriched with manure and wood ashes, when the days became warm.

E. L. D. Seymour
Garden Profits, 1911

Prune Weak Seedlings to Give Them Strength

In setting some plants in the soil, if of weak growth, it will be well to remove a portion of the top. This is universally done by Dutch gardeners, who remove all but the top leaves of cabbage and cauliflowers. It not only relieves the roots of the care of the top to a great extent, but by lightening the tops, the weight is removed from the stem, which is enabled to retain an upright position.

Ida D. Bennett
The Vegetable Garden, 1908

When you transplant leggy seedlings to the garden, remove a few leaves to keep the plants from breaking under their own weight. The seedlings' stems will quickly thicken and grow sturdy as they sprout new leaves.

Early Starts May Be False Starts

If one has an abundance of seed and does not care for the labor involved, then the chances of getting an early crop by early planting may be worthwhile. But as a general thing, seed planted when the soil has become warm and the nights are warm, will make more rapid growth to more than balance the difference in time, and can usually be trusted to overtake the earlier-planted seed plants.

Ida D. Bennett
The Vegetable Garden, 1908

Select Your Own Seed

Watch for any distinct seminal sport or break among the vegetables, and if any one plant strikes you as being in any way distinctly superior to its fellows, mark it for seed. Much more can be done by careful selection in this way than is generally supposed, especially if followed up year after year. This is the plan adopted by the best seedsmen; and in this way some of the finest strains of vegetable and flower seeds have been obtained.

F. W. Burbidge
Cultivated Plants: Their Propagation and Improvement, 1877

Editor's Note: If you want to save your own seeds, plant open-pollinated varieties. They'll come back true—hybrids won't.

Rediscover Cloches (or Bell Jars)

Cloches constitute one of the most conspicuous features of a French garden from October till May. At one time each cloche had a knob on top, as in the illustration. As, however, this acted as a lens for the sun, and burned the lettuces, etc., beneath, the knob has been dispensed with by all French market gardeners.

John Weathers
Commercial Gardening, 1913

Cloches aren't just useful, they're also attractive. Use them to decorate your garden or to make greenhouses for ferns and other woodland plants. You can occasionally find cloches for sale at flea markets and antique shops. Or see "Sources" on page 316 for ordering information.

Mud Makes Moving Transplants Easy

Cabbages and other plants may be safely transplanted in any weather, or time of day, by immersing the roots in mud made from rich soil the moment they are taken from the ground—provided the ground in which they are set is sufficiently moist at the time. It is best to take up as much of the soil with the roots as possible.

Genesee Farmer, 1838

Tuck Late Plantings In Tightly

An important element of success in July sowings is pressing the soil into close contact with the planted seeds. This is essential, for it causes the young plants to come up promptly, regularly, vigorously, and straight, instead of feebly, unevenly, and slowly, or else not at all, as often happens in midsummer when the soil is left loose and dry above the plantings.

E. L. D. Seymour
Garden Profits, 1911

Editor's Note: July is a good time to start fall crops such as broccoli, cabbage, and cauliflower. Firming the soil is one way to get your seeds off to a good start. Another tip for hot-weather sowing is to plant seeds near tall vegetables such as corn or sunflowers—they'll provide much-needed shade for your seedlings.

A Tepee for Tender Vegetables

With some protection, plants will thrive and come to maturity greatly in advance of plants which have not been transplanted. A double thickness of newspaper, coiled in a conical shape and held in place by earth placed on the edges, will serve very well. The paper may be left on during cold, windy weather, but must not remain too long, or the plant will become blanched and weakened. The paper can be held in shape by using nails as pins.

Benjamin F. Albaugh
The Gardenette, 1915

A newspaper tent is an inexpensive version of the traditional cloche or bell jar. It works by holding the earth's heat around newly transplanted seedlings. When the tents have served their purpose, you can spread them out and reuse them as weed barriers under bark mulch.

How to Time a Second Planting

To have a continuous succession of vegetables, make a new planting as soon as the last lot shows three inches above ground. This is a better method than planting ten days or two weeks apart, for different sowings of seeds may come up all at once if cold weather checks germination.

Loring Underwood
A Garden Diary and Country Home Guide, 1908

Succession Planting in Pots

In instances where the ground was not to be vacated early enough for the later planting, the sowings of the successive crops were made in flower pots, and the plantlets transplanted as soon as there was a vacancy; tomatoes, cucumbers, squash, bush limas, kohlrabi, and lettuce were treated in this way.

E. L. D. Seymour
Garden Profits, 1911

Mold-Free Melon Seeds

I have adopted the following plan in cleaning cucumber and melon seeds; and it is equally applicable for all pulpy fruits, if the quantity to be separated is not very large. Cut open the fruit and separate the seeds as cleanly as possible with the fingers, laying them on a coarse dry towel, in which they are to be rubbed until dry. The pulp quickly becomes absorbed by the cloth; but in some cases two towels may be necessary, one to absorb the bulk of the slimy pulp, and the other to thoroughly dry the seeds. Seeds so treated, and exposed for an hour in the sun on a sheet of paper, may be at once wrapped up and put away without any fear of mildew or moldiness.

F. W. Burbidge
Cultivated Plants: Their Propagation and Improvement, 1877

Plant Care and Harvest Hints

Water Roots Deep

Water to the bottom and extent of the roots, as much as may be. Wetting only the surface of the ground is of little use, and of some certain harm, as it binds the earth, and so prevents showers, dews, air, and sun from entering the soil and benefiting the roots as they otherwise would do.

Rev. Charles Marshall
An Introduction to the Knowledge and Practice of Gardening, 1796

A Soil-Stirring Experiment

If anyone wishes to try this experiment, and we have done it time and again, let two patches in a garden be treated in all respects alike, except in this—let one be hoed or raked every two or three days and the other not at all, or but once in the season. The result will satisfy any man better than a paper argument. Indeed, we have found it impossible to perfect some vegetables without constantly stirring the soil.

Henry Ward Beecher
Fruits, Flowers and Farming,
1859

Editor's Note: Continuous hoeing and raking did the trick for Beecher's garden, keeping weeds from getting a foothold and the soil from crusting over. You can get the same benefits for much less work by mulching your garden.

Reach between Crops with a Two-Pronged Hoe

The most effectual mode of stirring, and that now adopted by the best gardeners, is by the two-pronged fork or two-pronged hoe. Every crop, whether planted in rows, or sown broadcast, ought to be subjected to this operation once or oftener in the course of its progress to maturity. Small crops, where the distances between the plants are not wide, ought to be stirred by a fork of two prongs. A narrow hoe is the usual instrument, but this always tends to harden the ground below, and to form a sort of floor, which in many soils is impervious to air or rain.

J. C. Loudon
An Encyclopedia of Gardening, 1850

Editor's Note: You can make a two-pronged fork by removing prongs from a standard model with a hacksaw. For a two-pronged hoe, use an adjustable-tine cultivator (see "Sources" on page 316). These have from two to four bent tines, which you can extend or remove.

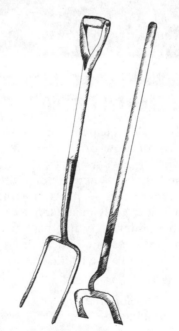

As odd as they look, a two-pronged fork (*left*) and hoe (*right*) do an admirable job of loosening soil around closely planted seedlings. Stirring up the soil keeps it loose and weed-free.

Clear Beds Quickly

As soon as your vegetable crops are past kitchen use, clear them out. Never suffer them to seed. A seed crop exhausts the soil more than two crops taken off in an edible condition.

The Gardener's Monthly, 1872

Editor's Note: For the most productive garden, this is good advice. But do make exceptions if you grow open-pollinated varieties and want to save the seed, or if you want to attract beneficial insects. Dill and parsley flowers are good sources of pollen and nectar for beneficials.

Strange But True

Take three onions, three carrots, about three turnips, one small cabbage, one bunch of celery, and one pint of stewed tomatoes. Chop all of the vegetables very finely, and set over the fire in four or five quarts of water; when these are thoroughly boiled, strain and add to the soup about two teaspoons of graham flour wetted in cold water; a small piece of butter, pepper, and salt; then boil again about twenty minutes, and it is ready for the table. This is for the vegetarian, or the man who is afraid of the juice of meat. But the vegetarian dies—and Graham himself is dead.

Detroit Post and Tribune, 1878

Editor's Note: "Graham" refers to Sylvester Graham (1794–1851), an advocate of vegetarianism. He promoted the use of coarsely ground whole wheat flour, which became known as "graham" flour, and is best remembered for graham crackers, which were also named after him.

can be as attractive as plantings.

You don't have to have green things growing in every season to make a garden. When your garden isn't green, mulching is a good way to make it look neat and prevent soil erosion. If you'd like a patterned look, use a variety of mulches to add interest and different colors.

Vegetables from A to Z

Artichokes

Time Harvest by Taste

No vegetable ought to be gathered till it has attained the requisite degree of maturity, or offered for use when it has begun to decay. What this degree is, often depends on the particular tastes of families: thus cabbages are most esteemed in Edinburgh, Scotland when fully headed and blanched; while in London, they are preferred open and green. Equal differences in taste as to peas, celery, lettuce, and, indeed, most other kitchen crops, might be noticed.

J. C. Loudon
An Encyclopedia of Gardening, 1850

A Well-Tilled Garden Is a Cheerful Garden

There is a pleasantness to the eye in new-broken earth, which gives an air of culture, and is always agreeable. This observation is particularly meant to apply in autumn, that the garden may not become dreary too soon, and so bring on winter before its time.

J. C. Loudon
An Encyclopedia of Gardening, 1850

Editor's Note: This notion of tilled soil for its own sake is similar to the Japanese practice of raking gardens of stones. Patterns in the soil or stones

Helping Artichokes Overwinter

Notwithstanding the fact that artichoke plants look well after several heavy frosts, they are not really hardy, although it is true that they stand a good deal of freezing. A new and different method of wintering which is not yet in general practice is to cut off all the tops and cover the crown with an 18-inch pot, inverted. This must be covered later with leaves or salt hay.

The Garden Magazine, 1908

Editor's Note: Salt hay is the dried grass taken from coastal marshes—ordinary straw will do.

Globe Artichoke as an Ornamental

The artichoke is beautiful, with its soft gray-green foliage, and masses with excellent effects with the tall-growing cannas, the aralias, and caladiums. The German people make pompoms out of the expanded and dried seed heads, adding pampas grass to fill their house vases. If they only forget to use cheap dyes to color them, the effect is good.

Meehans' Monthly, 1897

The globe artichoke's good looks earn it a trial in a mixed border. Even if you're away at harvest time, you won't miss out completely. Instead of harvesting a crop of edible flower buds, you'll get a collection of beautiful thistle-like blooms.

Recipe

A Tart of Artichoke Cream

When your artichoke bottoms are well boiled, beat them in a mortar and strain them through a colander with butter, the yolks of two eggs raw, salt, cinnamon sugar, and green citron, put them into a patty pan sheet with fine paste (pastry dough), but do not cover it all and when it is baked, ice it over with sugar and orange flower water and so serve it away.

Giles Rose
A Perfect School of Instructions for the Officers of the Mouth, 1682

Asparagus

An Effortless After-the-Harvest Backdrop

Asparagus usually looks best at the farther side of the garden, where its beautiful herbage makes a background border in summer and fall.

L. H. Bailey
The Principles of Vegetable Gardening, 1901

Blanch Asparagus for a Neat Treat

A few years ago white asparagus was in demand, but lately there has been little call for it. However, any one can have white asparagus by keeping the light away from it while growing. This can be most cheaply done by covering the bed thickly, about the first of April, with a coating of salt hay.

P. T. Quinn
Money in the Garden, 1871

Editor's Note: Gardeners value salt hay because it resists compaction and is free of weed seeds, but you can use any type of straw or hay for blanching asparagus. The object is to keep light off the plants with a light-weight material that lets air in and allows the shoots to grow.

Give Asparagus a Break

Some of the best growers now advise the breaking of the asparagus shoots rather than cutting them. There is no danger of injuring the crown, and the shoot will not break in the tough and stringy part, and therefore the product is sure to be tender and crisp.

L. H. Bailey
The Principles of Vegetable Gardening, 1901

Editor's Note: You can prepare many vegetables for cooking while you're in the garden, and save time and kitchen cleanup.

Heat Up Your Asparagus Crop

If you cover a few asparagus plants, or a lusty rhubarb, with a barrel and bank fresh stable manure up around it, you can be gathering those vegetables before their unprotected brethren are even awake and growing.

E. L. D. Seymour
Garden Profits, 1911

Editor's Note: You can substitute actively working compost for manure.

Get a jump on the asparagus season by warming your plants with hot compost or fresh manure. Put a barrel around the asparagus first to keep the manure from touching the plants. Fresh manure releases ammonia and other nitrogen compounds, which can "burn" if they come in contact with your plants.

Strange But True

Take the strongest spears, just as they show above the ground, and put dark green bottles over them. They must be put vertically, not more than half an inch in the ground, and therefore must be supported by sticks. Deprived of sun and air, the asparagus now quickly grows to the top of the bottle, and unable to grow higher, grows now along the walls of the bottle until the whole bottle is filled by it, and gets lifted from the ground. Now is the time to cut your asparagus and break the bottle.

The Gardener's Monthly, 1877

Editor's Note: Was this a hoax? A German periodical claimed that asparagus could be grown large enough to fill a wine bottle. But that article was treated as a hoax when reprinted in *The Gardener's Monthly,* a Philadelphia magazine.

When to Stop Picking Spears

The old rule to stop picking asparagus when green peas come is a good one.

American Agriculturist, 1879

Trap Crops Stop Asparagus Beetles

In asparagus beds being cut, leave small trap shoots; twice a week cut these and destroy.

L. H. Bailey
The Principles of Vegetable Gardening, 1901

Editor's Note: Hungry asparagus beetles tend to gather on young, uncut asparagus shoots. Go through the asparagus patch daily with a pan of very hot water, and shake the insects into it to destroy them.

Asparagus beetles appear in spring to feed on the tips of asparagus shoots.

Beans

Eyes Down for Earlier Harvests

Beans planted with the eyes *down* will make a quicker growth—other conditions being equal—than others.

E. L. D. Seymour
Garden Profits, 1911

Double-Crop Corn and Beans

How would a corn stalk do for a lima bean pole? Try planting a row of beans in a row of corn. Let the corn have a start of three weeks or so.

Farm Journal, 1888

Sunflower Bean Poles

If you find it difficult to procure good bean poles, spend a few cents for sunflower seed, start them early in the season, and transplant when a foot or more high to the bean hills—or rather where the bean hills are to be—sowing the beans around the sunflower. This, in one case at least, solved the problem admirably, with apparently no effect on the quality or yield of the beans. All that was necessary was to strip off the lower leaves of the sunflower stalk, that light and air might reach the bean vines.

E. L. D. Seymour
Garden Profits, 1911

Limas without Poles

By cutting off all the vines, or slender twining branches, the plant soon loses the disposition to climb up poles, and remains a thick-set bush, bearing as abundantly as if it were trained in the usual way.

The Gardener's Monthly, 1872

A Beautiful Bean Trellis

When the beans are up sufficiently high, I cultivate carefully until they start their runners, then go to the lumberyard and get three light 2 x 3 posts and 2 x 3s for a ridge pole. If my rows are 20 feet long, I put one post equidistant between the rows at each end, and one in the middle. Then I put the ridge pole as high on the posts as I can reach. I then split some short stakes about 15 inches long and drive them directly in the rows of beans in a slanting position about 3 feet apart. Then I run a string along these stakes, looping it on them to keep it from slipping, and from this string I pass strings over the ridge board to each bean hill, and the work is done; only I then carefully loosen up the soil, pull the earth from the center well up to the rows, and then let them run along the strings till they reach the top, which is the signal for pinching the runners off. When a little care is taken to do the work neatly, the growing beans are an ornament in the garden.

"Delta"
American Agriculturist, 1895

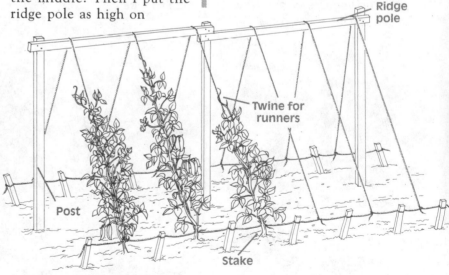

You can get pole beans to clamber up any rough sort of support, but this trellis will turn the vines into an ornamental feature of the garden. The structure is made from 2 x 3 studs. The posts should be as high as you can reach, plus another 2 feet for the end that will go in the ground. The stakes can be of any sort of wood. Use 6-penny nails (sold as 6d) to fasten the ridge pole to the posts.

Scarlet Runner Beans for Color and Flavor

The young pods of scarlet runner beans are tender and well flavored; and the seeds, green or ripe, are much esteemed in many localities. In Britain, the green pods only are used; on the Continent, the ripened seeds are as much an object of culture; in Holland, the runners are grown in every cottage garden for both purposes; while in France and Switzerland, they are grown chiefly for the ripened seeds. In England they cover arbors; are trained over pales and up the walls of cottages, which they enliven by the brightness of their blossoms; while every day produces a supply of wholesome and nutritious food for the owner.

Fearing Burr
Garden Vegetables and How to Cultivate Them, 1866

Cook scarlet runner bean pods like green beans, or dry the seeds. Don't forget the flowers—they're edible too, and their brilliant scarlet color adds visual punch to salads.

One Pole, Four Bean Plants

Any light rod is placed in the center of a place occupied by four pole bean hills, the hills being about three feet away from the base of the pole; a string is then led from each hill to the top of the pole, so that one pole does for four hills. The vines travel up the strings.

Meehans' Monthly, 1892

Simply Amazing Scarlet Alley

It is a great fashion in some parts of England to make scarlet runner beans border the garden walk. Very light poles are employed—not thicker than broom handles, and two are attached together somewhat like the letter X, only that the point of crossing is near the apex. When in bloom, it gives a solid sheet of scarlet flowers, which anyone who once sees will never forget.

The Gardener's Monthly, 1873

Editor's Note: You can use lengths of bamboo, saplings with the limbs removed, or inexpensive 1 x 3 lumber to make this attractive flowering alley. For a longer walk, add one or more Xs to the basic form until you reach the desired length. You'll get not only an arbor of brilliant flowers, but also lots of easy-to-pick beans to eat fresh or dried.

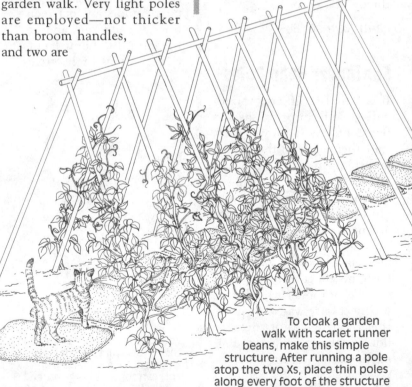

To cloak a garden walk with scarlet runner beans, make this simple structure. After running a pole atop the two Xs, place thin poles along every foot of the structure to support the vines.

Strange But True

The writer in the "Rural Intelligencer" stated that he had raised real coffee in Mount Vernon, Maine. It turns out that what he called coffee was nothing but a species of the chickpea. The same thing was produced in Maine as long ago as 1830, to our knowledge. It was said to have come from South America, and was recommended as a substitute for real coffee, which purpose it answered rather better than common peas.

Boston Cultivator, 1855

Gather Scarlet Runner Beans Straight

Many years ago I learned this piece of wisdom from an old cottager: "Gather your Runner Beans while they are straight." As the pods grow large and old they become curly in shape; any time before this occurs they are nice and tender.

Gertrude Jekyll
Home and Garden, 1900

A Tasty Bean to Eat

The scarlet runner bean, on account of its gay blossoms and decorative value, has many enthusiastic admirers. I had grown it solely on this account for a long time before I realized that it could be used as a vegetable, and a most delicious one at that. Remove the ends and strings, if there are any, and cut up the pod in small slices. Some cooks split them lengthwise. Cook in salted boiling water an hour or two, and before serving dress with butter, pepper, and salt or a cream sauce.

Laura B. Carpenter
The Garden Magazine, 1909

Editor's Note: Modern cooks have found that cooking vegetables less makes them tastier and more nutritious. Cook or steam scarlet runner beans for just a few minutes until they're tender-crisp, and they'll have a much better flavor than if you use Carpenter's recipe.

Eat Turtle Beans— Not Turtles

The ripe seeds of turtle beans are small, glossy black, somewhat oblong, and much flattened. They are used, as the name implies, in the preparation of a soup, which, as respects color and flavor, bears some resemblance to that made from the green turtle.

Fearing Burr
Garden Vegetables and How to Cultivate Them, 1866

A Test for Stringy String Beans

The stringiness in snap beans is, of course, to be avoided. One can tell whether beans are good or not by merely looking at the point that projects beyond the body of the bean. If it is limp or curved the bean will snap; if it is straight and rigid there will be a string.

Glenn Sevey
Bean Culture, 1914

Editor's Note: Most modern string beans are stringless, so you won't have to deal with stringy beans. If you're growing heirloom beans with strings, Sevey's advice is worth following.

The bean on the right, with its curved protrusion, will produce a satisfying snap. The bean on the left, with a straight point, will be stringy.

Beets

How to Tell When Beets Are Beat

Beets develop white lines or rings and lose their flavor when cooked, if they are allowed to get tough and woody.

E. L. D. Seymour
Garden Profits, 1911

A Tart of Beet Roots

First roast your beet roots in the embers and peel them very well, cut them in pieces and give them a boil with a glass of white wine and then beat them in a mortar, with a piece of sugar, a little salt, and cinnamon, and put them into fine paste with some green citron rasped and a piece of butter and do not cover it, but when it is baked, serve it with perfumed sugar and orange flowers.

Giles Rose
A Perfect School of Instructions for the Officers of the Mouth, 1682

Bigger Isn't Necessarily Better

Every year a great ado is made about monstrous beets—twenty and thirty pounders. There is no objection to these giants, unless they beget the idea that size is the test of merit. For table use, medium-sized fruits and vegetables are every way preferable; a beet should never be larger than a goose egg.

Henry Ward Beecher
Fruits, Flowers and Farming, 1859

Broccoli

The Fresher, the Better

We have frequently noticed an intensely bitter flavor in the broccoli sent to market, even when cooked in the most careful manner. Everyone who can should grow their own, and cut it an hour before dinner!

Mme. Vilmorin-Andrieux
The Vegetable Garden, 1885

Protect Broccoli from Heat

By the middle of June the broccoli heads will begin to form. If the weather is very warm, the heads sometimes "button" or run to seed. By bending some of the large leaves over the young heads, to shade them from the hot sun, the buttoning may be prevented.

P. T. Quinn
Money in the Garden, 1871

Editor's Note: Bend two or three large leaves over the forming heads just enough to break the skin of their midribs. You want the leaves to stay green, so damage them as little as possible.

Protect Broccoli from Cold

Sometimes broccoli does not head before there is danger of frosts, especially if growing vigorously. If taken up with small balls of earth, and set in a damp cellar, they will still perfect themselves.

The Gardener's Monthly, 1871

Strange But True

On the whole, broccoli gives little promise of becoming a prominent vegetable in this country.

John W. Lloyd
Productive Vegetable Growing, 1914

Brussels Sprouts

Cut, Don't Break, Brussels Sprouts

In gathering, brussels sprouts are frequently broken from the stems of the plants, and sometimes with a portion of the stem adhering to them. This is wrong, inasmuch as it destroys the second crop of young sprouts. A sharp knife should be used to cut off the sprouts, leaving as much spur as possible.

Mme. Vilmorin-Andrieux
The Vegetable Garden, 1885

Not fond of Brussels sprouts? Try pickling the small, cabbage-like heads to make a handy-sized snack food.

Buckwheat

Better than Beet Greens

Greens for buckwheat are easily obtained, easily prepared, and cook very quickly, and all whom I ever saw eat of them pronounce them fully equal, some deeming them superior, to beet greens. We gather buckwheat for greens anytime after it is large enough until nearly in blossom.

The Household, 1878

Editor's Note: Seed catalogs and members of an organization called Seed Savers Exchange offer seeds of buckwheat varieties with edible foliage. See "Sources" on page 316 for ordering information.

Harvest Buckwheat Seeds Still Green

The time to cut buckwheat is whenever about half of the kernels are ripe. Best to not wait for all to ripen. The greener grains, if almost mature, will harden after cutting.

Farm Journal, 1905

Editor's Note: Buckwheat seeds ripen at different times. If you wait for all of the seeds to be ripe, you'll probably lose some of the older ones. It's better to harvest early and bring home all of your crop.

Cabbage

Be Firm with Cabbage Seedlings

The rule among gardeners is that the cabbage transplant should be fastened (planted) so firmly that, when the edge of one of the leaves is taken hold of by the thumb and finger, the piece of leaf would be torn off before the plant could be pulled out of place.

P. T. Quinn
Money in the Garden, 1871

Old-time gardeners prepared cabbage seedlings for planting by dipping the roots in a mixture of composted cow manure and water. They made the mix thick enough that some of the goo adhered to the roots.

Preventing Cracked Cabbage

Cabbage heads that become of full size just before a heavy rain are the ones that burst. At the first indication of the outside leaves cracking, pull the head enough to break some of the roots, and lay the head on one side on the ground. This stops growth for a while, and gives us a second chance to use the cabbage before it is ruined.

Farm Journal, 1905

Give Cabbage a Second Chance...

Don't pull up your cabbages. Cut them off, leaving all the stalk you can, and in a short time a cluster of small heads will develop, which will provide you with some of the tenderest and most delicate cabbage you ever ate. You can afford to harvest these soon, while they are tenderest, for they represent a supplementary crop, a sort of free premium that you weren't, perhaps, expecting.

E. L. D. Seymour
Garden Profits, 1911

...And a Third Chance

Those who are fond of cabbage greens, in the spring, can have plenty of them by saving the stocks and heeling them in after the cabbages have been cut off during the fall. Early in the spring these stocks are taken from their winter quarters and planted out in some nook or corner of the garden. Very soon the young cabbage sprouts may be gathered in abundance, before spring vegetables are ripe.

P. T. Quinn
Money in the Garden, 1871

There's still life in your cabbage plants even after you cut off their heads. Dig up the stalks and roots that remain, and set them in a trench to keep them from freezing. Place mulch over the top for extra insulation. Plant the stocks back in the garden in spring for a harvest of early greens.

Keep Cabbage Coming

Cut your cabbages, if you have to give them away to your neighbors, before the heads get overripe and useless, and you will have a continuance of young and tender heads, which are greatly to be preferred to those which are large, white, and hard.

Mme. Vilmorin-Andrieux
The Vegetable Garden, 1885

Spare the Weeds and Save the Cabbage

When cutworms are very numerous, we have lost from a half to two-thirds of the plants. If the weeds are kept down only about the hill, and permitted to grow for a few weeks between the rows (although it has a very slovenly look), it will save the cabbages, etc., by giving ample food to the cutworm. When the plants grow tough in the stem the weeds may be lightly spaded in, and the surface leveled with a rake.

Henry Ward Beecher
Fruits, Flowers and Farming, 1859

Editor's Note: There's more than one way to stop cutworms. Handpick these night-feeding pests just after sunset, using a flashlight to spot them. Or, put cardboard or newspaper collars around young plants.

Cutworms feed by curling their bodies around plant stems. Once plants are older, the stems are too big for cutworms to wrap themselves around.

OLD-TIME WISDOM

Dining room etiquette. Should you find a worm or insect in your food, say nothing about it.

E. B. Davis and B. G. Jefferis
The Household Guide, 1891

Recipe

Pickled Red Cabbage

Hang up the red cabbage for a few days to dry, then shred the leaves, and put them in layers in a jar with a little salt, pepper, and ginger, and fill up with cold vinegar.

William Dick
Encyclopedia of Practical Receipts and Processes, 1872

Cook the Cabbageworm

Every worm visible upon the cabbages may be killed by the use of hot water at the temperature of 130°F. The water may be boiling hot when put in the watering can, but it will not be too hot when it reaches the cabbage leaves.

Clarence Moores Weed
Insects and Insecticides, 1891

Editor's Note: One or two seconds of a hot-water wash won't hurt your plants, but will sizzle cabbage worms. Use a plastic watering can and gloves when you try this so you don't burn your fingers.

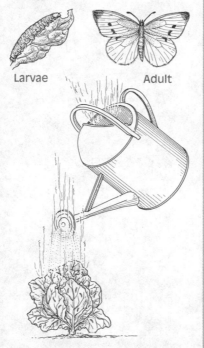

Imported Cabbageworm

Larvae   Adult

The velvety green worms that munch your cabbage plants are the larvae of a white butterfly known as the imported cabbageworm. As soon as you see the worms (or their dark green droppings), douse them with hot water or pick them from plants by hand.

Cardoon

A Treat for Artichoke Lovers

Cardoon is a perennial plant native to South Europe. The fleshy leaf stalks when blanched, as well as the thick fleshy main roots, are the edible portions. Plants are placed in holes or trenches about 1 foot deep, and from 4 to 5 feet apart. The space between the rows is utilized for quick-growing crops like radishes, early carrots, lettuces, dwarf beans, spinach, etc., which are taken off before the blanching process begins. Blanching takes place in autumn.

John Weathers
Commercial Gardening, 1913

Editor's Note: Cardoon tastes like its relative, the globe artichoke, but it's easier to grow. You'll need lots of room for these plants, since they can reach six feet tall and need at least two feet to spread out their prickly leaves. Given their size, interplanting makes good space-saving sense.

To blanch cardoon, start three weeks before harvest. Gather the leaves together with twine, and wrap them with straw or cardboard to keep light from getting inside.

If you like artichokes, you'll like cardoon. Fry, steam, or sauté the peeled leaf stalks, or use them to flavor soups or stews.

Strange But True

Digestion Times for Common Foods

	Hrs.	Min.		Hrs.	Min.
Apples, sweet	1	30	Butter, melted	3	30
Apples, sour	2	00	Goose, roast	2	00
Beans, boiled	2	30	Oysters, raw	2	55
Beets, boiled	3	45	Pork, raw	3	00
Cabbage, boiled	4	30	Tripe, boiled	1	00
Parsnips, boiled	2	30	Venison, broiled	1	35
Potatoes, baked	2	30			
Potatoes, boiled	3	30			
Turnips, boiled	3	30			

E. B. Davis and B. G. Jefferis
The Household Guide, 1891

Editor's Note: Cooks of the 1800s tended to boil their vegetables to death because these foods were considered difficult to digest. According to the authors, raw oysters and broiled venison steaks were less of a challenge for the stomach than boiled beets and turnips!

Timing Is Everything

With potatoes, cabbages, or corn, a week or ten days will make but little difference in the time of the first hoeing, provided the ground is in good heart. But with carrots this loss of time is irreparable, for, unless the ground between the rows is disturbed just when the carrots are coming up, the weeds will get ahead, and it will require a season's labor to make up the loss sustained by a few days' neglect at the commencement. "A stitch in time saves nine," and early and frequent disturbance of the ground materially lessens the expense of cultivating carrots.

P. T. Quinn
Money in the Garden, 1871

Cardoon Demands Delicate Cooking

Cooked in a delicate way, cardoon is excellent, but with the ordinary cook this, like many another good vegetable, is often spoiled. The degree of tenderness to which it is boiled should be studied, and the sauce should not be rank with salt and spice after the vulgar fashion.

Mme. Vilmorin-Andrieux
The Vegetable Garden, 1885

Editor's Note: Like most vegetables, cardoon is best if steamed or sautéed until it is tender-crisp. Overcooking turns vegetables to tasteless mush.

Carrots

Carrots for Tardy Gardeners

It's never too late to garden. Most people would give up all hopes of fresh vegetables, if the ground hadn't been broken by July. A safe crop to sow at any time during July is carrots. The roots do not need time to mature before cold weather, as they are excellent for the table when young and tender—the younger the better, indeed—before they reach full growth.

E. L. D. Seymour
Garden Profits, 1911

Are you tired of carrots served the same old way? A traditional alternative is to boil and then mash them with butter, salt, and pepper. Serve very hot.

Put More Color in Your Butter

The juice of the yellow carrot, when expressed by grating the raw root and pressing the juice through a cloth, makes an excellent and harmless color for butter, giving it the much-prized golden tint of early grass butter in the spring.

Ida D. Bennett
The Vegetable Garden, 1908

Editor's Note: Bennett may be referring to an heirloom carrot like 'Oxheart', which has a yellow core, but any carrot should do.

Cauliflower

Give 'Em a Drink

Cauliflowers should generally be watered in a dry season when they show fruit, in order to swell the head. In a light soil, this never should be omitted.

Rev. Charles Marshall
An Introduction to the Knowledge and Practice of Gardening, 1796

Celeriac

Recipe

Celeriac Salad

A most excellent autumn salad is celeriac well boiled, cut in slices like beetroot, mixed with a light mayonnaise sauce, half oil and half cream, surrounded by a wreath of garden cress.

Marie Theresa Villiers Earle
More Pot-Pourri from a Surrey Garden, 1899

Editor's Note: Celeriac tastes like celery, but you eat the roots rather than the stalks. Harvest celeriac roots when they reach two to four inches in diameter. You can use the leaves for flavoring since they also taste like celery. Garden cress (*Lepidium sativum*) has the peppery flavor of watercress.

Chicory

Grow Your Own Coffee Substitute

Coffee chicory is distinguished by its long, fleshy roots. After being properly cleaned, cut them into small pieces, dry them thoroughly in a kiln or spent oven (an oven that is still hot from baking), and store for use. After being roasted and ground, chicory is mixed with coffee in various proportions, and thus forms a pleasant beverage.

Fearing Burr
Garden Vegetables and How to Cultivate Them, 1866

Editor's Note: Since colonial times, Americans have grown chicory as an alternative to coffee. If you'd like to taste this treat without all the bother, look for instant coffee mixes that contain chicory.

When coffee is scarce, chicory makes a good substitute or filler. Even if you like your coffee straight, you'll enjoy growing chicory for its distinctive blue flowers.

Chicory Roots for the Table

At our inn we were informed that the chicory plant is raised from seed every spring. The tender leaves are used in salads early in the spring. The roots are considered fit for use when they are of the size of small carrots or parsnips; they are scraped and boiled, and eaten along with potatoes, with a sauce made with butter and vinegar.

Royal Caledonian Horticulture Society
Journal of a Horticultural Tour, 1832

Harvest Wild Greens from Waste Places

The young chicory leaves are eagerly sought for by Italians in our midst. Every morning, in season, these industrious persons are scanning the waste places for the young tops, with knife in hand and a large bag to hold their finds, in the same way that they gather dandelion tops earlier in the season.

Meehans' Monthly, 1902

Corn

Boil Corn *before* Husking

Remove the outer husks and strip back the inner, so that the silk may be removed; this should be very carefully done and the husks replaced. Put in boiling water and boil for twenty minutes and serve hot, first removing the husks. The object of leaving the husks on is that the corn, cooked in this way, is much sweeter than when the husks are removed.

Ida D. Bennett
The Vegetable Garden, 1908

OLD-TIME WISDOM

Plant corn by these clues. An old rule, and one that may be followed safely, is, plant first corn when the shadbush is in full bloom or when the leaves of the white oak are as large as a mouse's ear.

Loring Underwood
A Garden Diary and Country Home Guide, 1908

Editor's Note: This old saying is complicated by the fact that we have many shadbush or serviceberry species (*Amelanchier* spp.) growing in North America, and their blooms appear any time from March through August. So white oak leaves make a better guide. Another old-time tip suggests planting when the soil feels warm to your bare bottom—make sure the neighbors aren't watching!

Recipe

Coffee from the Cob

We got some nice wheat and sweet corn of a farmer, prepared and put it in the oven in flat tins to burn (roast slowly). After burning, grind it and set away in separate boxes. We generally put ours in paper bags and then in boxes, as it keeps the strength better. In making coffee, put in half and half of each, and sweeten with a little molasses.

The Household, 1878

Black Corn: How Sweet It Is

Black corn is a striking sight to anyone who has not seen it before. Ours caused considerable comment among our friends. It is suitable for a small garden, because it is very productive but does not take up much space. The stalks are short and slim and can be planted close together. It is one of the sweetest kinds, and bears a good-sized ear for a small-growing sort.

Boston Cultivator, 1872

Editor's Note: 'Black Aztec' is a black sweet corn variety that's still available. See "Sources" on page 316 for ordering information.

Recipe

Succotash, Cob and All

Take a pint of fresh-shelled lima beans; put them in a pot with enough cold water to a little more than cover them. Scrape the kernels from twelve ears of young sweet corn, first carefully removing every particle of silk; put the cobs in with the beans, boiling from a half to three-quarters of an hour. Then take out the cobs and put in the corn, boiling fifteen minutes. Season with salt and pepper to taste, a lump of butter the size of an egg, and half a cup of cream. Serve hot.

Ida D. Bennett
The Vegetable Garden, 1908

To Put the Pop Back in Popcorn

If the corn gets too dry, it will not pop. Immerse the ear one-half minute in water and it will pop nicely.

E. B. Davis and B. G. Jefferis
The Household Guide, 1891

Editor's Note: If you're trying to revive popcorn that's already been shelled, add a few drops of water to the jar the kernels are stored in.

A Test of Good Popcorn

A good sample of corn will increase about twenty times.

John W. Lloyd
Productive Vegetable Growing, 1914

Editor's Note: That is to say, if you cook 1 cup of good popcorn kernels, you should get 20 times that much of popped corn, or 5 quarts.

Recipe

Popcorn Balls

Pop the corn and leave it in the pan, rejecting all the unpopped kernels. Then take sugar or molasses and boil it until it becomes sufficiently waxy when dropped in water, so it will adhere to the kernels of the popcorn. Pour it while still warm on the corn and stir thoroughly. Then lift out with a spoon in such quantities as may be desired to roll into balls.

E. B. Davis and B. G. Jefferis
The Household Guide, 1891

Cucumbers

Water Automatically

Here is a method of watering cucumbers or melons that beats any surface watering, no matter how carefully done. Sink a tin tomato can (through the bottom of which a couple of small nail holes have been made) two-thirds of its depth in the center of the hill. Fill this can with water any time of the day you please; you do not have to wait until the sun goes down. The water is thus supplied to the plant in a gradual and natural manner, and at a normal temperature.

Farm Journal, 1906

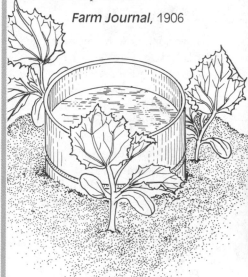

A few holes can turn a tin can into a simple irrigation system. Use it to give the roots of thirsty cucumbers and melons a steady supply of water. If the water percolates into the soil too slowly, try putting a couple of handfuls of mulch or compost in the bottom of the hole before lowering the can into place.

Grow Comely Cukes Just for Their Looks

Some gardeners make a special point of having a collection of plants of the cucumber family. They are all climbing vines, and require trellises for their support. The chief point of interest is in their fruit, some being round and others long, and of different shapes and varieties of color. A little patch of the different kinds of cucurbits will afford a fund of pleasure for a whole season.

Meehans' Monthly, 1897

Have a Cuke, on the House

I wonder how many ever tried planting two or three cucumber vines close to the house and training them up with strong strings. I had one this summer, trained up the side of the house like a vine, and it kept fresher and gave me more cucumbers than any one hill in open ground. This would be quite a scheme for one living in town with limited room for gardening.

Mrs. A. D. Babcock
Practical Farmer, 1902

Test Cucumber Seeds before Sowing

When the fruit is first cut, the seed should be put into a bowl of water, and that which swims on the surface is worthless; the good will sink to the bottom. This can only be depended upon at the time the fruit is first cut; if the seed has been dried and kept for any length of time, it will probably all swim, though it has not lost its vegetating properties.

William Dick
Encyclopedia of Practical Receipts and Processes, 1872

Old-Time Wisdom

Cucumber seeds age well. Seed from two to four years old is preferable to newer seed, which is more apt to run luxuriantly in vine, and the plants from which do not show fruit so soon or so abundantly as those from seed of a greater age. Seed which has been kept more than four years is sometimes found to be too much weakened.

J. C. Loudon
An Encyclopedia of Gardening, 1850

Cuke-in-a-Box

To raise early cucumbers, make boxes 8 inches square and 4 inches high; tack on bottoms so they can be easily removed; fill the boxes with rich soil; plant your seeds and keep them in the house until the weather becomes warm, watering them occasionally; then, having the ground in readiness, remove the bottoms and set the boxes on the ground, six feet apart, where you intend the cucumbers to grow; when the vines begin to put forth, cover the ground with straw as far as they will extend; this is to prevent the weeds from choking the plants, and the yield will be more extensive.

The People's Journal, 1854

1 × 4 boards

Remove bottom before setting out

6-penny common nails

With a hammer, nails, and scraps of lumber roughly ¾ inch thick and 3½ inches in width, you can slap together individual seedling flats for cucumbers. When attaching the bottom, don't drive the nails in all the way; let the heads protrude so that you can more easily remove the bottom boards when you set the plants out in the garden. Make sure you use untreated lumber for this project so chemical preservatives don't leach into your soil.

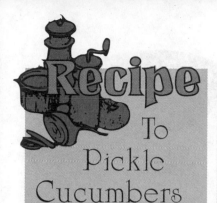

Recipe To Pickle Cucumbers

To 4 quarts vinegar, add 2 cups sugar; 3 nutmegs, grated; 2 large onions, sliced; ½ cup grated horseradish; 1 ounce mustard seed; 1 ounce celery seed; 1 ounce salt; ½ ounce mace; ½ ounce black peppercorns; 1 ounce allspice.

E. B. Davis and B. G. Jefferis
The Household Guide, 1891

When pickling cucumbers, feel free to omit the sugar in a recipe if you find that sweetness adds nothing to a pickle.

Late Cukes from May Cuttings

Cuttings of cucumbers may be struck in small pots of sawdust plunged in a bottom heat of 75° to 80°F, and will come in handy for late crops of fruit.

F. W. Burbidge
Cultivated Plants: Their Propagation and Improvement, 1877

Editor's Note: You can supply your cuttings with bottom heat in several ways. Electric heating pads or cables are the easiest modern devices for providing consistent bottom heat. But you can use a manure-heated hotbed if you'd like to try a more old-fashioned approach.

Cucumber in a Bottle

A hint for the boys: without detaching it from the vine, slip a small cucumber into a fair-sized bottle, and after it grows so as to fill the space, cut it from the vine. Folks will wonder how it got there.

Jacob Biggle
Biggle Garden Book, 1912

Editor's Note: And, presumably, the boys will wonder how to get the thing out. The cucumber can be retrieved only by breaking the bottle, and that means you'll risk getting a sliver of glass in the cuke. So it's best to enjoy the novelty of this trick without eating the cucumber.

Growing a big cucumber in a bottle with a small neck is the gardener's version of the old ship-in-a-bottle trick.

Roll Out the Barrel

Spade up the ground in a large circle. Take a barrel, with the bottom knocked out, and fill it two-thirds full of well-rotted manure. Plant cucumber seeds in hills around the barrel, and every day turn in upon the manure a pail or two of water. The water will soak its way through and keep the ground moist and rich.

Jacob Biggle
Biggle Garden Book, 1912

Editor's Note: Home centers often sell used whiskey barrels as planters. When the bottom of a planter gives out, you can try this hint. Your cucumbers will thrive since they'll get a manure-tea drink every time you water.

Radishes to the Rescue

Sow radish seeds in cucumber and squash beds, and you will not be troubled with the vines being eaten by striped cucumber beetles. As the radishes grow, they may be pulled for the table, for by that time the danger to the cucumbers and squashes from the bugs will be past. The radish seems to possess a pungency which is effectual in driving away the bugs.

E. L. D. Seymour
Garden Profits, 1911

Cucumbers as Mock Asparagus

When cut into quarters lengthwise, and tied in bunches and boiled, cucumbers make a good substitute for asparagus.

P. T. Quinn
Money in the Garden, 1871

Eggplant

Wax Makes Them Last

We have successfully prolonged the eggplant season until the end of November. To do this we select fruits with unbroken skins before frost injures them, dip the broken parts of the stems into melted paraffin, enclose each eggplant in a sound paper bag, and hang in the attic or other protected place until needed.

I. M. Angell
The Garden Magazine, 1908

Earliest "Eggs" Are Biggest

The first eggs are always the largest, the fruit growing smaller as the season advances; especially is this true when water and liquid manure is withheld.

Ida D. Bennett
The Vegetable Garden, 1908

Saving Eggplant Seed

The eggs should first be peeled, and then the part of the stem end that contains no seeds cut off. The balance is cut into small pieces and thrown into a tub or pail of water. Each of these pieces is then taken in the hand and tightly squeezed; this displaces the seed from the flesh, and when all the seed is separated in this way, the pulp is thrown away. The good seed will settle at the bottom of the vessel. When the seed is freed from the pulp, it should at once be placed on a fine sieve, or on a board, with a smooth surface, spread out thinly and set in the sun to dry.

P. T. Quinn
Money in the Garden, 1871

Potato Bugs Love Eggplant

The plants are often seriously injured by the potato bug, which eats the stem of the blossom at the point where it curves over. Whenever the bug appears early in the season, the plants should be gone over daily to catch and destroy it. The destruction of these first blossoms will make two or three weeks' difference in the maturing of the first crop and must be met energetically. These first bugs which appear lay their eggs on the underside of the leaves, and these must be looked for and destroyed and little subsequent trouble will be experienced.

Ida D. Bennett
The Vegetable Garden, 1908

Editor's Note: Mulch your eggplants with straw to help keep potato bugs away. Pick off the yellowish orange, black-striped adult beetles, and sweep the soft-bodied, pinkish grubs off plants with a broom. The grubs will get lost in the straw.

Recipe

Eggplant Fritters

A whole peeled eggplant is put into boiling water containing one tablespoonful of vinegar or lemon juice and a little salt. Cook until tender, then mash and drain. To each cup of eggplant add a well-beaten egg, ¼ cup of flour, salt, and pepper. Fry in small, thin cakes, browning well.

I. M. Angell
The Garden Magazine, 1908

American gardeners have been slow in warming to the eggplant as a vegetable. It was once thought of as more of an ornamental, especially the white varieties.

Garlic

A Pretty (Strongly Scented) Sight

Allium sativum, the garlic of the cook, is quite worth growing in the mixed border to provide large, pale lilac balls on yard-high stems, beautiful from their first appearance when wrapped in their pointed green night-caps, but more so when the time comes for a split and the escape of the flower buds, to be followed by six weeks of flowering, and even late in the winter the seed heads are attractive, as they have such a bold outline.

The Practical Farmer, 1904

Greens

Grow Clean Greens

Mustard and cress, which is so delicious at five o'clock tea or with bread and butter and cheese, many people will not eat because it is so often gritty. This certainly makes it horrid; and if the cress is washed it makes it very wet, often without getting rid of the grit. The best way to grow it is to make the earth very damp before sowing, press it down flat, and then sow the seed very lightly on the top, making a division between the mustard and the cress. Cover it with a tile, or something else to make it dark, till it has sprouted, and then cut it carefully, straight into the plate or small fancy basket in which it is to be served, without washing it at all. If grown in this way and carefully cut, there will be no grit whatsoever.

Marie Theresa Villiers Earle
More Pot-Pourri from a Surrey Garden, 1899

Recipe

Pottage of Chopped Greens

Mince very fine spinach, chives, parsley, marigold flowers, succory (chicory), strawberry and violet leaves, stamp them with cooked oatmeal in a bowl, put chopped greens in with it: you may either put broth or water to them; if water, boil a good piece of butter in it; put sippets (croutons) in the dish, and pour it over them.

Elizabeth Cleland
The Receipt Book of Elizabeth Cleland, 1759

Editor's Note: Pottage is oatmeal porridge. The marigold mentioned is now known as pot marigold or calendula.

Sprouts from the Garden

By "small salads" gardeners and cooks understand the small herbs, or very young plants, which are used in the seed leaves; such as cress, mustard, radish, and rape; also the lamb's lettuce or corn salad. Others, such as sorrel, are either potherbs or salad herbs. Sometimes the white cabbage (winter cabbage), lettuce, endive, and succory (chicory) are also sown, to be cut in the seed leaf. Sow very thick in drills, or on beds of very finely pulverized soil, watering in dry weather, to accelerate germination and the succulency of the plants. Early in spring sow under glass or in a warm sheltered situation. Observe, that a supply is wanted in most families throughout the year.

Cut off the seed leaves, and about half their foot stalks, as soon as the former are expanded. Some prefer letting small salading grow till one or two of the proper leaves appear, in which case it is of a stronger flavor.

J. C. Loudon
An Encyclopedia of Gardening, 1850

Editor's Note: We modern gardeners have the luxury of buying sprouts at the grocery store. But you can get fresher and more varied flavors by growing your own sprouts at home.

Corn Salad for Out-of-Season Greens

Corn salad is a beautiful plant when in flower. Flowers light blue, sometimes white. This plant, in its young state, when only the radical leaves have appeared, constitutes the corn salad of our tables. It is cultivated in great abundance in all the kitchen gardens near the city of Philadelphia, and is to be found plentifully in our markets during nearly the whole year.

William P. C. Barton
Barton's Florae, 1818

Editor's Note: Few people today could identify corn salad (*Valerianella locusta*) on their salad plate. But the plant has taken over the job of sowing itself in some areas, having spread to out-of-the-way places. It appears in nouvelle cuisine under the more exotic French name, mâche.

Use the spoon-shaped leaves of corn salad (also known as lamb's lettuce) to add a bit of minty flavor to salads in spring, fall, and winter.

Corn Salad Culture

Two or at most three sowings will be sufficient—a principal sowing at the beginning or towards the middle of August; a secondary sowing early in September, to furnish crops in winter and early spring; and a smaller sowing in spring, the close of February or over the course of March, if the plants are required in continuation throughout that season, though they are apt to get rank-tasted in warm dry weather.

J. C. Loudon
An Encyclopedia of Gardening, 1850

Editor's Note: Many seed catalogs carry corn salad, but they may offer it as a cover crop instead of a salad green. You may also find corn salad listed under one of its other common names, lamb's lettuce or mache.

Mole Hills Grow Great Greens

I have more than once found how sweet and tender and how little bitter is the whitened growth of a wild dandelion when it has been blanched and drawn out in length by having to grow through a mole hill.

Gertrude Jekyll
Home and Garden, 1900

Harvest Hints for Dandelions

In spring, after the growth has made some progress, the leaves may be cut, taking care to leave the central tuft to grow; several successive cuttings may be made the same season, and the plants will last for several years. When used for salad, the whole tuft or crown is cut, the center being tenderest; as this prevents future growth, the plants must be renewed annually.

American Agriculturist, 1882

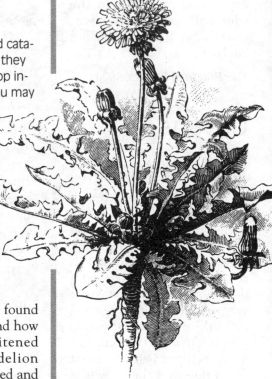

Dandelion flowers in your yard may drive you crazy, but the leaves make tasty salad greens if you grow them in your garden. Give dandelions a try, and harvest them before they put up their pretty yellow heads.

Taming the Wild Dandelion

The wild plants are usually small and with but few leaves, and the time required to prepare them for cooking is enormous. But if given room in which to grow on rich soil, and cultivated like other crops, the dandelion develops an immense mass of large, succulent leaves, and a much smaller number of plants is required to make a "mess of greens." Dandelions are cultivated in some private gardens. The seed is sown in early spring. As soon as the crop is harvested, the land should be plowed to kill out the roots and prevent any stray plants from going to seed.

John W. Lloyd
Productive Vegetable Growing, 1914

Editor's Note: Mail-order nurseries sell large-leaved dandelion varieties for eating. See "Sources" on page 316 for ordering information.

What's Up with Dock?

I want to speak a good word for a plant that is usually classed among the weeds. I refer to the *Rumex crispus*, or curled dock. Having a thick perennial root, it is one of the earliest plants to throw up its leaves in the spring, and these leaves form to my taste one of the best sort of greens that we have, cooked like spinach. It seems to me better than the colewort

(*Crambe cordifolia*) now so much eaten, and as it is perennial, it would be easier grown as a garden vegetable, and would come among the very earliest.

Dr. Seaman
Meehans' Monthly, 1892

Growing Hops for Greens

When the shoots of hops are about 6 or 8 inches high, before the leaves develop, they can be picked, tied together in a bundle, and cooked exactly like green asparagus. They have not much taste, but are pleasant in substance.

Marie Theresa Villiers Earle
More Pot-Pourri from a Surrey Garden, 1899

Hops Aren't Just for Beer

The young shoots of the hop, when blanched by covering them with earth, form an excellent substitute for asparagus, and are frequently eaten in the hop districts. The plant may be cultivated for this purpose in the kitchen garden, all that is necessary for its successful growth as a vegetable being a rich deep soil, and the earthing up of the shoots where they rise above the surface.

C. Pierpoint Johnson
The Useful Plants of Great Britain, 1862

Orach Adds Color to the Salad Patch

The leaves of orach are used as spinach. The stalks are good only while the plant is young; but the larger leaves may be picked off in succession throughout the season, leaving the stalks and smaller leaves untouched, by which the latter will increase in size. The spinach thus procured is very tender, and much esteemed in France.

J. C. Loudon
An Encyclopedia of Gardening, 1850

Editor's Note: Orach comes in many colors, but you can enjoy them only in salads—the plants turn greenish when boiled.

Left to grow through the season, orach may reach six feet tall and tower above your other vegetables. Most gardeners sow orach along with other greens in mesclun mixes and harvest it young for salad greens.

Cook Up a Mess of Purslane

The purslane, after being picked and washed, is put on a gentle fire to melt (wilt), without adding any water. When quite soft, add some salt (a very little) to taste. If too watery, pour it off; then add butter (a rather larger piece than the size of a walnut), and carefully mix a well-beaten egg; or, if this does not suit the taste, bind it with a little flour.

Marie Theresa Villiers Earle
More Pot-Pourri from a Surrey Garden, 1899

If you do much weeding, you probably know purslane, but it may come as a surprise to you that it's edible. The leaves and stems are thick and fleshy, which is why they survive when you uproot them with your hoe or toss them in your compost pile. You'll find that eating purslane is really the most effective method of weed control.

Shepherd's Purse for Boiled Greens

In Philadelphia, this plant is brought to market in large quantities in the early season. The taste, when boiled, approaches that of the cabbage, but is softer and milder. Those from the gardens and highly cultivated spots near Philadelphia come to a size and succulence of leaf scarcely to be believed without seeing them. They may be easily blanched by the common method, and certainly, in that state, would be a valuable addition to the list of delicate culinary vegetables.

Transactions of the Horticultural Society of London, 1830

Editor's Note:
Shepherd's purse (*Capsella bursa-pastoris*) is a widely distributed annual weed. You can easily identify it by the wedge-shaped seeds, which were once thought to look like purses carried by medieval shepherds. If you're curious about this wild plant that Philadelphians once liked so well, see "Sources" on page 316 for ordering information.

Watercress in a Pot

Almost any pot will answer. These you half fill with broken bricks, put on a layer of moss, and over that place good, rich soil, no matter how coarse, and well pressed down and rounded up; on the surface of this, bits of rooted cress or cuttings are dibbled in, about 3 inches apart. The pot sits in a saucer holding 2 inches of water. The newly planted pots are kept in the shade for a few days, and then exposed to full light and air; in summer the plants give a cutting in less than three weeks after planting, and give three cuttings in succession, when the pot is replaced by another started later.

American Agriculturist, 1876

Watercress prefers to grow in a babbling brook. If your property doesn't happen to have fresh water on it, you can raise this tasty plant in a pot placed in a shallow dish of water. Harvest watercress when the shoots reach four to six inches tall in spring. You can use the peppery-tasting leaves and shoots to liven up salads or sandwiches.

Horseradish

Horseradish and Early Cabbage

Horseradish cuttings may be planted at the first opening of spring, but since the plant makes the larger part of its growth late in the season, it is customary to hold them rather late and to plant them with some other crop. They are often planted in the rows of early cabbages. If the horseradish grows so rapidly as to interfere with the cabbages, the tops may be cut off two or three times early in the season. When the cabbages are off, the horseradish takes the land.

L. H. Bailey
The Principles of Vegetable Gardening, 1901

Editor's Note: A space hog like horseradish can take up more room than you can spare. By interplanting it with an early crop like cabbage, you get double use from the same space.

Quick and Deep Planting Technique

One very good method is to make a hole with a crow bar and drop the pieces of horseradish root into the hole, so that it is a foot or so beneath the surface.

Meehans' Monthly, 1893

Reining In Horseradish

As the horseradish is likely to become a bad weed, it is necessary that all the small roots be taken out of the land. When the crop is harvested, therefore, all the loose roots are picked from the furrow and destroyed.

L. H. Bailey
The Principles of Vegetable Gardening, 1901

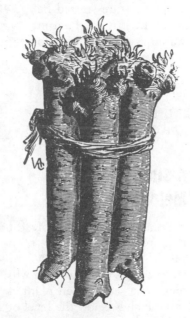

Just a smidgen of horseradish root, left in the soil in fall, can sprout in spring and spread like a weed throughout your garden. Remove *all* roots when you harvest in fall, or plant horseradish in a bottomless bucket, sunk in the soil, to keep the plant where you want it.

Keep Horseradish at the Ready

A few roots may be dug up and placed in a crock of water and will continue to grow and fur-

nish a pungent relish for weeks. It is only necessary to see that the water is changed occasionally, so that it does not become slimy, and horseradish will be at hand for immediate use without the trouble of going to the garden and digging it up each time it is wanted.

Ida D. Bennett
The Vegetable Garden, 1908

Only White Vinegar Works Right

Horseradish, when grated for the table, should be mixed with white wine vinegar, never with cider vinegar, as this gives it an unpleasant, dirty color.

Ida D. Bennett
The Vegetable Garden, 1908

Lettuce

In the Company of Cabbage

Head lettuce can be planted between the rows of early cabbage and also between the plants in the row. The lettuce is ready to cut just before the cabbage needs all the room.

John W. Lloyd
Productive Vegetable Growing, 1914

Editor's Note: You can interplant any early greens with your cabbage to make the best use of your garden space.

Romaine Reigns

Of late years the cos class of lettuce has nearly gone out of use. Those who know a good thing, however, when they see it, have still a tender regard for the memory of the old cos kind. It is far superior to the generality of lettuce such as we generally get. The reason for this comparative disappearance is probably the extra labor involved by the tying process. Cos requires to have the leaves tied up when the blanching process takes place in the center.

Meehans' Monthly, 1893

Editor's Note: It was customary to tie up the long leaves of cos or romaine lettuce ten or so days before cutting to bleach the color out of the center leaves. But that time-consuming technique is no longer in practice, so romaine is popular again.

For a taste of an old variety from the early 1800s, you can try 'Rouge d'Hiver', a deep red-colored romaine lettuce that's often used in mesclun salad mixes.

Jump-Starting Lettuce

Lettuce usually does best in a soil that is loose and warm, or one that the gardeners call "quick."

L. H. Bailey
The Principles of Vegetable Gardening, 1901

Melons

Give Melons a Late Start

Nothing is gained by very early planting and, indeed, flavor is frequently lost on account of the checked and weakened growth of the vines that are started before the nights become warm. A safe rule to follow is to wait until the trees are fully out in leaf before planting the seed.

E. D. Darlington
The Garden Magazine, 1908

A Simple Melon Forcing Bed

By making a square hole for manure, 20 inches deep, then putting on top of it two or three inches of soil, which will leave the seeds when planted three inches below the level of the surface—and placing over the top of this square opening a light of glass—a forcing bed is formed in the garden, which will be at once simple and effective as well as useful to keep off the bugs.

P. T. Quinn
Money in the Garden, 1871

Editor's Note: Fresh manure generates heat as it composts, and old-time gardeners put that free energy to work to warm their melon plants. You can use a spare storm window to trap the heat. Just be sure to take it off when days are sunny and bright to avoid baking your seedlings.

This simple forcing bed for melons will get your plants off to a quick start even in cool climates. It consists of a manure-filled hole, with low earth walls. A piece of glass laid on top of the walls traps the heat generated by the composting action below. When temperatures warm up, you can replace the glass with a floating row cover to keep bugs out and just a little heat in. Remove the cover when the plants flower.

Melon Warmers

In cold or mountainous regions, melons are hastened in the ripening process, and improved in flavor, by a piece of tile being placed under the fruit.

The Gardener's Monthly, 1871

Editor's Note: The tile works by collecting solar radiation. You can also use pieces of dark flagstone the same way.

Two Crops from One Melon Plant

When the fruit of the first melon crop is off, a second crop may be obtained from the stools (the lower stem, just above the crown), which often proves more effective than the first. As soon as the fruit is cut, prune the plant. Shorten the vigorous healthy runners at a promising joint, to force out new laterals, cutting about 2 inches above the joint. At the same time take off all decayed or sickly vines, and all dead leaves. Stir the surface of the mold (good, crumbly soil), and renew it partially, by 3 inches depth of fresh compost. Water the plant copiously.

J. C. Loudon
An Encyclopedia of Gardening, 1850

Trap Cucumber Beetles on Early Melons

In some cases, growers plant pumpkin or squash seeds in the field very early in order to attract the striped beetles where they may be killed, and the later frame-grown melon plants are then relatively safe.

L. H. Bailey
The Principles of Vegetable Gardening, 1901

Editor's Note: The seedlings that sprout directly from the garden soil aren't intended for a crop. They are simply a trap for any pests in the neighborhood. Gather and kill the striped cucumber beetles before you put out melons you've started in cold frames.

In spite of its name, the striped cucumber beetle has a varied diet that includes melon, squash, bean, and corn plants, plus the blossoms of many plants.

Homemade Citron for Your Next Fruitcake

Citron melon is employed in the making of sweetmeats (candied fruit) and preserves by removing the rind, or skin, and seeds, cutting the flesh into convenient strips and boiling in syrup which has been flavored with ginger, lemon, or some agreeable article. Its cultivation is the same as that of other kinds of melons.

Fearing Burr
Garden Vegetables and How to Cultivate Them, 1866

Citron melon isn't something you'd want to bite into raw. The flesh has to be candied by boiling pieces in a sugar syrup flavored with ginger or lemon. It is then ready for use in recipes like "A Tart of Beet Roots" on page 46.

Queen Anne's Pocket Melon

The perfume of this melon, which resembles that of other melons without being so strong, is rather agreeable as the fruit ripens, but the taste is not equally pleasant, and the plant is, consequently, only grown as a curiosity, or as an ornamental climber on trellises and arbors, or for covering bare slopes where the climate is warm enough.

Mme. Vilmorin-Andrieux
The Vegetable Garden, 1885

Editor's Note: The seeds of the pocket melon are still available through collectors (see "Sources" on page 316). The fragrant, attractively striped fruits grow to just three or four inches in diameter, and opinions vary on how good they taste.

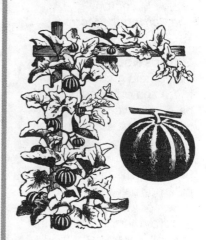

According to folklore, England's Queen Anne carried the fragrant pocket melon with her to mask body odor.

Mushrooms

Cook a Puffball?

Yes, the "puffball," or Lycoperdon (*L. perlatum* and *L. pyriforme*) is eatable and makes a very delicious dish. It should be steamed ten minutes, and then simmered in cream, or any sauce you like. Don't cut, but break it in flakes for cooking.

Lucy A. Millington
The Gardener's Monthly, 1878

Editor's Note: Use an illustrated field guide to identify these and other edible puffballs. The two species mentioned above are both pear shaped. The gem puffball (*Lycoperdon perlatum*) grows on the ground; the pear puffball (*L. pyriforme*) grows on decaying wood. Look for them in late summer and fall. Eat these puffballs only when they are young and pure white. If they appear at all yellowish inside, discard them—they are too ripe.

A Crop You Can Grow on Your Lawn

Mushrooms may be raised on the lawn. Plant the spawn two inches underground about June 1, and replace the sod. A warm, moist, but not wet condition of soil is the best.

Loring Underwood
A Garden Diary and Country Home Guide, 1908

Editor's Note: Mushrooms like moist, shady areas that are rich in decaying organic matter. You can order mushroom spawn from specialty growers (see "Sources" on page 316) to grow morels, shiitakes, or oyster mushrooms outdoors. Take care when you harvest, and pick only edible mushrooms. When in doubt, throw it out.

Okra

Keep Okra Hanging around All Winter

The okra pods can be kept for winter use, by slicing them and tying them up like dried apples.

P. T. Quinn
Money in the Garden, 1871

Editor's Note: Slice the pods crosswise, and string them up in a warm, dry area of the house. Toss them in soups or stews to rehydrate.

Harvest Hint

The time to cook okra is when the pods get a little larger than a pod of green peas, and until the pods get too tough.

The Household, 1882

Buyer beware: This old-time catalog picture tries to attract seed buyers by showing giant okra pods. These pods might make nice decorations, but only three-to four-inch-long pods will be tender and tasty.

Onions

By Seed or by Set, Onions You'll Get

If your soil is deep and very rich, onions can be grown in one season from the seed as well as from the set—we try it almost every year and never fail.

Henry Ward Beecher
Fruits, Flowers and Farming, 1859

Spot Ripe Onions by Their Tops

Onions are known to be ripe when a large share of the tops fall over. Pull, dry thoroughly, cut off the tops, and store in a dry, cool place.

American Agriculturist, 1884

Ongoing Onions

Onion sets prove useful in keeping the soil busy. If, whenever an onion is pulled, a set is thrust into the resulting space, there will be practically an unbroken succession of this popular vegetable.

E. L. D. Seymour
Garden Profits, 1911

Editor's Note: Onions help keep your soil loose and weed-free. Pop in an onion set whenever you have a spot of bare soil.

OLD-TIME WISDOM

A deodorant for hardworking hands. If you have been peeling onions, or doing any other work that leaves an unpleasant smell on your hands that will not wash off, hold them a moment in smoke of burned paper.

Farm Journal, 1885

Parsnips

Pretty as a—Parsnip?

Parsnips are an ornamental feature of the garden and may be grown to edge rows or beds of other vegetables if desired; they should occupy a prominent position in the garden, as their growth is lower than most other garden crops, and the beauty of the fernlike leaves makes them attractive at all times.

Ida D. Bennett
The Vegetable Garden, 1908

Parsnips like soil that's deep, loose, fertile, and well drained, just like carrots. Choose short-rooted varieties if your soil is heavy and longer-rooted types if your soil is good and deep.

Recipe

Parsnip Curry

Everybody grows parsnips, so far as I can make out, and hardly anyone ever eats them. Here is a receipt for anyone who does not dislike parsnips and does like curry. Boil some fine parsnips whole, without cutting them, wash and brush them, and put into just enough boiling water to cover them. Simmer till tender and till the water is nearly evaporated—about one hour and a half. Tear the parsnips into fine shreds with two forks. Sprinkle with cloves and a little dusted sugar. Have prepared apart a curry sauce. Pour this over the parsnips, warm up together, and serve with boiled rice.

Marie Theresa Villiers Earle
More Pot-Pourri from a Surrey Garden, 1899

Parsnips have a delicious, sweet, nutty flavor. It's a mystery why they aren't more popular. If you're not familiar with parsnips, buy a few and cook them like carrots. You'll be pleasantly surprised by their distinctive taste.

Recipe

Parsnip Fritters

Boil four or five parsnips; when tender, take off the skins and mash them fine; add to them a teaspoon of wheat flour and a beaten egg; put a tablespoon of lard or beef drippings in a frying pan over the fire, add to it a saltspoonful (a couple of pinches, to taste) of salt. When boiling hot, put in the parsnips which have been molded into small cakes with a spoon; when one side is a delicate brown, turn them over; when both sides are done, put them on a dish. These resemble very closely the taste of the salsify or vegetable oyster, and by many will be preferred.

Ida D. Bennett
The Vegetable Garden, 1908

Silverweed for Parsnip Lovers

The roots of this plant taste like parsnips, and are frequently eaten in Scotland either roasted or boiled. In the islands of Jura and Coll they are much esteemed, as answering in some measure the purpose of bread.

John Lightfoot
Flora Scotica, 1792

Editor's Note: Silverweed (*Potentilla anserina*) is a common yellow-blossomed wildflower. It gets its name from the unusual silvery color of the undersides of its leaves. If you can't find it in the wild and want to sample what was once a survival food on the two Hebridean islands mentioned above, see "Sources" on page 316 for ordering information.

Peas

Spread 'Em Out

In sowing peas, a common error is to sow them too thick: Each pea should be nearly two inches apart if the soil is rich, in order to have a very satisfactory crop of large pods. We hate to see the best half of mankind, namely, womankind, imposed upon by those gardeners who grow plenty of pods with no peas in them to "shell."

The Gardener's Monthly, 1872

Editor's Note: Another benefit of wide spacing is that your peas get better air circulation, which means less mildew.

Start Peas in Cold Ground

Sow peas as early as the ground can be worked in spring; old gardeners usually claim that they like to have the last snow find their peas in the ground.

Ida D. Bennett
The Vegetable Garden, 1908

Recipe

Peas in Turnip Cups

Peas as an entree may be served in cups made of boiled turnips, the turnips being first boiled whole and then removed from the fire, the centers scooped out, mashed, and served as a separate dish; the peas, boiled and dressed with a white sauce, or simply with butter, pepper, salt, and cream, and dusted with bread crumbs and a bit of butter, being returned to the oven for a moment to heat and slightly brown.

Ida D. Bennett
The Vegetable Garden, 1908

Pea Bush Boosts Harvests

When pea varieties of much taller growth are sown, a greater yield will be secured by bushing the plants, which is more economically as well as more strongly done if the planting is made in double rows. The staking, or bushing, should be furnished when the plants are three or four inches high. The stakes should be of equal height, and all straggling side twigs should be removed for appearance's sake.

Fearing Burr
Garden Vegetables and How to Cultivate Them, 1866

A traditional and easy way of supporting peas is with "bushing." Push twiggy branches into a garden bed firmly enough that they will stay in place through the months ahead. Plant peas on either side of the branches and they'll soon cover the bare wood with green.

Set Peas Super-Deep

Peas covered six or eight inches deep will produce twice as much as those covered but an inch; they continue to flower longer, and the vines are vigorous and do not lie down, as is often the case where shallow plantings are made. We have tested this matter, and therefore know from experience that if it is desired to get a large crop, the seed must be buried deep. Try it.

Utica Herald, 1865

Interplant Peas with…Peas

In a charming little garden in Charleston, South Carolina, garden peas grow side by side with sweet peas, and who must pick the one for his dinner is also tempted to feed his soul by picking the other.

Frances Duncan
The Joyous Art of Gardening, 1917

Pick Peas Perfect in the Pod

It is inexcusable that a gentleman having a garden of his own should be served with peas otherwise than in the very highest state of perfection, which they are not, if allowed to become too old, or even too large.

Fearing Burr
Garden Vegetables and How to Cultivate Them, 1866

Pluck 'Em Clean

Never pull your peas, but pluck them. Take the pod in the hand and break the pod from the vine with the thumb and first finger. Some pull them with an upward jerk, but this is likely to tear the vine loose from the support and often breaks or loosens it at the root, spoiling the remainder of the crop on that particular stem.

The Gardener's Monthly, 1875

Peppers

Peppers Keep Cheese Pest-Free

To prevent newmade cheeses from becoming fly blown and maggoty, take common garden peppers, let them be well dried and pulverized, then simmered in bacon fat thirty or forty minutes. Strain the fat off through a thin cloth, and it will be fit for use. When a cheese comes new from the press to the shelf, rub it all over with this preparation, and repeat it every time the cheese is turned, and ninety-nine in a hundred will be preserved free from skippers.

The Yankee Farmer, 1838

Editor's Note: Before refrigeration, cheese was vulnerable to fly damage. Skippers are the hopping larvae of a fly that is attracted to cheese.

Recipe

Prepared Cayenne Pepper

This is prepared from the pods of the chili or bird pepper. The ripe pods, dried in the sun, are placed in layers with wheaten flour in a dish or tray, and exposed in a stove room or half-cold oven until perfectly dry; they are then removed from the flour and ground to fine powder; to every ounce of this powder, 15 ounces wheaten flour are added, and made into a dough with a little tepid water and a teaspoonful of yeast; after fermentation is well set up, the dough is cut into small pieces, and baked in a slow oven until perfectly hard and brittle. It is then beaten or ground to powder, and forms cayenne pepper.

William Dick
Encyclopedia of Practical Receipts and Processes, 1872

Editor's Note: Nowadays, you can grind the dried fruits of 'Long Red Cayenne' peppers; into a powder using a food processor. (Take care when you work with cayenne peppers—the capsaicin, which makes them fiery, can burn your eyes and nose.)

Best Pepper Picks

There are twenty kinds of red pepper, but none of them better than the big mild bull-nose and the tiny cherry pepper, which is a nob of scarlet fire. Sow when the ground is warm, cultivate well, and gather when the pods show the least sign of turning. Thus they are stronger than when allowed to hang until a deep scarlet all over.

Emily Holt
The Complete Housekeeper, 1912

Recipe

Pickled Peppers

The pepper pods are picked while green, slit down on one side, and, after the seeds are taken out, immersed in salt and water for twenty-four hours, changing the water at the end of the first twelve. After soaking the full time, they are laid to drain an hour or two, put into jars, and boiled vinegar, after being allowed to cool, poured over them till they are entirely covered. The jars are then closely stopped for a few weeks.

Fearing Burr
Garden Vegetables and How to Cultivate Them, 1866

Potatoes

Bigger Crops from Bloomless Potatoes

The man who makes his potato ground feed flowers, prevents it feeding his children. Every ounce of matter consumed by the flowers is so much taken from the consumption of the family.

Henry Ward Beecher
Fruits, Flowers and Farming, 1859

Editor's Note: These days, putting food on the table doesn't depend on your potato harvest. If your time is more valuable than the size of your crop, let the flowers go—you'll still get plenty to eat. If you want to maximize your harvest, do keep the flowers picked off so the plants put their energy into spuds instead of blooms.

Milk Prevents Black Eyes

It may not be a matter of general information that in the spring, when the quality of potatoes has deteriorated, they are liable to show dark spots at the eyes when boiled. This may be prevented by the addition of a cupful of milk to the water in which they are boiled.

Ida D. Bennett
The Vegetable Garden, 1908

Recipe
Sweet Potato Confection

This is a southern recipe and will be found delicious. Wash and boil, with the skins on, 1 quart of medium, even-sized sweet potatoes; when tender, drain, peel and cut lengthwise about ¼ inch thick. For this quantity of potatoes you require ½ pound of good, sweet butter and 1 pound of light, dry brown sugar. Lay the potatoes in a large baking pan in layers, distributing the sugar and butter evenly. They must be watched and turned occasionally and care taken that the syrup does not burn. A medium oven is best.

Alice Chittenden
American Agriculturist, 1895

Quick-Start Potatoes

Potatoes can be sprouted before they are planted at all, being given thereby a tremendous start. The remarkable record of potatoes in seven weeks from sowing was made in this manner. A bushel of tubers which had developed half-inch sprouts was brought up from the

cellar and spread on trays in a light room where the temperature could be maintained between 40° and 65°F. The sprouts did not increase in length, but, with the surface of the tubers, took on a greenish-bronze appearance. On April 18, the seed was carefully planted in a light sandy loam, a pint of mixed hen manure and ashes being applied to each hill. The yield was fifteen bushels in seven weeks!

E. L. D. Seymour
Garden Profits, 1911

Sprouted green potatoes aren't for eating, but they'll give you a jump on the planting season. Cut potatoes in pieces, leaving at least one sprout per piece; then set them outside in loose soil. If your soil is heavy, plant the sprouted pieces shallowly and cover them with 10 to 12 inches of straw.

Recipe
Best Fried Potatoes

To have the fried potato at its best, one should boil medium-sized, new potatoes and remove them from the water as soon as done, allowing the steam to pass off, so that they may be dry and mealy, when they should be cut in dices and fried at once in hot butter or drippings. They should not be allowed to grow cold between the operation of boiling and frying and should be served at once on hot dishes.

Ida D. Bennett
The Vegetable Garden, 1908

Editor's Note: New potatoes are the young tubers harvested just after the plants start blooming.

Strange But True

When the potato is grafted on the tomato, which can be done by reason of the close relationship between the two plants, the potato roots continue to produce potatoes, while the tomato grafted on the potato stalk continues to produce tomatoes.

Meehans' Monthly, 1894

Recipes

Shaken Potato Salad

Potato salad in German fashion is thus made. Potatoes boiled in the "jacket" are peeled while warm, cut evenly into fine slices, and while still warm mixed with fine olive oil. After having drawn with this for a little while, add salt, pepper, chopped onion, and mix all this by shaking it up, as using a spoon would break the potatoes and make them unsightly; finally, add good vinegar, serve moderately warm.

The Household, 1879

Which is the best potato for potato salad? In 1871 P. T. Quinn, a practical horticulturist, recommended 'Early Rose' in his book, *Money in the Garden.* He called the 'Rose' one of the most popular early varieties, describing it as follows: "a large-sized potato, smooth skin, few eyes, flesh white, and steams or boils mealy." Another excellent and beautiful choice is the yellow-fleshed 'Yukon Gold'.

Potato Souffle

This makes an excellent lunch or supper dish and is suitable for company teas. To two cupfuls of cold mashed potatoes add ½ cupful of milk, a pinch of salt, a tablespoon of butter, two tablespoonfuls of flour, and two eggs, beaten to a froth. Mix until thoroughly light; put into a baking dish, spread a little butter over the top, and bake until a golden brown. The quality depends upon very thoroughly beating the eggs, so that the potato will remain light, like sponge cake.

Ida D. Bennett
The Vegetable Garden, 1908

Potato Puffs

Prepare the potatoes as for souffle (see the recipe above). While hot, shape in balls about the size of an egg; have a tin sheet well buttered and place the balls on it. As soon as all are done, brush over with beaten egg; brown in the oven. When done, slip a knife under them and slide upon a hot platter. Garnish with parsley and serve immediately.

Ida D. Bennett
The Vegetable Garden, 1908

Pumpkins and Gourds

Make Molasses from Pumpkins

Take pumpkins, boil them, press the juice out of them, and boil the juice to a proper consistency. There is nothing else necessary. The author has tasted this molasses, thinking it was the genuine kind, until the people of the house told him what it was.

John George Hohman
The Long-Lost Friend, 1819

Eggless Pumpkin Pie

The cooking books prescribe more eggs, to which there is no objection if the quantity of milk is increased accordingly; I have however eaten tolerable good pumpkin pies without any eggs at all.

"A Housekeeper"
Country Gentleman, 1854

For a great pumpkin pie, you don't need eggs, just a sweet pumpkin and plenty of spices. Choose a small pumpkin for the best flavor—they contain less water.

Strange But True

I found a man out in Prinevill who had established an industry of furnishing pumpkins of a given weight to ambitious farmers who desire to take prizes at the county fairs. How does he grow them? This pumpkin manufacturer feeds the pumpkins milk—just good, rich milk, and when the pumpkin has grown to the weight called for in his order from the ambitious farmer, he cuts it from the vine and turns it over to the one ordering it.

Every day he fills a quart vessel with milk, places it on the ground, and connects it with a slit in the pumpkin vine with a rubber tube. The vine draws in the milk by capillary or some other attraction. It was extremely interesting to go out in the evening and see the owner feed the pumpkins. The vines had become so used to it, and appeared to like the milk so well, that they actually rustled as the man with the milk approached. And when the milk had been consumed, the vines settled down for the night, as contentedly as a band of cows chewing their cuds.

Portland Oregonian, 1899

Engrave a Gourd

When a gourd is once scratched, the blemish will always remain, no matter how small it may be. Advantage may be taken of this, and a little engraving done on the gourd when it is small.

E. E. Wilcox
The Garden Magazine, 1906

Hanging Baskets from Gourds

Gourds are a very useful family. They are an ornamental feature of the summer garden, and afford an economic and unique addition to the winter's supply of plant receptacles, hanging baskets, low bowls for tulips, crocus, and other bulbs. Of the fruit of large-flowered ones the prettiest hanging baskets are made. Saw them in two when thoroughly ripe and dry, remove the pulp, scrape the shell clean and thin, and give a coat of green or brown shellac inside and out, and hang with brass chains. They are more satisfactory if the gourds are a year old and perfectly dry.

Ida D. Bennett
The Flower Garden, 1904

Use a hacksaw to cut a gourd's top off, drill holes in the bottom for chains, and presto—you've got a gourd hanging basket.

Radishes

Almost Instant Harvests

The radish seeds are to be first soaked for twenty-four hours and then placed in paper bags and exposed to the sun. They will begin to germinate in about twenty-four hours, and are then to be set in a box filled with well-manured earth, and moistened from time to time with lukewarm water. In five or six days the radishes will attain the size of a small onion.

The Gardener's Monthly, 1872

Radishes Make Good Companions

An excellent practice is sowing radishes and beets, carrots, or parsnips in the same row. The radishes germinate first, break any possible surface crust, and ripening rapidly, may be harvested before the permanent crop needs the space.

Fearing Burr
Garden Vegetables and How to Cultivate Them, 1866

Enjoy Radishes into Winter

A seed order in July! Who ever heard of such a thing? But that's no matter. Do you know the pleasure of having winter radishes? Sow the 'Black Spanish' winter radish between June 15th and July 15th.

The Garden Magazine, 1906

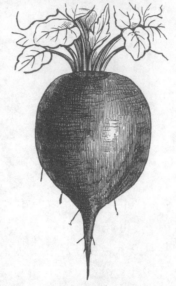

Stir-fry 'Black Spanish' radishes as you would Oriental radishes. They have a black skin and white flesh. Try newly introduced varieties of 'Black Spanish' types, like 'Nero Tondo', which are resistant to bolting (going to seed).

Grow Summer Radishes in Shade

Radishes usually suffer from the drought and heat incident to the summer, and, when grown at this season, are generally fibrous and very pungent. To secure the requisite shade and moisture, they are sometimes sown in beds of asparagus, that the branching stems may afford shade for the young radishes, and render them more crisp and tender.

Fearing Burr
Garden Vegetables and How to Cultivate Them, 1866

Rhubarb

Angelica Addition Makes Rhubarb Remarkable

If a small quantity of the leaf-stalks of angelica be cooked with rhubarb, the flavor of the compound will be acceptable to many who do not relish plain rhubarb. If the stems of angelica are young and juicy, they may be treated like rhubarb and cut up small, the quantity used being any proportion between 5 and 25 percent.

M. Grieve
Culinary Herbs and Condiments, 1934

Hang Rhubarb High

An old lady tells me she dries rhubarb every fall, when it is nice and tender. She prepares it as for pies, cutting it in bits about an inch in length, and stringing it as one strings apples to dry. Before using for pies in the spring, she soaks them overnight and the pieces fill out and become quite as good as new. They are very good mixed with stewed dried apples, seasoned with lemon or cinnamon, and make a pie that tastes like "something new under the sun."

Rosella Rice
The Household, 1878

Editor's Note: Drying rhubarb for pies is an intriguing idea, but cut the stalks in spring when rhubarb is at its best.

Rutabagas

Rutabaga Mash

Yellow turnips (rutabagas) are greatly improved when served mashed, by mixing with them a small quantity of Irish potato.

Farm Journal, 1911

Salsify

Salsify: An Oyster Substitute

When boiled and afterwards coated with rolled crackers and fried in butter salsify has a decided oyster flavor, from which the name vegetable oyster is derived.

Agricultural Service Co.
The Vegetable Garden, 1912

Asparagus Flavor from Salsify Shoots

The young flower stocks, if cut in the spring of the second year, and dressed like asparagus, resemble it in taste, and make an excellent dish.

Fearing Burr
Garden Vegetables and How to Cultivate Them, 1866

Editor's Note: Salsify is a biennial that flowers in the spring of its second year. The oyster-flavored roots are usually what gardeners are after, but the flower stalks can be a treat as well.

Salsify is a plant with a split personality. The tops taste something like asparagus and the roots a little like oysters.

Scorzonera: A Second Salsify

The roots of scorzonera will, some of them, be of a moderate size to begin taking up in August, others in September, but will not attain full growth till the end of October, when, and during the winter, they may be used as wanted: or some may be dug up in November, and preserved in sand under cover, to be ready when the weather is severe. The plants left in the ground continue useful all winter till the spring.

The outer rind being scraped off, the root is steeped in water, in order to abstract a part of its bitter flavor. It is then boiled or stewed in the manner of carrots or parsnips.

J. C. Loudon
An Encyclopedia of Gardening, 1850

Editor's Note: Scorzonera's flavor improves after a good frost. This plant is also called black salsify because the flesh beneath its dark skin tastes similar to salsify.

The edible roots of the scorzonera are somewhat snakelike, which led to its being known as the viper plant.

Recipe

Fried Oysters from the Garden

Scrape the brown skin from salsify roots, cut crosswise pieces perhaps half an inch thick, soak in salted cold water, drain off this, turn on boiling water just to cover, and cook until tender. Mash the vegetables as you would potatoes, add 1 or 2 beaten eggs, salt, pepper, and sufficient flour to make a batter. Fry in sufficient butter to keep from burning until they are browned, dropping a spoonful of the batter onto the griddle in imitation of fried oysters.

American Agriculturist, 1895

Spinach

Spinach as a Season Stretcher

Spinach is a crop which matures rapidly and is well suited to filling out either end of a season. It can be removed in time for the setting out of egg and pepper plants, or will easily reach the cutting stage on the same ground from which early potatoes, beans, etc., have been harvested.

E. L. D. Seymour
Garden Profits, 1911

Leave the Lid Off

In order that the spinach may retain its fine green color, the vessel in which it is cooked should not be covered.

Ida D. Bennett
The Vegetable Garden, 1908

Squash

A Late Start Foils Squash Bugs

Late-planted squash, I've discovered, often escape the black squash bugs.

Jacob Biggle
Biggle Garden Book, 1912

OLD-TIME WISDOM

Make the squash bug wear a scarlet letter! I am forced to carry on a continuous warfare with squash bugs, who, were I to let them alone for a whole day together, would perhaps quite destroy the prospects of the whole summer. It is impossible not to feel bitterly angry with these unconscionable vermin. For their own sakes, they ought at least to wait till the squashes are better grown. There is an absolute pleasure in taking vengeance on them.

Nathaniel Hawthorne
The American Notebooks, 1868

Editor's Note: Hold your temper! Cover seedlings with floating row covers to keep squash bugs off your plants.

A Little Gem of a Squash

The 'Little Gem' is a most excellent winter squash, and its small size makes it acceptable to small families, who find a large squash like the 'Hubbard' too much to cook at once. Taken in its green and partly grown state, the 'Little Gem' is really delicious and so far superior to the best kind of summer squash as to make it unnecessary to grow these varieties.

American Agriculturist, 1883

Strange But True

The movements of the squash vine when pressed by hunger or thirst are truly wonderful. During a severe drought, place a basin of water at night, say two feet from a strong vine, and in the morning it will be found bathing in the basin. Is not this an indication of thought in the vine?

The Household, 1883

Big Flavor from a Really Big Squash

The flesh of 'Blue Hubbard' squash is fine-grained, sweet, dry, and of most excellent flavor—in this last respect resembling that of roasted or boiled chestnuts.

Fearing Burr
Garden Vegetables and How to Cultivate Them, 1866

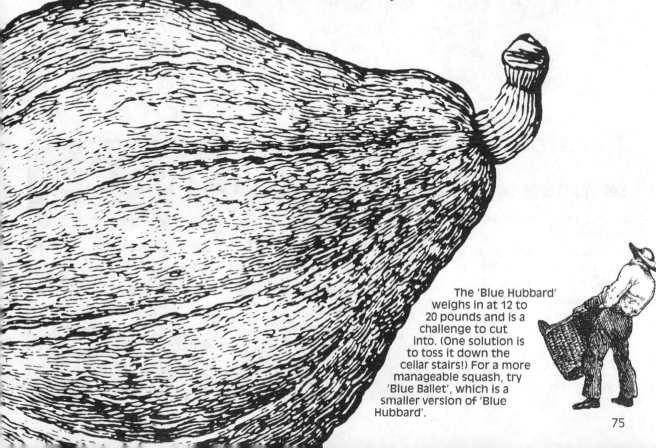

The 'Blue Hubbard' weighs in at 12 to 20 pounds and is a challenge to cut into. (One solution is to toss it down the cellar stairs!) For a more manageable squash, try 'Blue Ballet', which is a smaller version of 'Blue Hubbard'.

Recipe

Squash Biscuits

One pint strained squash, ½ cup yeast, 1 small cup sugar, and a small piece of butter the size of an egg. Beat the squash, butter, and sugar thoroughly, add yeast and beat again, add flour till quite stiff to stir with a spoon, let it stand overnight. In the morning put in gem pans, or make into biscuit, let rise, and bake. These should be eaten while hot.

Farm and Home, 1899

Oh, Bury Them Deep

"Leggy" plants can be made to give fairly good results by setting them deep and burying the larger part of the slender stem. But even then they are inferior to stocky plants.

Cornell Experiment Station
Bulletin 32, 1891

Editor's Note: To prevent tomato seedlings from getting leggy in the first place, give them plenty of light and avoid crowding them too close together in flats. Start tomatoes in separate cell packs so they'll have plenty of room to grow.

Transplanted Tomatoes Are Stronger

Replanting makes plants stocky. Tomatoes should be reset at least twice, and three times is better still.

Abner Hollingsworth
Farm Journal, 1888

Recipe

Tomato Honey

Select ripe yellow tomatoes, weigh them, cut them into pieces, and put into a porcelain kettle; for each pound allow the grated rind of one lemon. Simmer very gently for thirty minutes, then drain and press through cheesecloth. Measure the liquor and pour back into the skillet, and for each pint allow one pound of sugar, granulated, and four tablespoons of lemon juice. Boil twenty minutes or more till a thick syrup. Put in bottles or tumblers.

I. M. Angell
The Garden Magazine, 1906

Tomatoes

Set Tomatoes Out Late

Do not be in a hurry to plant out tomatoes. Often one cold night will check them so severely that, although planted in the open by the middle of May, they will not bear fruit sooner than plants put out as late as June 1st.

Loring Underwood
A Garden Diary and Country Home Guide, 1908

Strange But True

To many persons there is something unpleasant, not to say offensive, in the flavour of this excellent fruit, the tomato. It has however, long been used for culinary purposes in various countries of Europe. Dr. Bennett, a professor of some celebrity, considers it an invaluable article of diet, and scribes to it very important medicinal properties.

Mrs. Isabella Beeton
Mrs. Beeton's Book of Household Management, 1861

Fuzzy Dessert Tomato

As a dessert fruit, to be eaten out of hand, the peach tomato is by far the best. The ripe fruit has the shape, color, size, and even bloom of the real peach; the flavor is more sweet and fruity than that of most of the tomato family. Green peach tomatoes are excellent for pickles, because they are so firm and chop well, and because the vines are generally loaded when picking time comes.

I. M. Angell
The Garden Magazine, 1906

Editor's Note: Fuzzy peach tomatoes aren't for everyone, but they may suit your taste. See "Sources" on page 316 for ordering information.

A Barrelful of Tomatoes

Select a barrel, bore three or four holes in the bottom, sink the barrel about one-third its depth in the ground and pack the earth around it. Fill it about half full of fresh horse manure well tramped down and pour a bucket of hot water on this manure. Then put on 8 inches of good soil and then a mixture of well-rotted manure and rich black loam in about equal quantities, until you reach within about 12 inches of the top of the barrel; then heap up manure around the outside. Set three tomato plants in this and trim to two shoots each. Train one of these shoots from each plant to stakes or a nearby building, but allow the other three shoots to grow naturally over the sides of the barrel. Be careful to give plenty of water daily—a gallon each day will be none too much.

E. L. D. Seymour
Garden Profits, 1911

Well-rotted manure and loam

Soil

Composting manure

Stocked with composting manure and surrounded by more of the same warm stuff, the tomatoes in this barrel will produce sooner than plants set in garden beds.

Plant Tomatoes Twice

Make a second planting of tomato seed early in June, in an open-air seedbed, in order to have plenty of tomatoes after the early varieties have ceased to bear. Transplant this second planting to the rows as soon as large enough to handle. For this planting, I prefer an early variety, as the later-fruited sorts are often caught by the frost before they can ripen.

E. D. Darlington
The Garden Magazine, 1907

Editor's Note: Early-season tomatoes can ripen in as little as 55 days compared with 80 or more days for late-season varieties. Some early types to try include 'Early Girl', 'Siberia', and 'Oregon Spring'.

Recipe
Tomato Butter

Peel seven pounds of ripe tomatoes, add three pounds of sugar, a pint of vinegar, one ounce of ground cinnamon, ½ ounce of whole cloves; boil three hours. It may be kept without sealing, like apple butter, and makes a pleasing addition for a meal.

Farm Journal, 1885

Editor's Note: Despite this recipe's advice, you're better off preserving your tomato butter and apple butter in a hot-water bath. Early cooks weren't known for their safe preserving practices.

Twiggy Tomato Stakes Offer Support

It does not seem generally known that one of the best trellises for the tomato plant is a comparatively short straight stick, with short snags or spurs up and down it. A smooth straight stick will not permit the vines to be held up without slipping. Those, however, who have a little ingenuity could use smooth sticks, by first wrapping the tying material once around the stick before tying up the vines; this prevents the tying material from slipping down.

Meehans' Monthly, 1892

When you tie up your tomatoes, use old nylon stockings or soft, thick cord that won't cut into the stems.

Don't Stop at Scarlet Tomatoes

Even though the pink or crimson varieties are actually better than the scarlets, still we are sure that the scarlets will be the most popular. We see it in other things. Bright red is instinctively associated in one's mind with high quality. The crimson or purple fruits, as a matter of face, embrace some of the very best varieties, for instance 'Trucker's Favorite'.

L. and E. M. Barron
The Garden Magazine, 1906

Editor's Note: In a *Seed Savers Yearbook* (a catalog of seeds saved by volunteers), a gardener remarked that his father had grown 'Trucker's Favorite' for 40 years, then died without leaving a supply of seed. The son spotted a listing for it in the *Yearbook* and was able to carry on a family tradition. Of these tomatoes, he wrote, "Super flavor, good sliced or canned, prolific and dependable." See "Sources" on page 316 for information about Seed Savers.

Heirloom tomatoes offer gardeners a world of new tastes, scents, and colors. You'll find beauties like dark brown-red 'Black Krim' and 'Great White'.

A Window on Tomatoes in Winter

I prepared a seedbed in the sunniest spot in the garden. Three feet of the old soil was removed and replaced by two feet of manure, on top of which one foot of good potting soil was firmly packed. Early in February I planted seed of 'Chalk's Early Jewel' tomato, fitted over the top of the seedbed an old window sash, banked manure around the sides, and covered the glass with straw mats. As soon as the tiny plants appeared I gave them light, using the mats at night only. During warm, sunny days I raised the glass to admit air, so that the plants would harden. On May 6th I set in permanent places in the garden 110 thrifty plants, most of which were budded. I obtained a crop of unusually large tomatoes on June 21st.

Mrs. Joseph C. Brown
The Garden Magazine, 1909

Editor's Note: Mrs. Brown insulated her hotbed windows with straw mats, but you can use folded corrugated cardboard cartons instead.

'Chalk's Early Jewel' is a red variety, introduced in 1899 and still valued by gardeners who want an early crop of tomatoes. It's been dropped from commercial seed catalogs, but you can order it through the Seed Savers Exchange (see "Sources" on page 316).

Recipe

Dried Tomatoes

Housekeepers who have many tomatoes and few cans can easily preserve a large quantity of this very easily raised fruit by drying it. Scald and peel the tomatoes. Boil them slowly in a porcelain kettle, until the original quantity is reduced one-half. Then season them in the proportion of a teaspoonful of salt, and ½ cup of sugar to a gallon of stewed tomatoes. Spread on plates and dry quickly, without scorching. As the moisture dries away and the stewed fruit takes shape, scrape it up so that both sides may dry, and let the contents of several plates, heaped up lightly, stand in bright sunshine a little while before putting away. Store in bags and keep dry.

When wanted for use, put a small quantity soaking in considerable water several hours, or overnight. Stew in the same water long and slowly—keeping boiling water at hand to add if it grows thick and in danger of burning.

Faith Rochester
American Agriculturist, 1876

Give Green Tomatoes a Chance to Ripen

If the tomato fruits have not reached their full size, the whole plant may be pulled with the fruits on and hung in a barn or other dry place and the fruits will abstract nourishment from the vine and sometimes complete their ripening.

L. H. Bailey
The Principles of Vegetable Gardening, 1901

Take Tomatoes Indoors

Keep your tomato vines all winter, by cutting them back in the fall and storing them in dirt or sand. They should be kept moist, and away from any chance of frost action. The result will be a saving of three weeks or so in the ripening of the fruit the next year.

E. L. D. Seymour
Garden Profits, 1911

Leaning Tower of Tomatoes

We prefer a sloping trellis to a straight one for tomatoes. The illustration shows one made with wire. A trellis in this shape may be readily made by the use of stakes and poles. Drive stakes of suitable length into the ground for supports, and use any small poles that may be readily procured for the slats. These may be nailed to the supports, or lashed to them with small wire.

American Agriculturist, 1884

Editor's Note: This leaning tower of tomatoes takes less space than a row of tomato cages, and once it's covered with tomatoes, it's more attractive too. At harvest time, you'll find that the slats are easier to reach through than the wires of a tomato cage.

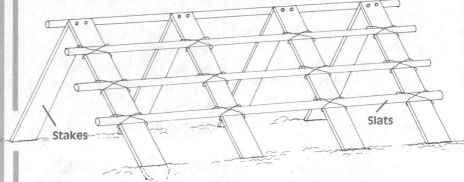

Tomato vines will easily scale the sloped sides of this trellis. Drive the stakes in deep if you'll be nailing the slats to them, or you'll knock them out of place as you hammer. You can also attach the slats as shown by wrapping them with wire.

Chow Chow

One peck of green tomatoes, three dozens of green peppers, one cabbage, one bunch of celery, ½ peck of onions, two cups of grated horseradish, one ounce of whole allspice, one ounce of whole cloves, one ounce of whole cinnamon, ¼ pound of mustard seed, one gallon of vinegar turned on boiling hot, after chopping all fine, and salt to taste. Put the cinnamon, allspice, and cloves in a bag and put it in the chow chow. The chopped tomatoes lay in salt and water overnight.

The Household, 1878

Save Sugar for Strawberries

Of course tomatoes should not be made sweet. Tastes differ greatly. We know a few persons who habitually use sugar upon the cooked fruit; for ourself, the least particle of sugar is at once detected, and the dish is spoiled. We should as soon think of putting salt upon strawberries as sugar upon tomatoes.

American Agriculturist, 1876

Editor's Note: This is one of those tips that tomato growers just can't agree on. Fresh tomatoes can be incredibly sweet without sugar,

but some cooks insist on the sweet stuff to cut the acid. Try a batch of sauce both ways and see what you think.

Tomato Pickles

Green tomatoes make a first-class pickle. First chop them into pieces, then squeeze off the juice, salt them, and let them stand over night. Chop some cabbage, salt it, and set aside also. Do the same with a few onions. The next day press out all the brine and put the chopped vegetables into an earthen jar, and pour over them: heated vinegar enough to cover, to which has been added a little sugar, some small pieces of horseradish, and little celery seed, some black pepper, a red pepper, chopped, and some mustard seed. The pickles will be ready to use in a week.

I. M. Angell
The Garden Magazine, 1906

Saving Tomato Seeds

It is by no means easy to clean tomato seeds, as they are firmly embedded in the mucilaginous pulp that is so difficult to detach.

One of the best means of obtaining clean tomato seeds is to cut away the outer rind and as much of the seedless pulp as possible. The remaining portion, full of seeds, should be rubbed between the hands and afterwards placed in a vessel containing cold water. Hot or even lukewarm water should not be used, or the seeds may be caused to sprout. The liquid should be churned round and round with the hand or a stick. This will detach a certain amount of pulp, which can be skimmed off. The seeds should then be laid out on sheets of glass or tin or stiffish paper and allowed to dry. When thoroughly dry they may be rubbed between the hands with some silver sand (fine white sand) and thus freed from all traces of dry mucilage.

John Weathers
Commercial Gardening, 1913

Watermelon

They're Not Older They're Better

While there are some seeds of vegetables which it is unsafe to rely on over a year old, it is also well established that there are others actually improved by age, and which seem when a few years old to run less to vine or top, and more to fruit or crop. The melon family is of this class; and for our own planting, we would *prefer* watermelon or cantaloupe seed four years old.

Rural Advertiser, 1865

Eat a Watermelon's Best End

The best part of a melon is the blossom end, the end opposite the stem. It is always the sweetest and most intensely flavored.

E. B. Davis and B. G. Jefferis
The Household Guide, 1891

Watermelon Ripeness Test 1

Unquestionably the flat, dead sound emitted by a melon when "thumped" is the readiest indication of ripeness, and the one most universally depended on. If the resonance is hollow, ringing, or musical, it is a certain proof of immaturity.

L. H. Bailey
The Principles of Vegetable Gardening, 1901

Ripeness Test 2

Put your foot alongside of the melon and snap your boot with your fingers and then the melon. If the melon is ripe, the sounds will be almost identical.

Farm Journal, 1885

Ripeness Test 3

Frequently on turning the melon and exposing the underside, the irregular white blotch formed where the melon has rested on the ground affords an indication of maturity. When this begins to turn yellowish and becomes rough, pimply, or warty, with the surface sufficiently hard to resist the fingernail when scratched, it is usually a fair sign of ripeness.

L. H. Bailey
The Principles of Vegetable Gardening, 1901

Ripeness Test 4

It is easy to tell whether a watermelon is thoroughly ripe or not, by drawing the thumbnail slightly over the melon, so as to scrape the thin, green skin. If the edge of the cut is ragged and the rind under the cut smooth, with a glassy appearance, the melon is ripe; but if the edges of the cut are smooth and the skin does not come clean off, the melon is not sufficiently advanced. It is said that a little practice on two melons, one ripe and the other unripe, will soon familiarize one with the knowledge required.

Meehans' Monthly, 1884

Watermelon Molasses

An article has been going the rounds of the papers about the practicability of making molasses from watermelons. We felt incredulous on the subject, but have recently been presented with a bottle of it by our friend. It was really a nice article, clear, sweet, and of a very pleasant flavor. He informed us the only process was to boil down the pulp to about one half. The boiling was continued for several hours.

The Pennsylvania Farm Journal, 1855

Editor's Note: Most watermelon recipes (like watermelon pickle) sound weird until you taste them. If you've got a glut of melons, molasses is worth a try.

Gardeners have come up with many ways of telling what a watermelon is like on the inside—without using a knife. Mark Twain suggested knocking on the skin and listening closely. If you hear a "punk," then it's harvesttime. If the response is "pink," then the melon is not yet ripe.

Herbs and Home Remedies

In the past, almost every plant was considered an herb. That's because early gardeners found ways to use most plants they encountered for food, medicine, dyes, or cosmetics. In this chapter you'll find common table herbs like rosemary and thyme, as well as fruits, nuts, trees, shrubs, and even weeds with herbal uses.

Herbs and Home Remedies

Gardening with Herbs

This Spring, Plant Herbs

All gardens should have beds of herbs. They are always looked for in the fall, and nearly always forgotten in the spring.

The Gardener's Monthly, 1873

Hyssop for an Herbal Border

Grown with catmint, hyssop makes a lovely border, backed with lavender and rosemary.

M. Grieve
Culinary Herbs and Condiments, 1934

Editor's Note: Catmint (*Nepeta cataria*) and hyssop will grow as tall as lavender and rosemary, so keep them pruned to form a tidy border.

Give Your Clothes an Herbal-Fresh Scent

Knot gardens were formed with a border of box, lavender, or rosemary, 18 inches broad at the bottom, and clipped so close and level at the top as to form a table for the house wife to spread out clothes to dry on.

Reginald Blomfield and F. Inigo Thomas
The Formal Garden in England, 1892

Herbs Underfoot

Herbs which perfume the air most delightfully, being trodden upon and crushed, are three; that is, burnet, wild thyme, and water mints (*Mentha aquatica*); therefore you are to set whole alleys of them to have pleasure when you walk or tread.

Francis Bacon
Utopian Garden, n.d.

If you'd like a knot garden to dry your clothes on, choose a design such as one of these shown. Draw a grid of evenly spaced lines over the design. Then make a similar but larger grid where you want your garden. Transfer the design from the drawing to the larger grid, square by square.

Strange But True

The leaves of <u>Mentha arvensis</u>, the corn (or field) mint when bruised smell like stale cheese. If you gather it because of its pretty dark rose-colored blossoms that appear in the late summer, your regret will last until you reach home and can thoroughly wash your hands.

Louise Beebe Wilder
The Fragrant Path, 1932

Editor's Note: A stink to one person is perfume to another. The leaves of this native mint are used to flavor jelly and sauces and were once used to keep milk from curdling. If you'd like to judge it for yourself, see "Sources" on page 316 for ordering information.

Find a Place for Herbs

Whoever owns a garden-plot ought to give a little space in it to herbs. A few stalks of dill, a root of tarragon, a marjoram clump, some sweet basil, a yard or so of caraway, thyme, sage, catnip, horehound, comfrey, and elecampane, give the last touch of homely comfort. Each and several, they must be picked just as they come into flower, dried in the shade, then put in tight paper-bags and hung in the airiest possible place. All that is, save the comfrey and elecampane, whose virtue is in the root, so they must be left where they grow until wanted.

Emily Holt
The Complete Housekeeper, 1912

While you're probably familiar with most of these herbs, you may not know elecampane. This four- to six-foot-tall herb blooms in summer, bearing yellow sunflowerlike blossoms. Its thick roots traditionally have been used to treat respiratory and digestive disorders. The roots can also be candied and eaten as sweets.

Fair-Weather Basil

Basil is sowne in gardens, and in earthen pots. It commeth up quickly, and loveth little moisture except in the middle of the day; otherwise if it be sowne in rainie weather, the seed will putrifie and grow into a jellie or slime, and come to nothing.

John Gerard
The Herball, 1633

Editor's Note: Basil isn't quite so picky as Gerard makes it out to be, though like most herbs it prefers well-drained soil. You can start seeds indoors six weeks before your last spring frost date, or direct-sow seeds in the garden after all danger of frost is past. Plant basil in a sunny spot with rich soil—amend the soil with composted manure before planting. This quick-growing herb comes in a variety of shapes, sizes, and scents. You'll want to sample cinnamon basil, lemon basil, and the striking, purple-leaved dark opal basil.

A Fragrant Walkway

Chamomile has been used to form green or carpet walks, planting it about nine inches or ten inches asunder; which naturally spreading, the runners are fixed by walking on them, or rolling.

J. C. Loudon
An Encyclopedia of Gardening, 1850

Decorate Your House with Hops

Very few persons know how graceful and pretty an effect is produced by the hop vine, when hanging over the wing of a cottage, or wreathing some rustic trellis of the farmhouse. This most rustic of all climbing beauties, whose rounded masses of green foliage and flowers fall into clusters as pretty as snow wreaths, is usually condemned to a pole in the kitchen garden. There are few things, in its way, which deserve a better place in the affections of those who live in the rural cottage or farmhouse than the hop.

Andrew Jackson Downing
The Architecture of Country Houses, 1850

Editor's Note: Both male and female hop plants produce flowers, but the females are the ones you'll usually see since they're used for brewing beer. Hops like soil that's well drained and rich in humus. Place the plants in full sun and where they'll get good air circulation; then stand back and watch them go. The vines can grow 6 to 12 inches a day.

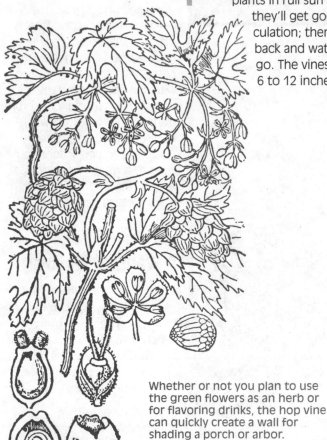

Whether or not you plan to use the green flowers as an herb or for flavoring drinks, the hop vine can quickly create a wall for shading a porch or arbor.

Plant Licorice with the Veggies

About 3 feet of space is given to each licorice plant, the ground between the rows being cropped with cabbages, lettuces, or other vegetables until the licorice fills all the space. Each year the tops are cut down close to the ground, and the soil is dug and manured between the rows. The crop is fit to harvest at the end of the third year.

John Weathers
Commercial Gardening, 1913

Editor's Note: Licorice (*Glycyrrhiza glabra*) is a legume, so it makes a good filler for vegetable gardens in Zone 9. In colder areas of the country, grow licorice as a greenhouse plant. Place the roots in deep pots and give them plenty of light. In cloudy weather, place plants under artificial lights to simulate long day length.

Grow the licorice plant for its uniquely sweet roots. To coax the flavor from the roots quickly, make shavings from them with a sharp pocketknife and simmer the pieces in boiling water. Or for a quick licorice fix, chew on a piece of root.

Use Rue for a Touch of Blue

Rue is a plant of rare beauty and elegance. It is the old time-honored medicinal herb, but is quite fit to serve a less material use in the garden world. Its delicately cut foliage shines with metallic lights that increase in luster as the season advances. Few finer accompaniments could be found for pink phlox, Michaelmas daisies (*Aster novae-angliae* and *A. novi-belgii*), or any flowers belonging to the magenta group.

Louise Beebe Wilder
Colour in My Garden, 1918

Editor's Note: Rue makes a stronger statement with its curiously shaped blue-green foliage than with its small yellow blooms. It's perfect for setting off pink, white, or purple flowers. Just be sure to wear gloves when you handle rue, since the oil in the leaves bothers some people's skin.

Plant a Garden Cushion of Thyme

Thymus serpyllum is the European wild thyme, sometimes called mother-of-thyme. There are numerous forms of it. The most lovely is *T. s.* 'Albus', an absolutely prostrate creeper, clinging as closely to a stone, as someone absurdly said, as its own skin, and powdering itself all over in summer with myriads of white blossoms. I have encouraged great mats of white thyme in my rock garden so that I may have them to sit upon while weeding, for its scent when thus pressed is given off freely and is most heartening and reviving during this somewhat arduous task.

Louise Beebe Wilder
The Fragrant Path, 1932

Herbs for the Table

Try Angelica Candy

The leafstalks and stems are candied by the confectioner. The use of the sweetmeat (candy) probably originated in the notion, prevalent in ancient times, that the plant possessed the power of averting or expelling pestilence, whence its high-sounding name, *Angelica archangelica*.

C. Pierpoint Johnson
The Useful Plants of Great Britain, 1862

Editor's Note: If you've got angelica on hand, you can make your own sweetmeats to decorate holiday breads or fruitcakes. Cut the stems into four- to five-inch-long pieces, and peel off the outer skin. Make a syrup of two cups water and one cup sugar, and bring it to a boil. Pour the syrup over the stems; let them cool and soak overnight. Then reheat the stems and syrup, and simmer until the angelica turns bright green. Drain and cool the stem pieces. Cut them up, and place them on breads and cakes before baking. Refrigerate unused pieces.

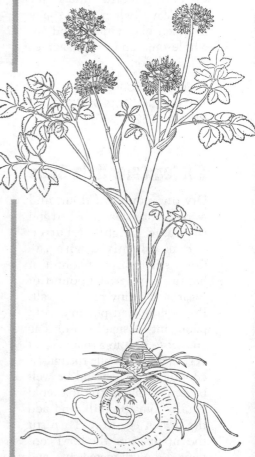

Angelica is a tall, fragrant herb that looks good at the back of a border. Cut off the flower stalks right after flowering, and your plants are sure to come back year after year. If you let them go to seed, the plants will die and you'll have to start them over again from seeds.

If you're nervous, put an angelica sprig in your pocket. In the Middle Ages, people carried angelica around as a charm to defeat witchcraft.

A Borage Swizzle Stick

The leaves impart a pleasant coolness to beverages in which they are infused, and are still an ingredient in several favorite liquors of local celebrity, as "cool tankard" and cider cup. Leaves when boiled may be eaten like spinach, and are wholesome and rather agreeable in flavor.

C. Pierpoint Johnson
The Useful Plants of Great Britain, 1862

Golden Calendula Buns

Dry one pound of flour, and work into it 3 ounces of lard and the same weight of butter. When well mixed with the flour, stir in a teaspoonful of baking powder, ¼ pound of sugar, and a tiny pinch of salt. Put some dried pot marigold petals into a small muslin bag and set to soak in a small cup of very hot milk. While the milk is cooling an egg should be well beaten. Remove the marigold petals from the milk and add the beaten egg to it. Then stir the mixture into the bowl containing the dry ingredients, and the whole should be beaten for some minutes—the longer the better. The mixture should then be put into bun tins and baked in a moderate oven.

M. Grieve
Culinary Herbs and Condiments, 1934

Editor's Note: Feel free to use vegetable shortening as a

Strange But True

The bay tree (<u>Laurus nobilis</u>) resisteth witchcraft very potently, that neither witch nor devil, thunder nor lightning, will hurt a man where a bay tree is.

Nicholas Culpeper
Culpeper's Complete Herbal, 1652

substitute for lard. And don't worry about drying your flour—it will work just fine straight out of the bag. Above all, don't confuse pot marigold (**Calendula officinalis**) with the common bedding plant (**Tagetes erecta**). Only the pot marigold will give you a good flavor and color for cooking.

Calendula, also called pot marigold, is an intriguing herb for imaginative cooks. Its bright, yellow-to-orange flower petals can turn buns and other baked goods a beautiful saffron yellow. Calendula petals have a slightly salty taste.

Cheaper Capers

The flower buds of the marsh marigold (*Caltha palustris*) form a safe substitute for capers; and likewise the young seed pods of the common radish; and the unripe seeds of the garden nasturtium (*Tropaeolum majus*). A species of spurge, common in gardens (*Euphorbia lathyris*) is vulgarly called caper bush, from the resemblance of its fruit to capers; and though acrid and poisonous, like the other plants of this genus, its seeds are sometimes substituted by the Parisian restauranteurs for the pods of the true capers.

J. C. Loudon
An Encyclopedia of Gardening, 1850

Editor's Note: Capers are the pickled flower buds of **Capparis spinosa**, a small, prickly Mediterranean shrub. With so many good caper substitutes, you can have caper flavor without tracking down the real plant. Just make sure you don't confuse this true caper with **Euphorbia lathyris,** which is poisonous but is sometimes called the caper bush.

How to Make Nasturtium "Capers"

Every morning pick the nasturtium seeds clinging fast to the stems they have grown on, and drop them into a glass jar half full of vinegar. Every day or two repeat the process until the seeds come up to the top of the vinegar. Then strain them out of that vinegar, and boil them lightly in some that is fresh. Then seal up as you do any pickle. Use in exactly the same manner as ordinary capers that are bought; and you will find them much more spicy and piquant. Care must be taken that the fruits are small when picked. If large enough to grow they will have a hard center, which is not so good for the purpose of pickles.

Caroline M. Brown
The Garden Magazine, 1906

Cooked Caraway Roots

The caraway roots are boiled in the manner of the carrot or parsnip, and by some are preferred to these vegetables, the flavor being considered pleasant and delicate.

Fearing Burr
Garden Vegetables and How to Cultivate Them, 1866

Candied Elecampane

Elecampane's principal consumption is in making a sweetmeat (candy) formed of the root candied with sugar, and highly esteemed by schoolboys and other consumers of such viands. The leaves were eaten by the Romans as a potherb; they are rather bitter and somewhat aromatic in flavor.

C. Pierpoint Johnson
The Useful Plants of Great Britain, 1862

Editor's Note: Elecampane (*Inula helenium*) is also known as wild sunflower. Its three- to four-inch-wide yellow flowers make it as welcome in the flower garden as in the herb garden.

Edible Flowers

In Turkey, and also in France, the flowers of the Judas tree are mixed with small salads; they have an agreeable acid flavor.

J. C. Loudon
An Encyclopedia of Gardening, 1850

Editor's Note: The Judas tree (*Cercis siliquastrum*) is more popular in Europe and Asia than in North America. But you don't need to go hunting for a Judas tree to enjoy its pink, pealike flowers in salads. The flowers of our native eastern redbud (*Cercis canadensis*) look and taste similar, and you can use them in the same way.

Lady's Bedstraw for Cheesemaking

The flowers of lady's bedstraw have a rather pleasant but strong scent. The plant has been used to curdle milk, either alone or with the juice of the stinging nettle.

C. Pierpoint Johnson
The Useful Plants of Great Britain, 1862

Editor's Note: The seventeenth-century herbalist John Gerard explained how this plant got the popular name "cheese rennet." He wrote that "the people of Thuscane do use it to turne their milkes and cheese, which they make of sheepes and goates milke, might be the sweeter and more pleasant to taste. The people of Cheshire especially about Nantwich, where the best cheese is made, do use it in their rennet, esteeming greatly of that cheese above other made without it."

You'll know lady's bedstraw (*Galium verum*) by its long, thin leaves that radiate out from the stems like the spokes of a wheel. It's a close relative of sweet woodruff (*G. odoratum*).

Nibble on Nasturtium Sandwiches

We call the attention of table epicures to nasturtium sandwiches, the effect being most novel, and to the palate most delicious, both green leaves and flowers being used.

David Landreth Seed Co. Catalog, 1914

Editor's Note: Nasturtium flowers will brighten your sandwiches in shades of bright red, orange, and yellow. The round leaves have a peppery taste.

Nasturtiums to Chew and View

The tall nasturtium is cultivated both for use and ornament. Its richly colored orange blossoms serve as a garnish for dishes, the young leaves are excellent for salad, and the green seed-pods, preserved in vinegar, make a pickle greatly esteemed by many. It is admirably adapted for a window or conservatory in winter, is a very rapid grower, and strikes (roots) freely from cuttings, but seeds sparingly. The flowers are large, trumpet-shaped, and in some species, are very brilliant and of many shades, from scarlet to black. It is a magnificent climber, running up to twenty or more feet high. Its chief glory is in covering arbors, trellis, and rustic work.

The Successful HouseKeeper, 1887

Recipe

Pickled Nasturtium Pods

Soak the green seed-pods of nasturtiums for three days in strong salt and water; then strain and pour boiling vinegar over them, omitting the spice. Vinegar for any pickle should never be allowed to boil over one minute.

The Successful HouseKeeper, 1887

Revive Parsley with a Haircut

If the growth of parsley becomes coarse in the summer, cut off all the outer leaves and water well. This will induce a new growth of leaves again, and may always be done when the plants have grown to a good size, as it encourages a stocky growth.

M. Grieve
Culinary Herbs and Condiments, 1934

Let Radishes Mark Your Parsley Rows

A few radish seeds, sown in the rows at the time of sowing parsley seed, will mark the lines so that a scuffle hoe can be run through before the weeds start.

E. L. D. Seymour
Garden Profits, 1911

Editor's Note: Parsley seeds take so long to germinate—up to six weeks—that weeds often beat them up out of the soil. The radishes germinate fast, and their presence will keep you from rooting out your parsley seeds along with the weeds. In addition to saving your parsley harvest, you'll get two vegetable crops from the same amount of space.

OLD-TIME WISDOM

Is parsley too slow to sow? The ancients held that parsley should never be sown but transplanted, as they claimed that the seed had to make a journey to Hades before it could again appear above ground, and, indeed, the tardiness with which it germinates would almost seem to bear out that idea.

Ida D. Bennett
The Vegetable Garden, 1908

Parsley Crisps

Crisped parsley is used for garnishing dishes. Pick and wash young parsley, shake it in a cloth to dry it thoroughly, and spread it on a sheet of clean paper and put in the oven. Turn the bunches frequently until they are quite crisp. Parsley is much more easily crisped than fried.

The Successful HouseKeeper, 1887

Fried Parsley

Wash and dry the parsley thoroughly; put it into the hot fat and let it remain until it is crisp; take it out immediately and drain it in a colander. If the parsley is allowed to remain in the fat one moment after it is crisp it will be spoiled. Parsley is best fried in a frying basket.

The Successful HouseKeeper, 1887

Try Turnip-Rooted Parsley

In this kind of parsley it is not the leaves, but the thick fleshy roots, which form the edible part of the plant. The flesh is white and somewhat dry. In flavor, it resembles the celeriac, or turnip-rooted celery, but is not so delicate.

Mme. Vilmorin-Andrieux
The Vegetable Garden, 1885

Editor's Note: An early variety of turnip-rooted parsley called 'Hamburg' is available through several mail-order firms. See "Sources" on page 316 for ordering information.

Parsley to the Rescue

The peculiar smell of parsley will neutralize the odor given to the breath by eating onions.

P. T. Quinn
Money in the Garden, 1871

Editor's Note: The smell of parsley is strong, but the taste is gentle. Try a little after dinner instead of a breath mint. The flat-leaved (Italian) varieties have the best flavor.

Parsley was once used as a remedy for many medical problems, perhaps because of its power of taming the scent of garlic and onions. It was even tossed in ponds to cure sick fish.

Put Purslane in Salads

Our common purslane, or pussley (*Portulaca oleracea*), is such a persistent weed in our country that no thought is given to it of any use in the service of man. In the Old World, where there is trouble in raising it, the list of valuable garden vegetables is hardly regarded perfect without it. When from three inches to four inches in height, the little plants are cut close down, and in that way washed and cooked as spinach. The young plants are also quite a pleasant addition to salads, especially to mixed salads, toning down, because so mild, the hotness of mustard and cress.

Meehans' Monthly, 1901

Purslane is a familiar weed, with fleshy stems and leaves and inconspicuous yellow flowers. It's a good source of vitamins A and C—something to consider before you yank it out of the garden. Eating purslane is probably the best way to control it, since any piece of leaf or stem that touches the soil will root and start a new plant.

Recipes

Rugosa Rose Marmalade

The fruit of *Rosa rugosa* is the most suitable for preserving as the pods (hips) are large, fleshy, and of high color. To make marmalade, the pods want to be picked fully ripe, yet before the frost touches them. Wash, trim, and seed the pods, cover with water, steam until tender, and strain. Mash through a colander with a wooden spoon, and add to 1 pint of the pulp ¾ pounds of granulated sugar. Put on to boil and constantly stir for twenty minutes or more, then fill in jars or jelly glasses.

Mrs. A. Millard
Meehan's Monthly, 1900

Editor's Note: The rugosa rose (*Rosa rugosa*) has unusually large hips, or pods, that are high in vitamins C, B, E, and K. The flowers have a strong clove fragrance and may be pink, white, purple, or yellow. The plants are hardy to Zone 2.

Rose Butter for Baking

Those who are fond of rose flavor for cooking will find the following much nicer than the rosewater one buys in bottles. Preserve the rose petals with salt. I gather the rose leaves from day to day, and place them with double the quantity of fine salt in a glass preserve can, carefully screwing the cover down after each addition. When I had collected all I could, I put the jar in a cool, dark place and shake it thoroughly once each day for a month. Then take a larger jar, put a layer of rose petals and salt on the bottom, on this place a pat of fresh, sweet butter, pack the rose leaves over and around it, strew salt over the whole, and cover air tight. In six weeks this will be ready for use. A little of this perfumed butter gives a delicious flavor to cake, and is also nice in apple or custard pies.

M. Maria George
The Household, 1882

A Conserve of Red Roses

Let your roses be gathered before they are quite blown, pound them in a stone mortar, and add to them twice their weight in double-refined sugar, and put them into a glass close stopped up, but do not fill it full. Let them stand three months before you use them, remembering to stir them once a day.

John Nott
The Receipt Book of John Nott, 1723

Editor's Note: Try this candied rose spread on toast or muffins for a sweet treat.

Strange But True

Sage is a happiness barometer. It is thought to follow the fortunes of the house, dwindling when evil days befall and reviving miraculously when things are bright again.

Louise Beebe Wilder
The Fragrant Path, 1932

Home-Cured Sage

We always raise our sage for home consumption, picking the leaves the first of July and again in September. The leaves are well washed and rinsed and then dried. Store the dried sage in paper bags. When wanted for seasoning, turn them onto a smooth surface (I use an oilclothed table) and roll the herb with a rolling pin until it is so finely pulverized that it nearly all sifts through a wire metal sieve. A handful of such home-cured sage is worth many times its weight of the yellowed, gritty, bitter stuff one buys.

Clarissa Potter
American Agriculturist,
1895

Salad Burnet Tastes Cool As a Cucumber

Burnet leaves are sometimes put into salads, and occasionally into soups, and they form a favorite herb for cool tankards. They continue green through the winter, when many other salad plants are cut off, or in a state unfit for use. Cut down all flower stalks not intended for seed.

J. C. Loudon
An Encyclopedia of Gardening, 1850

Editor's Note: Cool tankard is a drink made of watered-down wine and lemon juice. It is

flavored with herbs that have a cucumber taste, such as salad burnet and borage.

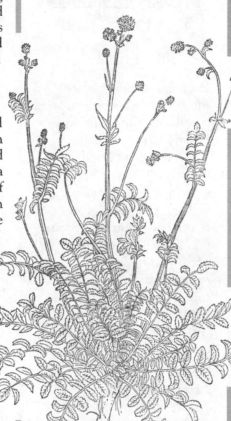

With its little scalloped leaflets, salad burnet makes an attractive addition to the herb or ornamental garden. Use it to border paths so you can smell its fresh cucumber scent when you brush against the leaves.

Put a few leaves in your salads and herbal vinegars for cucumber flavor without the burps. Or add a leaf or two to a glass of wine for a refreshing drink. A few minced salad burnet leaves will liven up your coleslaw recipe, or you can make a tasty side dish by mixing fresh burnet leaves with thinly sliced beets, freshly snipped dill, and yogurt.

When Fruit Is Scarce, Try Sorrel Pie

In *Rumex acetocella* (sheep or common sorrel), reddening barren hillsides and exhausted fields with its slender sprays of bloom, the thick, arrow-shaped leaves are pleasantly sour; in dearth of fruit, they are sometimes used with cracker crumbs as the basis of a sorrel pie.

Martha Bockée Flint
A Garden of Simples, 1900

Editor's Note: You can also use this common wild plant as a spinach substitute or to add piquancy to salads. If you plan to grow sorrel, plant French sorrel—it has larger leaves and an even better flavor.

The key to identifying common sorrel, a wild green, is the distinctive shape of the leaves. In outline they look something like little rocket ships or arrows.

Make French Sorrel Season Last Longer

As these herbs send up stalks in summer, cut them down occasionally; and cover the stool (the stem piece left after you cut the plant off just above the crown) with a little fresh leaf mold, to encourage the production of large leaves on the new stem. If, in two or three years, they have dwindled in growth, bearing small leaves, let them be succeeded by a new plantation.

J. C. Loudon
An Encyclopedia of Gardening, 1850

Editor's Note: This tangy, lemon-flavored herb reappears early each spring to form a manageable, bright green clump of leaves. Sorrel is versatile: You can steam it like spinach, or use it to liven up salads and soups.

Heat Up Tarragon to Warm Up Salads

In France tarragon is employed, on account of its agreeable pungency, to correct the coldness of salad herbs. It would be proper, towards the end of autumn, to transplant some full plants close under a south fence, to preserve them effectually in winter, and cause an earlier production of young tops in spring.

John Abercrombie
Abercrombie's Practical Gardener, 1818

Recipe
Tansy Pancakes

Put four spoonfuls of flour into an earthenware pan, and mix it with half a pint of cream to a smooth batter, beat four eggs well and put in, with two ounces of powdered sugar, and beat all well together for a quarter of an hour; then put in two spoonfuls of the juice of spinach and one of tansy, a little grated nutmeg, mix all well together, and fry them with fresh butter; garnish them with Seville oranges cut in quarters; and strew powdered sugar over them.

Richard Briggs
The New Art of Cookery, 1792

Editor's Note: Today you can use an electric mixer to beat the ingredients. You can get a juicy puree of spinach and tansy by squeezing wadded leaves in a garlic press. And as for the "spoonfuls" in the directions, try 12 heaping tablespoons flour, 2 tablespoons spinach puree, and 1 tablespoon tansy puree.

A small amount of tansy gives pancakes a nice peppery flavor, but don't get carried away—it has a strong taste, and large amounts can be toxic.

Serve Tarragon and Chives into Winter

All through November my salads have been nearly as good as in summer, from tarragon and chive tops being forced in the greenhouse. When once one has become used to the herbs in salad, it does seem so tasteless without them.

Marie Theresa Villiers Earle
More Pot-Pourri from a Surrey Garden, 1899

Editor's Note: If you don't happen to have a greenhouse, place pots of chives on a sunny windowsill. Tarragon is too large to make a good windowsill plant, but you can preserve its flavor in vinegar to add to your salads.

Tarragon has a strong taste, so it doesn't take too much to flavor vinegar, salad dressings, herbed butters, cream sauces, and soups. You can use the leaves fresh in salads or as a garnish for fish or any meat dish.

When you buy tarragon to grow, make sure it's French tarragon (*Artemisia dracunculus* var. *sativa*) and not the less flavorful Russian tarragon.

Recipes

Savory Herb Powder

Take fresh marjoram, basil, bayleaf, thyme, and parsley, and dry in the sun until brittle, pick carefully off the stalk, and rub the leaves into a fine powder. Add a small quantity of dried and pounded lemon peel, allowing one saltspoonful of salt and half a saltspoonful of pepper to each ounce of the powdered herbs. Take a piece of coarse muslin and sift the powdered mixture, then put in dry bottles and cork firmly. This powder is excellent for flavoring purposes.

M. Grieve
Culinary Herbs and Condiments, 1934

Editor's Note: If you don't have a salt-spoon handy, use 1/3 tea-spoon instead.

An Herbal Condiment

Take of nutmegs 1 ounce; mace, 1 ounce; cloves, 2 ounces; dried bay leaves, 1 ounce; basil, 3 ounces; marjoram, 3 ounces; winter savory, 2 ounces; thyme, 3 ounces; cayenne pepper, 1/2 ounce; grated lemon peel, 1/2 ounce; 2 cloves of garlic. All to be well pulverized in a mortar and sifted through a fine wire sieve, and put away in dry corked bottles. We made this last year, and used it frequently through the winter for flavoring a great many things, such as purees of cabbage, preserved French beans, soups, sauces, etc.

Marie Theresa Villiers Earle
More Pot-Pourri from a Surrey Garden, 1899

Editor's Note: The author credits this recipe to an earlier book, *The Gentlewoman*, published in 1864. When you try this herb mix, use dried or powdered garlic. Fresh garlic doesn't store well unless it's refrigerated.

Essence of Soup Herbs

Take lemon thyme, winter savory, sweet marjoram, and sweet basil, of each 1 ounce; grated lemon peel and eschalots (shallots), of each 1/2 ounce; bruised celery seed, 1/4 ounce; proof spirit, 1 pint. Digest for 10 to 14 days. A superior flavoring essence for soups, gravies, seasonings, etc.

William Dick
Encyclopedia of Practical Receipts and Processes, 1872

Editor's Note: For proof spirit, you can use standard brandy (without added flavoring), vodka, or high-proof, unflavored grain alcohol. By "digest," the author means to let the mixture sit in a dark place to allow the flavors to mingle.

Sun Salad Vinegar

A very good salad vinegar can be made of 3 ounces each of tarragon, savory, chives, and shallots, and a handful of the tops of mint and balm, all dried and pounded. Put into a wide-mouthed bottle or stone jar with a gallon of the best vinegar. Cork closely, set in the sun for a fortnight (two weeks), strain, press all the juice and vinegar from the herbs. Let it stand a day to settle, then strain through a filtering bag.

M. Grieve
Culinary Herbs and Condiments, 1934

Just as you brew tea using the sun's rays, you can make a solar vinegar by steeping herbs in a glass jar that's set in the sun.

Herb Teas

Sixteen-Herb Tea

Take:
1 handful fennel roots
1 handful parsley roots
½ handful borage roots
½ handful pennyroyal roots
½ handful violet roots
½ handful succory (chicory) roots
½ handful endive roots
½ handful hollyhock leaves
½ handful mallow leaves
½ handful garden mint leaves
½ handful powdered licorice root
1½ gallons water
Add to this:
3 spoonfuls anise seed
3 spoonfuls fennel seed
3 spoonfuls coriander seed
3 spoonfuls cumin seed
1 handful dandelion root
Put the above into 1½ gallons of water, boil until reduced to ¾ gallon, strain, and drink either warm or cold.

M. Grieve
Culinary Herbs and Condiments, 1934

Quick-Brew Herbs

Herb drinks should be made with boiling water in an earthen pitcher or tea-pot, and be drank after standing a few minutes without boiling. Long steeping makes them insipid and disagreeable.

Mrs. Cornelius
The Young Housekeeper's Friend, 1859

Chamomile Remedy

Chamomile leaves, stalks, and blossoms, are all medicinal, but, as a complexion specific, use the blooms alone. Pick them as soon as open, just as the dew dries off, spread thin upon a clean sheet, and dry in the shade. Put away in paper-bags hung where it is dry and airy. Use for headache, languor, lassitude, muddy skin, and slightly fetid breath. Take a handful of the dry flowers, put them in a china bowl, and cover with a pint of boiling water. Throw a cloth over the bowl, and let it stand in a warm place for two or three hours. Let the patient, when ready for bed, sip the tea very hot. This should be done three nights in succcession. It stimulates all the excretory glands, and especially those of the skin, gently but thoroughly, making the complexion velvet-soft, and of a fresh wholesome colour. It also gives lustre to the eyes; this, of course, where there is no serious disease.

Emily Holt
The Complete Housekeeper, 1912

Sweet-Scented Goldenrod Tea

In Pennsylvania the population of German descent still use the leaves of the fragrant goldenrod. This "mountain tea" has a faint perfume, pleasantly suggestive of its origin, and is sufficiently in demand to be an article of trade, gathered and cured in summer.

Martha Bockée Flint
A Garden of Simples, 1900

Editor's Note: This aromatic wildflower, which we call sweet goldenrod (*Solidago odora*), once excited interest for both its bold looks in the garden and its medical reputation. *Meehans' Monthly* noted in 1899 that "goldenrods are now becoming favorites for garden culture." A reader of the magazine reported that she had planted circular beds of sweet goldenrod that she had gathered, planning to compare their scents.

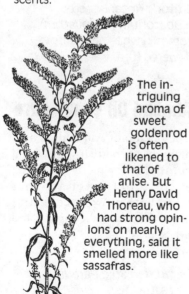

The intriguing aroma of sweet goldenrod is often likened to that of anise. But Henry David Thoreau, who had strong opinions on nearly everything, said it smelled more like sassafras.

Turn Ground Ivy into a Hot Drink

Take one ounce of the bruised fresh herb and infuse in a pint of boiling water, sweetening with honey, sugar, or licorice.

M. Grieve
Culinary Herbs and Condiments, 1934

Editor's Note: Chances are you yank a lot of this plant out when you weed your garden, so you might as well make use of it. Ground ivy is said to relieve headaches—whatever its medicinal properties, the scent is agreeable. To sweeten with licorice, buy the finely ground powder sold at natural food stores.

Some fast-spreading weeds are hard to dislike. Ground ivy, with its minty smell and tiny violet flowers, is one of them.

Black Tea with Hops

An infusion of hops is said to contain all the tonic, soothing, and nutritive properties of the hop, and when mixed with tea proper, counteracts tea's astringent and tannic properties.

Meehans' Monthly, 1891

Lemon Balm Brew

Lemon balm be comfortable for a moist and cold stomach, to open the stopping of the brain, and to drive away sorrow and care of the mind.

John Gerard
The Herball, 1633

Editor's Note: These claims for lemon balm may be a little extravagant, but there is medical evidence that the herb has a calming effect.

Give Me Liberty Tea

Most noteworthy among the substitutes adopted and first given the name of "Liberty Tea," were the leaves of the *Ceanothus americanus*, sometimes called New Jersey tea. The plant is not rare, although somewhat limited in range. One would not guess its secretions could have furnished a consoling cup to patriotic women. Certain it is, its infusion tasted now has no flavor beyond the slight twang from any growing bark.

Martha Bockée Flint
A Garden of Simples, 1900

Editor's Note: Liberty tea is made by steeping either fresh or dried leaves of New Jersey tea. The leaves do contain tannin, the astringent found in true tea, but they lack the intriguing taste—and caffeine—that would make this native drink a morning habit.

Oh, Say, Can You See, More Liberty Tea?

Many home-grown substitutes were used in Revolutionary times for tea; ribwort was a favorite one; strawberry and currant leaves, sage, thoroughwort, and "Liberty Tea" made from the four-leaved loosestrife. "Hyperion tea" was raspberry leaves, and was said by good patriots to be "very delicate and most excellent."

Alice Morse Earle
Home Life in Colonial Days,
1898

Editor's Note: Obviously there was no one single recipe for "Liberty tea." Good patriots made do with what was on hand. Be careful if you decide to try these tea substitutes. And steer clear of thoroughwort. This plant is better known today as blue cohosh, an herb that constricts the blood vessels of the heart. It can have a toxic effect on the cardiac muscle.

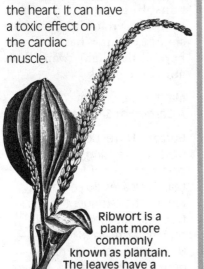

Ribwort is a plant more commonly known as plantain. The leaves have a mildly laxative effect.

Red Rose Tea

To impart a fine flavor to ordinary tea, place rose leaves in the tea canister.

William Dick
Encyclopedia of Practical Receipts and Processes, 1872

Speedwell for Sipping

An infusion of speedwell (*Veronica officinalis*), sage, and wood betony together is said to make an excellent beverage for breakfast, as a substitute of tea, speedwell having somewhat the flavor of Chinese green tea.

M. Grieve
Culinary Herbs and Condiments, 1934

Editor's Note: Hundreds of plants have been brewed over the years to find a cheaper substitute for East Asian tea. One of the more successful imitators is a wildflower, common speedwell.

Herbal Remedies

Harvest Hints for Medicinal Plants

Barks should be gathered as soon as they will peel easily in the spring. Leaves and herbs should be collected just before they begin to fade in autumn.

Flowers, when they first begin to blossom. Seeds, just before they are ripe. Roots may be dug at any time, thoroughly washed, cleaned, and dried.

E. B. Davis and B. G. Jefferis
The Household Guide, 1891

Herbal Cough Medicine

The following prescription is good for any kind of a cough. Boneset, flax seed, slippery elm bark, licorice, equal parts—say, an ounce each. Infuse thoroughly in water, simmering them together for a long time. This may be taken freely as an infusion, or molasses and sugar may be added to make a syrup, and when boiled it may be kept a long time in a corked bottle ready for use, and taken a teaspoonful at a time, whenever there is an inclination to cough.

The Household, 1878

Editor's Note: Boneset (*Eupatorium perfoliatum*) comes in white- and purple-flowered forms.

Almond Oil Cough Cure

The oil also of Almonds is used many ways, both inwardly and outwardly, for many purposes; as the oil of sweet almonds mixt with powdered white Sugar Candy, for coughes and hoarseness.

John Parkinson
Paradisi in Sole Paradisus Terrestris, 1629

Secret Apple Remedy

The paring of an apple cut somewhat thick, and the inside whereof is laid to hot, burning, or running eyes at night, when the party goes to bed, and is tied or bound to the same, doth help the trouble very speedily, and contrary to expectations— an excellent secret.

John Gerard
The Herball, 1633

For Nausea during Pregnancy

Use a small sack filled with all-spice and balsam, warmed, moistened with wine, and laid on the stomach.

Abraham Wagner
Specimen Book of Remedies, 1740

Editor's Note: Balsam is a fragrant resin produced by the balsam fir (*Abies balsamea*).

Cooling Barberry Water

Barberry water, made by pouring a cupful of boiling water on a large spoonful of barberry preserves, makes an excellent drink to use in cases of fevers and cold.

The Household, 1882

Editor's Note: Barberry berries are said to have anesthetic and antibacterial properties, which explains how they came to be used as a cold cure.

Strange But True

Insomnia is not a bane of our modern civilization alone. This little book, "The Queen's Closet Opened" (1656), shows that our ancestors craved and sought sleep just as we do. Here is a prescription to cure sleeplessness, which might be tried by any wakeful soul of modern times:

"Bruise a handful of Anise seeds and steep them in Red Rose Water, & make it up in little bags, & binde one of them to each Nostril, and it will cause sleep."

So anise-seed bags were used in earlier days for a purpose very different from our modern one; if your nineteenth century nose should refuse to accustom itself to having bags hung on it, you can "Chop Chamomile & crumbs of Brown Bread small and boil them with White Wine Vinegar, stir it well and spread it on a cloth & bind it to the soles of the feet as hot as you can suffer it." And if that should not make you sleepy, there are frankincense-perfumed paper bags for your head, and some very pleasant things made of rose-leaves for your temples, and hard-boiled eggs for the nape of your neck—you can choose from all of these.

Alice Morse Earle
Customs and Fashions in Old New England, 1893

Just a Spoonful of Basil Will Make You Feel Better

The later writers, among whom Simeon Zethy is one, do teach, that the smell of basil is good for the heart and for the head. That the seed cureth the infirmities of the heart, taketh away sorrowfulness which commeth of melancholy, and maketh a man merry and glad.

John Gerard
The Herball, 1633

Editor's Note: Add dried basil to sachets to sniff when your head (or heart) aches. Basil tea, made from a teaspoon of dried leaves in a cup of boiled water, may have a slight sedative effect.

Strange But True

This weed (black swallowwort) grows at the time when the swallows build their nests or eagles breed. If a man carries this about him, together with the heart of a mole, he shall overcome all fighting and anger.

John George Hohman
The Long-Lost Friend, 1819

Editor's Note: Black swallowwort (*Cynanchum nigrum*) is a climbing vine with purplish brown flowers. You can find it growing along roadsides from Ohio through New England. And if you're a gardener, chances are good you know where to find a mole.

Bergamot in the Bath

An ancient great aunt, barely remembered, used to pin her faith upon a bath in which branches of bergamot had been steeped to ease the stiffness of her tired old joints.

Louise Beebe Wilder
The Fragrant Path, 1932

Editor's Note: Both *Monarda didyma* and *M. fistulosa* are known as bergamot or bee-balm. The leaves of these mint family members have a citrus-like fragrance, and you can use them for making tea as well as scenting your bath.

Bergamot Balm

Bergamot and lemon balm are both garden herbs, and strongly sudorific; that is to say, sweat-provoking. Wisps of bergamot dry are good to keep away moths. Further, tender leaves of bergamot and balm, picked free of the stalks, and stewed slowly in very thick sweet cream for twelve hours, make a most excellent unguent salve for all sorts of angry and inflamed sores.

Emily Holt
The Complete Housekeeper, 1912

Blackberry Tonic for Stomach Upset

I remember well the stone jug of blackberry cordial made by our great-aunt Mary, that always stood upon a high shelf in my mother's clothespress. The dark and aromatic liquid used to be spooned out when occasion demanded to the children of the family to soothe the "griping griefs" of our imprudent young stomachs, and very warming and ameliorating it was. It was made yearly by mashing and straining the fully ripe berries until there was a gallon of juice, then sugar and allspice and cloves were added to taste and the whole cooked until slightly thickened. When nearly cold a quart of good brandy was added. During the making and for days thereafter the whole house was redolent of its stinging aroma.

Louise Beebe Wilder
The Fragrant Path, 1932

Other fruits are known to trouble stomachs, but blackberry has a reputation for quieting the insides. Drugstores still sell over-the-counter blackberry syrup as a gentle treatment for upset stomachs and diarrhea.

Summer-Complaint Cordial

This syrup is said to be a specific for the summer complaint gastroenteritis. From a teaspoonful to a wine glass, according to the age of the patient, must be given at intervals till relieved. To 2 quarts of juice of blackberries, add 1 pound of sugar, ½ ounce nutmegs, ½ ounce cinnamon, pulverized, ¼ ounce cloves, ¼ ounce allspice, pulverized. Boil together for a short time, and when cold, add a pint of fourth-proof (50-proof) brandy.

Farmers' Cabinet, 1837

Strange But True

Thrust the child having the whooping cough three times through a blackberry bush, without speaking or saying anything.

John George Hohman
The Long-Lost Friend, 1819

To Ease Your Pain, Bathe in Chamomile

The bathing with a decoction of camomile taketh away weariness, easeth pains to what parts soever they be applied.

Nicholas Culpeper
Culpeper's Complete Herbal, 1652

Kiss the Blues Goodbye with Borage

The leaves, flowers, and seeds are very cordial and help to expel pensiveness and melancholy that ariseth without manifest cause.

John Parkinson
Theatricum Botanicum, 1640

Editor's Note: When you're feeling sad, brew a strong tea by boiling borage leaves and stems in water. Use the tea to make lemon fruit ice, and you're sure to feel cheerier. Here's the recipe:

Bring 3 cups borage tea to a boil, and stir in 1¾ cups sugar until dissolved. Cool. Then add 1 tablespoon grated lemon rind and ¾ cup lemon juice. Pour into ice cube trays or a metal bowl and freeze.

Catnip Tea for Colds

Catnip is an excellent domestic remedy, and will produce active perspiration. Good for colds, headache, and similar diseases. Dose: Make a strong tea and drink before retiring.

E. B. Davis and B. G. Jefferis
The Household Guide, 1891

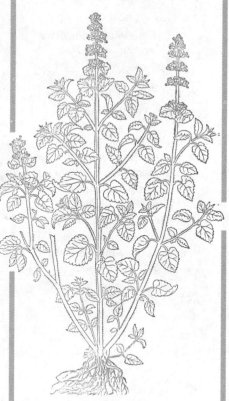

In contrast to its stimulating effect on cats, catnip is said to relax humans.

A decoction of chamomile is easy to make. Add 1 ounce dried herbs to 1 pint water that has been brought to a boil. Gently simmer the herbs for about 30 minutes, keeping the water just below boiling, and it's ready to use.

Chamomile Sunburn Soother

A decoction of its cream-tinted flowers was a much-used wash for sunburn.

Martha Bockée Flint
A Garden of Simples, 1900

Alert Traveler's Aid

It is reported that if such as journey or travel do carry with them a branch or rod of *Agnus castus* in their hand, it will keep them from weariness.

John Gerard
The Herball, 1633

Editor's Note: *Agnus castus* is actually the chaste tree, *Vitex agnus-castus*. This small tree has fragrant violet flowers that bloom all summer from Zone 6 southward. In cold winters the chaste tree may be killed to the ground, but it will come back from the roots and bloom on the new wood.

The leaves of the chaste tree (*Vitex agnus-castus*) are very aromatic, which may explain why sprigs were once thought to revive tired travelers.

Chicory for Red Eyes

The leaves of succory (chicory) bruised are good against inflammation of the eyes, being outwardly applied to the grieved place.

John Gerard
The Herball, 1633

OLD-TIME WISDOM

Banish warts with cypress spurge sap. In the old "grandmother's gardens," there was generally a patch of *Euphorbia cyparissias*, or "milk weed," grown especially for the purpose.

Meehans' Monthly, 1897

Editor's Note: Grandmother placed the milky sap of a broken stem on warts to make them go away. The sap may irritate your skin, and you should use caution when handling it. Note that this is not the common milkweed, but a plant better known today as cypress spurge. You'll find this spreading perennial growing wild in much of the north-central and northeastern United States.

Healthful Black Currant Jam

Many are the virtues of black currant jam and jelly. It was used by our grandmothers in gruel; it was given the children to eat when they had sore throats. A pitcherful of black currant tea, made by pouring boiling water over two or three tablespoonful of the jam, sweetened or not according to taste, was always kept on hand in fever cases, and made a delightfully cool and thirst-allaying drink.

The jam was made by using ¾ pound of sugar to a pound of fruit, and boiling over a slow fire till a little poured on a plate would set.

American Agriculturist, 1895

Both the fruit and the leaves of black currant have a pungent scent that either attracts or repels people. If you're a fan, try a few bushes as shrubs around the house. There are no thorns, so harvesting is a snap.

Sooth Nettle Stings with Dock

The soothing principle of dock leaves makes them useful in many ways. "In dock, out nettle," repeats the child who rubs them on his tortured hand.

Martha Bockée Flint
A Garden of Simples, 1900

Flaxseed Lemonade Cures Colds

Put 3 tablespoons of flaxseed in a little cheesecloth bag and sew it up. Let it simmer in a pint of water until it tastes like slippery elm, take out the bag, and add the juice of two lemons and 3 tablespoons of sugar. Cool before using. Drink freely of it if you have a bad cold or cough.

Meehans' Monthly, 1888

Editor's Note: Slippery elm is the slimy inner bark of a native elm, *Ulmus rubra*.

Quiet Coughs with Flaxseed Syrup

Take 1 teacupful of flaxseed, soak all night. In the morning, put in a kettle 2 quarts water, 1 handful licorice root (split up), ¼ pound good raisins (cut in half). Boil them until the strength is thoroughly extracted, then add the flaxseed, which has been previously soaked. Let all boil about half an hour more, watching and stirring, that the mixture may not burn. Then

strain and add lemon juice and sugar to taste. Take any quantity, cold, through the day, and half a thimbleful, warm, at night.

William Dick
Encyclopedia of Practical Receipts and Processes, 1872

For Soothing Sleep, Snooze on a Pillow Stuffed with Hops

Hops have long been known to possess soothing and sleep-producing properties. A cup of strong hop tea will produce pleasant sleep. Nervous and sleepless persons are often benefited by sleeping on a pillow of hops.

E. B. Davis and B. G. Jefferis
The Household Guide, 1891

Hoarse? Try Horseradish

Horseradish is an excellent remedy for hoarseness. Make a syrup by boiling the root, and add sufficient sugar to make it palatable. Dose: Two teaspoonfuls two or three times a day.

E. B. Davis and B. G. Jefferis
The Household Guide, 1891

Strange But True

The flowers of lily-in-the-valley put into a glass, and set in a hill of ants close stopped for the space of a month and then taken out, therein you shall find a liquor that appeases the pain and grief of the gout, being outwardly applied, which is commended to be most excellent.

John Gerard
The Herball, 1633

Editor's Note: All parts of lily-of-the-valley are poisonous—and that goes for the water they've been soaking in too. You're better off admiring and smelling the fragrant flowers than trying to use them medicinally.

Lily-of-the-valley is a trouble-free perennial for shady areas where choices for fragrant flowers are limited. The bell-shaped blooms appear in spring and are available in white or pink.

Hyssop Bandages

Hyssop is used of many people in the country to be laid unto cuts or fresh wounds, being bruised, and applied either alone, or with a little sugar.

John Parkinson
Paradisi in Sole Paradisus Terrestris, 1629

Lavender for a Level Head

The flowers of lavender picked from the knaps—I mean the blue part and not the husk—mixed with cinnamon, nutmegs, and cloves, made into powder, and given to drink in the distilled water thereof, doth help the panting and passion of the heart and prevaileth against giddiness.

John Gerard
The Herball, 1633

Mild Greens for Sweet Dreams

Lettuce is calming and beneficial to anyone suffering from insomnia.

Marie Theresa Villiers Earle
More Pot-Pourri from a Surrey Garden, 1899

Always Keep Mint on Hand

In order to have young leaves and tops of spearmint all the summer, cut down some advanced stalks every month, when new shoots will be thrown up; and to have dried balm for the winter, permit others to complete their growth and come into blossom. These last are to be cut as soon as the dew is off in the morning, for in the afternoon, and especially during bright sunshine, the odor of the plant is found to be much diminished. Dry the crop thus gathered in the shade, and afterwards keep it in small bundles, compactly pressed down, and covered with white paper. By the common mode of hanging up in winter in loose bundles, the odor soon escapes.

John Abercrombie
Abercrombie's Practical Gardener, 1818

Mint Heals Your Head and Belly

Two or three branches of spearmint taken in the juice of four pomegranates stays the hiccough. The dried powder taken after meat, helps digestion. Being smelled unto, it is comforting to the head. The decoction gargles in the mouth, cures the mouth and gums that are sore, and amends an ill-favoured breath. Mint is an herb that is useful in all disorders of the stomach, as weakness, squeamishness, loss of appetite, pain, and vomiting.

Nicholas Culpeper
Culpeper's Complete Herbal, 1652

Mugwort for Fatigue

The mugwort, *Artemisia vulgaris*, one of the humblest of plants in aspect, is of wide distribution. It was used in baths by the Romans, to remove fatigue and give suppleness. Pilgrims wore its leaves in their shoes, lest they be surbated (made sore).

Martha Bockée Flint
A Garden of Simples, 1900

Editor's Note: If you'd like to try a relaxing soak, place dried mugwort, agrimony, and chamomile in a small muslin drawstring bag. Hang the bag under the spout of your tub while you're running the water. Let the herbs steep awhile. Then remove the bag, squeeze it out into the tub, and climb in.

Mugwort has an unlovely name and green blooms that are easy to overlook. But once you experience its soothing ways, you'll be as fond of it as of showier herbs, especially when your joints ache from gardening.

A Spoonful of Mullein Syrup for Coughs

Mullein syrup, made with either honey or molasses, is still the remedy for coughs in many a country household.

Martha Bockée Flint
A Garden of Simples, 1900

Editor's Note: Mullein is a common weed with a commanding presence. The sight of its large, woolly leaves and six-foot-tall flower spikes should make you feel better, even if you don't use the flowers for cough medicine.

Onion for Better (Solitary) Sleep

For those troubled with sleeplessness, a raw onion, eaten just before retiring, will be found very beneficial in some cases.

Farm Journal, 1906

Editor's Note: A belief in the sleep-inducing properties of onions goes back centuries. John Gerard, in his famous English herbal of 1633, warned that onions "provoke overmuch sleep, especially being eaten raw."

Onion Syrup for Colds

There is nothing better than onion syrup for a severe cold. Peel and slice a good-sized, light-skinned onion and sift sugar over it, cover, and let it

Strange But True

To make a child merry hang a bundle of mugwort or make smoke thereof under the child's bed for it taketh away annoyance for him.

Peter Treueris
The Grete Herball, 1526

Editor's Note: Mugwort smoke, or any type of smoke, seems more likely to cause annoyance than relieve it. This herb has a sagelike smell, and Europeans once stuffed pillows with it to bring good dreams. Mugwort is not safe to use in teas or solutions for internal use, but you can use it in herbal baths to relieve aching muscles and joints.

stand in a warm place until the sugar draws the juice out.

American Agriculturist, 1895

Bathe Burns in Onion Juice

The juice taketh away the heat of scalding with water or oil.

John Gerard
The Herball, 1633

Treat Wounds with Soothing Parsley Salve

Take a handful of parsley, pound it fine, and work it to a salve with an equal proportion of fresh butter. This salve prevents mortification (gangrene) and heals very fast.

John George Hohman
The Long-Lost Friend, 1819

A Pennyroyal Headdress

A garland of pennyroyal made and worn about the head is of great force against the swimming in the head, the pains and giddiness thereof.

John Gerard
The Herball, 1633

Most herbs smell fragrant only when you bump, bruise, or step on them, but you can smell pennyroyal just walking by.

Plantain Stops Stinging Pain

All sorts of stings—whether from wasps, bees, hornets, or humble bees—should be sucked, to remove as much poison as possible; then have a slice of acid fruit, apple, tomato, or peach, or a crushed berry, or grape either ripe or green, bound lightly to the wound. If the pain is very severe, after a minute take off the fruit, wash the sting in warm water, and bathe it well in alcohol. Then wet a folded linenrag in either alcohol or vinegar, and bind on the sting. If neither alcohol, vinegar, nor fruit of any sort is at hand, try a bruised plantain-leaf. Change the application, whatever it is, every ten minutes until the pain subsides.

Emily Holt
The Complete Housekeeper, 1912

Strange But True

If the patient be too much sleepy put stinking things into his nose to waken him therewith.

William Turner
Herbal of William Turner, 1568

Editor's Note: This remedy was intended for people who had drugged themselves with opium, but no doubt it would also work for drivers who feel sleepy at the wheel.

Potato Poultice

I think nothing can equal grated potato as a poultice for any kind of sore that is expected to supperate, cooling it, is always at hand, quickly applied, changed without difficulty, never sticks, and keeps the skin soft and moist with reasonable attention.

Sarah E. Elliott
The Household, 1878

Quince Seeds Help Burns Heal

An excellent dressing for a small burn is made by turning about a tablespoon of boiling water upon a teaspoonful of quince seeds. When cool it makes a thick, clear jelly, with which to coat the burn.

The Household, 1878

Strange But True

The peony was believed by the Greeks to be of divine origin, an emanation from the moon, Diana's own gift to the Earth. Even now there exists a belief in its virtue, and the "anodyne (pain-relieving) necklaces" sold to prevent convulsions are made of beads turned from its solid rootstocks. They must be dug when "the decreasing moon passeth under Aries."

Martha Bockée Flint
A Garden of Simples, 1900

Editor's Note: According to Gerard's *The Herball* (1633), you don't have to bother making beads. Parents simply tied the fresh root around their children's necks to prevent epileptic seizures.

Sweet Raspberry Remedy

The raspberry flower stamped with honey and applied, is good for the inflammation of the eyes and the shingles.

William Langham
The Garden of Health, 1633

Editor's Note: To stamp the flowers, simply crush them with the honey using a pestle.

Rose Syrup for Melancholy

Steep new roses and then strain out the juice of it and add sugar therewith: this is the best making of syrup. In winter and in summer it may be given competently to feeble, sick, melancholy, and choloric people.

Anthony Askham
Herbal, 1550

Old-time remedies relied heavily on plant fragrances, which made the rose as valuable as any medicinal herb.

Sniff Roses before Retiring

Rosewater bringeth sleep which also the fresh roses themselves promote through their sweet and pleasant smell.

William Turner
Herbal of William Turner, 1568

Strange But True

Gold and precious stones were specially necessary "to ease the passion of the Heart," as indeed they are nowadays. In the 17th century, however, they applied the mercenary cure inwardly, and prepared it thus:

Take Damask Roses half-blown, cut off their whites, and stamp them very fine, and straine out the juice very strong; moisten it in the stamping with a little Damask Rose water; then put thereto fine powder Sugar, and boil it gently to a fine Syrup; then take the Powders of Amber, Pearl, Rubies, of each half a dram, Ambergreese one scruple, and migle them with the said syrup till it be somewhat thick, and take a little thereof on a knifes point morning and evening.

Alice Morse Earle
Customs and Fashions in Old New England, 1893

Rosemary to Boost Memory

Rosemary is for remembrance

Between us day and night,

Wishing that I may always have

You present in my sight.

From a traditional British song

Editor's Note: In *An Encyclopedia of Gardening* (1850), J. C. Loudon says about rosemary, "In some parts of the west of England and in Wales, sprigs are distributed to the company at funerals, as tokens of remembrance, and often thrown into the grave upon the coffin of the deceased."

A Wreath of Rosemary

Rosemary is a remedy against the stuffing of the head, that cometh through coldness of the brain, if a garland thereof be put about the head.

John Gerard
The Herball, 1633

Editor's Note: If the piny scent of rosemary doesn't clear your head, make rosemary tea to add to your bath—the volatile oils will get your blood flowing.

Strange But True

With onions, salt, and honey, walnuts are good against the biting of a mad dog or man, if they be laid upon the wound.

John Gerard
The Herball, 1633

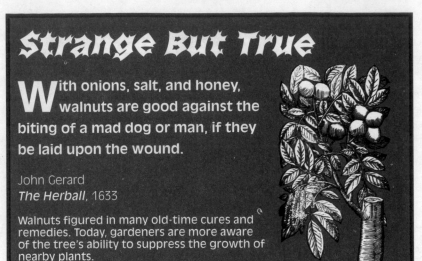

Walnuts figured in many old-time cures and remedies. Today, gardeners are more aware of the tree's ability to suppress the growth of nearby plants.

Rosemary Toothpaste

Take the timber of rosemary and burn it to coals and make powder thereof and rub thy teeth and it shall keep thy teeth from all evils.

Richard Banckes
Bancke's Herbal, 1550

Editor's Note: This herbal also suggests sniffing rosemary charcoal to "keep thee youngly." Rosemary oil does have antibacterial effects, but antiaging sounds like a stretch.

Sage Gargle for a Sore Throat

Combine very strong sage tea, ½ pint; strained honey, common salt, and strong vinegar, of each 2 tablespoonfuls; cayenne (pulverized), 1 rounded teaspoonful. Steep the cayenne with the sage,

strain, mix the other ingredients, and bottle for use, gargling from four to a dozen times daily, according to the severity of the case.

William Dick
Encyclopedia of Practical Receipts and Processes, 1872

Quiet Thyme

The distilled water of thyme applied with vinegar of roses to the forehead easeth the rage of frenzy.

John Parkinson
Theatricum Botanicum, 1640

Verbena Learning Aid

Infants bearing it shall be very apt to learn and they shall be glad and joyous.

Albertus Magnus
The Book of Secrets of Albertus Magnus, 1560

Vervain, the Party Herb

To make folks merry at ye table, take four leaves and four roots of vervain in wine, then sprinkle the wine all about the house where the eating is and they shall be all merry.

Peter Treueris
The Grete Herball, 1526

Violet Soak for Sleeplessness

For thee that may not sleep for sickness, seeth (boil) this herb in water and at evening let him soak well his feet in the water to the ankles. He shall sleep well by the grace of God.

Anthony Askham
Herbal, 1550

Fragrant Herbs for the Home

Fragrant Pillows

Pillows filled with sweet fern, balsam fir, rose leaves, and fragrant things of that sort are often found on sale and command good prices. Try making them.

American Agriculturist, 1895

Editor's Note: Sweet fern is a shrub, *Comptonia peregrina*.

Scented Herb Bouquet for the Blind

Think of the pleasure which could be given to the sightless by a posy of sweet-scented leaves, by southernwood, mint, balm, or basil, and when memory was thereby awakened in those who once had seen, what tender thoughts! If this book could influence the planting of an herb garden for the solace of those who cannot see the flowers of field and garden, then it will not have been written in vain.

Alice Morse Earle
Old-Time Gardens, 1901

Favorite fragrances can bring back sweet memories of summers past. This bouquet of southernwood (*Artemisia abrotanum*), mint, lemon balm, and basil is sure to stir up pleasant thoughts. Herb bouquets make unique decorations for dinner parties too.

Strange But True

The green boughs of willow with the leaves on them may very well be brought into chambers and set about the beds of those that be sick of fevers, for they do mightily cool the heat of the air, which thing is wonderful refreshing to the sick patients.

John Gerard
The Herball, 1633

Editor's Note: This idea may not be as farfetched as it seems since willow bark extract has been used to fight fevers from the first century A.D. on. Salicin, a substance derived from the willow, was used to develop aspirin.

Lavender for Lovely Linens

I remember, when a little girl in Baltimore, the pleasantest corners of the great open markets, for which that city is justly famous, were the lavender stalls where the pale aromatic spikes lay piled in great bunches that were eagerly bought by the fastidious housewives of the city to strew in their linen presses. We grew lavender in our old Maryland garden and the sheets in my mother's house always smelled of it. What sweet slumbers come to one between lavender-scented sheets!

Louise Beebe Wilder
The Fragrant Path, 1932

Editor's Note: If you like the aura of lavender around you, try placing a few sprigs of the fresh herb under the ironing board pad to subtly scent your clothes and linens.

Spicy Moth Repellent

Combine ½ pound of lavender leaves, ½ ounce each of dried thyme and mint, ¼ ounce each of ground cloves and caraway, and 1 ounce common salt. Tie up in a linen bag, which is hung in a wardrobe.

L. H. Bailey
The Horticulturist's Rule Book, 1895

Poor Soil for a Rich Scent

If lavender be planted in a dry, gravelly, or poor soil, its flowers have a powerful odor; while in a rich garden soil, although it grows strongly, it is apt to be killed, and the flowers have less perfume.

Royal Caledonian Horticulture Society
Journal of a Horticultural Tour, 1832

Orange Peel for Potpourri

An important ingredient in good potpourri is strips of Seville orange peel stuck with cloves. The peel is taken off and cut in pieces from end to end of the orange, so that each is about half an inch wide in the middle and two inches long; holes are pricked in it, and the shaft of the clove pressed in so that the heads nearly touch each other. The pieces are then packed into a jar firmly with the hand with sprinklings of salt in between and over the top.

Gertrude Jekyll
Home and Garden, 1900

To enliven a potpourri, try studding the peel of ordinary grocery-store oranges with cloves.

Strange But True

If anyone has to settle any just claim by way of a lawsuit, let him take some of the largest kind of sage and write the name of the twelve apostles on the leaves, and put them in his shoes before entering the courthouse, and he shall certainly gain the suit.

John George Hohman
The Long-Lost Friend, 1819

Editor's Note: Hey—it's worth a try!

Japanese Quince Sachet

The perfume of the fruit of the Japanese quince, *Cydonia japonica*, of our shrubberies, is almost roselike. Long ago as children we always kept a Japanese quince in the box with our little pocket handkerchiefs and thought the scent finer than any eau de rose that was ever bottled.

Louise Beebe Wilder
The Fragrant Path, 1932

Editor's Note: Wilder's Japanese quince is now known as *Chaenomeles japonica*. This spreading shrub forms a 6- to 10-foot-tall tangle of spiny branches. It's covered with bright red, pink, or white flowers in spring and produces 2½-inch-long, round yellowish fruits in fall. Japanese quince fruits not only smell good, they're also edible. You need to cook the fruits before eating them, but they are excellent for preserves and jellies.

Recovering Rose Oil

Take a large jar and fill it with clean flowers of roses. Cover them with pure water and sit it in the sun in the day time and take in at night for seven days or when the oil will float on the top. Take this off with some cotton tied on a stick and squeeze in a vial and stop it up close. Use either pure spring water or rain water and remember to cover the crock if it looks like rain. The oil or attar looks like a yellowish oily scum and should be removed daily.

Recipe Book, 1859

Editor's Note: The oily scum may sound unappealing, but it's the rose essence used in perfumes, sachets, and potpourris. It takes 60,000 roses to produce 1 ounce of pure essential oil, which is why rose oil is so expensive to buy. You can make a cheaper version by soaking rose petals in vegetable oil.

Sweet Potpourri

For any kind of potpourri I am always on the lookout for sweet materials such as shavings or sawdust of sandalwood or sweet cedar; all ingredients that have an enduring fragrance are good and welcome.

Gertrude Jekyll
Home and Garden, 1900

Valerian for Happy Cats

Valerian (*Valeriana officinalis*) has an effect on the nervous system of many animals as well as on man, and especially on cats, which seem to be thrown into a kind of intoxication by its scent. It is scarcely possible to keep a plant of valerian in a garden which these animals frequent. Although the odor is so disagreeable to Europeans, some of the Asiatic nations prize it as a delicious perfume.

C. Pierpoint Johnson
The Useful Plants of Great Britain, 1862

Editor's Note: You can make valerian-stuffed toys or pillows to make your cat happy. (Or steep leaves in hot bath water for a relaxing soak for yourself.)

Valerian has escaped the garden and can be found along roadsides. The plants grow to a graceful four feet tall, with pink flower clusters and divided leaves that make a nice addition to flower and herb gardens.

Herbal Cosmetics

Cream for Chapped Hands

Take house leek, sweet balsam, heal-all (self-heal, *Prunella vulgaris*), blue balsam blows (balsam poplar flowers), coolwort (possibly kale), rock liverwort (a hepatica), water scabish (scabious), red plantain, red clover heads, chamomile flowers, catnip blows, white poppies, kings clover, ground ivy, and put them all in an iron vessel. Add 3 pints cold water. Simmer gradually until it boils. Strain off the liquor and add 8 ounces fresh butter and 1 ounce beeswax to it and simmer till the liquor has evaporated, then strain through thick cloth.

Mary Ann Hill
Recipe Book, 1857

Editor's Note: This cream was used by the Shaker community at Hancock, Massachusetts. Some of the ingredients aren't clearly identified, but you could try the basic recipe with the ingredients you are familiar with. House leeks (*Sempervivum* spp.) are succulent herbs that are used as ornamentals in the garden. One of the most popular house leeks is known as hens-and-chicks (*S. tectorum*). White poppy (*Papaver somniferum*) is now sold as lettuce poppy.

Strange But True

Whoever loses his hair should pound up peach kernels, mix them with vinegar, and put them on the bald place.

John George Hohman
The Long-Lost Friend, 1819

The Sweet Scent of a Woman

The woman who wishes to carry about with her a delicate, almost imperceptible, fragrance that every one identifies with her (as is done by the heroines of the romantic novels, and very few besides), will do well to take her chosen perfume from among the unadulterated natural scents. Let her strew rose-leaves and sweet violets and lavender and citron-aloe and sweetbrier among her laces and gloves and ribbons. Let her keep her lingerie in drawers lined with orris-filled sachets, and choose for a handkerchief case a basket woven of the Indian sweet-grasses.

The Woman's Book, 1894

Splash On a Dash of Do-It-Yourself Cologne

Take of essence of bergamot and of citron each five drachms (drams), essence of lemon four drachms, essence of rosemary two and one-half drachms, essence of orange flower three drops, alcohol one quart; mix together. Those who prefer a fuller perfume may add five drachms of lavender.

The Successful Housekeeper, 1887

Editor's Note: A dram is equal to ⅛ ounce or 3.697 milliliters.

Bayberry Scrub Removes Sap

I discovered one convenient use the bayberries served—that if you got your hands pitched in the pine woods, you had only to rub a parcel of these berries between your hands to start the pitch off.

Henry David Thoreau
Journal IX, 1857

Editor's Note: In the northern woods, the northern bayberry (*Myrica pensylvanica*) is handy for a hand wash. In the southern United States, look for wax myrtle (*M. cerifera*), which is similar. Both plants have small, round, waxy fruits that are used to make bayberry candles.

Lobelia Hair Restorative

Put one-half pound pulverized lobelia herb in a bottle, add to it equal parts of whisky, brandy, and olive oil. Bathe the head once a day; it will prevent the loss of hair and is said to restore it.

Receipts of Material Medica, 1842

Editor's Note: Lobelia may be helpful as a hair-loss remedy, but it's not an herb to experiment with medicinally. Lobelia is a powerful poison if taken internally.

Quince Hair Pomade

The seeds covered with forty to fifty times their bulk of water and gently warmed, soon produce a thick mucilage used by perfumers and hair dressers. Many ladies prepare this for themselves, to keep the hair in place. It needs a little alcohol, or strong alcoholic liquor may be added, to keep it from souring, and it may be perfumed to one's taste.

American Agriculturist, 1883

Editor's Note: The author may be using Japanese quince (*Chaenomeles japonica*) or Chinese quince (*Pseudocydonia sinensis*) for this preparation. Both plants produce fragrant fruits that are used in preserves. Japanese quince is a low, spring-flowering shrub, and Chinese quince is a small tree.

Lavender Bath Soothes Dry Skin

An oil rub, especially if your skin is dry and harsh, will be most beneficial, and will help to put it into normal condition. The Greek bath, in which seven parts of pure olive oil and one part of lavender water are used, is exquisitely refreshing. Rub the mixture well into the skin, being careful to keep the body very warm; take this bath for three successive nights.

Dr. Emma E. Walker
Every Woman's Library, 1910

Saffron for a Warmer Skin Tone

If any person use saffron measurably it maketh in them a good color, but if they use it out of measure it maketh him look pale, and maketh the head ache and hurteth the appetite.

William Turner
Herbal of William Turner, 1568

Saffron comes from the saffron crocus (*Crocus sativus*). These days people aren't concerned with warming up their skin with saffron. Instead, this spice is used to give rice dishes a golden hue. Its flavor and color also go well with soups, stews, and herbal vinegars.

Beebalm for Clear Complexions

The Indians of the Winnebago tribes used a decoction of monarda leaves as a cure for pimples.

Louise Beebe Wilder
The Fragrant Path, 1932

Editor's Note: Make a decoction simply by pouring boiling water over the beebalm (*Monarda didyma*) leaves and letting them steep. Beebalm is a native member of the mint family. It has an aromatic fragrance and striking scarlet blossoms that appear in summer.

Cowslip Wrinkle Formula

Some women sprinkle ye flowers of cowslip with white wine and after disstill it and wash their faces with that water to drive wrinkles away and to make them fair in the eyes of the world rather than in the eyes of God, whom they are not afraid to offend.

William Turner
Herbal of William Turner, 1568

Editor's Note: Several plants share the common name of cowslip, but the plant Turner is referring to is most likely *Caltha palustris*, which is also known as marsh marigold. The leaves of this yellow-flowered herb are sometimes used as greens, and its flower buds are picked as a substitute for capers.

Quince Facial Cream

Take $^1/_3$ cup quince seed. Soak in tepid water until the gluten parts from the seeds. Stir once in a while carefully to avoid discoloration. Strain through a fine sieve or cloth, but do not squeeze. Add 2 full ounces of alcohol, $1^1/_2$ ounces of glycerin and oils or extracts of perfume according to liking. If oil is used, cut it in the alcohol first or it will not mix with the gluten. Thin with water if too thick. Beat it well and bottle tightly.

Unpublished Shaker recipe, Canterbury, N.H., 1800s

Editor's Note: This cream was marketed by the Shakers, a religious community that originated in England and came to America in 1774. Shakers are known for their herbal preparations and spartan lifestyle.

Rosemary Makes You Fair of Face

Many pretty rules may be found in old books and diaries, that are of New England, rules "to make the face fair" and to "make sweet the mouth." "Take the flowers of Rosemary and seeth (boil) them in White Wine, with which wash your face, and if you drink thereof it will make you have a sweet breath."

Alice Morse Earle
Customs and Fashions in Old New England, 1893

113

Flowers

Gardeners in the 17th and 18th
centuries had a lot of imagination,
especially when it came to flowers.
Their ideas for children's gardens
and water gardens and their hints
for using fragrance, color, and more
show that they not only
had a way with flowers, but
a sense of humor, too.

Flowers
Best Design Ideas

Blending Groups of Plants

Let one group of flowers run in behind another. If you plant large groups in a pear-shaped form with the narrow end slightly curved, and let the large end of the adjoining pear-shaped group run up to the narrow stem of its neighbor, you will produce the effect I suggest.

W. C. Egan
Making a Garden of Perennials, 1912

If you aren't sure how to blend one plant group with its neighbors, you need a system. Arrange the first group of plants in a rounded shape, such as a pear, amoeba, or kidney bean. Then keep repeating the shape along the bed for other plant groups, fitting the shapes together so one group runs behind another.

OLD-TIME WISDOM

Look to the clouds for inspiration. It is almost as easy to plant in pretty ways as in ugly ways if we take the trouble to think of it. There are hints to be gathered from the way wild plants arrange themselves, and even from the sky. Often a small cloud passing in the sky will give a very good form for a group, and be instructive even in being closer and more solid towards its center, as groups of narcissus in the grass should often be.

William Robinson
The English Flower Garden, 1883

Let Nature Be Your Guide

Flower gardens are generally too "fixed up"—too "fussy," as the ladies sometimes say. You have often stood on the bank of some beautiful stream and watched it, delighted, as it wound its graceful meandering course through the valley, lost to your view at some points by intervening trees, and again appearing in the distance like a bright silver thread. Let this be your model. Lay out your walks gracefully winding as the river; plant your flowers and shrubs and trees in little groups. Thus imitate nature, and the effect will be pleasing.

Genesee Farmer, 1850

Planning a Drift

A drift is a thin, longish line of plants, drawn diagonally across a straight border or placed in a slender bow in a long bed. It spreads the flowers in such a way that the sparest bloom will seem abundant. Twelve to eighteen plants make a sustaining drift that gives continuity to a border. Fifty to a hundred bulbs make a good drift.

Elsa Rehman
Garden-Making, 1926

Editor's Note: A drift calls attention to a single type of flower. By setting the plants out in a row that crosses the bed, you can tie the planting together and draw the eye from one end of it to the other.

Old-Time Wisdom

The origin of "drifts." Many years ago I came to the conclusion that in all flower borders it is better to plant in long rather than block-shaped patches. It not only has a more pictorial effect, but a thin long planting does not leave an unsightly empty space when the flowers are done and the leaves have perhaps died down. The word "drift" conveniently describes the shape I have in mind and I commonly use it in speaking of these long-shaped plantings.

Gertrude Jekyll
Colour in the Flower Garden, 1908

A Different Kind of Dribbling

Plants can be scattered through the border in a way that is sometimes called "dribbling in the plants." It is the effect that one gets when seed is scattered ever so thinly through the border and the plants crop up here and there delicately far apart. Such planting has the spontaneity with which Nature scatters her plants through the woodland. They are charmingly delicate when in bloom, and yet they are never missed when out of bloom. Plants of refined and delicate form are best for this use, plants like tulips and lilies of all kinds, various snakeroots and meadow rues, *Hyacinthus candicans* and *Delphinium belladonna.*

Elsa Rehman
Garden-Making, 1926

Editor's Note: *Hyacinthus candicans* is now known as the giant summer hyacinth (*Galtonia candicans*) and *Delphinium belladonna* as Belladonna delphinium.

Snow Shows Your Yard's Planting Zones

Take note where the snows always melt first—there the sun lingers longest and it is "early ground" compared to where the snows melts last, which is usually on the north or shade side of a clump of shrubbery, fence, or hedge. This will be the "late ground."

A. M. Kirby
Daffodils, Narcissus and How to Grow Them, 1907

Editor's Note: You can extend the flowering season by planting in both the warm and the cool microclimates of your yard. Patches of melting snow create a simple map for you to follow.

To Add Interest, Mix Tall and Small Flowers

In planting at boundary lines or at buildings, the taller flowers should be used at the back, but the semi-tall ones—say three feet in height—should occasionally be brought well toward the front in order to avoid stiffness and to add irregularity to the general effect.

W. C. Egan
Making a Garden of Perennials, 1912

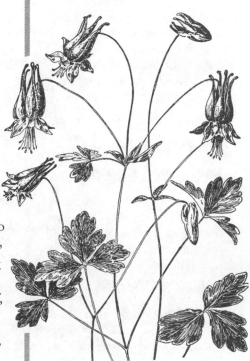

Break up the monotony of a planting by doing the unexpected. Plant a few tall, see-through flowers, like columbine (shown here) or Brazilian vervain (*Verbena bonariensis*), at the front of the flower bed to break up the rigid, stair-step look of small, medium, and tall plants.

Stretch the Bloom Season

If fortunate to have the same plant on the north side of the hill or wall, we have a difference of two or three weeks in the blooming of a plant.

William Robinson
The English Flower Garden, 1833

Editor's Note: By planting the same flowers on the north and south sides of a hill or wall, you can stretch out the blooming period. Plants on the warmer south side will bloom first, followed by plants on the cooler north side. It's an easy way to keep favorite flowers around longer.

Three Tips for Old-Fashioned Gardens

The beauty of an old-fashioned garden is due largely to the feeling of repose and settled-downness which it yields. Each plant looks as though it "belongs" where it is. There is plenty of background, and not too much episode. The "comfortably-at-home" effect is produced mainly by three causes:

Firstly, the presence of abundant deciduous trees and shrubs, giving infinitely varied effects of light and shade;

Secondly, the arrangement of the plants in bold groups of single species;

And thirdly, the provision of each separate plant with depth of suitable soil, and space to develop its individual form.

Harry Roberts
The Book of Old-Fashioned Flowers, 1904

Do You Have a Pet Plant?

Some seem anxious to obtain and grow everything. This is not best, especially where there is not a good deal of time and money to be devoted. A choice selection is best, and I like every cultivator of flowers to have a pet or hobby. Take, for instance, the pansy, and make it a pet. It will astonish you to see how flowers thrive under such petting, and what a wonderful exhibition they make of their gratitude.

Vick's Illustrated Catalogue and Floral Guide, 1872

Editor's Note: When time or space is short, specializing in one plant is a way to lower maintenance and give your garden an elegant look. Try growing mostly irises or salvias—you'll have all the color and size choices you need.

In Celebration of Singles

As flowers begin to be appreciated for their intrinsic worth—when we look *into* them rather than *at* them—our respect for double forms will be lost in our admiration for the single flower, perfect in all its parts as it was when it first beautified the earth.

C. L. Allen
Bulbs and Tuberous-Rooted Plants, 1893

Editor's Note: Periodically, gardeners return to simpler flowers. Wildflower gardens became popular in the 1870s, followed by a rage for cottage gardens and today's keen interest in heritage plants.

Create Graceful Curves with a Hose

A humble instrument with which to get good outlines for informal borders is the garden hose. Place stakes in your grass or open ground before shrub planting, to outline roughly the areas planned for flowering plants; then lay the hose either inside or outside of these stakes.

Louisa King
The Little Garden, 1921

Editor's Note: A garden hose makes a handy and flexible tool for experimenting with the shape of a new flower bed. Lay the hose on the site of your new bed, and arrange it to form an outline that you like. Push your lawn mower along beside the hose before you make a final decision about the border. You'll find that gentle curves are easy to mow, but tight curves make for maintenance headaches.

Tulipmania

Why not have fifty varieties of tulips, comprising practically all the important species and varieties so that everybody will want to come to your lawn party next spring and rave over the wonderful colors? Your whole family will get into the craze and you will become famous in your town as a connoisseur.

The Garden Magazine, 1906

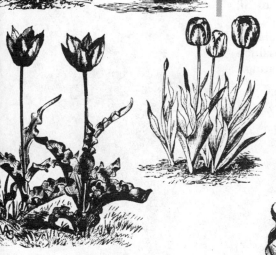

There's so much variation between the different varieties of a single plant that you can create an entire garden of one flower and never get bored. Make a planting of only salvias, for example, or only tulips, as shown here, using varieties with different heights, forms, and colors for a fascinating mix.

The Incredible Expanding Flower Bed

For a private botanic garden, the mode of grouping on turf is much the most elegant and it has this advantage—that, as the species belonging to the group are increased, it can be enlarged by appropriating a part of the turf.

J. C. Loudon
An Encyclopedia of Gardening, 1850

Editor's Note: Because gardens in the mid-1800s were often formally laid out, this hint must have sounded almost radical at the time. But its practicality is obvious: By placing a free-standing bed in the lawn, you can extend the borders as needed to accommodate new plants.

Spring Beds Need Fine Foliage

Gardens of spring flowers generally have a thin, poor effect for want of plants of important foliage. The greater number of them look what they are—temporary makeshifts. But herbacious plants of rather large growth with fine foliage in April and May are not many. The best I could think of are *Veratrum nigrum* (false hellebore), *Myrrhis odorata* (sweet cicely), and the newer *Euphorbia characias* var. *wulfenii* (spurge).

Louise Beebe Wilder
Colour in My Garden, 1918

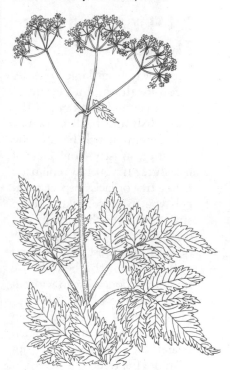

Use sweet cicely to fill out sparse beds in May. This 3-foot-tall plant appears on cue with graceful, fernlike foliage and a scattering of white blossoms.

Grass "Carpet" Keeps Gardens Looking Good

A flower garden formed on a groundwork of grass lawn has at all seasons a clothed effect; and though in winter the grass has a less lively tint, yet it still looks like a carpeted apartment with some of its more showy decorations awanting. The flower garden without grass is like a house which has not only lost its carpets, but nearly its whole furniture.

Charles H. J. Smith
Parks and Pleasure Grounds,
1852

Set Flowers and Trees Far Apart

Keep away from large trees. A vigorous elm and a perennial cannot eat and drink out of the same dish and both grow fat. The perennial will be the one to suffer, mostly from lack of moisture. If you have planted near a tree or lack of space compels you to do so, take a sharp spade and, each spring, cut deeply all along the edge of the flower bed nearest the tree, and pull out from the bed all the small tree roots you can without disturbing the plants. This applies to beds within eight or ten feet of a tree. For any bed much nearer, the cutting would be apt to injure the tree.

W. C. Egan
Making a Garden of Perennials,
1912

Perk Up Gardens with Potted Plants

In order to keep a mixed flower garden always gay, successive crops should be provided partially in pots. Plunged in the ground, and the tops of their pots covered with soil, no one can tell that the flower garden is not their constant station. To admit of this, a large reserve nursery is requisite, in which the plants must be kept in pots, and removed and plunged in the borders as wanted.

J. C. Loudon
An Encyclopedia of Gardening, 1850

Plants Patch Holes in Mixed Borders

There are ways of filling gaps by training plants down to fill the spaces. For this use, everlasting peas, tall perennial sunflowers, rudbeckias, and dahlias are especially accommodating.

E. T. Cook
Gardening for Beginners, 1901

Balanced Borders

Looking over my bright beds I still felt that there was something wrong, a haphazard, unrestful feeling about them. One remedy for this was discovered quite accidentally. It happened when I planted my ricinus or castor bean (*Ricinus communis*) in big clumps exactly opposite each other. I realized then that there must be balance in a garden. Just as when we put a pair of vases on a mantle piece, one at each end, we find the effect pleases, so in a double border a similar planting at stated intervals on both sides gives, not monotony, but restfulness.

Julia H. Cummins
My Garden Comes of Age, 1926

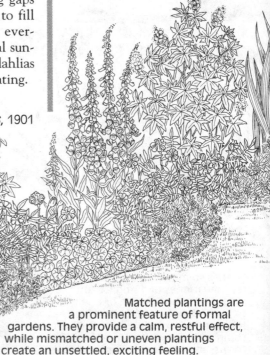

Matched plantings are a prominent feature of formal gardens. They provide a calm, restful effect, while mismatched or uneven plantings create an unsettled, exciting feeling.

Sunken Beds Use Less Water

Where there is an ample water supply the flower beds may be elevated a few inches above the lawn to make them more conspicuous; but where the seasons are hot and dry and water must be carried it is better to set them slightly lower than the lawn, so that all the available moisture may be utilized.

Ida D. Bennett
The Flower Garden, 1904

Separate Beds for Three Seasons of Blooms

I believe the only way it can be done is to devote certain borders to certain times of year; each border or garden region to be bright for from one to three months.

Gertrude Jekyll
Colour in the Flower Garden, 1908

Editor's Note: Despite Jekyll's discouraging words, you *can* create a single garden with three seasons of bloom. Mix early-blooming bulbs with perennials that have long bloom seasons and attractive seedpods and foliage. Baptisia (*Baptisia australis*) with its blue flowers, blue-green leaves, and showy seedpods is one good choice, and purple coneflower (*Echinacea purpurea*) with its rose pink blooms and spiny seedheads is another.

Babes in the Borders

White pinks are perhaps the best flowers for edging beds. They are covered with fragrant flowers in June and the silvery foliage is always attractive, even in winter. These unpretentious little flowers, which crouch at one's feet, appeal to one's protective instincts like helpless children. But they do their work marvelously well.

Wilhelm Miller
The Garden Magazine, 1909

Favorite Combinations

White and Lavender Light Up Late Summer

I have no combination more beautiful than that of white hydrangea flowering side by side with the pale little lilac wild asters of our northern fields.

Rose Fay Thomas
Our Mountain Garden, 1904

Editor's Note: Plant your favorite hydrangea with New England asters (*Aster novae-angliae*) for the late-summer effect Thomas so admired. Both the panicle hydrangea (*Hydrangea paniculata*) and oakleaf hydrangea (*H. quercifolia*) make a good match for asters. A sunny site with moist, well-drained soil suits this combination.

Gold and Lavender for Fall

I have often wondered, in the fall, when the pasturelands and fence corners were ablaze with the glory of goldenrod and asters, why no effort was made to bring this beauty nearer home. At last I tried the experiment. It has proved a grand success. In one corner of the yard I have a clump of both these plants, and in October they are a mass of brilliant color. Each year they increase in size, for I keep the grass away from their roots, and give them a rich soil to spread in. They keep the freedom of their native haunts in their new location, and bring into the garden a breath of the woods and the pastures.

Eben E. Rexford
The Homemaker, 1879

Editor's Note: In a sunny spot, mix a lavender aster such as Tartarian aster (*Aster tataricus*) or New England aster (*A. novae-angliae*) with a goldenrod such as Canada goldenrod (*Solidago canadensis*) or European goldenrod (*S. virgaurea*), and you'll get the bright, beautiful display that Rexford describes. If you're avoiding goldenrod because you think it causes hayfever, don't. Ragweed pollen is the culprit that causes your running eyes and nose. Goldenrod, which happens to bloom at the same time, takes the heat from allergy sufferers because its flowers are so conspicuous.

Brilliant Blue and Red Poppies, Too

One of the prettiest associations that came about by accident but is now permanently established is where blue flax (*Linum perenne*) grows among the jaunty Spanish poppy (*Papaver rupifragum*). They both have a grand blossoming for nearly two months in the spring and early summer and then for the rest of the season give little snatches of gay color now and then.

Louise Beebe Wilder
Colour in My Garden, 1918

Editor's Note: Set steel blue flax and brick red Spanish poppies in among summer-blooming perennials like salvias for a continuous show. Spanish poppies are hardy only to Zone 7, but you can substitute 'Allegro' oriental poppies (**Papaver orientale**) in colder areas.

Set a Green Stage

No prettier effect can be obtained than by planting bright-colored climbing roses with *Ampelopsis veitchii*. The latter forms a beautiful background of green for the gayly colored flowers, furnishing a more abundant foliage than the roses themselves.

Florence Beckwith
Vick's Family Magazine, 1902

Editor's Note: *Ampelopsis veitchii* is a variety of Boston ivy that is now known as

Parthenocissus tricuspidata 'Veitchii'. The leaves of this vine are smaller than the leaves of the species. They have a purple color when young, but later they change to green.

Variety Is the Spice of Life

The whole front of a bed is planted with a band some 8 feet deep and 20 yards long of *Iris florentina*, with every now and then a clump of *I. germanica* among them. At first it was all *florentina*, but a purple *germanica* got in by accident, and I saw how greatly its presence improved the general effect, which was rather too cold before, so I planted others at regular intervals.

E. A. Bowles
My Garden in Spring, 1914

Editor's Note: You can add interest to a mass planting of a single flower by mixing in a few blooms of another color. In this pairing, the lavender-white flowers of **Iris florentina** (now known as orris, **I.** x **germanica** var. **florentina**) are enhanced by adding a few purple blooms of flag, **I.** x **germanica**.

A Pastel Twosome for Summer and Fall

A color combination most subtle and beautiful has come to view: *Salvia farinacea*, a soft blue-lavender, with clustering spikes of palest pink stock very close to it. Let me commend

this arrangement as something rather out of the common, for I can hardly think this salvia is often met with in our gardens.

Louisa King
The Well-Considered Garden, 1915

Editor's Note: *Salvia farinacea*, the mealy-cup sage, is more common now than in King's day. It still makes a lovely sight mixed with pink stock (**Matthiola incana**) in a sunny border. Mealy-cup sage is hardy only to Zone 8, so gardeners in cooler zones grow it as an annual.

Sweet-Scented Groundcover for Vines

A newly made-up vine border sown with mignonette gives armfuls of joy, but is it good for the grapes? I hope so, because I like both the grapes and the mignonette, but even if it is not I should still wish to grow mignonette there as the crop I prefer.

E. A. Bowles
My Garden in Summer, 1914

Editor's Note: Mignonette (**Reseda odorata**) is an annual flower that grows only one foot tall, so it won't compete with your grapes or any other vines. Its white and orange flowers are inconspicuous, but their wonderfully sweet fragrance makes them welcome in any planting.

A Taste of the Tropics

One of the most charming beds imaginable for the lawn is made by planting the dark, velvety varieties of coleus in the center, and edging it with the gray centaurea. It should be raised somewhat, and if you can afford a canna for the center, you will be delighted with the brilliant and tropical effect.

The Household, 1878

Editor's Note: The gray centaurea is the familiar gray-leaved bedding plant we call dusty miller (*Senecio cineraria*).

Opposites Appeal

Orange zinnias and blue larkspurs make a good color contrast.

Loring Underwood
A Garden Diary and Country Home Guide, 1908

A Happy Accident

One summer I raised a thriving lot of young foxgloves and pink cup-and-saucer Canterbury bells, and, as good luck would have it—for I had never seen either of them before and was growing them chiefly for the sake of their names—I planted the foxgloves in the back of the hardy border and made an irregular group of the Canterbury bells in front of them. The effect when they bloomed the next June was one of the loveliest I have ever seen. For two weeks that corner of the garden reigned supreme and we realized as we never had before how much more beautiful a flower can be when it is planted with another that brings out its beauty of color and outline.

Louise Shaw
The Garden Magazine, 1908

Mix 'Em Up

Sometimes two kinds of plants are interplanted. Little patches of tiarella (foamflower) can be used with forget-me-nots, deep blue lobelia mingled with white pinks, annual candytuft mixed with sweet alyssum, ageratum distributed among nepetas (catmint). These plants are not placed alternately in a set pattern, but mixed up quite at random.

Elsa Rehman
Garden-Making, 1926

Editor's Note: You can create beautiful effects by mixing these or other flowers together haphazardly. Try odd-numbered groupings to avoid that patterned look. For example, plant one lobelia, then three pinks, and five lobelias in a row. For the next row, try a different grouping, such as three pinks and seven lobelias.

Foxgloves

Canterbury Bells

Both foxgloves (*rear*) and Canterbury bells (*front*) are biennials that are treated as annuals. Start seeds indoors six to eight weeks before your last frost date. Both plants have bell-shaped flowers, but foxglove blooms are spotted and Canterbury bell flowers are not. Plant these two- to four-foot-tall flowers in moist soil with partial shade.

A Pink and White Cutting Bed

Stocks, both white and pink, gladioli in the same two colors, snapdragons, *Lilium rubellum* and *L. speciosum* 'Magnificum' can be successfully planted together, and if the stocks and snapdragons are started under glass, they can, by proper feeding, be made to bloom continually from early in June until ice forms.

Helena Rutherfurd Ely
***The Practical Flower Garden**,*
1911

Editor's Note: The rose pink, funnel-shaped flowers of rubellum lily (*Lilium rubellum*) and the large crimson blooms of Japanese lily (*L. speciosum* 'Magnificum') add beauty and fragrance to this mix. All of the flowers listed are good for cutting and will give you blooms for bouquets all summer long.

Follow Sweetpeas with Nasturtiums

I often plant seeds of the climbing nasturtium in the row with the sweetpeas at a distance of one seed to the fist, the planting not being done until late May. The peas mature first, and after the best of their season has passed they are supplanted by the nasturtiums, which cover the dry vines and festoon the supporting brush with gorgeous color in early autumn.

Barbara
***The Garden, You, and I**,* 1910

Color in the Garden

Color Tests Let You Choose the Best

In planting for color effect the trial garden is a necessity. The space for it may be small. If the plants please, and the colors form an agreeable combination with the others already in the garden, their removal in the autumn from trial garden rows to certain spots in the garden proper is simple. A portion of the trial garden is kept for seed, and the balance for small collections of bulbs or plants.

Louisa King
***The Well-Considered Garden**,*
1915

Planting by Number Gets Color Ratios Right

The most satisfactory results in color are those in which the proportion is approximately one of yellow, to two of red and five of blue. Or, one of white and three of pink, to five of light blue. In either case the primary colors should be blended together by many times their combined quantity of tertiary colors—green, gray, etc.

Rose Fay Thomas
***Our Mountain Garden**,* 1904

Flower Gardener's Palette

Avoid placing rose-colored next to scarlet, orange, or violet. Do not place orange next to yellow, or blue next to violet. White relieves any color, but do not place it next to yellow. Orange goes well with blue, and yellow with violet. Rose color and purple always go well together.

***The Gardener's Monthly**,* 1874

Six Months of Color

Why not have something better than a kaleidoscope in your flower garden? Here are nine different color combinations that give flowers in succession from spring to fall—and no nerve shocks. September (H and I in the plan below) is a blank. That month in my garden calendar is bare of flowers of good perennials, or at least of any combinations good enough for this color border.

Louise Shawl
The Garden Magazine, 1908

Editor's Note: There are many excellent perennials you can use to fill in the blank in September (H and I in the plan below). Shawl must have forgotten about boltonia (***Boltonia asteroides***), a four- to six-foot-tall rounded plant with white daisylike flowers, and Joe-Pye weed (***Eupatorium purpureum***), which has clusters of rose-colored flowers and whorls of leaves on three- to six-foot-tall plants.

Common Name	Botanical Name	Height	Season	Color
A1 Forget-me-not	*Myosotis sylvatica*	6"	May 15	Blue
A2 Poet's narcissus	*Narcissus poeticus*	1'	May 15	White
A3 Hardy alyssum	*Aurinia saxatilis*	9"	May 1	Yellow
A4 White tulip		1'	May 1	White
B1 Lemon daylily	*Hemerocallis lilioasphodelus*	3'	June 1	Yellow
B2 German iris	*Iris* x *germanica*	2–3'	June 15	Yellow to purple
C1 Foxglove	*Digitalis purpurea*	4–6'	June 15	White and red
C2 Canterbury bells	*Campanula medium* 'Calycanthema rosea'	2–3'	June 15	Pink
D1 English larkspur	*Delphinium grandiflorum*	5–7'	July 1–5	Blue
D2 Madonna lily	*Lilium candidum*	4'	July 1	White
D3 Pink hollyhock	*Alcea rosea*	6–9'	July 1	Pale pink
E1 English larkspur	*Delphinium grandiflorum*	5–7'	July 1–5	Blue
E2 Coreopsis	*Coreopsis tinctoria*	4–5'	July 15	Russet and gold
F1 Cardinal flower	*Lobelia cardinalis*	3–5'	Aug. 1	Clear red
F2 Tiger lily	*Lilium lancifolium*	3–5'	Aug. 1	Yellowish pink
G1 Garden phlox (white)	*Phlox paniculata*	3'	Aug. 15	White
G2 Veronica	*Veronica longifolia*	3'	Aug. 15	Deep blue
K1 Wild purple aster	*Aster novae-angliae*	6'	Oct. 1	Purple
K2 African marigold	*Tagetes erecta*	4'	Oct. 1	Yellow

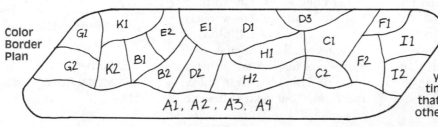

Color Border Plan

Follow this planting plan or make your own variation, and you'll have not only continuous bloom but colors that complement each other too.

125

Summer Seeding Makes Poppies Pop

Poppy seed sown in August gives richer-colored flowers than spring-sown seed.

Ida D. Bennett
The Flower Garden, 1904

Go Easy on Red and Scarlet

I have recently heard it advocated as a short cut to harmony that all red and scarlet flowers be banished from the garden. This, I think, would be sad indeed, for much of warmth and strength, of flash and spirit would depart with them, and our garden would be in grave danger of showing a wearisome suavity. But our effort must be to keep these stirring hues from overpowering the weak. In Nature, broadly speaking, we find that red and scarlet are rare, given to us a stimulants. Surely there is a lesson here.

Louise Beebe Wilder
Colour in My Garden, 1918

Managing a Red Bed

The term "red" as applied to flowers has a great latitude; it includes all tones ranging from orange-scarlet, pure scarlet and blood red, to those tinged with bluish shades. Therefore one needs to exercise much care in arranging places for the different plants. By keeping the orange tones at one end of the border and purplish tones at the other, uniting them by pure red, a certain color harmony can be maintained, but it is difficult. A red border involves many experiments and upheavals before it can be finally and satisfactorily arranged.

Helen R. Albee
The Garden Magazine, 1907

Floral Friends

Flowers have friendships. Whatever may influence these docile alliances, it isn't a proper sense of fitness of color; for tiger lilies dearly love to grow by crimson-purple phlox, a most inharmonious association, and you can hardly separate them.

Alice Morse Earle
Old-Time Gardens, 1901

Use Magenta in Moderation

Magenta is not bad in itself as many think, but it is used too much and in combination with its enemies, yellow and red.

John Dunbar
The Garden Magazine, 1906

Color Magic Saves Phlox

What commoner than to hear this exclamation as one wonders where a clump of tall phloxes have reverted to the magenta, despised of most of us: "What a horrible color has that phlox taken on!" But take that same group of flower stems, back it by the pale spires of obedient plant (*Physostegia virginiana* 'Rosea'), see that the phlox 'Lord Rayleigh' blooms beside it, that a good lavender like 'Antonin Mercie' is hard by, let some masses of rich purple petunia have their will below, with perhaps the flat panicles of large-flowered white verbena, a few spikes of the gladiolus 'Baron Hulot', and some trusses of a pinkish-lavender heliotrope judiciously disposed, and lo! the ugliness of the magenta phlox has been transmuted into a positive beauty and become an active agent toward the loveliness of the whole picture.

Louisa King
The Well-Considered Garden, 1915

Editor's Note: Lavender, purple, or white blooms of any kind can tone down too-bright colors.

Color Sweeps Beat Spots

Heterogeneous (mixed color) planting is often painful. Larkspurs, for instance, are far more beautiful when grown in great masses of each different shade, or with white Japanese iris (*Iris ensata*) and Madonna lily (*Lilium candidum*), than in smaller clumps in a border where many other colored flowers are planted.

Helena Rutherfurd Ely
The Practical Flower Garden, 1911

Free to Be Me

The "one-color" gardens that are at present enjoying a good deal of favor seem to me satisfactory mainly as achievements. They are apt to be monotonous in effect, are seldom truly harmonious, and fail to give the pleasure generally derived from gardens where all colours are blended and contrasted finely and where no lovely flower is shut out because it fails to offer a blue or a pink variety. It is important that each of us should feel free to express himself—his most extravagant, whimsical, ardent, honest self.

Louise Beebe Wilder
Colour in My Garden, 1918

Editor's Note: Wilder's best point is that you should feel free to express yourself, and that means using one or more colors as **you** choose.

Yellow Is Hard to Match...

Put yellows somewhere by themselves.

Jacob Biggle
Biggle Garden Book, 1912

...But Gets Along Well with Itself

Not all blue flowers may be safely used in each other's company and but few pinks unless they are of the same scale; but all yellow flowers, like the light of which they seem to be fashioned, blend and combine or flash back at each other with never a jar to the most sensitive eye.

Louise Beebe Wilder
Colour in My Garden, 1918

OLD-TIME WISDOM

Try this color illusion in your garden. The brilliant orange African marigold has leaves of a rather dull green color. But look steadily at the flowers for thirty seconds in sunshine and then look at the leaves. The leaves appear to be bright blue!

Gertrude Jekyll
Colour in the Flower Garden, 1908

The Unifying Power of Blue

A predominance of one color is a good way of achieving a harmony. To make but a single example, a garden of annuals. Zinnias and snapdragons, stocks and petunias, marigolds and calendulas, poppies and larkspurs and phlox make but a pleasant medley until ageratums and blue salvias are added in abundance to become the unifying element. Blue seems to be almost the very best color for this use.

Elsa Rehman
Garden-Making, 1926

Editor's Note: Other good blue flowers for unifying plantings include forget-me-nots (*Myosotis sylvatica*) and veronica.

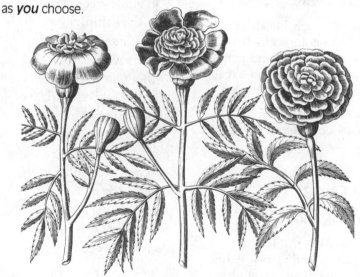

Yellow flowers in any shade from butter colored to golden look good together. Marigolds are perfect for do-it-yourself color experments. Mix together as many different varieties as you can find, and you'll still end up with a harmonious planting.

Strange But True

I am inclined to believe that lobelia is the least pleasing blue flower that blossoms. I never see it in any place or juxtaposition that it satisfies me. Wherever you find it growing in a garden, you never want it in that place.

Alice Morse Earle
Old-Time Gardens, 1901

Editor's Note: The brilliant blue of annual lobelia doesn't seem to bother modern gardeners. You'll find this popular plant used in hanging baskets, containers, and flower beds throughout the United States. If lobelia's blue is too bright for you, set the plant in a shady spot. Its blue color looks calmer set against a green background of ferns or groundcovers.

beholder an impression of tranquil unity and accord.

Louise Beebe Wilder
Colour in My Garden, 1918

Editor's Note: Wilder recommends blue lyme grass (*Elymus arenarius* 'Glaucus') as one of the best gray-leaved plants for the border, even though its leaves are usually described as blue. Whether you see it as blue or gray, this 1- to 3-foot-tall grass is an excellent ornamental that's hardy from Zones 4 to 10. It's not fussy about soil and will grow in either sun or light shade.

Red Shrinks Beds, Blue Stretches Them

Blue flowers planted in the rear of the garden increase its apparent size, while white, bright yellow, and scarlet, by bringing the background nearer, decrease it. Monkshood and the tall blue larkspur are excellent for rear beds.

Ida D. Bennett
The Flower Garden, 1904

Editor's Note: Landscape painters use warm colors—red, orange, and yellow—to make objects look as though they are coming forward. And they use cool colors—blue and violet— to suggest distance. You can create the same effect in your flower bed.

　　Steer clear of monkshood (*Aconitum* spp.) if children visit your garden—it's poisonous. But feel free to use other tall

blue perennials like salvias (*Salvia* spp.) to make your garden look bigger.

Purple Makes Peace

Purple of a rich bluish cast is one of the colors which bind instead of separate, and purple it is which becomes an excellent focal color for the garden.

Louisa King
The Well-Considered Garden, 1915

Gray Calms Clashing Colors

I am ever on the lookout for new gray-leaved plants. A free use of these quiet-toned plants seems to soothe all the conflicting elements of the garden into a happy relationship and creates in the mind of the

OLD-TIME WISDOM

Think green. Did you ever think how monotonous and gaudy flowers would seem without green foliage to set off their beauty? Have all the green things you can in the garden, particularly at the back of flower beds and borders, and take as much pains in protecting foliage of plants from insects as you do the flowers.

Loring Underwood
A Garden Diary and Country Home Guide, 1908

How Green Was My Garden

It is said that green is the last color to be appreciated even by the most aesthetic, and it is significant that the Japanese, who are more sensitive to color than any other people, and are unequalled in their flower art, plant whole green gardens wherein few flowers unfold to stir the cool tranquillity. "Be less Lavish" is often good advice to the gardener.

Louise Beebe Wilder
Colour in My Garden, 1918

Plant Choices Stretch the Color Season

In arranging my garden I have adopted a color scheme by which pink, red, blue, and yellow flowers are planted separately and by a careful selection of plants it is possible to have a continuous bloom of the same color throughout the season. With all of these, white flowers are used to harmonize the colors.

Helen R. Albee
The Garden Magazine, 1906

White's a Sight at Night

The white border is my greatest delight; the flowers grown in it are exquisite at night as well as in the daytime.

Helena Rutherfurd Ely
The Practical Flower Garden, 1911

To Blend Colors, Add White as a Buffer

White may be introduced to harmonize any two colors together.

J. C. Loudon
An Encyclopedia of Gardening, 1850

White Diamonds

Great care should be taken to have a liberal sprinkling of white, for the white in the flower kingdom is what the diamond is in the mineral world, necessary as a setting for all other colors, as well as for its own intrinsic worth.

Barbara
The Garden, You, and I, 1910

Editor's Note: Barbara suggests trying this experiment. Fill a tall jar with blue larkspur, and then watch how their color comes alive when you add stalks of white foxgloves or Canterbury bells. Bouquets are a good way to pretest color schemes for your flower garden. Combine flowers you'd like to plant to see how they look together.

A garden filled with shades of green can be extremely attractive, if you use a variety of plant sizes and shapes to add interest. This shade garden features Virginia creeper, growing along the wall. In front of the wall are plantings of ostrich fern (*Matteuccia pensylvanica*), blue star (*Amsonia tabernaemontana*), variegated fragrant Solomon's seal (*Polygonatum odoratum* var. *thunbergii* 'Variegatum'), Jack-in-the-pulpits (*Arisaema triphyllum*), variegated hostas, and lady's-mantle (*Alchemilla mollis*).

Pastels Glow at Night

What flowers will be the most effective for a night garden? White ones, first of all; and if any others are to be used, let them be of the palest pink or yellow—any pale color that will stand out well in the moonlight; red or blue, never. The effect will be almost unearthly in its loveliness by night. The backbone of the night garden is phlox. The *Nicotiana affinis*, too; *Lilium auratum*, *L. speciosum* var. *album*, and *L. candidum* also.

Amelia Leavitt Hill
Garden Portraits, 1923

Editor's Note: *Nicotiana affinis* is flowering tobacco, which is now known as **N. alata**. **Lilium auratum** is the goldband lily, **L. speciosum** var. **album** is the Japanese lily, and **L. candidum** is the Madonna lily.

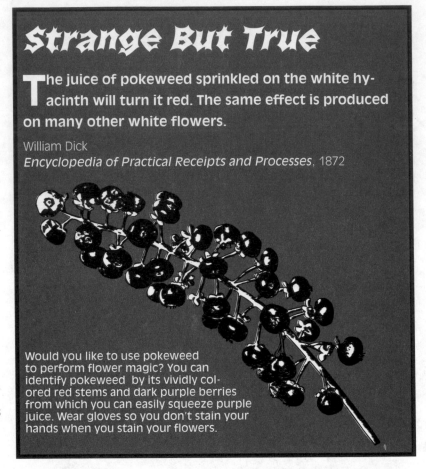

Strange But True

The juice of pokeweed sprinkled on the white hyacinth will turn it red. The same effect is produced on many other white flowers.

William Dick
Encyclopedia of Practical Receipts and Processes, 1872

Would you like to use pokeweed to perform flower magic? You can identify pokeweed by its vividly colored red stems and dark purple berries from which you can easily squeeze purple juice. Wear gloves so you don't stain your hands when you stain your flowers.

White and pale-colored flowers are at their best at night when the moonlight reflects off their petals. Add night-blooming flowers such as evening primroses (*Oenothera* spp.) and moonflower (*Ipomoea alba*) to Hill's list, and you'll attract the fascinating moths that pollinate these late-night prima donnas.

Make Your Own Mix

It is best to buy flower seed in separate colors, and when transplanting from the seed bed, combine as required.

E. T. Cook
Gardening for Beginners, 1901

Editor's Note: Prepackaged color mixes are fine for informal plantings, but if your design calls for specific colors in specific places, a do-it-yourself mix is the way to get what you want. Mix plants together as seedlings for accurate results.

Stick with Seasonal Colors

In the natural progress of the seasons we have certain colors predominating at certain periods. The earliest color scheme of the garden, as of the world beyond its walls, is yellow and white; this is followed by the rose color of late spring and early summer when fruit blossoms and then roses adorn the world. Next come the blue and yellow of midsummer which deepen to scarlet, gold, and purple as autumn lavishly spreads the colors.

This natural scheme of color we may modify or accentuate as much as we like, but to choose it as a sort of underlying theme much simplifies our work, since there are always plenty of good and willing flowers decked in the prevailing colors of the season. Let us not try to have a blue garden or a yellow garden in late May and early June; let us revel in a pink one.

Louise Beebe Wilder
Colour in My Garden, 1918

Follow the Rainbow

In no way can you get so much real power of color, by which is meant strength, richness, and brilliancy, as by beginning very quietly at the ends of the borders with cool bluish foliage and flowers of tender coloring, white, pale blue, and palest sulfur yellow; and from that to stronger yellows; then by a gradual crescendo to rich orange; and from that to the *forte* and *fortissimo* of scarlets and strong blood-crimsons; and then again descending in the scale of strength to the pale and tender coloring.

E. T. Cook
Gardening for Beginners, 1901

Growing Blooming Plants

Annual and Perennial Rule-of-Thumb

If it be an annual, do not let it make seeds; if it be a perennial, do not let it make leaves.

Meehans' Monthly, 1897

Editor's Note: What's behind this advice? By pinching off an annual's blooms before it forms seeds, you force the plant to keep producing flowers and get a better show. Annuals will keep putting out flowers in an attempt to make seeds. Perennials often have showy seedpods, so you may want to let them go to seed—you'll still get a nice display. Perennials do need some leaves, but they typically must be divided and have their leaves pruned back so they won't outgrow their garden spaces.

Help for the Half-Hardy

If you have no cold frame for half-hardy plants, they may be laid in by the heels, i.e., taken up, and the roots laid into a trench, the tops sloping at an angle of about twenty degrees, and then covered with earth. The soil should cover about half the stem.

Henry Ward Beecher
Fruits, Flowers and Farming, 1859

Editor's Note: Heeling plants in is a good way to hold them over temporarily (for one or two weeks). You can crowd the plants together so they don't take up much space or planting time. The soil protects the roots from cold spells until you're ready to set the plants in their permanent home.

A Word to the Water-Wise

Water should be applied thoroughly when given and then withheld until the plant is nearly dry again. This produces a stocky growth, with well-ripened wood, capable of producing healthy bloom. To keep a plant consistently wet may produce a quick growth, but it will be a soft one, incapable of the best results.

Ida D. Bennett
The Flower Garden, 1904

Editor's Note: Bennett's watering tip is for woody perennials such as salvias (*Salvia* spp.) and chrysanthemums.

A Thumb Is Valuable in a Pinch

Your thumb is worth about twenty dollars during July for the purpose of pinching chrysanthemums, cosmos, and dahlias. That's the way to keep them from growing tall and scraggly. Begin in June and make them compact, shapely, and full of flowers.

The Garden Magazine, 1908

For bushy mums and other perennials, pinch back the plant's tips once or twice during the summer. In the North, make your pinches before July 15; in the South, make them before August 15 so the plants have time to set new flower buds.

A Manure Pile Is like Money in the Bank

Don't try to grow good flowers in a poor soil. Always have a little pile of manure in some outer corner. It is as convenient as money in the purse.

Vick's Illustrated Catalogue and Floral Guide, 1872

Editor's Note: A pile of composted manure is priceless when it comes to soil improvement. Use an inch of this black gold as mulch around your flowers each year and watch them flourish.

Good and Proper Staking

Thoughtful staking has much to do with the well-furnished appearance of the borders. No plant should have its slender branches gathered into a stiff bunch and tied tightly to a stake. A flower stem should never be fastened more than halfway up its length.

Louise Beebe Wilder
Colour in My Garden, 1918

The Art of Staking Asters

Staking, which is a much neglected art, is peculiarly necessary to the success of the aster garden. Staking demands an intimate knowledge of plant forms. It is all the more piteous, then, to see asters tied tightly to stakes and hopelessly strangled. In one garden I know, ordinary tomato-plant hoops were used for staking the asters. Well hidden by the foliage, they held the stems sturdily upright and yet they left the bushes free to express their own loose-branching character.

Elsa Rehman
Garden-Making, 1926

Strap a flower to a stake, and it will look as though it is choking. But if you support bushy growth with a cage, the stems can curve naturally and the flower will look graceful.

Flower "Girdle" Gives Hidden Support

If the plant to be supported is a maze of side branches, like the cosmos, a row of stout poles, a little lower than the bushes, should be set firmly behind them, the twine being woven carefully in and out among the larger branches, and then tightened carefully, so that the whole plant is gradually drawn back and yet the binding string is concealed.

Barbara
The Garden, You, and I, 1910

Develop Your Own Special Flower

If you want a delightful recreation and lots of fun, and would like to possess a flower entirely new in color or form—and certainly in your estimation finer than any your rival neighbors have ever seen—make a reserve bed in some sunny spot and raise hybrid delphiniums. These delphiniums, or garden larkspurs, possess the blood of two or more species and as a result are inclined to "sport," producing flowers of various forms and colors, entirely different from those of the parents.

W. C. Egan
Making a Garden of Perennials, 1912

Editor's Note: The plants Egan recommends for creating new varieties are hybrids between two or more delphiniums. You can try growing *Delphinium* x *elatum* and *D.* x *belladonna* for your experiments.

When Only the Best Seed Will Do

In saving seed, only that from the best flowers should be taken. It is too often the practice to gather any seed that ripens, without regard to the flower which produced it; and the chance is greatly in favor of the seed coming from the poorest flowers, the best having been gathered in bloom.

Edward Sprague Rand
Seventy-Five Popular Flowers and How to Cultivate Them, 1872

Brighten the Roads for Travelers—and Bees

Got any flower seed or bulbs left? Plant them along the public road far from any houses, where they may rejoice some weary traveler and brighten life for even a bee.

Farm Journal, 1910

Flowers as Fundraisers

At the end of September and in October every amateur gardener finds it necessary to divide the plants in at least a part of the garden. It occurred to me last fall to save the little plants that seemed hardly worthwhile replanting, also those that had grown too large and the sturdy varieties which threatened to crowd out their neighbors, and sell them all, devoting the proceeds to a charity.

Plants that may be advantageously thinned out, the seedlings or divisions to be sold in small pots or flats, are: larkspur, forget-me-not, columbine, evening primrose, foxglove, and hollyhock. The following plants may be divided into clumps and sold: pyrethrum, German and Japanese iris, *Hemerocallis flava*, *Funkia subcordata*, pink spirea, monarda, *Phlox subulata*, and tall perennial phlox.

Anna Gilman Hill
The Garden Magazine, 1908

Editor's Note: *Hemerocallis flava*, the yellow daylily, is now known as *H. lilioasphodelus*, and *Funkia subcordata* as *Hosta plantaginea*.

Batten Down the Beds

When sudden clouds darken a hot June sky, the gardener and I, taking plenty of twine, hurriedly tie into sheaves the taller and more delicate flower stems such as delphiniums, Canterbury bells, pyrethrums, physostegias (obedient plant), and taller phloxes, and other especially precious things. Taller or shorter stakes are hastily driven in, and this support and close tying has saved for us many a raceme and panicle of later bloom.

Louisa King
The Well-Considered Garden, 1915

Shelter from the Storm

Long beds of plants—as Japanese iris, pansies, and the like—may be protected by taking narrow boards eighteen or twenty inches long, with a notch cut in one end, the other end being pointed and driven into the ground; set these at intervals through the center of the beds; place the poles lengthwise over the beds, their ends resting in the notches, and arrange evergreen boughs across the poles on each side to shed rain.

Ida D. Bennett
The Flower Garden, 1904

20" Stake

Notch for pole

Poles

Make this simple framework to support an evergreen canopy over cold- or wind-sensitive plants. If you don't have boughs to spare, use tall, stiff weeds from fall fields. (Make sure they aren't bearing seed!) Use pruned limbs or saplings for the poles.

Hedge Your Bets: Sow Twice

I planted abundantly of flower seeds—just before a drought. I neither covered the earth with mats, nor watered it—supposing that the seeds would come up after the first rain. But, in a cheerless and barren garden, I have learned that *heat* will kill planted seeds, and that he who will be sure of flowers should not depend upon only one planting.

Henry Ward Beecher
Fruits, Flowers and Farming, 1859

Editor's Note: Water seeds right after planting and mulch seedlings shortly after they sprout to avoid the disappointment Beecher faced. If water is scarce and seeds are cheap, a second planting isn't a bad idea.

A Dose of Charcoal for Better Color

Powdered charcoal is not only healthful for plants, when applied to their roots, but will darken the colors of roses, petunias, and other flowers.

New York World, 1878

Editor's Note: Charcoal is sometimes used in soil mixes for potted plants. It improves drainage and adds minerals and nutrients, which are probably the reasons for the improved flower color. You don't have to use powdered charcoal for good results—small pea-sized or slightly larger chunks will do the trick and are less messy to apply. Add 1 part charcoal to 15 parts potting soil.

Ideas for Window-boxes

Climbing Vines Beautify Boxes

Grand effects may be produced by the use of climbing vines as window plants, which can be trained outside in summer on wire or strings. Notable among these are *Cobaea scandens*, *Ipomoea noctiflora*, or moonflower, and Maurandyas (*Asarina* spp.), purple and white.

Peter Henderson
Practical Floriculture, 1913

Editor's Note: All of the vines Henderson recommends are tender perennials that are grown as annuals north of Zone 9. **Cobaea scandens** is the cup-and-saucer vine, which gets its name from the cup-shaped purple or white flowers it bears. The moonflower has huge, fragrant white blooms that open at night; it's now known as **Ipomoea alba**. Maurandyas include a number of plants in the genus **Asarina**, which have trumpet-shaped blooms.

Strange But True

I have seen, in certain parts of the city, sunflowers growing successfully in windowboxes, and admired the wise thought of their owner, who shut out the squalid street from his sight by a solid wall of green reaching the entire length of his window.

Amelia Leavitt Hill
Garden Portraits, 1923

Two-Season Display

A good plan is to have two boxes; starting one in the house in March, that it may be ready to place as soon as danger of frost is past; and the second in June, that it may be ready to replace the first when needed. For the latter the vines started in the house in April will be available. Maurandya (*Asarina* spp.), black-eyed Susan vine (*Thunbergia alata*), and the like, and many flowers from seed, will have reached sufficient size to be used for the second box. Plants that have been carried over from another season, or purchased from the florist, will be necessary for the first boxes.

Ida D. Bennett
The Flower Garden, 1904

Geraniums for Wind-Blown Boxes

Petunias are easily whipped by wind; geraniums are not.

The Garden Magazine, 1907

Give Them Something to Talk about

To have a better windowbox than your neighbors, grow something different from the hackneyed stuff kept by the small local florist: the white or blue moonflower, lemon verbena, *Gazania rigens*, *Maurandya barclaiana*, or *Thunbergia alata*. They are no harder to grow, and will be an agreeable change from frenzied magenta geraniums, gaudy coleus, etc.

The Garden Magazine, 1908

Editor's Note: The fragrant trumpetlike blooms of white moonflower (*Ipomoea alba*), sharply scented leaves of lemon verbena, and bright daisylike flowers of gazania (*Gazania rigens*) are enough to cause a sensation. Add a maurandya (*Asarina barclaiana*), for its long, trumpet-shaped, pink, purple, or white flowers, and a black-eyed Susan vine (*Thunbergia alata*), for its orange and black blooms, and the neighbors will really sit up and take notice.

Expand a Room with a Windowbox

The outside windowbox is a thing of beauty. So greatly does it add to the cheerfulness and apparent size of the rooms under the windows of which it is placed that I should advise its use whenever practicable.

Ida D. Bennett
The Flower Garden, 1904

Fill a windowbox with low-growing flowers for color in a bleak room or with climbing vines for privacy.

OLD-TIME WISDOM

Beware of young urban blossom nappers. Do not put flowers into boxes that are within the reach of children in large cities.

The Garden Magazine, 1907

Spring Flowers in Veranda Boxes

It is quite impossible to raise crocuses, hyacinths, and other bulbs in veranda boxes unless the whole box containing the bulbs is placed underground in the fall and kept there until March. Many people have planted hardy bulbs in veranda boxes and left them exposed to outdoor air all winter, but I have never heard of any result but failure.

The only objection I know of to this method is that the boxes are very heavy to lift, but this may be obviated by potting the bulbs.

Henry Maxwell
The Garden Magazine, 1908

Editor's Note: A veranda box looks the same as a windowbox, but it's attached to a porch instead of a house.

Gardens for Children

Flowers for the Young (and Young at Heart)

Fast and plenty of bloom are the chief requisites for the children's garden. To wait a year for results from perennials is beyond the patience of even the most serious minded of children. So let annuals be the order of the day. Among the first of the blossoms to be included should be the nasturtium, which blooms fairly soon from seed, and which combines the advantages of being practically indestructible and of furnishing a mass of bright color.

Amelia Leavitt Hill
Garden Portraits, 1923

Strange But True

There was a love divination by lilacs which we children solemnly observed. There will occasionally appear a tiny lilac flower, usually a white lilac, with five divisions of the petal instead of four—this is a Luck Lilac. This must be solemnly swallowed. If it goes down smoothly, the dabbler in magic cries out, "He loves me"; if she chokes at her floral food, she must say sadly, "He loves me not."

Alice Morse Earle
Old-Time Gardens, 1901

Guaranteed Good Plants for Kids

Plant	Days to Result	Remarks
Beet early	50–70	Requires little care
Beet late	140–150	
Lettuce	21–65	Most satisfactory
Radish	18–45	Easy to cultivate
Bachelor's button	40–50	Always succeeds
Nasturtium	45–60	Blooms profusely
Zinnia	50–60	Good colors, blossoms late

The Garden Magazine, 1909

Editor's Note: Quick and easy flowers and vegetables are tops for children's gardens. Choose red-leaved lettuce to put extra color in the planting, and add some cherry tomatoes for color and quick snacks. Other good plants for children's gardens are sunflowers, which come in a variety of sizes from 2-foot-tall dwarfs to 15-foot-tall giants, and peas, which make good eating straight from the vine.

Curiouser and Curiouser

Love-in-a-mist (*Nigella damascena*), in spite of its daintily cut foliage and pretty blue flowers, is primarily a curiosity and will charm every new generation of children as long as the race survives.

Thomas McAdam
The Garden Magazine, 1907

Aside from its name, what makes love-in-a-mist so charming? Its puffy, purple-striped seedheads for one thing, and the airy bracts that pillow its blue flowers for another. Both the seedheads and the flowers of love-in-a-mist make interesting features in bouquets.

Please-Touch Flower

Among hardy herbaceous plants, the *Physostegia virginiana* (obedient plant) is particularly desirable. It has the singular character of permitting its flowers to be placed in any direction, without springing backwards; and this peculiarity is always interesting to children of small size, as well as to children of a larger growth.

Meehans' Monthly, 1897

Editor's Note: Obedient plant has spikes of pink flowers on three- to four-foot-tall stems. It grows in sun or partial shade and spreads quickly.

Bring On the Bugs

If children were early introduced to the wonders of insect life—ants, bees, butterflies, moths, etc.—I think they would fear them as little as the ordinary housefly, which is really more objectionable than many of them. I know some who dare not pick certain flowers for fear of an earwig, which from its silly name they believe to be really a dangerous enemy.

Marie Theresa Villiers Earle
More Pot-Pourri from a Surrey Garden, 1899

Editor's Note: Earwigs look fierce because they have a pair of pincers at the tip of their abdomen. They use the pincers to grab ants that attack them from behind. Earwigs won't crawl in your ears, despite the old wives' tale, and they rarely damage crops. Like many insects, they have an undeserved bad reputation.

Lilac Necklaces

Lilac petals make such lovely necklaces, thrust within each other or strung with needle and thread.

Alice Morse Earle
Old-Time Gardens, 1901

Bog and Water Gardens

Celebrate the Skunk Cabbage!

Who loves skunk cabbage? Only bees and artists and Thoreau. Yet it is malodorous only when bruised, the coloring of its hoods is unsurpassed, and it is undoubtedly the first wildflower of the year, preceding the hepatica by a month or more. On a great estate near Philadelphia is a two-acre bog garden where skunk cabbage is appreciated, especially for its foliage effect before the trees leaf out. New England asters were planted among them to hide the cabbage leaves during their period of coarseness.

Henry Maxwell
The Garden Magazine, 1907

Iris That Like Wet Feet

Iris laevigata and *I. kaempferi* delight in rich wet soil, where the plants will grow to a height of four and one-half feet. When they flower, in June and July, there is nothing in hardy plants that can rival them. The plants grow well at the edge of the water, and thrive equally well when planted in shallow water.

Peter Bisset
The Book of Water Gardening, 1905

Editor's Note: For a beautiful effect, plant rabbit-ear iris (**Iris laevigata**) in shallow water—up to eight inches deep—at the edge of a pond. Japanese iris (sometimes offered as **I. kaempheri** but now known as **I. ensata**) likes conditions a little drier—it thrives at the pond's edge or in damp meadows.

OLD-TIME WISDOM

Let a cow firm your pond floor. Probably the simplest way of constructing a lily pond where the lay of the land and soil are favorable is to mark out a desired area, remove about two feet of soil, and turn the cattle on it. With stiff clay soil this will in a few months give a bottom sufficiently hard to hold water.

Ida D. Bennett
The Flower Garden, 1904

To Make a Bog Garden

For those who are fortunate enough to have a stream through their garden the task will be easy, for then all that is necessary to do is to remove the soil to a depth of about 3 feet, and fill the hollow so made with about 6 inches of coarse stones, a little charcoal, and a compost made up of about equal parts of peat and fibrous loam, with a little sand and broken stones added. It will be necessary, of course, to spread the water from the stream over the bog garden in such a way that it can reach all parts; the most efficacious method is to cut small channels running from the stream on either side, in the way the farmer irrigates his fields. Another plan, if the channels are considered unsightly, is to lay pipes with a number of holes bored in them a couple of inches below the surface of the ground and connected with the stream.

Lewis B. Meredith
Rock Gardens, 1914

Editor's Note: Inexpensive plastic drainage pipe will work to spread water through a bog garden. It comes ready-made with holes, but you may want to place 1/4-inch mesh screening over the uphill end of the pipes to prevent leaves and litter from clogging them. If you don't have a stream, a bog garden is a good choice for drainage areas that stay too wet for anything else to grow.

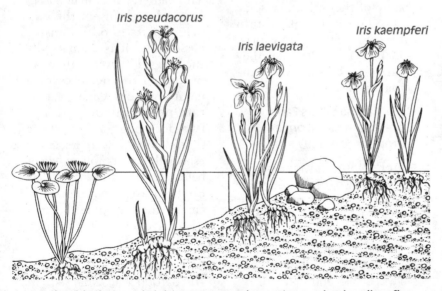

Iris pseudacorus

Iris laevigata

Iris kaempferi

Another iris that can brighten your pond or water garden is yellow flag (*Iris pseudacorus*). Its vivid yellow flowers bloom in early spring on four-foot-tall stems. You can plant yellow flag at the water's edge or up to ten inches under water.

Half-Barrel Water Garden

A half barrel is set on bricks in the garden, and is filled with a mixture of garden earth, sand, and well-rotted manure. The water lily roots are set in this, and covered. Water is added gently, and a little at a time, every day or two till the tub is filled. The handsome round leaves, four or five inches in diameter, soon appear and fill the tub. Several blossoms delight us with their beauty. When cold weather approaches, water is allowed to dry off, and the tub is placed in the cellar and watered at long intervals during the winter. In the spring, the roots are separated, and about half the increase put back into the tub in a fresh mixture of earth.

The Gardener's Monthly, 1872

Editor's Note: Hardy water lilies are easy to grow in containers since they are shallow rooted. You can plant water lilies in shallow (six- to eight-inch-deep) pots that hold eight to ten quarts of soil. Use heavy soil, not a light potting mix, and top it with gravel to keep the soil in place. Submerge the pots in your half-barrel of water, and you can bring them inside for the winter instead of the entire barrel.

Commuter's Water Lily

The night-blooming waterlilies, which we may properly term the lotus group, open their flowers between seven and eight P.M., and they remain open until from nine to one o'clock of the following day. These are therefore preeminently the busy man's waterlilies; the proper kinds for the suburban dweller who is away from home and garden throughout the day.

The Garden Magazine, 1905

Editor's Note: You can grow night-blooming water lilies in a pond or half-barrel in your backyard—place them where they'll get 5 to 6 hours of sunlight a day. Night bloomers are tropical plants that can't survive frost. So buy new plants each year, or store the tubers in a cool room (55°F) in jars of distilled water over the winter.

You don't need a large body of water to enjoy the exotic flowers and floating leaves of water lilies. Mail-order catalogs offer a wide variety of water lilies and water-garden supplies to get you started. See "Sources" on page 316 for ordering information.

Night-blooming water lilies are not lotuses (*Nelumbo* spp.), although this one is called the Egyptian white lotus (*Nymphaea lotus*).

Asters for the Water's Edge

Aster novae-angliae delights in deep moist soil, exposed to full sunshine. The plants are very effective in the late fall months, when covered with their showy attractive flowers. They can be grown from seed sown in spring or by division of the roots in spring or fall.

Peter Bisset
The Book of Water Gardening, 1905

Editor's Note: New England asters (*Aster novae-angliae*) thrive near ponds or boggy areas since they need evenly moist soil. These three- to six-foot-tall perennials are covered with purple daisylike flowers from late summer through fall.

Best Bulb for Stream Banks

For naturalizing along the banks of streams none is better than the various forms of *Narcissus poeticus*. The old Pheasant's Eye is so inexpensive that it may be put in by the thousand and looks lovely gleaming among the young fern fronds in the short grass.

Louise Beebe Wilder
Colour in My Garden, 1918

Editor's Note: In the wild, the pheasant's eye or poet's narcissus grows in wet meadows, so it's suited to moist situations in your yard. This fragrant, white-petaled flower is known as the pheasant's eye because of its short, red-rimmed cup or corona. There are several heirloom varieties of poet's narcissus available—look for 'Actaea', 'Cantabile', 'Felindre', and 'Milan'. Pheasant's eye is an excellent choice for naturalizing in Zones 3 through 7. (It will grow in Zone 8 if you give it a northern exposure.)

Enjoying Your Flowers

Judge a Flower's Scent by Its Color...

White flowers stand highest in number among fragrant species, next yellow, then red, and lastly blue. And it is among white flowers that disagreeable odors are most seldom found, while orange and brown are frequently unpleasant in scent. It is also worthy of notice that many of the scents among white flowers are only pleasant when in very small quantity, and become absolutely disagreeable when intensified; this is the case especially with the hawthorn and white lily.

The Gardener's Monthly, 1872

...But Don't Judge a Flower by Looks Alone

For the sake of its perfume a blossom may be tolerated here which on account of its appearance, or the lack of it, would otherwise be rigorously excluded—such as, for example, the wallflower or the mignonette.

Amelia Leavitt Hill
Garden Portraits, 1923

Editor's Note: Both wallflower and mignonette are grown as annuals. They prefer cool temperatures and sun or partial shade. The wallflower is not nearly as unattractive as Hill would have you believe. It has clusters of yellow, orange, red, or purple flowers on 2- to 2½-foot-tall stems. Mignonette has spikes of inconspicuous orangey flowers on 1-foot stems. Its fragrance is so sweet, you won't mind that it isn't showy.

Sniff Pinks at Night

The common pinks yield increased fragrance during the hours between sunset and sunrise, and are then frequently visited by moths.

Harry Roberts
The Book of Old-Fashioned Flowers, 1904

Strange But True

The whole elder plant has a narcotic smell and it is not prudent to sleep under its shade.

Good's Family Flora, 1854

Editor's Note: Good is referring to the European elder (*Sambucus nigra*). The flowers of this multistemmed shrub have a heavy odor, and the leaves smell bad when bruised. This elder isn't all bad, though. The plant's black fruits are often used in homemade wine and jelly, and some varieties, like 'Filigree Lace', are quite attractive.

Try These Tulips for Scent

Many of the wild tulip species are fragrant, and these are most fascinating to grow. Some of the sweetest are: the wild British tulip, *Tulipa sylvestris* (that has a scent like hot-house violets), *vitellna*, with the bouquet of oranges, and *didieri* with a fragrance of sweetpeas.

Louise Beebe Wilder
Colour in My Garden, 1918

Editor's Note: The wild yellow-flowered British tulip (*Tulipa sylvestris*) is still easy to find, but *T. vitellna* and *T. didieri* are not. As replacements you can try *T. aucheriana*, a tiny tulip (four to eight inches tall) with flat, scented pink flowers and *T. patens* (also known as *T. celsiana* var. *persica*), a sweet-scented yellow tulip that grows five inches tall. When you buy "wild" tulips, make sure they are grown commercially and not gathered from the wild.

Be Forewarned about These "Fragrant Plants"

Some flowers are never agreeable to my fussy old nose. Phloxes smell to me like a combination of pepper and pig sty, most brooms of dirty, soapy bath sponge, hawthorn of fish shop, and meadowsweet of curry powder.

E. A. Bowles
My Garden in Summer, 1914

Editor's Note: Let your nose be the judge before you discard a plant on Bowles's advice. A broom (*Cytisus* spp.) or meadowsweet (*Filipendula* spp.) that offends one person may not be disagreeable to another.

This Stock Performs Nightly

The night-scented stock (*Matthiola bicornis*) is a hardy annual with a small unpretentious pink flower which gives off a delicious odor at night. It was one of the pleasant surprises of last year's gardening. One of the family expressed the opinion that the flowers were no prettier than radish blossoms, to which, it must be confessed, they do bear some resemblance, only they are larger. But when evening approached, the rather sprawling plants seemed to stiffen and straighten, and the flowers, which until then had been utterly without fragrance, suddenly exhaled a most entrancing odor, as charming as it was unexpected.

Florence Beckwith
The Garden Magazine, 1906

Night-scented stock is sometimes offered as *Matthiola bicornis*, but it is more correctly known as *M. longipetala* subsp. *bicornis*.

Old-Time Wisdom

Try garden aroma-therapy. There is nothing more conducive to health then the subtle aroma of certain blossoms. I can at times lay my head down with an inexpressible relief beside some of the pets of my garden, and feel a power most grateful and unmistakable while smelling some of the tiniest blossoms of all.

Rev. E. P. Powell
The Gardener's Monthly, 1873

Mignonette could easily have been one of Rev. Powell's "pets." This 1-foot-tall annual has ⅓-inch-wide orangey blooms with a wonderfully sweet scent.

Latin Names for Picky Noses

There are many plants whose unhappy secret is advertised by the Latin specific terminations *foetidus*, bad smelling;

graveolens, heavy scented; and *hircine*, goatlike odor.

Louise Beebe Wilder
The Fragrant Path, 1932

Editor's Note: Look for Latin names when you buy plants. Not only will you get a clue about what the plants are like, you'll also be sure you are getting the plants you want. Common names change depending on the area you live in, but scientific names are the same worldwide.

Creating Beautiful Bouquets

Few or Many in an Arrangement?

There are flowers that depend for beauty upon the strength of numbers, as well as those that make a more individual appeal. The composite flowers—daisies, asters, goldenrod—belong to the class that take naturally to massing, while the blue flag, meadow and wood lilies, together with the spiked orchises, are typical of the second.

Barbara
The Garden, You, and I, 1910

Keep Cut Violets Longer

Violets which fade quickly with the usual care will keep fresh several days if they are excluded from the air and kept in a cool place at night. They should be put loosely into a bowl of fresh water, then covered with another bowl large enough to fit tight to the rim, or to the table on which the receptacle stands, and left in a cool or even cold room.

Penelope Kay
The Garden Magazine, 1908

Week-Long Bouquets

My idea of a really useful cut flower is one that will last for a week, so that once a week I may have a field day among the flower vases, and have them washed and filled with water for me to start afresh on Saturday mornings. There are many little tricks for choosing those that will last the best. The most obvious is that in gathering composite flowers one should choose those in which only a ring or two of the disc florets have opened.

E. A. Bowles
My Garden in Summer, 1914

Editor's Note: Composite flowers are those like asters, daisies, and sunflowers. Most have two types of flowers in each flower head: ray flowers, which look like petals, and disc flowers, which make up the center of the flower head.

Strange But True

Bouquet-making has always been considered an art, but it has remained for the Parisians to discover that it is really a science. We are told that "a bouquet is a symphony of odors" and that to properly "construct" the bouquet it must consist of a foundation odor placed in the center around which is placed a complementary odor, then a number of other odors to give character to the basic odor. This is perhaps the reason why the old-style French bouquet was a mass of lesser bunches of different flowers, and like a parti-colored cauliflower. Let us discard the idea and stick to art!

Gardener's Monthly, 1878

A Perfect Pairing

The large pink and white hibiscus, with a generous handful of long-stemmed pink, crimson and white cosmos, makes an ideal bouquet for a high glass vase. Placed in front of a large mirror, the effect in form and color is hardly surpassed by the choicest exotics.

Ida D. Bennett
The Flower Garden, 1904

Pick Least Fragrant Flowers for the Table

A few flowers in a wineglass of water are also often placed at each plate. In choosing flowers for this purpose, or for table decoration of any kind, those of too high perfume are not desirable, as their odors, with the heat of the lights and the steam of the food, are apt to be sickening.

The Household, 1882

Use White for No-Fail Flower Arrangements

It has ever been a matter of wonder to the workers in flowers how such a preponderance of white is required. The most beautiful colored bouquets have always a large proportion of white in their composition.

Peter Henderson
Practical Floriculture, 1913

Editor's Note: White makes a good buffer between bright colors and shows off more colorful flowers to advantage.

Melon Bouquet

A very novel bouquet may be made by taking an unripe melon, cut off one end, stand it up on the cut part, then surround with the stiff leaves of the peony, and stick the melon full of dahlias and asters.

Henry T. Williams
Window Gardening, 1881

Until the fruit flies come calling, you can use a melon as a novel base for cut flowers. Tap holes for the stems with a skewer, and set the melon on a plate to catch any drips.

Bouquets Shouldn't Compete with Dinner

A dinner table decorated heavily with sweetpeas spoils my dinner, as I taste sweetpeas with every course, and they are horrible as a sauce for fish, whilst they ruin the bouquet of good wine. The scent of fresh flowers in rooms is one of the joys of life if sufficiently understood and controlled.

E. A. Bowles
My Garden in Summer, 1914

Editor's Note: So what can you use to decorate your table? Any flowers without a strong scent, such as zinnias, nasturtiums, coneflowers, and snapdragons.

Stop Staking Glads

I was greatly interested to learn that florists prefer for cutting in some cases the gladiolus whose stems are allowed to bend and twist as they bloom. A hint of this kind may be valuable for some of us who grow this superb flower mainly to put about our houses. It is easy to see the agreeable variety of line afforded for such purposes by the gladiolus which has not been strictly staked.

Louisa King
The Well-Considered Garden, 1915

Wildflower Bouquet

Comparatively little attention is paid to this flower, false Solomon's seal (*Smilacina racemosa*), by those who go to the woods in spring in quest of wild blossoms. Perhaps the rather coarse appearance of the plant in contrast to the grace of the anemones, violets, crowfoots, etc., which everyone loves to gather, causes us to pass this humbler beauty by. Yet, if a dozen or so of the plants are broken off and bunched together, the effect of the delicate white bloom amid the luxuriant green leaves is somewhat akin to that produced by a handful of lily-of-the-valley, though on a much larger scale. Such a bouquet put in a large vase makes a useful adornment for a hall or roomy apartment, and will last for a number of days.

Meehans' Monthly, 1897

False Solomon's seal adds grace to bouquets with its arching stems and showy white plumes. Plant it in a moist, shady part of your garden.

Lace in a Vase

The umbels of white flowers of the wild carrot (Queen-Anne's-lace) are very pretty in vase decorations, yet how few persons would think of gathering them for that purpose! Nevermind the smell of its peculiar fragrance—if fragrance it may be termed.

Meehans' Monthly, 1901

Editor's Note: Even weeds can be beautiful in bouquets. Mix Queen-Anne's-lace with purple or blue flower spikes from a butterfly bush or salvia plant for an attractive informal display. You probably won't mind the fragrance of Queen-Anne's-lace since it's very faint. Test it with your own nose—you may find it refreshingly grassy scented.

Dinner Party Tip

Tulips light up extremely well under artificial light.

Amelia Leavitt Hill
Garden Portraits, 1923

Early Picking Keeps Peonies Perky

To make peonies last longer, cut them twenty-four hours before you want to use them. Carry a pail of water to the beds and drop them in at once, immersing the whole stem. Then keep them in the cellar or cool room till needed.

The Garden Magazine, 1908

Give Your Garden a "Brake"

A brake patch is a treasury to be drawn from when arranging tall flowers like foxgloves, larkspurs, hollyhocks, and others that have little foliage of their own.

Barbara
The Garden, You, and I, 1910

Editor's Note: Brake, or bracken (*Pteridium aquilinum*), is a sturdy fern that grows in waste patches where little else thrives. Like all ferns, it makes a fine filler for bouquets.

Pansies Prefer Sand

The best results may be obtained by filling a shallow dish or bowl with sand, thoroughly wet, and standing each pansy upright in it. Treated this way the cut pansy will last several days.

Amelia Leavitt Hill
Garden Portraits, 1923

Rx for Tired Bouquets

Flowers that have stood in a vase for a day or so can be greatly refreshed if taken from the vase at night, thoroughly sprinkled and wrapped, stems, blossoms and all, as closely as possible in a soaked cloth, and laid aside until morning. A bit of each stem should be cut off, as soon as the end hardens; this ought to be done twice a day.

Jacob Biggle
Biggle Garden Book, 1912

Glads Keep Going and Going...

The gladiolus lasts in water perhaps longer than any other flower, and, constantly opening new buds as it does so, affords a pleasant variety to the ordinary cut flower in the house, whose story is generally one of sad deterioration from day to day.

Amelia Leavitt Hill
Garden Portraits, 1923

Keep Vase Odor Away

For preserving flowers in water, there is nothing so good as finely powdered charcoal. It keeps the water from all obnoxious odors.

Henry T. Williams
Window Gardening, 1881

Editor's Note: You can buy powdered charcoal at garden centers and pet stores. But to keep vase flowers really fresh, remember to change the water.

Hot-Water Bath Revives Cut Roses

Roses which have dropped before their time—as, for example, when worn on the dress—may be revived if the stems, after being trimmed, are placed for ten minutes in almost-boiling water and then removed to cold water.

Jacob Biggle
Biggle Garden Book, 1912

Shakespearean Floral Code

There's rosemary, that's for remembrance...

and there is pansies, that's for thoughts.

William Shakespeare
Hamlet, IV, 5, 174

Parting Bouquet

A beautiful bouquet, a fitting tribute to a departing friend, is composed of sweet pea and forget-me-not. Use the pink and white sweet pea. The sentiment of this flower is, "Must you go?"

"Daisy Fields"
The Household, 1882

OLD-TIME WISDOM

Send this hidden floral message: "I trust you will find consolation, through faith, in your sorrow; be assured of my unchanging friendship."

E. B. Davis and B. G. Jefferis
The Household Guide, 1891

Editor's Note: Which flowers can you use to send this message? Scarlet geranium, passionflower, purple hyacinth, and arborvitae.

The Language of Flowers

A bouquet of flowers can be made to represent almost any sentiment.

Arborvitae: unchanging friendship

Camellia: loveliness

Candytuft: indifference

Carnation, white: disdain

Clover, four-leaf: "Be mine"

Clover, white: "Think of me"

Clover, red: industry

Columbine: folly

Daisy: innocence

Dead leaves: sadness

Fern: fascination

Forget-me-not: "Remember me"

Fuchsia, scarlet: good taste

Geranium, horseshoe: stupidity

Geranium, scarlet: consolation

Geranium, rose: preference

Goldenrod: "Be cautious"

Heliotrope: devotion

Hyacinth, white: loveliness

Hyacinth, purple: sorrow

Ivy: friendship

Jasmine, white: amiability

Lily, day: coquetry

Lily, white: sweetness

Lily, yellow: gaiety

Lily, water: purity of heart; elegance

Lily of the valley: unconscious sweetness

Monkshood: "Danger is near"

Myrtle: love

Oak: hospitality

Orange blossoms: chastity

Passionflower: faith

Primrose: inconstancy

Rose: love

Rose, Damask: beauty ever new

Rose, yellow: jealousy

Rose, white: "I am worthy of you"

Straw: agreement

Straw, broken: broken agreement

Sweetpea: depart

Tuberose: dangerous pleasures

Thistle: sternness

Verbena: "Pray for me"

Witch hazel: a spell

E. B. Davis and B. G. Jefferis
The Household Guide, 1891

You can put together a complex message with flowers. For example, witch hazel, white lilies, ferns, and white hyacinths mean: "You cast a spell on me with your loveliness and sweetness. I am fascinated."

Keep It Simple

1. Never allow more than two sorts of flowers together under any possible circumstance. The best effects seem to be won by combinations of light and heavy blossom. Thus asters and *Amaryllis belladonna* (belladonna lily) go very beautifully together; cactus dahlias and cosmos, or eupatorium (Joe Pye weed), are a pleasant mixture if the color is properly considered. You want lightness and delicacy of form in the smaller flower, richness of hue and dignity in the larger.

2. To mix sweetpeas is a relic of the past and not good. Keep them separate in their colors.

3. With roses you must put nothing but their own leaves. Never mix roses. You always do, of course, like nearly everyone else; but try a bowl of the different sorts alone, and you will perceive the force of this advice. A dinner-table of one rose is a pleasant thing but adorn it with a dozen varieties and you sink into the commonplace at once.

4. Never overdo the leaves in your vases. It is a relic of mid-Victorian times, when we used maidenhair fern with everything and thought it lovely.

Eden Phillpotts
My Garden, 1906

Bloodroot for Flatterers

The bloodroot has been employed in emblematic floral language to represent "flattery's smile." The appropriateness of the association is manifest to all familiar with the short duration of the flowers. In a very little while after the expansion of the blossom, the petals fall, just as the early withering of flattery's smile is reputed to do.

Meehans' Monthly, 1900

Revive Floral Travelers with a Deep Drink

When flowers arrive from any far distance, the stalks should be prepared with a long slanting cut, or be slit up in order to expose a larger surface to the water, and they should be plunged deep in the water, right up the flower itself, and left all night.

Gertrude Jekyll
Home and Garden, 1900

Pack Roses Right

I should say that the very best way of packing roses and violets is to stand them in water for two hours after being cut and bunched, and to pack them in tins lined with any fresh leaves—rhubarb, cabbage, lettuce, spinach, dock, or any leaves that are large and cool and succulent. There is a handsome dock that I grow for this and other like purposes as well

Strange But True

A friend received through the post office a roundish, irregular package, which on examination proved to contain a large potato. Further investigation showed that the potato had been cut in two and the insides scooped out, and in the cavity were found flowers—pansies, geraniums, and others—as fresh and bright as if they had been gathered within an hour, although their journey across the continent had occupied fifteen days.

The Gardener's Monthly, 1877

as for its merit as a plant of fine foliage—the monk's rhubarb (*Rumex alpinus*). The leaves are large and tough and pliable.

Gertrude Jekyll
Home and Garden, 1900

Fresh Hand Bouquets

Small bouquets for the hand soon fade if no effort is made to give them moisture. But a wrapping of a bit of wet cotton batting, fastened lightly about the ends of the stems, will suffice to keep them in good condition. Take a small vial, partly fill it with water, and place the flower stems therein. Then cover the vial by tying a ribbon around it. Flowers used in decorating the hair and the dress can be kept bright and fresh in the same way.

Henry T. Williams
Window Gardening, 1881

Sweet Scents Make Noses Gay

There is no sweeter nosegay than one made of such a fragrant rose (if there be any as fragrant) as 'Gruss an Teplitz' and a leaf of rose geranium. Tucked into the belt or through the buttonhole or carried in the hand on a warm day, it enlivens and refreshes one amazingly.

Louise Beebe Wilder
The Fragrant Path, 1932

Editor's Note: 'Gruss an Teplitz' is a red rose from the 1890s that will climb up to 12 feet tall with the support of a wall or arbor. The rose geranium is a scented geranium with leaves that smell like rose blossoms. It's just one of the many fragrances that scented geraniums come in—peppermint and lemon are other favorite scents. See "Sources" on page 316 for ordering information.

Goldenrod Garland

This is simply an arrangement of several bunches of dried goldenrod, one above another, in a corner of a room, and extending nearly to the ceiling. It is used as a repository for a collection of handsome cards or photographs, which are tucked in among the branches in careless profusion. The goldenrod is first made up into several long-stemmed bunches, each tied separately with wire or thread the color of the stems. Then the bunches are tied to a slender wooden rod, loosely so that the stalks droop forward and spread so as to fill the corner. It is kept in position on the wall by tacks driven through the ends of the rod.

Goldenrod, if dried head downward in a dark place, will never shatter and be almost as pretty as when growing.

American Agriculturist, 1891

Strange But True

The skunk cabbage (<u>Symplocarpus foetidus</u>) has generally been regarded as a sort of joke among spring flowers, although there are those who hail with pleasure the appearance of its purple streaked hoods in the bogs of late winter. That it is by no means undeserving of a place, however, in the spring bouquet, was made manifest this season to the writer, who saw cut specimens of it set in vessels of water in at least two windows fronting on business thoroughfares in Philadelphia. The cuttings had been made at a point six or eight inches below the vase of the spathe, so as to include both flowering and leaf stalks. The effect was really striking and picturesque.

C. F. Saunders
Meehans' Monthly, 1898

Editor's Note: It's okay to harvest plants from your own property, but leave wild skunk cabbages in the wild. The plant's distinctive odor comes from bruised leaves or flowers. If you can carefully unearth a specimen, it will be less apt to scent your house.

Heuchera for the Table

In the depth of winter Heuchera foliage is fresh, and even in a growing state. The leaves in a cut state are of great service for table decoration, doing duty repeatedly around dishes, etc., either with or without flowers; after being so used, if placed in water, they may be kept a fortnight in good form.

John Wood
Hardy Perennials and Old-Fashioned Garden Flowers, 1884

Editor's Note: Plants in the genus *Heuchera* go by the common name of coral bells. They are perennials with rounded, heart-shaped, or triangular evergreen leaves, which are often beautifully colored. Most heucheras are hardy from Zones 3 to 8 and prefer moist, rich soil and shade.

Try using goldenrod instead of the refrigerator door as a setting for photos and postcards.

Try Trillium, for a Change

In a cut state, for dressing "old-fashioned" vases, nothing could be in better character than trillium, a few leaves of yarrow, daylily, or similar foliage being all it will require.

John Wood
Hardy Perennials and Old-Fashioned Garden Flowers, 1884

Ammonia Magic

The natural color of flowers may be altered by exposing them to the diluted fumes of ammonia. Most of the blue, violet, and light crimson flowers turn to a splendid bright green. Dark crimson clove pinks turn black, other dark red flowers turn dark violet, and white flowers turn sulfur yellow. The change of color is especially beautiful when the flowers are variegated or the single petals possess a different color. As soon as the new color is fully developed, the flowers must be dipped into cold water, where they will keep their new shade from two to six hours; by degrees their natural color returns.

The Household, 1882

Flowers to Make You Feel Better

Do not send all white flowers, or flowers with a heavy perfume, to the sickroom. Bright flowers are better. Notice the cheer in a pot of golden daffodils or a bunch of hepaticas. A charming thing is a handful of Japanese morning glory buds picked and sent the night before, that the invalid may watch their unfolding in the morning.

Ida D. Bennett
The Flower Garden, 1904

Here's a bunch of daffodils that are sure to light up a sickroom. They're called yellow hoop petticoat since the flowers have a petticoat shape. They grow only five inches tall, so they're perfect for pots or rock gardens.

There's Nothing Fairer Than Roses and Ferns

Give me a bouquet of perfect wild rosebuds within a deep fringe of maidenhair fern to set in a crystal jar where I may watch the deep pink petals unfold and show the golden stars within; let me breathe their first breath of perfume, and you may keep all the greenhouse orchids that are grown.

Barbara
The Garden, You, and I, 1910

Preserving Special Blooms

To Make Flowers Last, Try Sand and Heat

To dry flowers that they may keep their colors, may be done by an old and tried way. They are placed erect in a box deep enough that their tops will not extend beyond, then sand is poured slowly and carefully around them until they are covered, when the box should be placed in a slow oven subjected to a continuous light heat for two or three days, at the end of which time they will be dry and still have their original colors.

Meehans' Monthly, 1897

Editor's Note: You can help cuplike flowers like roses hold their shape by spooning sand in and around each bloom. For tall, spiky flowers like snapdragons, pour sand gently over the blooms until they're buried—some flowers on the back side may get slightly smashed.

Rather than keep your oven on for a few days, try placing the drying box on top of a furnace or alongside a baseboard heater to keep warm.

Solar Flower Preservation

Several methods of preserving the natural color of pressed flowers have been suggested, but the best, it is said, is that used in the New York Botanical Garden. After the specimens have been under pressure for a day or two they are laid in papers heated in the sun, and this is repeated until the drying is completed. This, it is said, preserves the colors perfectly.

Retail Druggist, 1902

Wax Flowers

Dip the flowers in melted paraffin, withdrawing them quickly. The liquid should be only just hot enough to maintain its fluidity, and the flowers should be dipped one at a time, held by the stalks and moved about for an instant to get rid of air bubbles. Fresh-cut flowers, free from moisture, make excellent specimens in this way.

William Dick
Encyclopedia of Practical Receipts and Processes, 1872

Capture Summer's Scent

If next winter you wish a pleasant reminder of this fragrant weather, pack rose leaves now in a jar and sprinkle each layer with salt. Keep them in a fancy jar with a glass stopper.

Leave out the stopper awhile and your parlor will smell like June.

Farm Journal, 1884

Blanch before Pressing

If you attempt to dry them, some plants, like stonecrops, orchids, and other succulents, will live for months, and then the leaves and flowers will rot away in dreary blackness, giving only a few dry sticks for one's trouble. The best way to effect this desirable taking of life is to dip the specimen for a few seconds in boiling water. After taking it from the water, the specimen may be allowed to dry a little before putting it in a press.

Meehans' Monthly, 1898

Flowers A to Z

Annuals

Turn Annuals into Perennials!

There is no annual but may be made to last for many years, if only the flowers are pinched off before they fade, and before they have an opportunity of forming seeds. It is the production of seed that exhausts life, and is always a strain on the vital powers of any plant.

Meehans' Monthly, 1892

Editor's Note: This is an experiment to try with potted plants since most annuals are not winter hardy.

Not Everybody Loves Annuals

Geraniums and coleus became popular because public taste had begun to demand material for a special gardening purpose—to ornament home grounds with the smallest possible expenditure of thought and pains. It would be easy to show that the practice of "bedding out" is, in the long run, the costliest and most troublesome which can be adopted for the adornment of a garden.

Mariana Van Rensselaer
Art Out-of-Doors, 1893

Editor's Note: Bedding out, or setting out large plantings of annuals, is still popular, but as Van Rensselaer says, it is a lot of work. Annual flowers need deadheading to look their best plus plenty of water and fertilizer. Perennial plants are often less fussy, and you don't have to replant them every year. See "Perennials" on page 155 for suggestions on which plants to grow and how to care for them.

A Quick Screen

There are some situations where a low hedge or screen is very useful and ornamental. I don't know of anything that will make a prettier hedge, supported by neat brush, than the sweetpea. The amaranthus (amaranth) makes a fine ornamental hedge; the foliage is dark, rich, and some varieties two- or three-colored.

Vick's Illustrated Catalogue and Floral Guide, 1872

Editor's Note: Ornamental amaranths grow from one to five feet tall, depending on the species. Their flowers range in shape from fuzzy, drooping cattails to feathery, upright plumes.

Plant a sweetpea hedge the same way you start peas for eating. Set pea brush (twiggy sticks) throughout the area you want your sweetpeas to grow, and let the brush support the climbing vines. Or, for an even more attractive look, support sweetpeas on a trellis.

What Is a Biennial?

We have often heard complaints of the foxglove dying out; and there seems to be popular ignorance of the nature of biennial plants. An annual is suited to the popular comprehension; it is sown, it blooms, ripens seed, and dies; so is a perennial, which cares for itself, and blooms year after year; but why a plant should live through the winter, and then die, is a mystery.

A biennial is only a longer-lived annual; the plant takes more than one season to produce its flower; that done, it ripens seed, and dies. By sowing the seed every spring, a succession of blooming plants is kept up; and though some die every year, others are always ready to take their place.

Edward Sprague Rand
Seventy-Five Popular Flowers and How to Cultivate Them, 1872

Geraniums for Late Color

Frosts, with us, are due in early September. Heliotropes are apt to blacken then, Japanese anemones to receive that baptism of cold from which they do not recover. To offset such diminishings of the garden's color, I keep hidden away back of some white spruces a number of pots of the good geranium 'Mrs. E. G. Hill'. These, when set among the foliage of plants which have done their duty by the garden, give a look of gaiety at once, and help enormously to prolong the feeling of summer which with each day becomes more dear.

Louisa King
The Well-Considered Garden, 1915

Editor's Note: 'Mrs. E. G. Hill' may be hard to find today, but you can substitute any of hundreds of geraniums as an instant reinforcement.

Best Geranium

I would advise everyone to try and get the old 'Prince of Orange' pelargonium (geranium). There is nothing like it, but it is not easy to get, as gardeners do not understand that it requires to be treated like an ordinary flowering pelargonium, rather than like the hardier sweet-leaved kind. It wants well cutting back at the end of the summer, and then growing on in rather more heat than the ordinary sweet-leaved pelargoniums. This little care and constantly striking young plants in the summer will prevent its dying out. Of the fifteen to twenty kinds of sweet-leaved geraniums which I possess, I consider it the most valuable and the best worth having.

Marie Theresa Villiers Earle
More Pot-Pourri from a Surrey Garden, 1899

Editor's Note: This geranium's small, scalloped leaves have an orange scent that's as delightful as the fragrance of any scented geranium. See "Sources" on page 316 for ordering information.

Nasturtiums Are All the Rage

Study nasturtiums now! The time has come for intelligent flower lovers to stop planting mixed nasturtiums and study the named varieties, for the nasturtium is the "coming flower" among annuals and is being bred to as high a pitch of perfection as the sweet pea. Visit a good collection now and note which you like best.

The Gardener's Monthly, 1878

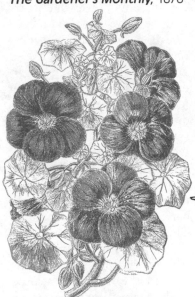

Nasturtium is a soup-and-salad flower. You can use it in the kitchen to add visual kick and a peppery piquancy to both soups and salad greens. Use both the fresh flowers and the young leaves.

A Flower for the Vegetable Patch

Mignonette (*Reseda odorata*) is the most popular flower grown solely for fragrance. Because of its lack of beauty and its desirability for cutting, it is best planted in the vegetable garden where it can be grown in larger quantities and with less care. Its great weakness is its short season of bloom, as it quickly runs to seed in hot weather. Therefore, select moist soil and water freely.

The Garden Magazine, 1907

Vacationing Phlox

Should you mourn because the phlox (*Phlox drummondii*) is just coming into bloom when you are leaving home for two or three weeks, nip off the heads, and the side shoots will have a display nearly ready to greet you upon your return.

H. G. Taylor
The Garden Magazine, 1906

In his catalog for 1872, James Vicks wrote of the flowers he sold, "*Phlox drummondii* would be my choice over any annual or perennial." This annual phlox is still a favorite, with clusters of flowers in almost every imaginable color.

Self-Sown Verbenas

If one does not care to go to the trouble of sowing verbena seed in the spring, the last year's bed may be cleared of the old plants in early spring, the surface soil containing the self-sown seeds may be removed, and the bed spaded with a coating of old manure, when the surface soil is to be spread on again and watered. The seedlings will come up too thick to remain, but they can be thinned out, and the surplus transplanted when a couple of inches high.

P. S. Lord
American Agriculturist, 1893

Bulbs

Mound Your Beds

In making bulb beds remember this: have the surface rounded to give drainage as well as to display the center mass.

The Garden Magazine, 1908

Lighter Soil for Bulbs

The general error in bulb culture is that the soil is made too close (heavy), causing the bulbs to rot, or be thrown out of the ground by the frost. In the preparation of a bed for bulbs, an addition of one fifth common building sand may be made with advantage.

Edward Sprague Rand
Seventy-Five Popular Flowers and How to Cultivate Them, 1872

Some Plants Don't Like Pampering

The more the uneducated gardening mind cares about a plant, the more it turns to manure and mulching; but in many cases it does more harm than good—notably with aconites, daffodils, scillas, etc. What they all want is moisture and protection at the growing time. Drying ever so much in the summer does them good rather than harm, and they never do well in a bed that is hosed or watered to suit other things.

Marie Theresa Villiers Earle
More Pot-Pourri from a Surrey Garden, 1899

Scillas are among those plants that can largely take care of themselves. They rate as the least picky of bulbs about shade. The Cuban lily (*Scilla peruviana*) shown here is an unusual scilla with a short, stout stem and a mass of 50 to 100 small starlike flowers. Grow it in pots north of Zone 7.

Keep Bulbs in the Garden

I am convinced that even rich men have no aesthetic right to scatter costly bulbs in wood or meadow. You cannot make hyacinths look like wildflowers. It is a common practice to put tulips and Easter lily bulbs after forcing into woods or meadows, but they never fit. The only places for them are the reserve garden and the mixed border. You cannot use costly material in wild gardening effects without ostentation because you violate the law of fitness.

T. McAdam
The Garden Magazine, 1908

A Daring Color Combination

A very daring experiment this was, but one which proved so interesting in rich color that it will always be repeated. It consisted of sheets of Siberian squill (*Scilla sibirica*) planted near and really running into thick colonies of Dutch crocus (*Crocus vernus* 'Purpureus Grandiflorus'). The two strong tones of color are almost those of certain modern stained glass. The brilliancy of April grass provides a fine setting for this bold planting in a shrubbery border. The little bulbs should be set very close, and the patches of color, in the main, should be well defined.

Louisa King
The Well-Considered Garden, 1915

Editor's Note: Siberian squill flowers are deep blue, while the blooms of 'Purpureus Grandiflorus' crocuses are deep purple. Masses of these bulbs planted under trees or bordering fresh green grass are showstoppers.

Why Crocuses Don't Bloom

Many complaints are made by amateurs of their crocuses not flowering; there is really but one cause of failure when a new bed is made; that is, the work is too long delayed. They must be planted as soon as the corms can be procured after their arrival from Europe. They usually commence growth by the first of September, and if planting is long deferred the germ is destroyed; for grow they will, whether in or out of the soil.

C. L. Allen
Bulbs and Tuberous-Rooted Plants, 1893

A Host of Wild Daffodils

All of the wild types of daffodils are favorites for naturalizing, as they show no deterioration, as do the larger flowering modern garden hybrids when grown wild.

A. M. Kirby
Daffodils, Narcissus and How to Grow Them, 1907

Editor's Note: Many wild daffodils will naturalize or spread with no help from you. See "Sources" on page 316 for ordering information.

Get Glads to the Vegetable Garden!

Gladioli have no business in a flower border. They have no decent foliage or habit and besides, tender plants don't fit in a hardy border. Grow them in your vegetable garden, in rows, where you can cultivate them with a wheel hoe, and where stakes don't matter so much.

The Garden Magazine, 1906

Lilies Like Rhododendrons

An English idea about bulbs that can be applied in any yard large enough for a bed of rhododendrons is to grow lilies in the same bed. This combination enables you to have gorgeous color about your house for three months after the rhododendrons have ceased to bloom. The first cost is heavy, but the beds need to be dug only once.

Wilhelm Miller
The Garden Magazine, 1909

Editor's Note: Lilies like this arrangement since the shrubs keep their roots cool and shaded.

A Tulip-Planting Tool

That the tulip roots (bulbs) may be planted exact, I prepare a board 6½ inches wide, the length of the width of the bed. On the edges of the board I mark the distances the bulbs are to be planted from each other, by sawing in a notch; thus, three inches from the end, for the first, and from that seven inches, until the whole number, seven, are made, which will leave three inches on the other side.

Joseph Breck
The Flower-Garden, 1860

Digging Tulip Bulbs

As soon as the segments (petals) fall I snap off the seed heads, and it is wonderful how soon one can lift after the loss of their seedpods has removed all inducement to keep their roots actively at work.

E. A. Bowles
My Garden in Spring, 1914

Editor's Note: Removing seedheads is a good idea, since the plants put their energy into the bulbs instead of into making seeds. You'll have better flowers next spring for your efforts. Bowles dug his bulbs and removed them from the bed, a laborious task that's necessary only if you plant intensively. You can leave your bulbs in place if you let the leaves yellow completely before pulling them from the ground.

Prevent Muddy Tulips with a Good Diet

Tulips become deteriorated by improper culture, by feeding them too highly with stimulating manures. This causes the colors to run together, and the flower becomes what the florist denominates "foul" and they can only be restored to their former beauty by planting in a pure, loamy soil for a few years.

Joseph Breck
The Flower-Garden, 1860

Editor's Note: Too much fertilizer makes bulbs concentrate on growing leaves instead of gorgeous flowers. Use a sprinkle of blood meal in fall (2 pounds per 100 square feet of area planted) if your bulbs need a nitrogen boost, and save the manure for your vegetable garden.

Stick with Species Tulips in Wild Gardens

Only sharp-petaled tulips look like wild flowers. Darwins are so cheap that many people will be tempted to plant them by the thousand, but in my opinion they are too gardenesque because they have rounded petals.

Thomas McAdam
The Garden Magazine, 1908

Editor's Note: Darwins are now grouped with cottage tulips and are called single late tulips. They have large blooms on 18- to 24-inch-tall stems. Use them as bedding plants for masses of bold, bright color in May. For rock gardens and wild gardens, the smaller wild or species tulips look more at home.

Wild Dark-Eyed Tulips

There is no surer sign of wildness in a tulip than the bold black eye formed by the spots at the base of the petals. This black eye has been bred out of all modern tulips by centuries of relentless persecution. The reason is that a dark eye generally goes with dark stamens, and the bursting of the latter soon litters the cup of the flower with an untidy mass of powder which stains the flower a muddy color. But when your point of view is that of naturalizing tulips on a great scale so as to produce a gorgeous sheet of wild flowers, these spots become a joyful sign of wildness, and they may be black, brown, blue, violet, or dark green.

The Garden Magazine, 1908

Wild tulips are typically smaller than cultivated varieties, and they often have pointed petals and a dark central eye. When you purchase wild tulips, make sure the bulbs are nursery grown and not collected from the wild.

Perennials

Don't Forget Foliage

For a grouping of plants having foliage very similar yet with sufficient differences to awaken particular interest in the whole, the yucca, iris, daylily (*Hemerocallis* spp.), and blackberry lily (*Belamcanda chinensis*) will be found suitable, and will furnish flowers of their several kinds from earliest spring till fall, with scarcely any interruption.

Meehans' Monthly, 1902

Editor's Note: When you choose perennials, consider which have the best flowers, but don't ignore the leaves. In your garden, beautiful blooms will catch your eye first—interesting leaves, though, will keep your attention once the flowers have faded.

Be Patient

Too much is expected of perennials the first year, as a rule. Persons used to setting out coleus and geraniums, which are well started, neat, and showy from the beginning, look for the same in the herbaceous perennials, forgetting their entirely different character.

Meehans' Monthly, 1902

Editor's Note: If you can't wait for your perennials to flower, fill in the spaces between plants with colorful annuals. You'll have your instant color and your perennials, too.

Fresh Seeds Grow Best

The fresher the seed of any perennial, the surer the germination. August is the best month in the year for sowing seeds of hardy perennial flowers, because the seeds that you get then are fresher and will therefore germinate more quickly.

Thomas McAdam
The Gardener's Monthly, 1878

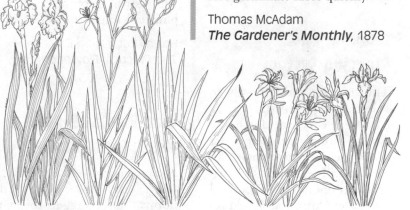

These daylilies, yuccas, irises, and blackberry lilies all have attractive strap-shaped foliage. The leaves are a mixture of different lengths, widths, and shades of green to make the planting even more interesting.

Three-Year Itch in the Perennial Beds

It comes about, with the most successful of hardy mixed borders, that at the end of the third season, things will become a little confused and the relations between certain border-brothers slightly strained. Personally, I believe in drastic measures and every third or fourth year, in late September, or else April, I have all the plants carefully removed from the beds and ranged in rows of a kind upon the broad central walk. Then, after the bed is thoroughly worked, manured, and graded, the plants are divided and reset.

Barbara
The Garden, You, and I, 1910

Editor's Note: The author, known only by her mysterious pseudonym, adds that the left-over plants are "a sort of horti-cultural wampum" that can be traded with neighbors for other plants.

A Perennial Planting System

The simplest and best way to select the perennials for a garden is this. Set down the twelve months in their order and write down two names for each month—one for the first half and one for the second. I don't mean that you should restrict your garden to twenty-four kinds of flowers altogether, but I do mean that is more than enough for massing, and

one's first concern should be for the big masses—not for variety. The reason for this is that the most beautiful gardens are those in which one kind of flower dominates the whole garden at a time, and then gives away to another big mass, and so on; while the weak, petty, restless gardens are the ones that have too many different kinds and not enough of any one.

Wilhelm Miller
The Garden Magazine, 1908

Color-Code Your Perennials

I always mark the plants whose seeds I wish to save by tying white strings about the stems when in full bloom as a sign to all that blossom must not be cut. I tie black upon the plants that are to be cast out in the autumn; scarlet upon the very bright red phloxes; a pink-and-white string upon all those of pink-and-white varieties.

Helena Rutherfurd Ely
The Practical Flower Garden, 1911

Hide Shabby Leaves with Strong Growers

Some perennials—the bleeding heart and the perennial poppy—have ragged foliage after blooming and require some tall bushy plant to be placed in front and around them to hide their shabbiness. Strong-

growing perennials—aster, or the biennial *Rudbeckia triloba* (thin-leaved coneflower)—are good for this purpose.

W. C. Egan
Making a Garden of Perennials, 1912

Lots of flowers and branches make the thin-leaved coneflower the perfect coverup for faded perennials.

Make a Leaf Quilt for Perennials

A poultry-wire fence about eighteen inches high can be placed around a bed of hardy flowers and the bed piled with leaves.

W. C. McCollom
The Garden Magazine, 1908

Editor's Note: This easy leaf mulch will keep your perennials from heaving out of the ground when temperatures freeze and thaw. Chopped or shredded leaves work best—use a three-inch-deep layer to protect your plants.

Best Bellflower

Perhaps the prettiest bellflower is *Campanula persicifolia* (peach-leaved bellflower), with its many stems of fragile bells. It has the usual violet-blue and white forms and if these are allowed to sow themselves about the garden we shall get intermediate shades all the way from the deepest blue to the curious skimmed-milk hue so often displayed by these intermarrying campanulas.

Louise Beebe Wilder
Colour in My Garden, 1918

The peach-leaved bellflower blooms in summer in Zones 3 through 7. Its bell-shaped flowers open on tall stalks that hold the blooms above the 4- to 8-inch-long leaves. Plants grow 1 to 3 feet tall in either sun or partial shade.

Long-Blooming Bellflower

Campanula persicifolia, the peach-leaved campanula, is a bellflower that proves to be especially valuable, as it is a continuous bloomer for almost a month.

Meehan's Monthly, 1901

Develop Your Own Columbine

Columbine hybridizes too readily, so that, unless a particular species is kept far apart from others, there is no telling what its offspring will be like. But this is a fault on the right side; for, although one may be disappointed with many seedling columbines that are grossly inferior to a beautiful parent, yet there is always a good chance that some will be superior; and the ordinary amateur, by merely saving seed from the best varieties and without any skill in hybridization, may in a few years obtain a splendid strain of columbines. Indeed, he may, if he cares to give up a good-sized plot of ground to their culture and if he selects his seed judiciously, obtain a race of plants surpassing most of those sold by the florists.

A. Clutton-Brock
Studies in Gardening, 1916

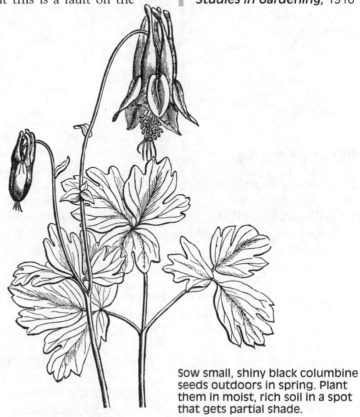

Sow small, shiny black columbine seeds outdoors in spring. Plant them in moist, rich soil in a spot that gets partial shade.

Wintering Echeverias

Echeverias which have served for borders, beds, or floral inscriptions during summer, if potted to pass the winter, are liable to rot. A method of preserving them, which occupies practically no room whatever, is to shake out the earth from their roots when taken up in autumn, and suspend them heels up or anyhow, in small bunches, on strings stretched horizontally, like linen hung up on a line to dry.

The Gardener's Monthly, 1876

Editor's Note: These short, tender perennials resemble fleshy hens-and-chicks. They form rosettes of succulent gray or green leaves and have pink, red, or yellow flowers that bloom in spring and summer. Store the plants in an attached garage or enclosed porch where the temperature doesn't go below freezing.

Foxgloves Forever

There are flower varieties little known to the casual gardener which will give you of their beauty lavishly all summer, and for many summers, in return. "Give us a chance!" they seem to cry. First of all these tempting blossoms comes the foxglove. This flower is, of course, familiar to everyone, but it is astonishing how many persons neglect to raise it because of the care which it is supposed to require. As a matter of fact, nothing is easier to grow. A bed of foxgloves, once started, will practically, like the brook, "go on forever."

Amelia Leavitt Hill
Garden Portraits, 1923

Heliotrope "Trees" Add Fragrance Indoors

Few plants are more useful for piazza (porch) decoration than heliotropes, when grown in standard or tree forms. The rich mauve color of the flowers and their delicious fragrance make the heliotrope a favorite with everyone. Even under a heavily shaded piazza or in a hallway they will keep well for two or three weeks, after which they should be placed outdoors in a sunny position, pruned back a little, syringed two or three times daily, and carefully watered. Within a month they will again be a mass of bloom. Four good crops of flowers can thus easily be secured between May and October. In March or April secure a few small, vigorous plants. All flowers and side shoots should be carefully removed, and the stem tied to a stake sufficiently stout to keep it firm.

W. N. Craig
The Garden Magazine, 1906

Editor's Note: A standard is a plant trained to grow on a single stem like a tree. Keep leaves and side shoots pruned off the stem, and add new ties every three inches as the plant grows. Repot the heliotrope as needed, adding a bigger stake each time until the plant reaches the height you want. When your standard is tall enough, pinch out the terminal bud so the top will bush out and not grow higher. Prune and pinch the heliotrope as needed to form a rounded head.

Keep Hollyhocks— At a Distance

There is nothing in the line of flowers which can give a greater brilliancy to a garden than a clump of hollyhocks. Coarse, you say? Well, yes, perhaps they are not as refined in their appearance as some other flowers. I would not advise you to plant a bunch of them in front of your parlor windows, but among shrubbery whose season of bloom is over, they are very effective. If they had been recently introduced from Japan, and were offered at $5 a root, you would be crazy to have one, and forget all about their coarseness.

Eben E. Rexford
The Household, 1878

Editor's Note: If you haven't tried hollyhocks in a while, give them another look. There are double- and single-flowered forms available in bright or pastel colors. The plants grow five to six feet tall and make an excellent carefree screen or backdrop for a sunny border.

Trumpeting Tufted Pansies

The best of all, perhaps, for artistic use are the tufted pansies (*Viola cornuta*), which are delightfully simple in color— white, pale blue, or lavender, and various other delicate shades. Almost perennial in character, they can be increased and kept true, and they give us distinct and delicate color in masses as wide as we wish, instead of the old "variegated" effect of pansies.

William Robinson
The English Flower Garden, 1883

Tufted pansies grow 4 to 12 inches tall and are hardy from Zones 6 to 9. Choose your favorite colors, from the cherry red of 'Arkwright Ruby' to the sky blue flowers of 'Blue Perfection'. The flowers appear in spring and grow best in light shade and moist, humus-rich soil.

Another Vote for Tufted Pansies

Tufted pansies (*Viola cornuta*), or violas, have smaller flowers than the ordinary kinds and will actually bloom freely through our hot summers. I wish everyone who reads this article would try some tufted pansies in a rose bed next spring.

Wilhelm Miller
The Garden Magazine, 1909

Plant Penstemon for Months of Blooms

For their varied color, profuse flowering, and graceful habit, pentstemons have a high value for our flower beds, especially as their beauty covers five months, commencing in June with the charming blue *Penstemon procerus* and finishing with the endless varieties of *P. hartwegii* in shades of rose, scarlet, and crimson, whose beauty holds its own even in November, after more-fragile plants have perished.

William Robinson
The English Flower Garden, 1883

Editor's Note: Robinson's recommendations may work in England, but the two penstemons he mentions are hardy only in the southern United States. For long periods of bloom and hardy plants, try common beardtongue (**Penstemon barbatus**), which grows in Zones 3 through 8, and foxglove penstemon (**P. digitalis**), which is hardy from Zones 4 to 8. Penstemons like well-drained, humus-rich soil and will grow in sun or partial shade.

OLD-TIME WISDOM

Do not disturb the peonies. These plants require several years to recover after being moved, and only actual necessity should lead to their disturbance, certainly not the requests of friends and neighbors to dig them up and divide. Better buy a root to give away, if reluctant to refuse, than injure the plant.

Ida D. Bennett
The Flower Garden, 1904

Tree Peonies Are Worth the Wait

One of the most desirable tub plants is very rarely seen, namely the tree peony. As usually seen in gardens, they do not make much of a show, because it takes many years before they can grow to large specimens. Each shoot only makes two or three buds a year. But in five or ten years, a bush in flower presents a striking appearance. A large tree peony is usually considered of great value. It is a never-ceasing object of growing interest.

Meehans' Monthly, 1897

Get in Tune with Phlox

An interesting experiment would be a garden made up entirely of varieties of phlox; beginning with the lovely colors now obtainable in the *P. subulata* group, next the fine lavenders of *P. divaricata*, then an interim of good green foliage till 'Miss Lingard' of the *P. decussata* section made its appearance, to be followed by the full orchestra of the general group of violets and purples (basses); mauves, lavenders, and pinks (violas, cellos, and brasses); and the range of whites (flutes and violins).

Louisa King
The Well-Considered Garden, 1915

Editor's Note: The moss pink (*Phlox subulata*) produces masses of bright pink, blue, or white flowers on 4- to 8-inch-tall plants; wild blue phlox (*P. divaricata*) grows 10 to 15 inches tall and has evergreen leaves; *P. decussata* 'Miss Lingard' is actually a variety of wild sweet William (*P. maculata*), which has pure white flowers and grows 24 to 30 inches tall.

Protect Your Pinks

A January like the present, 1870, will be death to half the pinks (*Dianthus* spp.) in the country. We have kept them finely under a thin covering of pine needles.

Edward Sprague Rand
Seventy-Five Popular Flowers and How to Cultivate Them, 1872

Best Perennial Screen

The best hardy perennial for a screen is the plume poppy (*Macleaya cordata*) and it does equally well in the shade and in the full sun. The leaves are light green above and a silvery white underneath. The creamy white flowers are borne in plumelike spikes which need not be removed after the blooming period, as the seed vessels are also pretty. The plume poppy grows six to eight feet high; will grow in any soil; and when once established its suckers are hard to eradicate—therefore, it belongs to the wilder parts of a garden.

W. P. Longland
The Garden Magazine, 1907

A Poppy Coverup

Oriental poppies leave terrible blanks in the wake of their brief brilliance, but we meet the difficulty by planting gypsophila between the poppies and Michaelmas daisies behind. It is astonishing how close together plants will grow and not suffer any appreciable inconvenience.

Louise Beebe Wilder
Colour in My Garden, 1918

Editor's Note: Annual baby's breath (*Gypsophila elegans*) can easily cover up poppies' departure with its bushy 10- to 18-inch-tall stems and clusters of white or pink flowers. Michaelmas daisies are asters, either *Aster novae-angliae* or *A. novi-belgii*. Both asters have violet flowers and can reach 6 feet tall.

Roses

The Best Rose Is a Blackberry

The best rose bush we can get is not a rose bush at all. The best rose bush is a blackberry bush. Here, at this season, our blackberry bushes are snow white with bloom—great big blossoms, and so many of them. Then, when this wealth of bloom is past, which lasts fully three weeks, we see the green fruit forming, then the berry turning red. But when the bloom falls from the rose bush, we have nothing but green leaves left. In most cases, not even a hip.

F. K. Steele
Meehan's Monthly, 1901

Train a blackberry up a trellis beside your house, and it can fool you into thinking it's a wild rose, until harvest time.

Roses Like to Watch the Sun Rise

The best place for a real rose garden is a southeastern slope. Roses love the early morning sun.

Frances Duncan
The Joyous Art of Gardening, 1917

Let Roses Choose Where to Grow

We must primarily choose places for the roses rather than roses for the places.

Charles MacFarland
The Rose in America, 1923

Editor's Note: Roses do best and need the least maintenance when you plant them where they get good air circulation, plenty of sun, and a well-drained, humus-rich, loamy soil.

Roses Deserve Their Own Garden

Some people have a liking or hobby for hybrid roses, and the lawn is dug into beds and roses planted in every conspicuous place. The roses are beautiful when in bloom but at other seasons they are a group of straggling briars. The best way to have roses is to set apart an area especially for them, or plan a rose garden.

Herbert J. Kellaway
How to Lay Out Suburban Home Grounds, 1915

Hide Those Roses!

There are more mistakes made in arranging roses than any other plants. It is usually wrong to put roses in the front yard, either in beds near the house, or as borders for lawns or walks, because the rose bush is not a graceful bush and it has so many enemies that it must be covered more than half the time with unsightly powders or spraying material. The rose belongs in a garden where its misfortunes can be hidden from the public gaze and its troubles more easily dealt with.

Wilhelm Miller
The Garden Magazine, 1907

You can avoid the bother of soap and baking soda sprays if you plant healthy, disease-resistant roses. Rugosa roses (*Rosa rugosa*) are tough and particularly disease resistant. They grow 3 to 6 feet tall and are hardy to Zone 4. The clove-scented flowers may be single or double, and the rose hips are extra-large and showy.

Little Bulbs Brighten Rose Beds

I have often been asked, What should be put into rose beds to enliven their dull branchiness for early spring?

Strong clumps of winter aconites planted very deep, to be succeeded, when the aconites are only bright green tufts of leaves, by large, pale crocuses, white and light lavender, are as good a combination as I know; and when they die down a fresh top dressing can be lightly forked into the roses without hurting the bulbs.

Marie Theresa Villiers Earle
More Pot-Pourri from a Surrey Garden, 1899

Editor's Note: Winter aconites (*Eranthis hyemalis*) grow only three to eight inches tall. Their one-inch-wide flowers are bright yellow and are among the first blooms to greet you in spring. How deep should you plant them? They're small bulbs, so two inches should do it.

Don't Plant a Rose Graveyard

A rose garden is usually the worst-looking kind of garden there is, because the stakes and labels look like the stones in a graveyard. Use iron stakes, or prune your plants so they won't need stakes.

The Garden Magazine, 1906

Roses Are like Robins

Thousands of people who love roses are afraid to grow them because they may imagine it requires too much skill. A great deal of this may be laid at the door of our old-school gardeners who, from narrow-mindedness, have tried to envelop everything pertaining to floriculture in mystery. The main factor required is good plain common sense.

Should dry weather set in, give them a liberal soaking of water once a week, for roses are like robins, they like the best water there is and plenty of it. It will also very greatly help them to produce continuous bloom if they are heavily mulched with well-composted manure or chopped straw; even a coat of coarse dry grass is better than nothing. In the following spring, after all frost is past, go over them, shorten back any long shoots, and cut out any dead tips that may appear. Renew the mulching in the spring as soon as pruned.

American Agriculturist, 1895

Can You Spot a Sucker?

A careful lookout should be kept for suckers, or growth from the root on which the stock is grafted; for roses, of course, do not ordinarily grow on their own roots. These growths may be recognized by their thorny stems, and by the seven leaves which they put out in contrast to the grafted stock, which has but five.

Amelia Leavitt Hill
Garden Portraits, 1923

Sucker Pruning Tip

If one has wisdom enough to recognize rose "suckers" from the roots, and resolution enough to cut them out, then a wide range of budded roses is possible. But if one cannot tell a sucker when he sees it, he never should get roses except on their own roots.

Frances Duncan
The Joyous Art of Gardening, 1917

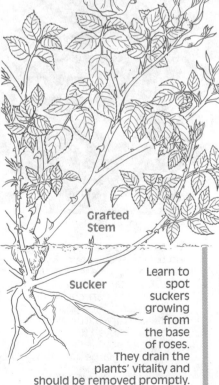

Grafted Stem

Sucker

Learn to spot suckers growing from the base of roses. They drain the plants' vitality and should be removed promptly.

Pegged Roses Produce More Flowers

Peg down roses where a heavy mass of flowers is desired. The side shoots push more freely for this treatment.

The Gardener's Monthly, 1876

Coaxing Stingy Roses

Hardy perpetuals or monthly roses often fail to give more than a few early spring flowers at the tips of the branches. If the plants are in good condition, and the branches of some length, peg the ends down to the ground with a clothes pin or stick, as the tendency in rose growth is for new wood to start from the highest point. Bending the end down brings the highest point at the middle of the branch, which will then break and bloom.

Ida D. Bennett
The Flower Garden, 1904

Editor's Note:
Perpetuals or hybrid perpetual roses have large, mostly double flowers. They bloom in shades of pink, maroon, or white in early summer and in fall. Some varieties like 'Mrs. John Laing' are very fragrant. As a bonus, this one is disease resistant too.

Roses from Cuttings

My first attempt at raising roses from cuttings was made last fall and it was very successful. I got fifty cuttings of twenty varieties of roses, teas, hybrids, etc., being careful to have two or three buds on a cutting. These I stuck into the bed, leaving one bud well above ground. A common glass jar was placed firmly over each cutting and there it remained until the weather was warm and settled in May. In the late fall when other plants were mulched I had the jars surrounded with manure about halfway up. Out of the fifty cuttings not more than six failed to root and grow. They have grown wonderfully the past summer and many have produced fine blooms.

Anna K. Cummins
The Garden Magazine, 1908

When starting roses from cuttings, keep the flower buds pinched off until the young plants can get established.

Cold Roses Go Green

Beginners are often perplexed as to why their roses should come with green centers. The most common cause of this troublesome occurrence is spring frosts. At pruning time, especially when the season is early, one is tempted to leave young promising growths, but unfortunately the frost comes and so injures the embryo buds that these green centers are the result.

E. T. Cook
Gardening for Beginners, 1901

Best Old-Time Roses

Cabbage rose (*Rosa centifolia*)

Cinnamon rose

Common China rose, or monthly rose

Sweetbrier, or eglantine (*R. eglanteria*); the single flowering form is the one to get

Scotch rose (*R. spinosissima*)

'York' and 'Lancaster'

Damask rose

Yellow roses: Austrian yellow, Persian yellow or wreath rose, and yellow Scotch rose

White rose (*R. alba*)

Maiden's Blush, or Blush rose

Common Moss rose

Frances Duncan
The Joyous Art of Gardening, 1917

Editor's Note: This checklist of roses for an old-fashioned rose garden includes some of the all-time favorites. If you're trying to find these roses, here are the names you should look for.

The cinnamon rose is *Rosa cinnamomea*, the China rose is *R. chinensis*, the Damask rose is *R. damascena* and 'York and Lancaster' is a variety of the Damask rose (*R. damascena* 'Versicolor'). The Austrian rose is *R. foetida* and 'Persian Yellow' is a variety of it called 'Persiana'. The Scotch rose (*R. spinosissima*) comes in many colors, but there are yellow forms. 'Maiden's Blush' is a variety of the white rose (*R. alba*), and common moss roses are natural sports developed from the centifolias or cabbage roses (*R. centifolia*).

Grow a Rose "Tree"

I have learnt from cottage gardens how pretty are some of the old roses grown as standards. I have taken the hint, and have now some big round-headed standards of the lovely 'Celeste' and of 'Madam Plantier' that are worth looking at, though one of them is rather badly shaped this year, for my handsome Jack (donkey) ate one side of it.

Gertrude Jekyll
Wood and Garden, 1904

Editor's Note: Standard roses are plants trained to grow on a single upright, treelike stem.

Strange But True

Dorothy Perkins' roses require no care whatever, as may be gathered from the fact that some railroads are at present planting them broadcast to cover unsightly railway cuts.

Amelia Leavitt Hill
Garden Portraits, 1923

Editor's Note: Yes, there was a time when railroads, gas stations, and post offices displayed creative gardening. 'Dorothy Perkins', by the way, is a rambler with small pink double blossoms.

Best-Colored Climber

The pink of the wild rose is at once the most luscious and delicate color in all the kingdom of flowers, and it is all too rare. The fine climbing rose, 'American Pillar', comes very near to being pure rose color.

Louise Beebe Wilder
Colour in My Garden, 1918

Editor's Note: You can count on this sturdy climber to put out a profusion of two- to three-inch-wide, deep pink flowers with white centers. The blooms have almost no fragrance, but the masses of flowers, disease-resistant foliage, and red rose hips more than make up for the lack of scent.

Rediscover the Damask Rose

Fifty years ago they tell me it was hardly possible to find a garden in which the Damask rose did not grow. Now you can hardly find it anywhere. The new roses have crowded it out. And yet I heard a great rose grower say not long ago that we never have had a sweeter rose or one combining more good qualities. You see how it goes—the new ones are fashionable, and the older ones are forgotten.

Eben E. Rexford
The Household, 1878

Despite predictions that they would be forgotten, the Damask roses remain popular for their perfumey scent. Many Damask roses bloom only once a year, so try to choose varieties such as 'Autumn Damask' or 'Rose de Rescht' that are repeat bloomers. Plants grow 4 to 7 feet tall and are hardy to Zone 3.

Chimney Roses

From the first of May until the middle of June I have great clusters of pink roses on a chimney. A big wood fire burns night and day in this chimney all winter. When the killing frost comes, the leaves do not all drop off, but turn yellow, with tints of red or bronze and some stay on until the new growth starts in the spring. I have tried several varieties on this chimney, but the best is 'General Washington', a climbing pink clustered rose.

H. A. Tate
The Garden Magazine, 1907

A Green Rose

The Green Rose, *Rosa chinensis* 'Viridiflora', is but little grown, yet it is very interesting as one of the most perfect illustrations of phyllode (petals acting as a leaf), for every one of its many rows of petals has become as green and firm in texture as its leaves. I greatly like its shapely emerald green buds for cutting to arrange with other roses whose own are too precious to nip in the bud, and would not be half so elegant and attractive, for the Green Rose manages to make the most of its own charm, and the buds open very slowly, and remain a long while. When fully open they turn a dingy olive with dull purple streaks here and there; they are no longer beautiful.

E. A. Bowles
My Garden in Summer, 1914

Chain Up Your Roses

A lovely effect may be obtained by means of an ordinary iron chain, run loosely through a series of plain iron posts, at the foot of each a 'Lady Gay' rose has been planted. If these be trained over the chains, the result will be, during June, a series of festoons of a solid mass of exquisite pink, which will be visible at a considerable distance.

Amelia Leavitt Hil
Garden Portraits, 1923

The 'Lady Gay' rose seems to have slipped from commercial catalogs. But you can train any climbing rose or rambler of your liking along a chain.

Best Rose for Hedges

Among the roses, the first place for a beautiful flowering hedge plant must be given to 'Marie Pavie'; of compact growth, neat foliage, and with myriads of small white flowers which are produced from early spring until after a heavy frost. Set the plants two feet apart and shear very slightly, just sufficient to keep them in good shape.

Prosper J. Berckmans
The Garden Magazine, 1907

Moss Rose Lament

Welcome as we do the many advances made by florists in connection with new flowers and new varieties of flowers, one has often to regret the neglect into which the old favorites fall. The disappearance of the beautiful moss rose is especially a case in point. Few flowers have suggested more beautiful sentiments; few flowers have been more universally beloved; but simply because they were not ever-bloomers the moss rose has fallen into disuse. If someone would only undertake and succeed in raising a good ever-blooming moss rose, surely his fortune would be made.

Meehans' Monthly, 1897

Editor's Note: When this article appeared, the Victorian fascination with the moss or cabbage roses had passed. We are still waiting for an ever-blooming variety, but nurseries continue to stock moss roses for their double flowers and exceptionally sweet fragrance. Moss roses take their name from the mossy growth that covers the outside of their flower buds.

Wichuraiana Roses

Do not forget to put the Wichurian rose in your vine garden. No vines, I believe, trail over level ground and slopes quite as lovingly as the Wichurian roses, nor is there another vine quite so happy for such usage in and out of flower. When I use Wichurian roses on a terrace slope, I like sometimes to use the Scotch or Burnet rose, *Rosa spinosissima*, as a hedge at the top, for the two are charmingly similar in flower and in foliage.

Elsa Rehman
Garden-Making, 1926

The wichuraiana rose (*Rosa wichuraiana*) is vigorous but susceptible to mildew. It blooms late in the season and can easily cover a bank with its 10- to 12-foot-long canes. The variety 'Dorothy Perkins' was at one time one of the most popular climbing roses in America. You may find 'Dorothy Perkins' and other old wichuraiana roses growing in cemeteries. These roses were so popular for cemetery use that they are also known as memorial roses.

Fruits and Nuts

What's the newest fruit craze? Tasty heirloom varieties. Let your gardening forebears guide you into growing the most flavorful apples, berries, peaches, pears, and nuts ever, as well as some less common delicacies such as currants, dewberries, and quinces.

Fruits and Nuts

Better Berries

Blackberries

Tame Your Brambles

To save tearing flesh while tying prickly canes, and the expense of posts and wires, cut out all three-year-old canes of blackberry and raspberry bushes, pinch out tips of young shoots when 2½ feet high, and they will make compact, branching bushes next year.

The Garden Magazine, 1906

Editor's Note: Individual bramble canes grow vegetatively their first growing season, then flower, fruit, and die in their second growing season. New canes emerge each year to replace the old ones. The author did his pruning in the third growing season and removed all the dead canes. Modern-day fruit growers get a jump on pruning and trim out two-year-old canes right after they harvest the fruit.

Keep Fresh-Picked Berries Shaded

Beware of exposing blackberries to the sun after they are picked. Sunlight soon turns the black, shiny fruit to a rusty, dull, unpleasant-looking red.

Farm Journal, 1905

Editor's Note: Preserve the look and taste of your home-grown berries by refrigerating them immediately after you pick them. Wash berries just before you use them.

Dewberries

A Very Good Dewberry

A variety called 'Lucretia' is considered a very good dewberry. The chief value of this class lies in its earliness. Those who grow 'Lucretia' for market, however, do not find it very profitable, as dewberries have to be supported on stakes, while blackberries are usually stiff enough to be self supporting. For the amateur who does not care so much for the little time taken in the cultivation of the fruit, so long as he has something superior, the dewberry is a very good fruit to grow.

Meehans' Monthly, 1894

The dewberry is basically a trailing blackberry. It has prickles instead of thorns and produces tasty, thimble-size fruits 1 to 2 weeks before upright blackberries. The canes need support and are best grown on a trellis. 'Lucretia' is still a popular variety today. See "Sources" on page 316 for ordering information.

Take Time to Trellis Your Dewberries

There are few gardeners who care to take the trouble of trellising dewberries. This is the proper method—braced posts at the ends with intermediate stakes between, twelve feet apart, and number-14 wire stapled to the posts, three or four strands. Then the thorny vines, cut back to four feet, are tied on vertically to the wires. About gathering time, the new growth should be cut back, so as to get the rampant growth out of the way for easy picking. After the picking, cover the ground around the wires with leaves, straw, or hay, and let them go and grow to suit themselves. The following February, prune to straight stems, and tie to the wires again.

F. K. Steele
Meehans' Monthly, 1902

Raspberries

Oats as Raspberry Mulch

A subscriber speaks highly of the practice of sowing oats in the fall among raspberries. Of course the winter kills the oats but they afford a mulch for the soil.

Farm Journal, 1885

Recipe

Refreshing Raspberry Drink

A most delicious and refreshing drink for hot weather is made from a half gill (¼ cup) of raspberry vinegar in a glass of cold water. The vinegar is exceedingly easy to prepare and the surplus berries from the berry patch may be utilized in this way. After carefully picking over the berries, place them in a stone jar (not earthenware) and pour into the jar enough vinegar of a good quality to just cover the berries. Let this stand for twenty-four hours, then strain through a cloth. To each pint of juice add one pound of sugar and boil gently for half an hour, removing the scum. When cold, bottle and seal, and if this is done correctly, the vinegar will keep for two years.

I. M. Angell
The Garden Magazine, 1908

Editor's Note: In *The Fragrant Path* (1932), Louise Beebe Wilder recalls, "Raspberry vinegar was made in every home in my youth and when diluted with water and finely crushed ice is a most refreshing and innocuous summer drink."

Plant Black Raspberries in Spring

The black raspberry must always be set in the spring, and very shallow. The reason for this is that the black variety roots from the tip, forming a tuft of leaves and buds, and these must be left uncovered in planting.

E. P. Powell
The Orchard and Fruit Garden, 1914

Black raspberries don't spread by suckers as red raspberries do. When you want to increase the size of your planting, try tip layering in midsummer—this works for trailing blackberries, too. These brambles will root if you peg their branch tips to the ground with a piece of wire or a clothespin. Leave the tip uncovered, but place soil over the pegged part of the branch. Once the roots are established (usually by late fall), cut the new plant free from the mother plant. You can just let it grow or transplant it to a new location.

For Big Raspberries, Sacrifice the Suckers

The fruit of the raspberry may be obtained of a very large size, other circumstances being of the most favorable kinds, by destroying all the suckers; but in this way, the plant being destroyed, a double plantation is wanted, one to grow only suckers, and the other fruit.

J. C. Loudon
An Encyclopedia of Gardening, 1850

Bramble canes die after they fruit; so unless you start new plants from suckers, your berry patch will die out. Most people shoot for moderate-size fruits and let some suckers grow. If you want prize-winning berries, cut all the suckers, as Loudon suggests, and keep a separate suckering patch to start new plantings.

Nip Raspberry Suckers in the Bud

With the exception of from four to six canes in the hill, treat all red raspberry suckers as weeds, cutting them down while they are little, before they have sucked half the life out of the bearing hill. The first tendency of most varieties of newly set red raspberries is to sucker immoderately; but this gradually declines, even with the most rampant, and under good culture the fruiting qualities improve.

E. P. Roe
Success with Small Fruits, 1881

Strawberries

Hot Strawberries Grow Faster

A strawberry bed in the open ground will yield fruit nearly two weeks earlier if a low glass frame be put over the plants. A very little heat tickles the strawberry, and will make it laugh in delicious berryness.

The Gardener's Monthly, 1873

Editor's Note: You can make simple cold frames to warm your strawberry beds by resting old storm windows atop rows of hay bales. The bales should be placed end to end, snug against one another to conserve warmth.

Raised Bed Yields More Strawberries

This strawberry wall is 3 feet, 6 inches wide at the base, and of such a height that the sides and ends form an angle of 45 degrees. The outer surface of the wall is formed of small course stones, or bricks, and the interior is filled up with soil. Early in every August the wall is taken down and replanted.

J. C. Loudon
An Encyclopedia of Gardening, 1850

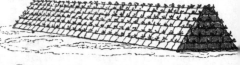

This raised bed will produce more strawberries than the same amount of flat ground. Place plants every six inches. Water the berries through the small trench along the top. Fruit grown with this system will be free from sand and earth.

Watering Strawberries without a Hose

For a small garden bed which cannot be systematically irrigated, water can be supplied effectively by hand. In this case, a small hole should be dug by the side of each hill, or every 2 feet in the row. Into this should be poured, slowly, not less than 1 or 2 quarts of water. When this is absorbed, draw over a little dry earth to prevent evaporation.

E. P. Powell
The Orchard and Fruit Garden, 1914

Start New Strawberries on Top of Old Ones

The strawberry runners are allowed to cover the beds with plants as thick as they can stand. In autumn, the beds are covered with earth from the alleys to the depth of 2 inches or 3 inches. In the following spring, the runners shoot through the covering with vigor, producing very strong foliage, and in due season, an abundance of large and finely flavored fruit. The first year of this plan is less productive than the succeeding ones.

J. C. Loudon
An Encyclopedia of Gardening, 1850

Which Strawberry Grows Best?

No fruit is more fickle about its habitat than the strawberry. Each region has favorite varieties; the same sort may give radically different results on neighboring farms.

S. W. Fletcher
Strawberry-Growing, 1917

Editor's Note: This advice holds true today: There isn't a one-kind-fits-all strawberry. There are hundreds of varieties available, so consult your local extension agent, plant nurseries, and neighbors for recommendations. Then try out several varieties and see which works best.

Strange But True

To keep off the birds how simple, how certain, how small is the cost of a cat on a small chain sliding on a wire, and giving the animal the walk up and down the whole length of the strawberry beds. A small kennel placed in the middle of the walk affords her a shelter and a home for her kittens.

The Gardener's Monthly, 1872

Alpine Strawberries Stretch the Season

The red and white Alpine strawberries possess the advantage of ripening, when properly managed, through autumn till winter; we have seen a dish of good fruit picked on the first day of December.

The Genesee Farmer, 1838

Alpine strawberries (*Fragaria vesca*) are a type of wild wood strawberry. Their berries are not large but are sweet and highly fragrant, and birds tend to overlook the white variety.

Perk Up Strawberry Jelly with Juice

When making strawberry jelly, add some currant juice. It will improve the flavor and the firmness of the jelly.

Farm Journal, 1906

Wash Frost Away

If the strawberry ground is wet thoroughly, either by sprinkling or by irrigation, the evening before a frost is expected, the danger is lessened since the increased amount of water vapor in the air raises the dew point.

S. W. Fletcher
Strawberry-Growing, 1917

Editor's Note: Modern-day fruit growers protect their crops using an automated variation of this technique. They water plants lightly all night long with a sprinkler on a fine-mist setting. They usually start watering when the temperature dips to 34°F and stop at sunrise.

Mulch Strawberries against Frost

The winter mulch may be used for frost protection in two ways. If it is left on the strawberry plants late in the spring, or until they begin to bleach, the blossoming season is retarded and the danger from frost lessened thereby. The mulch also may be used to cover the plants when a frost is threatened. This method has been used more than any other since 1557, when Thomas Tusser wrote in his *Five Hundred Points of Good Husbandrie*:

If frost do continue, take this for a law,

The strawberries look to be covered with straw,

Laid overly trim upon crotches and bows,

And after uncovered as weather allows.

S. W. Fletcher
Strawberry-Growing, 1917

Towel Strawberries instead of Rinsing

To wash strawberries spoils the fragrance of the fruit and thus despoils us of half our gastronomic pleasure. Sand may be removed from the berries without washing by bouncing them about in a damp cloth just before they are served.

Louise Beebe Wilder
The Fragrant Path, 1932

Terrific Tree Fruits

Start a Fruit-Grower's Club

A rural club, by whatever name it may be called, should be formed in every neighborhood. Once a week in winter, this should bring together all who are engaged in the cultivation of the soil. At such gatherings, fruit culture will form a topic of frequent discussion, and many useful facts be elicited. Information as to the peculiarities of the neighborhood can only be had on the spot, and local experience is of much more value than general treatises.

American Agriculturist, 1883

Perfect Tree Planting

More than half the losses in tree planting, and fruit trees especially, arise from their being planted too deep. It is much the better to plant the tree so that it shall, when the whole is complete, appear just as deep as before, but standing on a little mound two or three inches higher than the ground about. This, when the mound settles, will leave it nearly on a level with the previous surface.

Peter Henderson
Henderson's Handbook of Plants, 1890

Include Fruits in Your Landscape

The pear tree, the quince, the medlar, and the mulberry are surely entitled by their beauty to a place in the garden. It is only since nature has been taken in hand by the landscapist and taught her proper position that these have been excluded.

Reginald Blomfield and
F. Inigo Thomas
The Formal Garden in England, 1892

Editor's Note: A pear tree will grace any yard, as will the quince (*Pseudocydonia sinensis*). Mulberries are beautiful trees that attract birds. Their fruits and the birds' droppings are very messy, so set this one well away from the house.

The medlar (*Mespilus germanica*) is a sometimes thorny hawthorn relative that grows about 20 feet tall. It has white flowers and apple-shaped fruits that are edible after they are nearly rotten—they're mostly used for preserves.

Fruit Trees Need Elbow Room

Crowded orchards produce fruit, as a rule, that is not up to full flavor because the sunshine has not a chance to perform its full mission. Where the evil exists an ax should accompany the pruning saw on its rounds among the trees. In such cases the space occupied by some of them is worth more than the trees.

American Agriculturist, 1891

Where to Site Fruit Trees

I always feel a desire to ask the author of a treatise on fruit-growing, who starts off with "in planning for a home orchard, choose a slightly rolling, well-drained area, preferably sloping to the south, with a deep, loose soil not too heavy, underlaid by a gravely clay subsoil, and within easy hauling distance of the barnyard and railroad"—I always want, I say, to ask him what we are going to do if such a piece of land is not on our farm to choose, or whether we had not better take our neighbor's front lawn, which seems to answer the requirements.

E. L. D. Seymour
Garden Profits, 1911

Editor's Note: Then, as now, fruit growing is easier said than done. Even if you can't give fruit trees the perfect site, don't let that stop you from growing them. You may not get the same level of production as a commercial orchard, but you'll harvest plenty of tasty fruit to feed your family.

Pruning with a Chisel

I take a carpenter's framing chisel and put a long handle on it, so that I can stand on the ground and reach many of the limbs from the ground. And for any that are to large to cut off with a thrust with two hands, I take a mallet to drive with. The cuts heal quicker than when cut with a saw.

Farm Journal, 1911

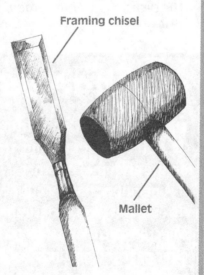

Framing chisel

Mallet

Framing chisels are heavy-duty tools, used for cutting the ends of posts and beams in timber-frame construction. For this tip, you need a chisel with a socket for its handle. Replace this short handle with one from a garden rake or hoe. Use a mallet with a head of rubber, wood, or leather to pound the end of the handle.

Don't Judge Trees by First Fruit

The fruit produced by a seedling tree in the first year of bearing affords by no means a fair criterion of its future merit. If a pear or an apple possess promising qualities—a white and heavy pulp—it may be expected, in the second, third, and subsequent years, greatly to improve in size and flavor.

Royal Caledonian Horticulture Society
Journal of Horticultural Tour, 1823

Apples

How to Tell a Keeper

Usually, a firm-fleshed apple with a rough skin is a good keeper.

F. H. Valentine
The Garden Magazine, 1907

Editor's Note: Apple varieties with rough, corky skins are often called "russets." Because of their appearance, they are rarely grown commercially today. But back before cold storage, russets were important for stretching the fresh apple season. You can still buy russets to grow, but if you'd rather just taste, look for these apples at farmers' markets or order fruit from Applesource. (See "Sources" on page 316.)

OLD-TIME WISDOM

Be not a variety collector. Certainly the rage for having a numerous collection of apples has too much prevailed of late. It were better to be contented with a few good kinds that produce well in most seasons, than to plant many sorts for the sake of variety.

J. C. Loudon
An Encyclopedia of Gardening,
1850

Long-Keeping Cider

Russet cider is the slowest to ferment of any. If made late in the season, and kept in a cool place, it may be kept nearly all winter. One man said that he thought it would keep ten years if kept at just the freezing point. The quality is very good, too.

F. H. Valentine
The Garden Magazine, 1907

Editor's Note: Russet cider is pressed mostly from russet apples. Good choices for cider include 'Golden Russet', a medium-size yellow fruit with a sweet flavor, and 'Herefordshire Red Streak', a small apple with streaks of red and yellow and a semisweet taste. If you don't have your own home-size press, find a cider mill that will process your russets for a per-gallon fee.

Spare That Old Tree

If fruit trees are very large, very old, and very haggard, it will be a problem whether they had not better be cut down, and a new orchard planted. This will be a disagreeable conclusion, and should not be reached too promptly. An old apple tree is a very homeful affair. If possible save a few of them. Remember that old associations cluster about an orchard. If you conclude to renovate them, first of all cut out the dead wood and the suckers. In nine cases out of ten you will find that the ruin has been wrought by allowing a growth of young shoots all over the limbs and the body of the tree.

E. P. Powell
The Orchard and Fruit Garden,
1914

Oven Baked Applesauce

Pare, quarter, and cut the apples open, put into a large bowl or earthen pudding dish, sprinkle sugar between the layers, pour in a cup of water, cover with a plate, and bake in a slow oven for several hours.

The Household, 1878

Strange But True

We here saw one of the most uncommon efforts in the art of grafting, that of inserting an entire tree on the stump of another.

A neighbor having cut down an apple tree about fifteen feet high, a desirable kind, he immediately selected a stock of similar dimensions, and, cutting it over near the ground, placed on it the foster tree; supported the tree by stakes; and excluded the air from the place of junction by plastering it with clay, and afterwards heaping earth around it. The experiment succeeded perfectly.

Royal Caledonian Horticulture Society
Journal of a Horticultural Tour, 1823

Top Six Apples

In preparing this list in order of ripening, we have reference to the most desirable qualities both of trees and fruits—the hardihood, growth, and productiveness of the trees, and the size, flavor, and beauty of the latter.

1. 'Duchess of Oldenburgh'
2. 'Porter'
3. 'Hubbardston Nonesuch'
4. 'Rhode Island Greening'
5. 'Baldwin'
6. 'Roxbury Russet'

The People's Journal, 1854

Editor's Note: These apple varieties are still available from nurseries and are still worth growing. All six have a lot of personality; they'll hold on to their distinctive flavors even when you bake them in a pie.

Be Sure Apples Are Ripe

Cut up an apple of the average ripeness of the crop, and examine if its seeds have become brown or blackish; if they remain uncolored, the fruit is not ready for pulling.

J. C. Loudon
An Encyclopedia of Gardening, 1850

An Apple Tree Bower

Single apple trees sometimes form great bowers with their own branches alone. There is a beautiful specimen of this kind in Rochester, New York. It is an old tree of the 'Twenty-Ounce Pippin' variety. At the height of seven or eight feet its branches spread horizontally, and finally bend to the ground on all sides, enclosing in deep shadow a circular space forty feet wide; an arched opening is made on one side.

Frank Jessup Scott
The Art of Beautifying Suburban Home Grounds, 1870

Editor's Note: The image of a room within the branches of an old tree is a lovely one. If you'd like to grow this apple tree bower, 'Twenty-Ounce Pippin' trees are still available. For other hints on making outdoor rooms from trees, see "Tree 'Houses'" on page 200.

Strange But True

Tell your future with apple seeds. An ancient trial of my youth was done with apple seeds; these were named for various swains, then slightly wetted and stuck on the cheek or forehead, while we chanted:

Pippin! Pippin! Paradise!
Tell me where my true love lies!

The seed that remained longest in place indicated the favored and favoring lover.

Alice Morse Earle
Old-Time Gardens, 1901

Editor's Note: "Pippin" is a traditional British term for an apple seed.

Tidy Apple Pies

To prevent the juice from apple pies running over, thrust little funnels of white paper into the cuts on top, through which the steam may escape, and the juice boil up, and then run back into the pie again when it stops cooking.

Farm Journal, 1892

Provide apple pies with an escape route for boiling juices, rather than make the top crust (or oven) a sticky mess. Cut small, rounded holes in the crust to help the little paper funnels keep their form without tape.

Gentle Apples for Sensitive Stomachs

Certain sorts of apples are more digestible and better suited to weak stomachs than others. Among the most tender and light are the 'Melon', 'Peck's Pleasant', 'Rambo', 'Early Joe', 'Baily Sweet', 'Sweet Paradise', etc.

William G. Waring
The Fruit Grower's Handbook, 1851

All of these old-time apple favorites are still available except for 'Sweet Paradise'. See "Sources" on page 316 for ordering information.

Applesauce: Better Late than Sorry

Beware of early applesauce. There is a temptation to make sauce of the early apples before they are really fit. Do not be in a hurry about it. Better to wait a few days longer than to run the risk of an attack of bowel trouble.

Farm Journal, 1905

An Edible Crabapple

There are few kinds of fruit trees which are greater bearers, which produce more elegant flowers, or make a finer display of handsome and valuable fruit, than the apple tree called the Siberian crabapple. When fit to gather, the fruit is far from having an unpleasant taste, being destitute of the bitter flavor that characterizes the common crab of this country. The taste is a clear, pleasant sour, and the fruit makes one of the most delicate preserves with which we are acquainted.

Genesee Farmer, 1838

Editor's Note: The Siberian crabapple (*Malus baccata*) bears yellow fruits with a blush of red—they're favorites for both jelly and pickling. The tree's white blossoms start out as pink buds and are particularly fragrant. Unfortunately, the Siberian crabapple is susceptible to scab. The variety *himalaica* is less susceptible if you'd care to try it.

Recipe

Apple Molasses

We have made excellent molasses by boiling down the juice of sweet apples, pressed and boiled as soon as possible after grinding.

William G. Waring
The Fruit Grower's Handbook, 1851

Editor's Note: This concoction is not true molasses, of course, which is made from sugar cane, but a thick liquid resembling apple butter. Try spreading it on toast, or use it as a special treat on warm biscuits, pancakes, or waffles.

OLD-TIME WISDOM

Send fruit instead of flowers. In rural communities not so long ago an apple stuck full of cloves was called a "comfort apple" and was sent to bereaved families as an expression of sympathy.

Louise Beebe Wilder
The Fragrant Path, 1932

Recipe

Indian Apple Bread

We recently partook of some most excellent Indian corn bread baked in large loaves, and the following method of making it was given. After the meal is prepared (ground), pour some boiling water on it till it is wet. Put in six steamed sweet apples to a loaf, a little yeast, milk, and enough middlings (coarse wheat flour) to render it capable of being kneaded. Let it rise, and then bake it three hours at least.

Genesee Farmer, 1838

Editor's Note: Most early recipes are vaguely written. This one has little to say about quantities, so you're on your own. The wheat flour contributes gluten to the mix and helps to make the loaves more breadlike. As for the six "sweet" apples, any common supermarket variety will do, though sweet-tasting heirloom apples such as 'Calville Blanc d'Hiver', 'Pound Sweet', and 'Tolman Sweet' will give you extra flavor and a taste of history.

Snap Those Suckers

At times, suckers are cut off with an ax or knife, but this is not permanent, as it leaves a little stump from which a new supply is sent forth the following year. The better way is when the trees are in full leaf to grasp each sprout separately, bend it over at an angle of forty-five degrees from the tree, and pull it loose from the trunk. The operation is greatly aided by pressing the boot between the tree and sprout. When thus removed they are not liable to sprout again.

American Agriculturist, 1894

Editor's Note: If you prune a tree heavily, you are apt to get a small forest of suckers—thin, fast-growing shoots that divert the tree's resources from growing fruit. Remove the suckers while they're young.

Recipe

Cider Cake

1 cup boiled cider
1 cup currants
2 cups brown sugar
6 cups flour
1 cup molasses
2 eggs
1 cup butter
2 teaspoons saleratus

Boston Cultivator, 1865

Editor's Note: Here's a recipe that's long on quantities and short on directions, so follow any standard apple cake recipe. Saleratus is a leavening agent made of potassium or sodium bicarbonate, but you can use baking soda as a substitute.

For cooking, it's hard to beat dessert apples like this one called 'Wismer's Dessert'. Like most dessert apples, it holds its flavor and appearance in pies and applesauce. This particular apple originated in Canada in 1897. The fruits are medium to large and colored yellow with stripes of bright red.

Cherries

Recipe

Delicious Dried Cherries

To make delicious dried cherries, perhaps Morellos are the best. Stone, and allow half as much sugar by weight. Let it lie on them till the juice begins to flow, then put them in a preserving kettle, and when thoroughly heated through, remove the cherries and spread on dishes. Cook the syrup an hour, then put the cherries in again and cook a quarter of an hour. Drain them out again and spread thinly on dishes in the sun. Boil the syrup until thick as honey, and put away in a covered jar. Keep the cherries in the sun, turning each day, pouring over them some of the syrup until all is dissolved and they are dry, then pack away in jars. Keep in a cool, dry place.

Farm Journal, 1892

Editor's Note: The 'Morello' is an English cherry variety from 1629 that's still available. The juicy, tart, dark fruits are wonderful for cooking. Once they are fully ripe, the cherries have a sweet flavor.

Strange But True

Baron Munchausen relates that, running out of shot he loaded his gun with cherry stones, and the next year saw the deer he had fired at, covered with young cherry trees sprouting from all parts of its body.

Meehans' Monthly, 1895

Cherry Pits for Planting

Cherry pits intended for planting should not be allowed to dry much after they are taken from the fruit. They should be washed clean and sufficiently dried in the shade to prevent mold; then mixed with clean, moist sand and buried in a dry place, covering with a few inches of earth. These pits may be planted either late in the fall, or early in the spring as soon as the frost is out, sowing them thinly in rows three feet apart.

Farm Journal, 1905

Mulberries

Best Mulberry

Of all the numerous varieties I have tested, I like the 'Downing' best, because it is of the largest size and has a rich, subacid sprightly flavor, somewhat like that of a well-ripened blackberry. It is said, however, that this old and at one time general favorite is now becoming scarce in the nurseries, owing to its being rather difficult to propagate.

A. S. Fuller
American Agriculturalist, 1894

Editor's Note: 'Downing' yields large, sweet pink berries that are good for making pies and jam. Trees grow to just 15 feet tall. This variety is hard to find, but it is still available. See "Sources" on page 316 for ordering information.

Peaches

A Mulch Mattress Saves Peaches

We have known a whole peach orchard to be mulched, and the owner thought its cost was more than repaid by saving the fallen fruit from bruises.

Peter Henderson
Henderson's Handbook of Plants, 1890

Peaches from Pits

I have planted peach pits for 30 years. Here is my way to plant pits. Take an old tin can with both ends off. Place halfway in the ground in the flower bed. Put into the can a handful of pits, then a handful of soil. In the spring, when the sprouts are 3 inches high, pull up the can, give a downward shake, and the little trees will fall. Transplant in rows in the flower bed.

Rhoda Cummins
Farm Journal, 1906

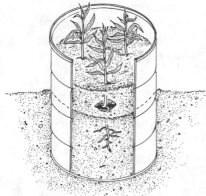

A coffee can makes a handy "pot" for starting peach trees. The peach trees you buy are grafted onto rootstocks that make them grow smaller or that give them more cold hardiness or pest resistance. Home-grown trees won't have those attributes, but they're fun to grow.

Winter-Proof Peaches

The Canadian practice is to cut off the large roots on two sides of the compass points; the roots of the two opposite sides of the compass then twist without breaking, so that the tree can be bent completely under the sur-

face of the ground and covered with earth.

Meehans' Monthly, 1891

Editor's Note: You *could* bury your peach tree each winter, but it's easier to grow a miniature tree in a container and move it to a protected area, like a garage, for the winter.

Recipe
Peach Leather

Peach leather is handy to add to school lunches. Pare and cut the peaches in halves, and allow a quarter of a pound of sugar to each pound of fruit. Slowly stew until smooth; spread on dishes and set in the sun until a rather stiff paste is formed. Thickly sprinkle with sugar and roll like a jelly cake. Keep in jars in a cool, dry place.

Farm Journal, 1894

Peach Pits Add a Hint of Almond

Two or three peaches with the stones left in them, in each jar of canned peaches, will give a delicate almond flavor to the rest.

American Agriculturist, 1885

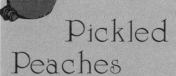

Recipe
Pickled Peaches

To seven pounds of peaches allow one quart of vinegar, and three or four pounds of sugar, white or brown, spiced with cinnamon and cloves, whole, if convenient. Bring the vinegar to a boil, adding a few peaches; when reduced a little take out these peaches and add more. When done, pour the juice over the whole.

The Gardener's Monthly, 1879

Pears
Mulch and Manure Mean More Pears

Unobserving people are not aware of the great benefit of mulching, and the rapid and powerful effects of liquid manure. The treatment was extended to some dwarf pears: one tree, five years from the bud and 4½ feet high, bore 83 pears the last season, which made a heaping pailful. Was not that a *gem* in the garden?

L. L. Pierce
Boston Cultivator, 1865

Try a Trained Pear for Good Looks and Taste

Don't let the backyard fence spoil the effect of your pretty garden. People have come to think it a necessary evil, but it isn't; it can be reformed. To make the espalier shown, plant dwarf pear trees, one at each post of the fence. The branches are trained along wire stretched between the posts.

Frances Duncan
The Joyous Art of Gardening,
1917

An espalier is a plant trained to grow flat against a wall, fence, or trellis. The formal branching pattern of espaliered fruit trees can ornament an uninteresting south-facing fence. Add a bench, and the fence will no longer seem like barrier, but a positive feature of the yard.

Test for Pear Ripeness

The proper season for harvest is easily known, by the ripening of a few full-grown, but worm-eaten, specimens, which fall soonest from the tree.

Peter Henderson
Henderson's Handbook of Plants, 1890

Editor's Note: Injured fruit tends to ripen first. Therefore, these pears alert you to the fact that the rest of the crop will soon be ready to pick.

Best Fruit Perry

The harsher sort of pears produce the best perry (pear cider); the redder and more tawny they are, the more they are preferred; and crab apples mixed with them are said to improve the quality.

Samuel Morewood
A Philosophical and Statistical History of the Inventions and Customs of Ancient and Modern Nations in the Manufacture and Use of Inebriating Liquors, 1838

Editor's Note: Or, as Louise Beebe Wilder puts it in *The Fragrant Path* (1932), "While the best apples make the best cider, the poorest pears seemingly make the best perry."

'Flemish Beauty' Pear

The fruit is large, the skin a little rough, pale yellow, with marbling and patches of light russet. Not very fine grain, but juicy, melting, very sweet and rich. The 'Flemish Beauty' is one of the most superb pears in this climate, sometimes measuring twelve inches in circumference. The tree is very luxuriant, and bears early and abundantly.

The People's Journal, 1854

Editor's Note: This pear was originally known as the "Sweetmeat of the Woods" because of its sweet, aromatic, musky flavor.

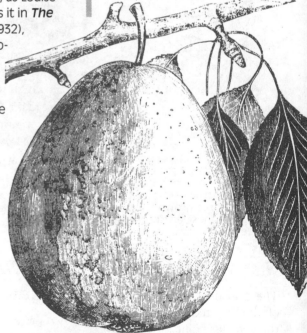

You often hear people talk about heirloom apples, but not much is said of old-time pears. This one, 'Flemish Beauty', was once among the best-known varieties and is still available. It's hardy to Zone 3.

Ripen Pears Properly

Those pears which ripen very soon after gathering are much improved by being taken from the tree before quite mature, while late-ripening kinds like to stay on as long as possible. Some ripen better in a dark room and others in full light. In nothing is skill more at home than in the proper ripening of pears.

Meehans' Monthly, 1891

Plums
Backyard Fruit Tree

A few trees can be crowded into corners, where other fruit trees would not find room, or would become the prey of insects. In city yards the plum is an ideal fruit tree. It is the poor man's tree, rising out of pinched yards, and hanging over ash heaps and wash tubs.

E. P. Powell
The Orchard and Fruit Garden, 1914

Proper Plum Picking

The operator grasps the stem and not the fruit itself. In this way he does not remove the delicate bloom, and does not injure the fruit when pulling it from the spur.

L. H. Bailey
The Principles of Fruit-Growing, 1909

Editor's Note: The bloom is a whitish, waxy covering, especially noticeable on dark plums. It readily shows fingerprints.

Recipes

Flower Pot Plum Cake

One pound of flour, quarter pound of butter, quarter pound of sugar, quarter pound of dried currants, three eggs, half pint milk, and a small teaspoonful of carbonate of soda. The above I make weekly; it is excellent. The cakes are always baked in a common earthen flower pot saucer, which is a good plan.

Country Gentleman, 1854

Editor's Note: What? No plums? Raisins and dried currants, when used in desserts, are called plums. For more on currants, see "Vines and Bush Fruits" on page 182.

Pickled Damson Plums

Six pounds of damsons, six pounds of sugar, two quarts of vinegar, quarter ounce of cinnamon (stick), quarter cloves, one onion (about as large as a nutmeg), half tablespoonful of cayenne tied in muslin, and a little salt.

Put all except the damsons into a pan, and boil; then pour the liquid over the fruit, and allow the whole to remain until the next day, when strain it, putting the fruit back into a basin; boil up the liquid, and pour it over the fruit again. Let the whole stand for another twenty-four hours, and on the third day boil for four or five minutes. Strain and press through a sieve, to remove the stones and skins. The pickle will then be ready to bottle for use.

Martha Bockée Flint
A Garden of Simples, 1900

Strange But True

It is said that hanging a scythe in a plum tree, or an iron hoop, or horseshoes, will insure a crop of plums. **This ought to be investigated.**

Henry Ward Beecher
Fruits, Flowers and Farming, 1859

Vines and Bush Fruits

Currants

Many tips that work for currants also work for gooseberries, so make sure you read both sections even if you're growing only one fruit or the other.

Keep Cuttings Moist

If cut a week or two before using, and packed in moss slightly damp, cuttings of currants and gooseberries root much more rapidly when placed in the ground than if put in at once on cutting.

Meehans' Monthly, 1893

Editor's Note: Rather than digging up moss, try using moist, shredded newspaper or excelsior (fine wood shavings). That way you'll have moist cuttings and can still admire the moss growing in the woods.

Don't Neglect Currants

In some places there has grown up a practice of leaving red currants to grow uncut; it is claimed that they crop more heavily. The practice has as much to recommend it as any other "do nothing" policy has. The test of

experience proves that the fruit loses in color and size; the bushes become lanky and flop about, so that the fruits are mostly on the ground, splashed by every rain, and made an easier prey for the birds.

John Weathers
Commercial Gardening, 1913

Cover Delays Currants

Cover a few currant bushes with muslin or burlap before the fruit ripens, and you can eat currants in August.

Farm Journal, 1906

Editor's Note: By draping the currant bushes to shade them, you slow the ripening process and delay the harvest.

De-Scenting Currants

The European black sorts of currants are very seldom grown in America; the odor of the plant and the flavor of the fruit are very disagreeable to most people. But this odor and flavor can be removed from the fruit by scalding and it then makes a jam which is preferred to red currant jam by many.

S. W. Fletcher
The Garden Magazine, 1906

White Currant Is Tops

The best of all currants in point of quality as far as I have tested the different kinds is 'White Imperial'. This is not a good market variety, because

the color seems to be objectionable.

H. E. Van Deman
Green's Fruit Grower, 1902

Editor's Note: A century later, this variety remains popular— for a white currant. Americans still seem unenthusiastic about white currants, even when they're as full flavored and beautiful as the 'White Imperial'.

Don't let the color put you off. White currants have a delicate flavor and glow like translucent jewels.

Recipe

Decorative Frosted Currants

Currants are very nice "frosted" for dessert or tea. Select large berries, pick them carefully from the stems without breaking, and spread on a platter. For a quart, beat the white of an egg to a stiff froth, and stir in a tablespoon of sugar. Drop slowly over the currants, that all may be wet, and let them stand ten minutes. Sift sugar over them, and in an hour, if they seem dry on top, shake the platter sufficiently to turn the fruit. If there is not sugar enough on the platter, sift on more. Dry another hour, and shake gently into a colander in order to let the loose sugar shake through. Put the berries carefully into a glass dish, and keep cold until ready to serve.

Emily Hayes
The Household, 1882

Currant Air Freshener

The black currant may be forced in pots. In Russia this is often done for the sake of the fragrance of the leaves.

J. C. Loudon
An Encyclopedia of Gardening, 1850

Currant "Trees" Are More Attractive...

Much taller and more ornamental currant and gooseberry trees can be obtained by grafting any variety we wish on the Missouri species (*Ribes aureum*). These can be made pretty and useful ornaments of the lawn, as well as of the garden.

E. P. Roe
Success with Small Fruits, 1881

...And More Productive Than Bushes

A novelty indeed to see currants and gooseberries, that we are usually obliged to look down at, growing where the fruit could be examined without stooping, and where a good share of mankind could look up at it. The stock used to graft upon is the Missouri currant, *Ribes aureum*, well known in cultivation as an ornamental shrub with very fragrant yellow flowers. The advantages for this treatment are:

1. Great fruitfulness
2. Great size and excellence of the fruit
3. Freedom from the borer
4. The ability to raise the fine large English varieties without mildew
5. Cleanliness of the fruit
6. The highly ornamental character of the trees

American Agriculturist, 1876

Editor's Note: You don't have to graft currants and gooseberries to the Missouri currant to grow attractive standards, as the next tip shows.

Train Them as Trees

We advise those who are careful in such matters to train their currants and gooseberries to a *tree form*; let a cutting be set, rub out all the buds but two or three at the top; at about twelve or fifteen inches from the earth let the branches put out, and never permit suckers to grow, or branches to stand lower than this. The stem, in a few years, will become strong enough to withstand winds and sustain its own top.

E. P. Powell
The Orchard and Fruit Garden, 1914

If trained as a small tree, the gooseberry will benefit from better air circulation, which discourages mildew. And you'll have an easier time pruning and harvesting.

A Mix Makes the Best Currant Jelly

The jelly from white currants is red, but of a lighter shade than that made from the red varieties. It is well to make a mixture of one-fourth red and three-fourths white.

E. P. Powell
The Orchard and Fruit Garden, 1914

Recipe

Bachelor's Plum Pudding

Four ounces of grated bread, the same of currants and apples, 2 ounces of sugar, three eggs, a little essence of lemon, and ground cinnamon; boil three hours.

Country Gentleman, 1854

Editor's Note: Despite its name, you won't find any plums in this recipe. In desserts, currants and raisins are called plums.

Neat Tip for Unruly Bush Fruits

It is a neat custom to tie the branches of currants and goose-berries together, in order to give next year's growth a compact appearance. The work may be done in winter, whenever the branches are not brittle with frost.

Abner Hollingsworth
Farm Journal, 1892

Editor's Note: Annoyed by the scraggly appearance of currant or gooseberry bushes in your tidy yard? Tie them up loosely; then prune any stray branches that spoil the effect.

Elderberries

Punch Up Elderberry Pie

The elderberry fruit furnishes "pie timber" (filling), which is a favorite with many. Lacking acidity in itself, it must have this supplied. Boiled cider or rhubarb are the most common attendants for this purpose.

Meehans' Monthly, 1902

The Versatile Elder

The young buds, before expanding, are pickled and eaten as a substitute for capers. The pith is employed for making balls for electrical experiments.

C. Pierpoint Johnson
The Useful Plants of Great Britain, 1862

Figs

Tipsy Figs Ripen Rapidly

In Italy, a wound with a knife is sometimes made on the broad end of the fig, or a very small part of the skin of the fruit removed for the same purpose. Brandy is also sometimes applied, by dropping a small quantity in the eye of the fruit.

J. C. Loudon
An Encyclopedia of Gardening, 1850

Editor's Note: In Zones 5 through 7, fig lovers go to extraordinary lengths to keep their fig plants from freezing, burying the plants or building protective boxes and piling them high with straw mulch. If you get a good harvest, you can use the excess figs for fig preserves, which are wonderful for desserts.

According to Loudon, the fig tree's milky sap can be used as a vegetable rennet for making cheese and as an ointment for destroying warts. Better to just eat the delicious fruits straight off the tree, which you can do in Zones 8 through 10.

When Is a Fig Ripe?

The old rule for judging the ripeness of figs was to observe if a drop of water was hanging at the end of the fruit; a more certain one is to notice when the small end becomes of the same color as the large end.

J. C. Loudon
An Encyclopedia of Gardening, 1850

Figs through the Winter

Protect the branches of fig trees during winter by wrapping strips of old newspapers round them, and afterwards attaching the branches to a wall. This covering is removed towards the later end of April. The branches are previously loosened and pruned to reduce to a minimum the quantity of paper and labor required.

J. C. Loudon
An Encyclopedia of Gardening, 1850

Gooseberries

Intensive Weeding

It is not easy to get couch grass and some other weeds out of the gooseberry roots. I prefer to dig up a weedy plant, tear it to pieces, make it thoroughly clean, and replant the parts.

Donald Van Vliet
American Horticulturist, 1888

Shady Companions for Gooseberries

Try a shaded situation by planting gooseberries among rows of Jerusalem artichokes in the direction of east and west.

J. C. Loudon
An Encyclopedia of Gardening, 1850

Gooseberries thrive in cool temperatures. If your summers are too hot, shade the plants with Jerusalem artichokes. But be aware they are invasive and will take over in a garden situation. You can dig Jerusalem artichoke tubers after the first fall frost and eat them raw in salads, stir-fried, or cooked like potatoes.

Gooseberry Basics

The gooseberry delights in three things: a very rich soil, a shady position, and a free circulation of air. Hilltops are the best sites.

E. P. Powell
The Orchard and Fruit Garden, 1914

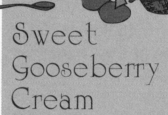

Recipe

Sweet Gooseberry Cream

Boil a pound of green gooseberries; drain, and when cool press through a fine sieve; sweeten to taste with white sugar and add double the quantity of sweet cream whipped stiff. Serve in little china or glass cups with sponge cake or lady fingers.

American Agriculturist, 1891

Editor's Note: This recipe calls for not-quite-ripe gooseberries, not a green variety. Many gooseberry varieties develop a pinkish blush when they are fully ripe, but a tarter stage is often preferred for cooking.

You don't need much space to grow enough fruit for this delightful dessert—one gooseberry bush will yield about ten pounds of fruit.

Gather Gooseberries without Scratches

The thorns of gooseberries are bothersome to the picker if he is to reach in for the berries. But if he lifts up a branch with one hand and picks the berries, which are mostly on the lower side of the branch, with the other hand, he will avoid scratches.

S. W. Fletcher
The Garden Magazine, 1906

For Gooseberries the Size of Goose Eggs

The Lancashire connoisseur, Forsyth, when he is growing for exhibition, places a small saucer of water immediately under each gooseberry, only three or four of which he leaves on a tree. This he technically calls suckling.

J. C. Loudon
An Encyclopedia of Gardening, 1850

British gardeners competed for generous prizes awarded annually to growers of the biggest gooseberries. In this case, the fact that Forsyth removed all but three or four berries probably accounts for their large size—rather than the saucer of water.

Recipe

Gooseberry Jam

Carefully look over the berries, set aside the largest of the fruit, and remove stems and ends. Enough of the remaining fruit must be mashed and strained through a cloth to make half a cupful of juice. To this amount allow 1½ pounds of sugar.

This is such a large quantity in comparison to the amount of liquid that in order to prevent burning, place the saucepan in another of boiling water for ten or fifteen minutes. This will commence the melting process, and it can then be very easily brought to a boil on the stove. Skim, and boil five minutes, stirring constantly.

Drop in carefully one-half pound of the selected berries and simmer for six minutes longer. Remove the fruit on a skimmer to the jelly glasses, being careful not to break them. Boil the syrup five minutes longer or until thick and fill up the tumblers.

Laura B. Carpenter
The Garden Magazine, 1908

Grapes

'Concord' for Beginners

Send to a nursery for a 'Concord' vine. Of course many grape fanciers will ridicule our choice of the 'Concord'. But we want grapes, and plenty of them, and whoever has a 'Concord' vine will be quite sure of these. 'Concord' grapes are vastly better than no grapes. We still believe that the 'Concord' is the best grape for the beginner.

American Agriculturist, 1884

More than a century later, the vigorous 'Concord' is still widely grown. And grape growers are still lifting their noses at it. The grape does have the distinctive scent of grape jelly, often described as "foxy."

See-Through Grapes

The most transparent grapes are the most ripe.

J. C. Loudon
An Encyclopedia of Gardening, 1850

Bottled Grapes

An English gardener cuts his grapes with long stalks and keeps the bunch with this stem in a bottle of water, in a cool place long into the winter months.

The Gardener's Monthly, 1872

"New" May Not Be "Better"

It appears to me we are in danger of losing sight of many very excellent varieties of grapes, and other fruits as well, simply because they are old. Nurserymen give the highest praise to the novelties because there is money in them, and the people will buy what the nurserymen praise.

Abner Hollingsworth
Farm Journal, 1885

Editor's Note: Older varieties of fruit often have aromas and flavors that their modern counterparts can't match. New varieties do have some excellent qualities like disease resistance; but for that old-time flavor, there's nothing like the taste of heirloom grapes such as 'Muscat' and 'Petite Sirah'. These old varieties are still available today.

Thinning Grapes

As soon as the bunches have berries as large as BB shot, the thinning should be taken in hand. For this purpose there is nothing much better for holding the bunches still while the berries are being thinned than a piece of a bamboo cane about six or nine inches long, cut with a neat little fork at one end and the rest of it shaved down to a fine handle. To get a bunch just right, the thinner must carry in his head an idea of the size the finished berry should be.

John Weathers
Commercial Gardening, 1913

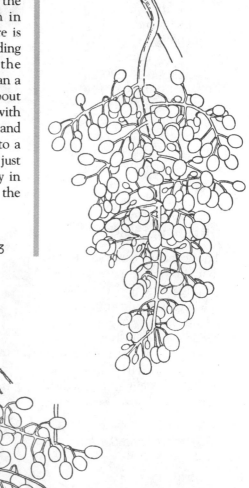

Thin grapes when they are still very small, so the individual berries in a cluster will reach their maximum size. How do you know which grapes to remove? Imagine how much space each grape will take up when it's ripe. Then remove enough of the grapes surrounding that fruit so it has room to grow. A cluster is shown before (*above*) and after (*left*) the thinning process.

Quince

*The term "quince" is used for two different fruits, the Japanese quince (*Chaenomeles japonica*) and the Chinese quince (*Pseudocydonia sinensis*). Both plants produce fragrant fruits that are used in jellies and preserves. Japanese quince is a low, spring-flowering shrub, and Chinese quince is a small tree.*

Unforgettable Fruit

The wonder of horticulture is that the quince has remained so long just a quince. In fact it is less of a dessert fruit than it was in the days of Henry VIII. Yet as a baked dish it is unsurpassed. Cut it open while still hot, spread with butter and sugar, and you will have a dish that you will never forget.

E. P. Powell
The Orchard and Garden,
1914

The Chinese quince (*Pseudocydonia sinensis*, formerly *Cydonia sinensis*) is a large shrub or small tree that grows 10 to 20 feet tall. It has pale pink flowers in spring, 5- to 7-inch-long pear-shaped fruits, and beautiful peeling bark. Unfortunately, this plant is very susceptible to fire blight. It will grow in Zones 6 to 8.

Recipe

Quince Sauce

Pare, core, and weigh; first stew soft in water and then add as many pounds of sugar as there were of the uncooked fruit, and simply scald through. Pour off the water and cover the fruit with a syrup of a pound of sugar to a pint of water. Boil up quickly, then take the fruit out carefully, and put it into preserving jars. Pour the syrup over it and close the jars tightly. Many like a sauce with a large proportion of apples better than the pure quince.

American Agriculturist, 1883

Recipe

Easy Quince Bake

Rub the fuzz off with a coarse cloth, but do not pare or core them. Pack in a granite basin; half fill it with fresh, sweet cider; cover it closely and bake for half a day in a moderate oven. An hour before they are done, add a cupful of sugar to each four quinces and baste with the syrup. Serve cold with cream.

Farm Journal, 1910

Editor's Note: One Chinese quince tree will produce a bushel of fruit, which is enough for several delicious desserts. Quinces need full sun and well-drained, somewhat rich soil. Pick the fruits in fall when they are fully colored and fragrant—they'll probably still be hard. Handle the fruits with care since they bruise easily. Refrigerate quinces and they'll last up to two months.

Dried Quince Drink

Scalding and soaking the dried fruit in water makes a good substitute for tamarind water—a very acceptable, cooling acid drink.

American Agriculturist, 1883

Recipe

Quince Blancmange

Pare 2 pounds of quinces, but do not core them, then throw them into cold water. Drain them and put them into a saucepan, pouring over them two quarts of cold water. Place the saucepan on the fire and let the quinces simmer gently. When they become quite tender set them away in a bowl, together with the liquor (juice) until the next day. Then put them in a cloth or jelly bag and strain the juice without pressing the fruit, suspending the cloth or bag over a pan. When all the liquor has dripped through, put it into a saucepan and to every pint of the juice add 1½ ounces of gelatin and 9 ounces of granulated sugar. Now let the ingredients simmer gently until the gelatin is dissolved. When the juice becomes jellied, pour it into a bowl and stir into it very gradually ¾ pint of rich cream, stirring the two quickly together and continuing to stir until the whole becomes nearly cold. Have ready an oiled mold or one that has been soaked in cold water. Pour the blanc-mange into it and chill until it sets.

American Agriculturist, 1894

Perfect Fruit Preserves

These tips will help you make better jellies and marmalades from a variety of fruits. If you're interested in preserving a specific fruit, see the recipes in each fruit category.

Add Flavor with Scented Geraniums

In my youth during jelly-making time the leaves of rose geranium were made use of to give point and flavor to certain otherwise rather insipid jellies, apple among them. A leaf was put in the bottom of each glass before the boiling syrup was poured in.

Louise Beebe Wilder
The Fragrant Path, 1932

Editor's Note: One reason to take up the hobby of collecting and growing scented geraniums is that you can use the fragrant leaves to flavor teas, jellies, and cakes. Place leaves in the bottom of a cake pan before you pour in the batter to give pound cake or other desserts a rose or lemon flavor. Or if you're more adventurous, choose flavors like apricot, lime, or strawberry.

Fruit Gumdrops

A clever housewife has perfected a new way of preserving fruit, as delectable looking squares and discs made of golden and ruby-tinted jellies. These gelatinous cubes have the consistency of a fresh gumdrop, and hold the delicate flavors of peach, strawberry, pear, or plum marvelously well. The principal feature in their preparation is the careful boiling of the fruit pulp until the desired consistency is reached, which, by the way, requires a very delicate adjustment of sugar and sense. The hot, thick preserve is then poured into large pans where it must remain undisturbed for ten hours, after which, if it has jellied properly, it can be cut like cheese.

Farm Journal, 1904

Editor's Note: By using gelatin, you can avoid all the boiling and delicate adjustments this recipe calls for. Start by soaking 2 tablespoons plain gelatin in ½ cup cold water. In a separate saucepan, heat ¾ cup fruit juice to boiling and stir in 2 cups sugar. Add the soaked gelatin. When the sugar and the gelatin are dissolved, bring the liquid to a boil for 10 minutes. Pour the syrupy liquid into a chilled pan, and let it harden for 12 hours. Cut the hardened syrup into shapes with a hot knife, and roll the pieces in granulated sugar.

Double Straining for Clearer Jelly

When making jelly, much pulp is often pressed out with the juice. A good plan is to cover a bit of hoop with cheesecloth, and set it upon the bowl that is to receive the juice. This double straining—the last allowing the juice to go through without pressure—will give the clear jelly so much prized by housekeepers.

Farm Journal, 1906

Free Jelly Jar Labels

Whenever an unsealed envelope comes in your mail, cut off the gummed flap and put it away in a box. You will find these useful for jelly labels.

Farm Journal, 1909

Jelly and Marmalade, All at Once

It is most convenient with crab apples and plums to make jelly and marmalade from the same fruit, and both are the nicer for this separation of juice and pulp. One thus saves squeezing the fruit juice through a jelly bag. I let the plums drain through a colander, but the stewed crab apples are hung up in bags to drain all night. The juice is then ready to be measured and boiled before the addition of a "pound of sugar for pint of juice"—a *scant* pound for ap-

ples and plums. The pulp remaining in the bag or colander is rubbed through a sieve or colander, to remove seeds and skins, and only needing to be boiled a short time with the sugar (3/4 pound, or a little less, to a pound of pulp), when it is thick and firm enough to put away. The rule is to use 3/4 pound sugar for one pound of fruit.

American Agriculturist, 1879

Editor's Note: Jellies are made from fruit juice, while marmalades are made with bits of fruit. Make both treats at once, as this tip suggests, and you'll save fruit and time. Follow your favorite recipes for canning instructions.

Grow Nicer Nuts

A Mixed Nut and Fruit Orchard

Nut trees are often planted 10 feet apart each way, but better results are likely to be obtained at 12 feet apart each way. The intervening space may be cropped with gooseberries, currants, or raspberries, or vegetable crops until the nut trees require all the ground to themselves.

John Weathers
Commercial Gardening, 1913

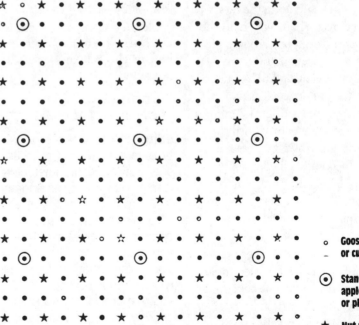

o **Gooseberries or currants**

⊙ **Standard apples, pears, or plums**

★ **Nut trees**

This diagram, representing roughly one-quarter acre, shows how you can efficiently interplant nut and fruit trees with bush fruits like gooseberries or currants.

Filberts

Filbert Walkways

Filbert walks and arches, so productive and pleasing, were welcome inclusions in the old gardens. Latterly, filberts have been neglected, but results equal to those read of in the old garden books might still be secured. Filbert nuts look most effective planted 1½ to 2 feet apart in rows, though the heaviest crops are secured by planting not less than 4½ to 5 feet apart.

Thomas H. Mawson
The Art and Craft of Garden Making, 1907

Editor's Note: To use filberts (hazelnuts) as hedges framing a walk, allow them to grow as shrubs with multistemmed trunks.

Walnuts

Restore Walnuts with a Milk Bath

Before you send walnuts to table, if you find that they have become shrivelled, steep them in milk and water for six or eight hours before they are used; this will make them plump and fine, and cause them to peel easily.

J. C. Loudon
An Encyclopedia of Gardening, 1850

Harvest Walnuts Fast for Better Taste

A great many persons have an idea that this nut is strong tasting, and hard to digest. But it should be gathered immediately after it is ripe, and not allowed to remain in the hull. It should not even be allowed to remain on the tree till it falls off. *Dry it quick* and it is a very different nut from what is commonly found.

The Gardener's Monthly, 1876

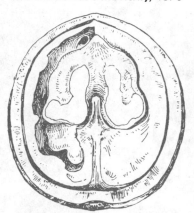

To get to the meat of a fresh walnut, you have to remove a husk, then the shell. Wear gloves when you handle the husks or they'll stain your hands.

Use Young Walnuts for Pickling

Walnuts should be taken for pickling while the internal parts remain tender and fleshy, which may be ascertained by probing them with a pin or needle.

J. C. Loudon
An Encyclopedia of Gardening, 1850

Recipe

Walnut Ketchup

Take young, tender walnuts, prick them in several places, bruise them with a wooden billet, and place in a jar with sufficient water to cover them, adding a handful of salt for every 25 walnuts; stir them twice a day for 14 days; then drain off the liquor into a saucepan. Cover the walnuts with boiling vinegar, crush to a pulp, and strain though a colander into the liquor in the saucepan. Add, for every 2 quarts, 2 ounces each black pepper and grated fresh ginger, 1 ounce each cloves and nutmeg pounded fine, a pinch of cayenne, a shallot minced fine, and a thimbleful of celery seed tied in a muslin bag. Boil all together for an hour, and when cold, bottle. In the above manner, an excellent ketchup may also be made from butternuts.

William Dick
Encyclopedia of Practical Receipts and Processes, 1872

Editor's Note: "Handfuls" of salt is too liberal for modern palates. Try a recipe published in the 1930s that calls for 8 ounces of salt per 200 walnuts.

Trees, Shrubs, and Vines

Early gardeners knew how to get the most out of every plant. In their planting schemes, they even paid attention to the scents of trees! Follow this old-time advice to get the best plants for big or small yards. Choose from fanciful topiary tree houses, practical hedges and windbreaks, and long-blooming vines to beautify your landscape.

Trees, Shrubs, and Vines

Trees in the Landscape

Fall for Tree Shopping

You will be welcome at the nursery in fall, but not during the spring rush. Visit the nurseries and select your trees, shrubs, and fruits when it can be done most intelligently. You will have more varieties to select from. You can see which kinds stand summer drought.

The Garden Magazine, 1907

Editor's Note: You also may find leftovers at bargain prices, such as a flat of leggy azaleas for a dollar each.

Match Trees to Terrain

Round-headed trees suggest solidity, and suit with gently undulating ground. Drooping or weeping trees are lovely by still water because their reflections complete a curve. Trees with rugged contours, such as Scotch firs, accentuate rugged ground.

Madeline Agar
Garden Design, 1912

Editor's Note: Scotch fir is actually a pine, *Pinus sylvestris.*

Naturally Formal Trees Need No Pruning

Clipped trees are not always absolutely necessary to a formal scheme. There are conifers and shrubs which have naturally a decided geometrical outline; the best is unquestionably the Irish (or English) yew, *Taxus baccata.*

Thomas H. Mawson
The Art and Craft of Garden Making, 1907

Editor's Note: Most yews you'll see are pruned into geometric shapes, but they don't have to be. Instead of pruning, choose well-shaped dwarf yews for a formal look without all the work. Try three-foot-tall 'Nana' if you'd like a triangularly shaped plant; 'Fastigiata' for a tall, narrow (four to eight feet wide), columnar look; or 'Repandens' for a short (two to six feet tall) but wide-spreading evergreen. Dwarf and slow-growing evergreens of all kinds often have neat shapes. They're good choices for formal gardens and plantings.

Pick Trees with Ear Appeal

The birches have a small, quick, high-pitched sound; so like that of falling rain that I am often deceived into thinking it really is rain. The voice of oak leaves is also rather high-pitched, though lower than that of birch. Chestnut leaves in a mild breeze sound much more deliberate; a sort of slow slither. Nearly all trees in gentle wind have a pleasant sound, but I confess to a distinct dislike to the noise of all the poplars, feeling it to be painfully fussy, unrestful, and disturbing.

Gertrude Jekyll
Home and Garden, 1900

Editor's Note: British gardening great Gertrude Jekyll was having serious problems with her eyesight at the time of life when she wrote this book. She obviously compensated for her loss by choosing plants that appealed to her other senses.

Fragrant Foliage for Close Encounters

We would suggest, as worth trial, where there is ample space, the mode of arranging by odors; the ancients are said to have paid particular attention to this in mixing their trees. Every one must have experienced a difference in this respect between walking in a pine forest, a plantation of balsam poplars, a birch copse, and beside sweet briar and juniper hedges. An arrangement of this kind, depending on the smell of the buds and leaves, rather than of the flower, would have its effect the greater part of the year, especially after showers.

J. C. Loudon
An Encyclopedia of Gardening, 1850

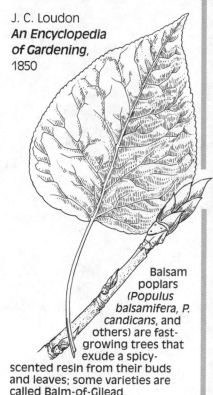

Balsam poplars (*Populus balsamifera, P. candicans*, and others) are fast-growing trees that exude a spicy-scented resin from their buds and leaves; some varieties are called Balm-of-Gilead.

Strange But True

Our common sweet gum tree, <u>Liquidambar styraciflua</u>, is one of our finest forest trees and one deserving more general cultivation on the lawn. Its beautiful star-shaped leaves are very fragrant when bruised, or after a shower when young. This is the tree whose rough, corky-ridged branches are sold in the streets of New York as the "Alligator Plant." These pieces of stick are sold by the thousands every season to unsophisticated city men, with about as much chance of growing as their fence pickets.

Peter Henderson
Henderson's Handbook of Plants, 1890

OLD-TIME WISDOM

A tale of two trees. What is the noblest combination of forest trees in America? Some say oak and pine. People often remark that "oak and pine love to touch elbows." It is said that the bluejays help to perpetuate this partnership by hiding acorns in pine stumps.

The Garden Magazine, 1909

Editor's Note: This deciduous tree and evergreen combination will give your yard color and interest all year long. Oaks and pines are also good sources of food and shelter for birds and other wildlife.

The Ugly Sapling

Nurserymen but seldom recommend the Kentucky coffeetree to persons desiring a choice ornamental tree, and this is because of its poor appearance while young, of a salable size. Up to the age of five or six years, it is but little more than a straight, rough-barked pole, with perhaps a branch or two attached in anything but an attractive manner. But a little later in life the rugged branches become more numerous and symmetrical, and have a personality that will make friends for the tree.

Meehans' Monthly, 1902

Editor's Note: The coffeetree (*Gymnocladus dioica*) has been used in parks as a shade tree. Coffee-deprived Civil War soldiers roasted the beans for a handy (but noncaffeinated) substitute.

A Tree That Deserves Greater Attention

No deciduous trees are so effective as the comparatively little-known fern-leaved beech (*Fagus sylvatica* 'Asplenifolia'), which stands severe cutting and trimming; the light pea green of the foliage in spring is delightful, and in the summer, when it has taken on soberer hues, there is much to admire in the beautiful narrow serrated leaves and its peculiarly neat habit.

Thomas H. Mawson
The Art and Craft of Garden Making, 1907

OLD-TIME WISDOM

Raise trees, as well as kids. All young married people beginning life in the country should start at once to raise trees if their place is of any extent. By middle life, when grandchildren come, the trees will not only be splendid specimens, but will be monuments to the ancestral forethought and love of beauty.

Helena Rutherfurd Ely
The Practical Flower Garden,
1911

Two Top Trees

There are two trees, great favorites of ours, natives of this country, which are not half so generally known, admired, and planted as they deserve to be. We mean the mossycup oak (*Quercus macrocarpa*) and ashleaf maple or box elder (*Acer negundo*). The mossycup's great recommendations are, first, its rapid growth, its fine sized foliage (which is two or three times as large as that of most other oaks); and its very large and handsome acorns, curiously tufted or fringed at the edges of the cup. The ashleaf maple is perfectly hardy, takes root almost at once, and makes a thick head of foliage very speedily; its foliage is of a peculiar lively, light green, which gives it a striking and marked appearance among other trees; while its long racemes of pale green seeds, which hang all summer on the tree, and the peculiar pea-green bark of the young wood, are all features of novelty and interest.

The Horticulturist,
1847

You can spot the mossycup oak by the odd fringe on its acorns and its huge leaves. In time, it makes a grand lawn tree, with a well-shaped, spreading head.

The seeds of the ashleaf maple or box elder attract birds, and you can make sugar from the tree's sap. For well over a century, homeowners have grown a variegated variety in their yards. See the following tips for details.

A Maple for a Moonlit Night

One of the most beautiful sights among trees is a fine specimen of our variegated ash-leaf maple or box elder, seen by moonlight.

The Gardener's Monthly, 1877

Editor's Note: The foliage of the variegated box elder (*Acer negundo* 'Variegatum') shows up at night because the leaves are edged with white.

Variegated Show in Late Summer

I have never felt the disgust for variegated foliage evinced by so many good gardeners. Towards the end of summer, and before the autumnal hints begin to brighten them up, most of our shrubs and trees become very heavy in their tone of green, and we miss the contrasting shades of spring vegetation. Then the value of silver elm or *Acer negundo*, and of golden-leaved shrubs is apparent.

E. A. Bowles
My Garden in Spring, 1914

Editor's Note: It's not clear which elm Bowles was referring to, but there is at least one variegated form of the smooth-leaved elm (*Ulmus carpinifolia* 'Variegata') and the Scotch elm (*U. glabra* 'Variegata'), and there are many variegated varieties of *Acer negundo*, which is better known as box elder.

Best Broadleaf Tree for Late Shade

For comparatively late leafing, where as much of the early summer sunshine as possible is wanted, plant the white oak (*Quercus alba*). It makes rather a spreading head, becoming one of the most effective trees for shade in the course of years.

Leonard Barron
The Garden Magazine, 1907

A Word against the Soft Maple

The choice of this tree is one against which the tree lover should protest. The soft maple is a fast grower, but is awkward in its habit, short lived, and brittle and frail. It is not as decorative as many of its sturdier brethren, and when so many better trees are to be had at no greater trouble or expense, its popularity is not to be understood.

Amelia Leavitt Hill
Garden Portraits, 1923

Editor's Note: The soft maple Hill is referring to is the silver maple (*Acer saccharinum*).

Strange But True

Weeping trees are very much overplanted in this country. During the 1870s no yard was complete without a collection of these curiosities. Even today you may often see a place that is nothing more than an outdoor museum composed of such oddities, which are scattered indiscriminately through the yard. The worst freak is the Kilmarnock willow (Salix caprea 'Pendula'). At first it forms a ball on a stick, like an "all-day sucker," and later the branches droop dolorously to the ground. Its grief is exaggerated, like that of hired mourners.

Thomas McAdam
The Garden Magazine, 1907

A Tree Worthy of Dr. Seuss

Standards can be obtained with mushroom-shaped heads of *Taxus elegantissima* 'Aurea' grafted onto the Irish yew, the heads of a bright golden color contrasting admirably with the dark green of the Irish yew below.

Thomas H. Mawson
The Art and Craft of Gardening Making, 1907

Editor's Note: The first yew named here, *Taxus elegantissima* 'Aurea', is now known as *T. baccata* 'Elegantissima'. It's just one of several golden-leaved varieties of the English yew. The Irish yew is *T. baccata* 'Fastigiata', a variety that was discovered in Ireland about 1780.

For a Mountain Ash, Go Native

The ruddy brown bark of our native mountain ash (*Sorbus americana*), and its immunity from insect pests and disease, are two characteristics which should give it preference over the dull ashen bark and bug-ridden foliage of the European species (*S. aucuparia*), the one generally sold by nurserymen.

Herbert Durand
Wild Flowers and Ferns, 1925

Editor's Note: The European mountain ash continues to be the one you're likely to find when visiting a nursery. Check mail-order companies for the American mountain ash. See "Sources" on page 316.

The European mountain ash produces beautiful orange-red fruits in fall that are favorites of birds. This tree is susceptible to many diseases, so try a healthier option, the American mountain ash. You'll find that it looks similar but has fewer problems. It grows 10 to 30 feet tall.

The Lightning Rod Tree

In Holland, the Lombardy poplar (*Populus nigra* 'Italica') is often used as a lightning rod and is planted near haystacks and isolated farmhouses. This poplar has the habit of growing nearly vertical; as soon as the rain falls the water runs along the branches and forms a constant stream of water from the top to the ground. Lightning finds in the stream of water a safe conductor towards the ground.

P. Ouwerkerk
Meehans' Monthly, 1902

A Lightning-Proof Tree for the Yard?

Willows are never struck. Longpointed or spear-shaped leaved trees always indicate a tree that is lightning proof.

John Hugh Ross
Meehans' Monthly, 1902

Editor's Note: Take this bit of wisdom with a grain of salt—nature is never predictable. Note the following tip.

No Tree Is Lightning-Proof

It is sometimes stated that certain kinds of trees are never struck by lightning; there is, however, no foundation for this idea.

J. C. Loudon
An Encyclopedia of Gardening, 1850

Tips for Placing Trees

A Natural Effect

It is told of landowner Robert Marnoch that he once horrified an up-to-date forester by taking a bundle of Scotch firs by their roots and throwing them with all his force, requesting him to plant each tree on the identical spot where it had alighted. It may be easy to take exception to this method, but at any rate the result would not be in any way stiff, formal, or constrained.

Thomas H. Mawson
The Art and Craft of Garden Making, 1907

Think 5, 7, or 11 When Planting

When trees are set out in any regular or geometric formation, the mind irritatingly falls to arranging them. It is politic to plant groups with odd or indivisible numbers such as five, seven, or eleven.

Thomas H. Mawson
The Art and Craft of Garden Making, 1907

Editor's Note: Geometric arrangements are best for formal plantings. Odd-numbered plantings look more relaxed and suit informal yards.

How Should You Arrange Your Trees?

The easiest way is this. When trees are to be planted, take tall stakes, six feet perhaps, stick them in the ground where you think you want the trees, then go off at a distance and look.

Frances Duncan
The Joyous Art of Gardening, 1917

Editor's Note: Use cut branches or stakes with paper bags tied on top to help you visualize bushy trees.

Group Gregarious Evergreens

It must not be forgotten that in a state of nature, evergreens are gregarious; growing together, they shelter one another. If put out in the open, exposed on all sides to the wind, the sun, and the weather in general, the hardiest of even these hardy things have a hard time of it.

The Gardener's Monthly, 1877

Move a Tree without Digging

Often one can alter the place of a young tree a few feet by bending its head down gradually till it touches the ground, and then pegging it underground till it roots and the old stem can be cut away.

Gertrude Jekyll
Home and Garden, 1900

A Dangerous Tree

The purple beech is normal in shape and normal in texture, but its abnormal color puts it on the list of eccentric, and therefore dangerous, trees. Rightly used, it may very beautifully assist the effect of a garden picture; wrongly used, it may ruin it entirely. It should never figure in a distinctly rural picture; and in a gardenesque picture it should never look as though accident had determined its place, for everyone knows that it is not a natural species. Its place is in definitely ornamental, well-tended, "polished" grounds near a house.

Mariana Van Rensselaer
Art Out-of-Doors, 1893

How Far from the House?

A house should not be nearer to a wood than fifty yards, but may be within half that distance of a mere row of trees.

John Arthur Hughes
Garden Architecture and Landscape Gardening, 1866

Editor's Note: You can grow a single row of trees near your house without making it dark and damp. A single row allows light and air in, yet still acts as a barrier to the elements and passing traffic. But you should allow more distance between your house and a forest. A patch of woods that's too close can overpower your house and shade out all other plantings.

Set Off Early Blooms

Flowering trees that bloom before the leaves should have an evergreen background.

The Garden Magazine, 1907

Editor's Note: For example, set off the blooms of a dogwood with a dark green Canada hemlock (*Tsuga canadensis*) backdrop.

Trees for Small Lots

There is no greater fallacy than that which leads to crowding a place with young trees, for immediate effect, with the idea of cutting out the superfluous ones when they become crowded. The idea is a capital one—the trouble is, people will not carry it out. In fall, (the landowner) puts off the cutting until spring, and in spring he finds a ready excuse for postponing it until the next fall, and so it goes on, the trees grow up as a thicket, and the beauty of the whole is spoiled.

Fortunately for owners of small places, there are trees especially suited to them. The Norway spruces (*Picea abies*) possess most excellent qualities. The Conical spruce, or Conica (*P. abies* 'Conica'), is one of the most popular of all the small evergreens. We are not surprised that this could be so, as its exceedingly neat and compact habit, and its pleasing color, joined to a very dwarf stature, all make it a desirable small evergreen for small places.

Meehans' Monthly, 1878

Tree "Houses"

A Hemlock Arbor

Arbors or arches can be made much more quickly with carpentry and lovely vines, but the permanent and more unusual structures made with living trees must nevertheless be more interesting. We would suggest that four hemlocks be planted at the intersection of two walks, say five or six feet apart. By cutting back the side branches, to within one foot of the trunk, the growth at the tops will be increased so that in five or six years they may be tall enough to allow the opposite diagonal corners to be twisted together. The fragrant and graceful foliage of the hemlock can thus be made to embower retired seats, or make quaint openings for diverging paths.

Frank Jessup Scott
The Art of Beautifying Suburban Home Grounds, 1870

To join hemlock trees to form a living arbor, trim the side branches back and twist the tops together. Create a curved shape by tying the trees together at three points, as shown here.

A Living Gateway

The figure below represents two hemlocks which have been planted two feet away from, and on each side of, an ordinary gateway. After five or six years' growth they may be high enough to begin work upon. A crotched stick about two feet shorter than the distance of the trees apart is stretched from one to another, from six to seven feet from the ground, and fixed there to keep the tops apart up to that point.

Frank Jessup Scott
The Art of Beautifying Suburban Home Grounds, 1870

If you are willing to get out the stepladder, you can prune young hemlocks into formal shapes such as the one above.

Train two hemlocks into a gateway by tying their tops together at a height that will allow people to pass comfortably below. To form a graceful arch, the trees must be about 11 or 12 feet high. After the trees are firmly entwined at the top, which is usually in about 2 years' time, you can start clipping the sides and tops to form an arch.

The figure below shows how a hemlock archway would look in 20 years after planting, if the trees were allowed to develop somewhat naturally after their artificial character was well established. Such arches increase in quaint beauty as they grow old.

You can produce the formal effect above by joining, then twisting, and tying together the side branches of two hemlocks to form the arch. Let the main stems grow to form two spires; then start trimming to form and maintain the shape. A topiary gateway of this kind takes lots of patience and lots of time, but it makes an amazing entrance for a formal garden. It's a good hobby if you enjoy training and pruning plants and want to express yourself artistically.

A Picnic Grove of Pines

If it is desired to make an ever-green umbrage (shelter) in which to take tea out of doors in summer, it may be provided by planting four white pines, say twelve feet apart each way; and when they are from eight to ten feet high, cutting their leaders out so as to leave a tier of branches as nearly as possible at the same height on the four trees. The following year see to it that none of these upper branches turn up to make leaders, and if necessary tie them down to a horizontal direction. By attending to this for two years the top tier of shoots will make a horizontal growth, which will meet in a few years overhead, and form a tablelike top of foliage.

Frank Jessup Scott
The Art of Beautifying Suburban Home Grounds, 1870

Grow a Hemlock Palace

Suppose six trees to be planted at the corners of a hexagon ten or twelve feet in diameter. Let them feather naturally to the ground on the outside of the group, and trim to within one or two feet of the trunks on the inside. When twelve feet high, pass a rope around the circle, on a level, two or three feet below their tops, so as to draw them towards the center of the circle as far as the main stems may be safely bent, which will probably be about three feet inside of the perpendicular. If the circle is twelve feet in diameter, this will leave six feet unenclosed at the top. The rope is to be left around them until the trees have grown five to six feet higher, when another binding will bring their tops together; and if they are long enough they may be twisted together.

Frank Jessup Scott
The Art of Beautifying Suburban Home Grounds, 1870

Editor's Note: There's a little more work involved in making a hemlock palace than mentioned here. Once the trees are tied in place, you'll need to prune the sides and top each year to form and keep the shape you want.

You can make your own domed temple! Pull and tie 6 trees together at the center to make them grow as one. Cut back the branches that grow from the upper sides of the curved stems to prevent them from becoming leaders and trim as needed. It will take 12 to 15 years to perfect a pavilion like this one.

A Mulberry Tea Room

Teas weeping mulberry (*Morus alba* 'Pendula') is a weeping form of the white mulberry. A specimen grown near Philadelphia is about nine feet in height, and permits of room for six or eight adults with chairs within its drooping branches.

Meehans' Monthly, 1897

Editor's Note: Teas weeping mulberry is still available. (See "Sources" on page 316 for ordering information.) The tree can reach 15 to 20 feet tall, but you won't have to wait that long to enjoy a tea party under its pendulous branches.

The Playhouse Tree

The most famous example of a living playhouse is the Camperdown elm (*Ulmus glabra* 'Camperdownii'). This makes a famous playhouse for the children, and even adults have been known to take tea under its grateful shade. It is generally grafted at the height of six to eight feet, and the branches zigzag outward and downward until they reach the ground.

Thomas McAdam
The Garden Magazine, 1907

Editor's Note: To create a playhouse of your own, plant this odd elm in a spot with rich, moist soil. The grafting is done at the nursery—so all you have to do is watch the tree spread its hanging branches and move your tea table in place once the elm is big enough.

A Sassafras Bower

The sassafras is eminently adapted to form a useful bower, as it naturally assumes a parasol-like top, grows rapidly, and dispenses with its bottom limbs quickly. Six thrifty trees will grow into a perfect canopy, of the size suggested within five years, if their central stems are cut back, and kept to a height of about eight feet. For the next five years all the upright growth at their tops should be annually cut back, so that the trees will not exceed twelve feet in height. Afterwards they may be allowed to grow naturally; but their greatest beauty will not be attained in less than fifteen or twenty years.

Frank Jessup Scott
The Art of Beautifying Suburban Home Grounds, 1870

A leafy bower isn't hard to make. Choose straight-trunked trees with wide-spreading branches, such as sassafras, redbud, or flowering dogwood, and keep their tops pruned back and lower branches pruned off.

Strange But True

Not far from Vianen, we noticed, on a lawn fronting a neat house, some lime trees with their stems painted with alternate bands of black and white, by way of ornament!—the only instance we have met with this absurdly bad taste, which, however, we believe, is common in North Holland.

Royal Caledonian Horticulture Society
Journal of a Horticultural Tour, 1832

Grow Your Own Trees

Johnny Walnut-Seed

If, along in October, one gathers a bag of walnuts, removes the green shells, and, going about the place, makes here and there a hole in the ground some two or three inches deep with a pointed stick or crowbar, drops in a nut, and presses the soil down with his foot, the next year he will have a vigorous shoot; the following year the tree will begin to grow, and in an astonishingly short time whoever has followed this practice will be rewarded by a fine lot of young black walnut trees upon his place.

Helena Rutherfurd Ely
The Practical Flower Garden, 1911

Harvest Tree Seeds in October

The following tree seeds, amongst others, should be ripe this month, and are best sown as soon as possible after being gathered—horse and Spanish chestnuts, walnuts, and oaks. Kinds that would suffer by spring frosts, such as beech, maples, etc., should be kept till sowing time.

F. W. Burbidge
Cultivated Plants: Their Propagation and Improvement, 1877

Hardwoods from Seed

The deciduous tree seeds that germinate most easily are maple, catalpa, ash, linden, birch, oak, walnut, and hickory.

Helena Rutherfurd Ely
The Practical Flower Garden, 1911

Strange But True

The top view represents a tree as it usually comes from the nursery. The trunk is not at all protected by the narrow top, but is left exposed to wind and sun, which work havoc. The lower illustration shows an arrangement for bringing the limbs into proper position. The frame is made by driving four posts three feet apart at the ground, and five feet at the top, their height corresponding to that of the tree. The cross strips can be cut from any odd pieces on hand. Attach rope with broad strips of cloth to avoid injuring the bark or contracting the growth. Let the limbs be drawn down gradually, a little at a time, through the growing season.

American Agriculturist, 1884.

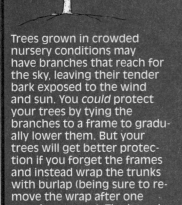

Trees grown in crowded nursery conditions may have branches that reach for the sky, leaving their tender bark exposed to the wind and sun. You *could* protect your trees by tying the branches to a frame to gradually lower them. But your trees will get better protection if you forget the frames and instead wrap the trunks with burlap (being sure to remove the wrap after one growing season). The branches will gradually move into protective and pleasing positions on their own. You can buy burlap wrap from nursery-supply catalogs. See "Sources" on page 316 for ordering information.

Horizontal Cuttings Root Best

In respect to the choice of cuttings, those branches of trees and shrubs which are thrown out nearest the ground, and especially such as recline, or nearly so, on the earth's surface, have always the greatest tendency to produce roots. Cuttings, then, are to be chosen from the side shoots of plants, rather than from their summits or main stems.

J. C. Loudon
An Encyclopedia of Gardening, 1850

Free Trees for the Taking

The finest tree seedlings are to be found on low ground or along the banks of streams, where there is moisture and protection of undergrowth from too-strong sun.

Helena Rutherfurd Ely
The Practical Flower Garden, 1911

Editor's Note: Transplanting wild tree seedlings from your own property is a good way to get extra trees for your yard. Before you move trees from anywhere else, make sure you get permission from the landowner first. And *never* remove wild plants of any kind from state or federal parks or land. Wild tree seedlings in public areas need protection, since they help hold the soil along stream beds and provide food for wildlife.

A Bed for Evergreen Seedlings

It is not generally understood that the conifers, both the white and red pine, the Scotch pine, and the native hemlocks, can be easily raised from seed. Cones may be gathered in September and spread upon a sheet in a light room of a tool house or other dry place where they will dry; the seeds will fall out from the cones and can then be collected and stored though the winter in boxes. The seed bed should be made in the same way as are the seed beds for flowers. When the ground is warm, about the time that we would plant beans in the vegetable garden, the seed should be sown thickly in drills.

Over the bed and resting upon the tops of four stakes, a screen made of lath should be laid to protect the young seedlings from the too-strong sun of the summer.

Helena Rutherfurd Ely
The Practical Flower Garden, 1911

Editor's Note: In natural conditions when conifers seed themselves, they are protected from the weather by the pines overhead. You can provide this same effect with a cover of lath screens—remove them after the first frost at the end of the growing season.

Grafting for Amateurs

Inarching is simply drawing together the branches of two trees growing side by side, slightly shaving the bark down to the wood, and then fitting the two shaven sides closely together and tying them tightly. In a few weeks the two branches will be united together when the one desired may be cut from the parent's stem. The same thing is accomplished by the use of a bottle of water which keeps the graft moist in the same way as if it were really attached to the mother plant.

Meehans' Monthly, 1892

Editor's Note: This is a handy tip if you want to graft a rare tree or shrub variety onto a more common seedling rootstock. If you've never grafted plants before, experiment with rose bushes first to see how the process works; then you're ready to move on to other plants.

This variation on inarching uses a bottle instead of a parent plant to give the graft moisture. Once the plants have bonded, the bottled portion of the graft can be cut away.

Caring for Trees

Plant with a Firm Hand (or Heel)

Trees properly planted need no staking. The fact that a tree needs staking is a proof that it was not properly planted. In nurseries, where it is presumable planting is thoroughly understood, a man stands with a rammer while one is putting in the earth, and hammers the earth in as tightly as though he was hammering in a post. This packs the earth in more tightly than can be done by either feet or hands.

Meehans' Monthly, 1892

Editor's Note: This old-time method is thoroughly up-to-date. The latest research shows it's best to avoid staking whenever possible. Hardware stores and home centers often carry heavy metal bars with flattened ends for tamping.

Snow Job

Many evergreen trees are injured by heavy snowstorms. See that the snow is shaken from the lower limbs that are bent down with its weight. If this is not done, a high wind may break many of the handsomest boughs.

Loring Underwood
A Garden Diary and Country Home Guide, 1908

Spare Old Trees

It is a mistake to destroy old trees because they are worn out. A tree is frequently picturesque in its old age. Use the old trunks as supports for climbing roses. There is something about old apple trees that roses seem to like, and the combination has in short time a charming effect.

E. T. Cook
Gardening for Beginners, 1901

A Second Life for Christmas Trees

The Christmas tree and other small evergreens will keep their freshness all winter if transferred to the open air, and they may serve to produce a pleasing effect if placed where they appear to be growing naturally.

Loring Underwood
A Garden Diary and Country Home Guide, 1908

Editor's Note: Old Christmas trees have lots of uses. Ask your neighbors for their leftover trees; then arrange them in your yard to test out new landscape plans. Or cut off the branches and use them to protect tender plantings from wind and snow. They'll stay green all winter and add a welcome touch of green to an otherwise bleak scene. You can even take the trees to a recycling center and have them ground up into a wonderfully scented mulch.

Hints for Hedges and Windbreaks

Trees and Shrubs for a Rustic Hedge

In a pastoral landscape it is a source of delight to meet with mixed hedges of holly, thorn (hawthorn), privet, hornbeam, and beech, the various alternating hues and tints appealing strongly to those of the painter's imaginative sense; nor would such a hedge be out of place in the wild garden.

Thomas H. Mawson
The Art and Craft of Garden Making, 1907

Control Hungry Hedges

It is an excellent plan to build a wall some three feet deep on the border side of the hedge. This prevents the hedge from absorbing the nutriment from the border, and gives a narrow walk next to the hedge. Where this plan is too costly, it is advisable to have a grass walk several feet wide between the hedge and the border.

Thomas H. Mawson
The Art and Craft of Garden Making, 1907

Two Hedges in One

Where one side of a hedge has a northern exposure, or is much shaded by trees, it may be well to vary the form so that side shall present a broader surface to the vertical light to compensate for the lesser sunlight, as shown. The two sides of a hedge are rarely seen at one view, so that its apparent symmetry will not be marred; and this difference of form may be recommended as a pleasing variety—giving the beauty of two forms of hedge in one—as well as for the purpose of equalizing the vigor of the two sides.

Frank Jessup Scott
The Art of Beautifying Suburban Home Grounds, 1870

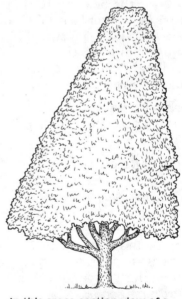

In this cross-section view of a hedge, the side on the left faces the north and gets more shade. Cutting it at a broader angle helps the north side get more light so it stays as vigorous as the sunnier south side.

The Best Way to Shape a Hedge

It may be interesting to compare the difference between the section adopted respectively by nurserymen and by the architect. By a little care, the advantages of the one might be combined with the primness of the other, the plants encouraged to form a good bottom by training to a point. The top can then be gradually brought out to the square, as the bottom gets denser.

Thomas H. Mawson
The Art and Craft of Garden Making, 1907

Editor's Note: Mawson's point is that a nurseryman concentrates on a healthy shape, while an architect is more likely to focus on an artistic shape.

Homeowners often let the top of a hedge spread, resulting in plants that are thin at the bottom. By training your hedge to a point, as shown with the dotted lines, you can encourage the lower part to fill out. Once it does, let the top grow into a squarer shape. But always keep the top of the hedge narrower than the bottom so sunlight can reach the lower branches.

Graft a Living Fence

In a state of nature, two branches rubbed together by the wind become bruised, and if they afterwards remain quietly resting on each other during the growing season, their inner barks easily unite. This is probably the most ancient of all kinds of grafting. Two young trees or branches are bent towards each other, and at the point where they cross a wound is made in each, as shown. The parts are then united exactly, and bound together, so that neither air nor water can penetrate between them. This mode of grafting is used when it is wished to unite the branches of the same tree, or young trees, for the purpose of forming a hedge.

J. C. Loudon
An Encyclopedia of Gardening, 1850

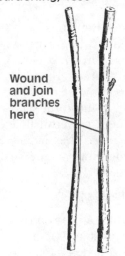

Wound and join branches here

By wounding, then joining the branches of one tree to another, all along a row, you can make a living fence of interlocking branches.

Diagnosing an Ailing Hedge

Most failures in old hedges are traceable to impoverished soil or to the plants having been set out too high in the first place; planting deeper than they were in the nursery helps in the formation of a dense base.

A. T. Raven
The Garden Magazine, 1907

Editor's Note: So what's the cure? Mulch your hedge plants with compost. Put an inch or two of good compost around your hedge each year, and you'll improve the soil and protect sensitive feeder roots from sun, wind, and mowers. Mulch also keeps weeds away and prevents the soil from drying out too fast.

Lovely Looping Laburnum Hedge

I regret that I have no place to make a laburnum hedge, planting them about three feet apart and arching them over one after the other and fastening the head of each to the arched back of the next.

Gertrude Jekyll
Home and Garden, 1900

Editor's Note: Laburnums (*Laburnum* x *watereri*), or golden-chain trees, are small European trees that produce beautiful long bunches of yellow pealike flowers. The pods contain toxic seeds, so keep them away from children.

Cedar Hedge Stops Cattle and Boys

The red cedar (*Juniperus virginiana*), for hedges, possesses advantages over almost every known tree or shrub. Unlike the various species of thorns, it is not subject to the attacks of caterpillars; it possess great advantages over the honey locust in the closeness and compactness of its growth; and in short, is not injured nor touched by any insect or large animals, and in durability and beauty is perhaps unequaled. It is indeed of slow growth; but this difficulty is in a great measure overcome by employing a fertile soil, and cultivating the ground about it. The branches are so completely interlaced as to be perfectly impenetrable to cattle; and from the innumerable fine prickly leaves, any attempt of boys to scale it would be next to impossible.

Monthly Genesee Farmer, 1836

Head Off Livestock with Hawthorns

The hawthorn, of all other thorns, is the best calculated for forming a good fence. The plants should, at least, be three years old, with good roots, and put down in single rows, allowing 14 inches between each plant. Such a hedge, if properly attended to, will in six years be proof against sheep and cattle; but if neglected for the first two years, much art will be required to form it afterwards into a good fence.

John Evelyn
Silva, 1777

Editor's Note: Get your hedge off to a good start by pruning the plants back to one foot tall immediately after planting. This encourages side branches to form, which you'll need for a good thick hedge. Keep the plants well watered the first year or two, and prune the tops back when they sprout up. Don't let the plants put on more than a few inches of top-growth the first two years to make sure you get enough lower branches.

Honey Locust Hedge Has Its Place

The honey locust is a hardy, vigorous tree with formidable thorns over every part of it. If well grown, we know of no other plant that would form such a complete and powerful hedge in a short time. The plants are fit for hedgerows at one year from the seed.

Genesee Farmer, 1850

Editor's Note: As *The Garden Magazine* put it in 1907, a honey locust hedge is "bull strong, horse high, and pig tight." Honey locust thorns can destroy lawn mower tires in a hurry, so use this tree as a hedge only in areas that don't require mowing.

Fierce Osage Orange Fence

In the best farm districts of Pennsylvania the progressive farmer still sticks to the osage orange fence. The Chester County farmer uses a corn knife or hook to trim the hedges. The are cut twice a year—hay time and harvest. A man can cut a mile a day.

Meehans' Monthly, 1892

Editor's Note: A corn knife looks like a wide, blunt-end sword, and a corn hook looks like a short, blunt-end scythe.

The osage orange (*Maclura pomifera*) bears one-inch-long thorns and was a widely used hedge tree before barbed wire caught on. The odd, inedible fruits have a convoluted surface that looks something like a brain.

Graceful White Pine Hedge

If one wishes to make a hedge of white pine, the ground should be trenched in the same way as it is for any other hedge, and the young plants then set out two feet apart. They will grow rapidly, and in a short time will form a hedge five or six feet in height and three or four feet wide at the base, and be an object of the greatest beauty. It needs trimming but once a year.

Helena Rutherfurd Ely
The Practical Flower Garden,
1911

Transition Trees

For protection and shelter from northerly storms, the hemlock and Norway spruce, white pine, Austrian pine, Scotch fir, etc., are very serviceable, and give an expression of comfort and security in winter not obtainable by any amount of deciduous trees. They are most expressive when kept in a manner separate from deciduous trees, still the boundary line need not be abrupt; the deciduous cypress and larches are very appropriate connecting links, combining the general conical form and outline of the evergreens with the leafless habit of the deciduous, forming a complete and pleasing whole.

The Progressive Farmer, 1855

Where to Put Windbreaks?

Almost every country home needs a windbreak of trees, the exceptions being where hills check the air currents, or a natural grove can be utilized for the purpose. In regions of low temperature, place it on the cold side of the house. In mild latitudes, place it so as to shield the premises from the most prevalent and dangerous winds.

American Agriculturist, 1895

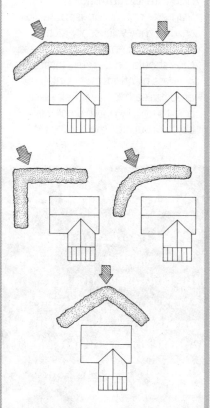

Windbreaks may take several shapes to offer the most protection. Use a long rope attached to a stake to lay out curved forms. The arrows indicate the prevailing wind.

A Tangled Hedge of Trumpet Vines

It is to be regretted that this fine vine (*Campsis radicans*) is so common and old-fashioned that no one seems to appreciate it sufficiently to bring it up to its really magnificent possibilities. When grown as a shrub, no finer plant for a hedge could possibly be desired. For this purpose the plants should be set about three feet apart, or even closer, if it is desired that the hedge should be useful as well as ornamental.

Ida D. Bennett
The Flower Garden, 1904

Editor's Note: To turn this shrubby vine into a hedge, set plants close together and keep stray branches pruned back. The traditional trumpet vine has reddish orange flowers, but if that's not your color, try the yellow variety, 'Flava'.

A Windbreak for Wide-Open Spaces

Deciduous trees of almost any quick-growing hardy variety will answer for a windbreak, but require more land than do evergreens, a grove 50 to 100 feet wide being necessary.

American Agriculturist, 1895

Editor's Note: You need more of these trees as a buffer because they lose their leaves in fall—just when you need protection from the wind.

Superior Shrubs for Your Yard

Pick the Pinkshell Azalea for Truly Pink Flowers

The only pink azalea I have ever seen that is entirely free from any suggestion of magenta is *Rhododendron vaseyi* (pinkshell azalea). The lovely species grows wild only in North Carolina, and was not discovered until long after the Civil War. It blooms more profusely than any other native species, the whole bush being covered with flowers, and it attains an extreme height of fifteen feet.

Thomas McAdam
The Garden Magazine, 1907

Handle Day-Glo Azaleas with Care

Beside a house of reddish brown was an unhappy azalea—aflame in that crimson magenta which, as far as quarrelsomeness is concerned, carries a chip on its shoulder—and not even an evergreen between to break the violence of a color effect which would almost have knocked down a Japanese gardener! Far from enjoying the blooming of the unfortunate plant, one could only be thankful when it was over.

Frances Duncan
The Joyous Art of Gardening, 1917

Editor's Note: *Meehans' Monthly* (1902) also urged caution with high-powered azaleas: "Good judgment should be exercised. Flowers will completely cover the plant with a dazzling brilliancy that in such a dwarf, compact plant has a heavy effect which does not always harmonize with its surroundings. Planted singly amongst other shrubs, they will usually please the eye at all times; but en masse they should be carefully located."

Mass plantings of bright-flowered azaleas do have their place but it's usually not in small yards. Large groups of the shrubs look good beneath pine plantings and beside ponds and lakes where the water tones down their exuberant colors.

Revive the Pearl Bush

May is the time for the blooming of the most important of our well-known flowering shrubs. But one shrub, as beautiful as any of these and as easily grown, seems to be forgotten. This is *Exochorda* x *macrantha* 'The Bride'—related to the spireas. Its pearl-like buds have earned it the name of pearl bush, but its whole lovely bloom should before now have secured it a place in every good garden.

Gertrude Jekyll
Colour in the Flower Garden, 1908

Strange But True

This peerless pink azalea is familiarly known in New England as the honeysuckle, the swamp pink, and the May apple. The latter name comes from the irregular excrescence, pale green and glaucous, growing on the leaves when stung by an insect, which there deposits its eggs. Cool, crisp, and juicy, they are the delight of children, and put for a day in spiced vinegar, make the first pickles of the year.

Martha Bockée Flint
A Garden of Simples, 1900

Editor's Note: This native azalea is now known as roseshell azalea (*Rhododendron prinophyllum*). Its pink blooms have a clovelike scent that delights gardeners from Zones 3 to 8.

A Flowering Shrub for August

Flowering shrubs that will come to one's help in mid-August are none too plentiful, so those that make a bright display are of great price; *Genista aetnensis* (Mount Etna broom) is one of the best, and for an old specimen has so many good points—among them I reckon a trunk that is a veritable tree, graceful pendant branches, slender twigs of a rich green, a delightful habit of bearing its bunches of flowers scattered evenly over the whole plant, and a delicious scent to crown it all.

E. A. Bowles
My Garden in Summer, 1914

Editor's Note: This shrub is hardy only from Zone 7 southward. Mount Etna broom looks practically leafless, but has fragrant, golden yellow flowers.

Shrubs for Poor Soil

We often hear people say their soil is so poor they cannot raise anything. This is a common excuse for bleak surroundings. The following shrubs will grow well in poor, dry soil: beach plum (*Prunus maritima*), sumac, Japanese rose (*Rosa rugosa*), woad wax (*Genista tinctoria*), sea buckthorn (*Hippophae rhamnoides*), groundsel shrub (*Baccharis halimifolia*), and laurel-leaf willow (*Salix pentandra*).

Loring Underwood
A Garden Diary and Country Home Guide, 1908

Don't Plant a Joseph's Coat of Shrubs

Far too many places are disfigured by an accumulation of abnormally colored plants, with striped or blotched or speckled foliage, and especially with foliage of those sickly yellow hues which in nursery catalogs are poetically called "golden." A single plant of this sort may often produce a pretty effect, if grouped among others of a normal tint—as a slender golden honeysuckle climbing amid others of ordinary kinds. But to mingle reds and yellows, streaks and spots, is to destroy all peacefulness and unity as well as all naturalness of effect.

Mariana Van Rensselaer
Art Out-of-Doors, 1893

Green Doesn't Always Go with Green

Even when shrubs of a normal hue are adhered to, there is still need for selection. The different shades of green should be well distributed. Each should harmonize with its immediate neighbors. A dark blue-green should not come in contact with a light and rather yellowish green; there should be a medium tint to make a transition between them. Nor does a pale grayish green harmonize well with a yellowish tinge, although against a dark blue green it may look well.

Mariana Van Rensselaer
Art Out-of-Doors, 1893

Sumac Is Super

In England, our native American sumac is highly prized and sells at high prices, just as we pay large sums for shrubs and plants from Japan and China. The leaves give it a palmlike appearance through the summer, and certainly we have nothing more gorgeous through the fall. Then, in winter, its large bunches of crimson berries give tone and color to the monotony of the outlook, and, when shown off by a background of evergreens, have almost the effect of flowers.

Eben E. Rexford
The Household, 1879

Editor's Note: The author is referring to either staghorn sumac (**Rhus typhina**) or smooth sumac (**R. glabra**). The plants are similar, but staghorn sumac has fuzzy stems and smooth sumac doesn't.

With its graceful compound leaves and dramatic crowns of red berries, staghorn sumac creates as nice a show in summer and winter as it does in fall when its leaves turn brilliant red and orange.

Perfume a Bedroom with Missouri Currant

The yellow-flowering Missouri currant is quite out of fashion and is somewhat straggly of habit, but as a perfume distillery it is not to be surpassed. It is one of the shrubs I like to plant beneath my chamber windows. It is delicious to waken to its spicy morning greeting.

Louise Beebe Wilder
The Fragrant Path, 1932

The yellow flowers of the Missouri currant (*Ribes aureum* or *R. odoratum*) will spread the scent of cloves over your yard. The leaves turn scarlet in fall.

Here's a Currant That Smells like Cloves

Ribes aureum, or Missouri currant, is an old plant, which is a high recommendation with those who look upon old plants as connoisseurs look upon old wine—nothing can surpass its fragrance when in flower.

The Progressive Farmer, 1855

Editor's Note: This native yellow-flowered shrub is also known as buffalo currant, golden currant, and Idaho buffalo currant. A related shrub that has also been called Missouri currant is now sold as either the golden or the clove currant (*Ribes odoratum*). It offers a similar clovelike scent and has larger yellow flowers.

Light Up the Night with White

One garden which I know is always associated in my mind with a little thicket, about ten feet in height, of the white-stemmed bramble (*Rubus biflorus*), which, on a moonlit evening, is a most impressive sight.

Harry Roberts
The Book of Old-Fashioned Flowers, 1904

Editor's Note: The white-stemmed bramble is a Himalayan shrub with foliage that's very pale on the underside and white canes that stand out in winter. It is also known as the whitewashed bramble or twin-flowering raspberry and bears amber or orange fruit. See "Sources" on page 316 for ordering information.

Plant Bright-Barked Shrubs for Winter Color

The quickest and cheapest way to get winter color in the city yard is to plant shrubs with brightly colored bark. Near a swamp edge you can find red-twigged dogwood (*Cornus sericea*), or the purple-barked kinnikinnick or silky dogwood (*C. amomum*). If you cannot find any plants small enough to move, take cuttings about ten inches long of these and the yellow-barked willow (*Salix alba* 'Vitellina') and put them in sand and water until they root. Then plant them in soil.

Evelyn Prince Cahoon
The Garden Magazine, 1908

Strange But True

I once heard a woman say, "If I am worried about anything I simply cannot endure the odor of box, it affects me so that I want to scream. At other times I like it."

Louise Beebe Wilder
The Fragrant Path, 1932

Editor's Note: The woman quoted is unusual in that she *sometimes* likes the odor of boxwood flowers. Most people either like the smell (or don't notice it) or hate it. Those that can't stand the scent compare it to the reek of cat urine.

Strange But True

I do by no means commend the scent of elder (European elder, <u>Sambucus nigra</u>), which is very noxious to the air. We learn that a certain house in Spain, seated among many elder trees, diseased and killed almost all the inhabitants, which, when at last the trees were grubbed up, became a very wholesome and healthy place.

John Evelyn
Silva, 1777

Editor's Note: The foliage has a disagreeable smell, and the scent of the blossoms doesn't appeal to everyone. But the black fruits of the elder are used to make wine and jelly. This elder is similar to our native tree, the American elder (*Sambucus canadensis*).

Best All-Around Spirea

Spirea x *vanhouttei* (Vanhoutte spirea) is the most useful, hardy, showy spirea, as far north as Ontario. As a single individual on the edge of a lawn, showing the graceful outlines when in bloom, it can hardly be surpassed.

John Dunbar
The Garden Magazine, 1906

Vanhoutte spirea is popular because it has showy white flowers and it's tough as nails.

Another Vote for Vanhouttei Spirea

Frequent praise is bestowed on various spireas, and in fact as a whole they are indispensable among shrubs. But it is seldom that *vanhouttei* is mentioned. In the writer's estimation—and many others would willingly concede its worth—it is the best of the shrubby spireas. The leaves have considerable resemblance to the maidenhair fern, which at once speaks favorably for it.

Meehan's Monthly, 1899

Editor's Note: Vanhouttei spirea went on to become one of the most popular spireas. This versatile plant has bluish green leaves and masses of white flowers in spring. It prefers full sun and grows 6 to 8 feet tall in Zones 3 through 8.

Can Your Yard Handle 'Anthony Waterer'?

The tyrant of spireas with flat flower clusters is 'Anthony Waterer', which came with a whoop about 1895 and has almost bullied the others out of cultivation simply because it has the deepest, and therefore the showiest, color of them all. I like crimson-purple-magentas at dusk as well as any man, for they are softened in a mellow light, but all through the long sunny day they are harsh, artificial, gaudy. Anything that has a twenty-horsepower color and blooms all summer is just the thing for small parks in big cities, but why spoil our front yards by edging the shrubbery with these spireas?

W. E. Pendleton
The Garden Magazine, 1908

This much-maligned spirea (*Spiraea* x *bumalda* 'Anthony Waterer') wasn't a passing fancy. More than a century after its introduction, it remains a garden-center standard.

Best Viburnum for Winter Berries

I have a collection of every kind of hardy viburnum but the one that cheers me most in winter is what the nurserymen call *Viburnum opulus* (European cranberrybush). There are other viburnums with red berries that last all winter but this is the only one I can afford to have in big masses. Besides, it has the largest berries.

Jabez Tompkins
The Garden Magazine, 1908

Use Gobs of Gray Leaves

To be wholly effective, these sober-hued plants should be used with a fairly lavish hand, not dotted about among gayer colors where their quiet sway would scarcely be felt. They are most effective among light-colored flowers, mauves and pinks, pale buff, and particularly with white flowers.

Louise Beebe Wilder
Colour in My Garden, 1918

Editor's Note: Many shrubby herbs such as santolina, rosemary, and rue have grayish foliage. Larger shrubs with gray leaves include Russian olive (*Elaeagnus angustifolia*), Jerusalem sage (*Phlomis fruticosa*), butterfly bush (*Buddleia davidii*), and willows such as silver willow (*Salix alba f. argentea*, also known as *S. a. 'Sericea'*), coyote willow (*S. exigua*), and rosemary willow (*S.elaeagnos*).

Caring for Shrubs

Cut Back Cut-Leaved Sumac

We know of no cut-leaved shrub or tree that, in departing from its normal condition, so effectually disguises itself as does the cut-leaf sumac. This is a form of the common smooth sumac, *Rhus glabra*, as delicate and refined in its aspect as the other is coarse and common. As a lawn plant it should always be grown with a single stem, cutting it back each fall, to get a start as near the ground as practicable; if allowed to branch, it loses much of its beauty.

American Agriculturist, 1876

Cut-leaved sumac (*Rhus glabra* 'Laciniata') leaves are deeply cut, which gives them a delicate, fernlike appearance. Come fall, bright scarlet fruits and brilliantly colored orange, red, and purple foliage make this shrub a real knockout.

Weigelas Love Water

One thing let every lover of the weigela note. Most flowers love abundant moisture, but the weigela is a perfect glutton for drink.

The Gardener's Monthly, 1877

Editor's Note: To conserve precious moisture, mulch your weigelas with chipped or shredded bark or a layer of compost.

Weigelas like plenty of water but make sure they're planted where they won't drown. Give the shrubs a well-drained site in full sun. They'll grow six to nine feet tall and at least that wide. Weigelas produce pink or red trumpetlike flowers on arching branches in May and June.

Shrubs, Fast and Slow

Separate the slow growers from the quick growers, for the former are soon crowded to death by the latter in the ordinary mixed border. The quick growers are privet, spirea, mock orange, hydrangea, golden bells (forsythia), deutzias, red-twigged dogwood—anything you can buy inexpensively. The reason you can buy them so cheaply is that they can all be easily raised from cuttings. Typical slow growers are lilacs, Japanese maple, pearl bush, Japanese redbud, dwarf horsechestnuts, and azaleas.

Louise Beebe Wilder
Colour in My Garden, 1918

Editor's Note: The pearl bush is *Exochorda racemosa*, the Japanese redbud is what we now call the Chinese redbud (*Cercis chinensis*), and dwarf horsechestnut is now known as bottlebrush buckeye (*Aesculus parviflora*).

Tip-Root Forsythias for Fountains of Flowers

The English get great masses of forsythia for landscape effect by putting a stout stick in the center of each plant, and drawing in the stems at a height of three feet or so. This allows the upper parts of the stems to reach over and take root at the tips. Thus these

shrubs layer themselves and give rise to new plants, eventually forming large colonies.

Henry Maxwell
The Garden Magazine, 1907

Creating the Natural Look

A good simple rule for the informal planting of shrubs is this: Straight rows should be avoided. A laborer or novice, when told this, will arrange the plants in a zig-zag manner, thinking that he is placing them irregularly, the result often being almost the same as that of two rows. If the group is being planted along a straight line, the distance of plants from this line ought to be somewhat as follows: two feet, four feet, five feet, three feet, one foot.

Louisa King
The Little Garden, 1921

Train the Dogwood to Stay Down

One of the most beautiful plants for massing for fall colors is the common dogwood, cut down and kept pinched low. It has a far more beautiful color than when it grows up in the normal way.

The Gardener's Monthly, 1877

Editor's Note: In fall, the leaves of the flowering dogwood (*Cornus florida*) turn shades of red, orange, and yellow. For the mass planting effect described above, prune the tops of young trees back in late winter or early spring to keep them growing bushy and low. If you don't have time for that much fussing, let your dogwoods grow naturally, and you'll get good fall color on a taller plant.

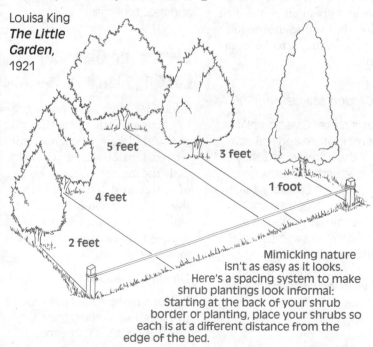

Mimicking nature isn't as easy as it looks. Here's a spacing system to make shrub plantings look informal: Starting at the back of your shrub border or planting, place your shrubs so each is at a different distance from the edge of the bed.

Bog Plants That Don't Need Wet Feet

The wild- or downy bog rosemary (*Andromeda glaucophylla*), which always has "wet feet" in native conditions, does splendidly with me in a light, sandy soil and forms a much neater shrub than I ever saw in the wild. Another plant which can be grown quite well in light, loamy, moist soil, is the leather cap or leatherleaf (*Chamaedaphne calyculata*). The one-sided spikes of nodding white flowers appear with the first warm spell of spring. Flowering a little later, and of smaller size, the Labrador tea (*Ledum groenlandicum*) usually grows in shade in sphagnum bogs. It never looks happy unless grown entirely in peat or humus and given an abundance of water, but it does not require a boggy condition to be comfortable.

John Dunbar
The Garden Magazine, 1906

Editor's Note: Give bog plants the temperature and soil conditions they prefer, and they can thrive without growing directly in water. Labrador tea, for example, prefers a cool, moist, acidic site. Though it grows native in swamps, you can also satisfy this plant's needs in spots that are drier, like a wooded site with moist, acidic soil.

Cut Old Hedges in Half

If you have the courage of your convictions you can restore that ragged arborvitae hedge of yours to density and symmetry by cutting it back severely. A ten-foot arborvitae hedge that is bare at the base can be cut back to five feet, and new branches will come right out of the hard old wood. Is there any other evergreen hedge of which you can say this?

The Garden Magazine, 1908

Editor's Note: Actually, yews (*Taxus* spp.) can take as drastic pruning as arborvitaes (*Thuja* spp.). But the author is on the right track: Most evergreens can't take such severe pruning. When you're stuck with an old overgrown hedge made up of either of these evergreens, hard pruning can make them bushy and beautiful again.

Encourage Oleander Cuttings with Oats

Oleander slips may be rooted by cutting a little slit in the end of the slip, large enough to put an oat kernel in; put the slip with the kernel in it in a bottle of water and hang it up in a shady place. Soon little rootlets will appear, and it may then be planted in earth without removing the oats.

Farm Journal, 1884

Editor's Note: It's actually not the oats, but keeping the slit in the cutting open that encourages rooting. If you don't have any oats handy, you can substitute any other oat-size seed.

Oleanders (*Nerium oleander*) are southern shrubs that are hardy only in Zones 8 through 10. They produce pink, red, or white flowers in summer and fall on 6- to 12-foot-tall plants.

Buy, Don't Steal, Mountain Laurels

The urgent appeals of the wildflower preservation societies for the protection of the laurel should be heeded by every admirer of American plants and American scenery. Even the little seedlings, which transplant readily, should be left undisturbed, in the hope that they may survive the depredations of the wild-flower Huns. Nurserygrown plants are always of better habit than plants taken from the wild and much more floriferous.

Herbert Durand
Wild Flowers and Ferns, 1925

Editor's Note: The laurel or mountain laurel (*Kalmia latifolia*) has glossy evergreen leaves. It was particularly popular as a Christmas green, which may explain why people so eagerly gathered it from the wild. There are so many beautiful mountain laurel varieties available from nurseries that there's no reason to look for plants in the wild. You can choose pink-, red-, or white-flowered varieties to decorate your yard.

Tough Love for Lilacs

It is utterly useless to cut small sprays from declining lilacs and expect the plants to bloom. They will start out bravely but will soon droop. With the lilac I always cut off a whole bush at the ground, and have yet to fail in having a wealth of exquisite bloom.

Gertrude L. Whitlock
The Garden Magazine, 1906

Editor's Note: Lilacs bloom on new wood, so you'll get more flowers if you cut out large, old branches and let new branches sprout. Healthy shrubs will come back after being cut as Whitlock advises, but older shrubs need a kinder, gentler approach. For these, prune out one-third of the biggest branches each year.

Choosing and Using Vines

Look for the Very Best Clematis

The most wonderful of them all, to me at least, is *Clematis* 'Henryi'. I saw it but once, and yet each recurring memory of it has a thrill. It was in a garden beside a border of blue flowers. A *Clematis* 'Henryi' had flung a branch of great star-shaped white blossoms over a balustrade.

Elsa Rehman
Garden-Making, 1926

Editor's Note: *Clematis* 'Henryi' has stood the test of time. It's still a favorite of gardeners and is widely available at nurseries and through mail-order catalogs.

Give Passionflowers Plenty of Space

Passionflowers (*Passiflora* spp.) are best adapted for large structures; in small greenhouses close pruning becomes necessary, and the plants consequently cannot develop their true characters.

Peter Henderson
Henderson's Handbook of Plants, 1890

Warm the Passionflower with a Wall

The hardy passionflower, *Passiflora caerulea*, from its beauty and distinctness, deserves to be grown wherever the climate permits. It is not so suitable for arbors or trellises as for walls; the heat from the walls aids in ripening the wood, and so enables it to withstand the winter. A southern aspect is best for it.

William Robinson
The English Flower Garden, 1883

Editor's Note: The hardy passionflower is also known as the blue passionflower. This tender tropical vine is hardy only in Zones 8 to 10, but you can grow an equally pretty passionflower, called the maypop (*Passiflora incarnata*), as far north as Zone 5.

Passiflora caerulea is an evergreen vine native to Brazil. It has to be coddled with mulch and protective coverings to make it through a temperate winter.

Don't Fear the Creeper

For some reason, perhaps because of its climbing habit and its inappropriate popular name of American ivy, the Virginia creeper is often feared as something poisonous. It climbs a tree trunk somewhat as does the poison ivy, but is easily distinguished and is entirely harmless. One should remember that the Virginia creeper has five fingerlike leaflets that are suggestive of the fact that one's own five fingers can safely handle it; while the poison ivy has but three.

Charles S. Newhall
The Vines of Eastern North America, 1897

According to the *Vick's Catalogue* for 1884, "the cultivation of the simple Virginia creeper has done more to beautify American villages and rural homes than any fifty plants in existence."

Strange But True

The rapid growth of the kudzu vine created at the time great astonishment. But we have very little doubt but that if the hop vine were given a fair opportunity to compete in growth with our kudzu visitor from Japan, it would show quite as admirable a record.

Meehans' Monthly, 1897

Editor's Note: Patriotic pride must have influenced the editors at *Meehans'*. Our hop vine is no match for the aggressive kudzu, as we learned in the century that followed.

A Kiwi for You (and Your Cat)

A species of kiwi, *Actinidia polygama* (silver vine), has leaves at the ends of the growing shoots that change on the upper surface to a glistening white, making it a most strikingly beautiful vine. Cats are especially fond of it, and protection of wire netting needs to be put up to keep them from tearing the vines in pieces.

Samuel T. Maynard
Landscape Gardening as Applied to Home Decoration, 1899

Editor's Note: Male plants have the prettier leaves, but you'll need to grow female silver vine too if you want a crop of small, edible, greenish yellow fruit. The flowers are creamy white and sweetly scented. Young plants may not show their silvery coloring until they mature, so keep the cat away until the plants are well established. The leaves do contain a compound similar to that in catnip.

Make a Hedge of Matrimony Vine

The matrimony vine (*Lycium halimifolium*) is hardier than the privet, a richer green, and bears brilliant scarlet fruits in winter. After a few years of pruning and training it is self-supporting. The leaves appear earlier in the spring than do those of the privet. The plants stand trimming excellently, the foliage and flowers being greatly increased thereby.

Aldred Scott Warthin
The Garden Magazine, 1908

Editor's Note: The matrimony vine is more of a trailing shrub than a vine. To train the plant into a hedge, support it on an arbor or fence. Prune back wayward branches to create the shape you want.

This Jasmine's a Star

It is to be regretted that some flowers, which would be household pets, are burdened with very hard names. One of these is the *Trachelospermum jasminoides*. As a pot or tub plant for the decoration of summer gardens, few things are more acceptable; and in the South, where it is free from frost, or nearly so, it is one of the most desirable of hardy climbers. The white, waxy flowers have a delicious odor.

Meehans' Monthly, 1898

Editor's Note: This twining vine has picked up a few common names since 1898, including confederate jasmine and star jasmine. Give it moist soil, a shady site, and a trellis, and this plant will quickly form a screen. In Zone 9 star jasmine can reach 30 feet tall, but you can keep it in bounds in warm or cool climates by growing it in pots. Where it's hardy, star jasmine makes an attractive groundcover if you cut the tips back a couple of times a year to encourage branching.

A Native Bittersweet that's No Longer Neglected

I have never understood why persons of excellent taste should neglect our native vines. A very desirable vine is the American bittersweet (*Celastrus scandens*). It has beautiful, bright foliage, which is seldom infested with insects. During the later part of the season its clusters of scarlet berries, enclosed in orange husks, which part and disclose the fruit within, are showy enough to suit anyone. These berries hang on all winter if the birds let them alone. For verandas and porches, the bittersweet is quite equal to the Virginia creeper, and that is high praise.

Eben E. Rexford
American Agriculturist, 1884

Editor's Note: The American bittersweet wasn't neglected for long. It disappeared from parts of its range because it was so aggressively gathered by commercial nurseries.

Place this vigorous vine where it won't get out of control. Fences and dead trees make good choices for it to climb on since bittersweet can choke living trees and shrubs. You'll need both a male and a female plant if you want to grow the attractive fruits. When you buy American bittersweet, make sure you don't confuse it with oriental bittersweet (*Celastrus orbiculatos*), which is an even more rampant grower.

A Natural Veranda

A strong plant of Dutchman's-pipe (*Aristolochia durior*) or Virginia creeper run up on a tree trunk about ten feet high, and then carried in a festoon across to another tree, makes a novel and pleasing object in a garden. A wire must be stretched across from tree to tree to support the vine at first.

Elias A. Long
Ornamental Gardening for Americans, 1884

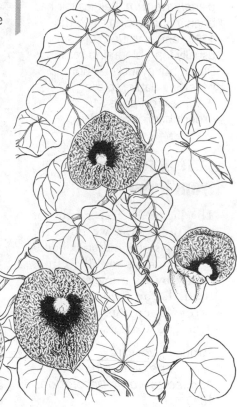

Dutchman's-pipe is a traditional climbing vine for shading and ornamenting porches. The plant gets its name from the curious pipe-shaped flowers it produces.

Longest-Blooming Honeysuckle

The Belgian or Dutch honey-suckle has the longest season of bloom. It begins in early spring and lasts all summer. Frequently its beautiful fragrant pink or reddish flowers can be gathered as late as December in the South. It is of vigorous growth and may also be grown as a shrub.

The Garden Magazine, 1908

Editor's Note: This variety of honeysuckle is also known as Dutch woodbine (*Lonicera periclymenum* 'Belgica'). It has been in cultivation since the 1700s and is valued for its un-usually long blooming season. Dutch honeysuckle is not widely available, so see "Sources" on page 316 for ordering information.

Boston Ivy Is Far from Home

The Japanese creeper is by far the finest vine we have for covering stone and brick build-ings. It grows rapidly, clings firmly by its numerous disk-tendrils, and does not run across openings formed by doors and windows.

Samuel T. Maynard
Landscape Gardening as Applied to Home Decoration, 1899

Editor's Note: Japanese creeper (*Parthenocissus tricuspidata*) is usually called

Boston ivy, despite the fact that it's native to Japan and China. Its shiny leaves turn bright red in fall, and birds like the blue berries that appear in summer. This vine grows in Zones 4 to 8 and can reach 60 feet tall if it has a large enough wall or tree to climb. Japanese creeper is a tough vine that tolerates most soils, wind, pollution, and sunny or shady sites.

When you want a leafy wall cov-ering that's not as dense as the standard Japanese creeper or Boston ivy (*Parthenocissus tricus-pidata*) shown here, try the small-leaved varieties 'Veitchii' and 'Lowii'. They don't grow as vigorously as the species, and their leaves are purplish when they're young.

Best Flowering Vine for Commuters

For the busy suburbanite, who is away from his home during the day, and whose only mo-ments of gardening are in the early morning or the evening, the moonflower (*Ipomoea alba*) is especially good. The great, saucerlike, white blossoms, six inches across, open in the evening and stay open all night or until the direct sunlight strikes them.

William C. McCollom
Vines and How to Grow Them, 1911

The moonflower is a tender perennial vine, but you can grow it as an annual in northern areas. Start seeds indoors in early spring to get a head start on the growing season. This vine will grow in sun or partial shade and can reach eight to ten feet tall. The large, showy blossoms smell somewhat like cloves. If you'd like to plant other evening-blooming flowers with the moonflower, try the yellow-flowered evening primroses (*Oenothera* spp.).

Choose Vines That Suit Your Color Scheme

The color of the house is a matter of which, in planting, the gardener should take notice.

For a House of White Clapboards with Green Shutters:
 Wild grape
 Wisteria
 Roses—'Debutante' (a pink-blooming rambler) or Wichuraiana (a long-blooming, white-flowered creeper)

If the House Is of Red Brick
 Wisteria
 English ivy (if south of New York)
 Sweet autumn clematis (*Clematis maximowicziana*, also offered as *C. paniculata*)
 Fruit trees grown against the walls

Against a House of Colonial Yellow
 Wild grape
 Actinidia or kiwi (a peculiarly rich green)
 American bittersweet (*Celastrus scandens*)
 Clematis

The Small Frame House Painted Dark Red
 Actinidia or kiwi
 Boston ivy or Japanese creeper
 Japanese honeysuckle (*Lonicera japonica* 'Halliana')

The House of Unstained Shingles
 Prairie rose (a pink, late-flowering American native)
 Virginia creeper
 Boston ivy or Japanese creeper

Frances Duncan
The Joyous Art of Gardening, 1917

Flowering vines are gorgeous, but not every one will complement the color of your house. Some devoted gardeners change the color of their trim or their entire house to suit the shade of a favorite flower. It's easier to match the plant to the house color, though. Here, clematis vines cloak a traditional porch. The most common clematis colors are shades of purple that go well with pale-colored paints.

Decorate Shrubs with Flowering Vines

Often stiff, unbroken masses of rhododendrons and evergreen flowering shrubs will be more varied if delicate flakes of clematis (white, lavender, or claret red) or the bright arrows of the flame nasturtium come among them here and there in autumn.

William Robinson
The English Flower Garden, 1883

Editor's Note: Clematis is a well-behaved vine that won't smother shrubs. You can train the vine to grow over shrubs so its flowers add color to an otherwise green scene.

Shades of Gray Set Off Clematis

Clematis is particularly effective when massed upon the walls of a house that is painted a color that well sets off the peculiarly rich color of the blossoms—a soft gray color affording a beautiful background for the rich purple of the most commonly seen clematis.

Webb Connell
American Agriculturist, 1895

Editors Note: If your house does not happen to be gray, select a clematis of a different color. With red, white, and blue varieties to choose from, you can match this vine to any paint color.

Up against the Wall

I have a lantana at the corner of my house which I wished to spread over the two walls and flatten against them. I nailed loops of cloth to the wall, ran a piece of white grocer's twine through it, hitched one end to a branch of the vine and the other to an old horseshoe—not too heavy as the vine is very fragile. I have several of these slings in use and they slowly, gently, and continuously train the vine to the desired position.

W. C. Woolworth
The Garden Magazine, 1907

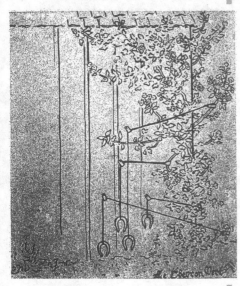

Lantana is hardy only in Zone 8 and south, but you can use Woolworth's training system for hardier vines. If horseshoes are too heavy for weights or too hard to find, use clay flower pots to pull your vine into shape. Protect the vine's stems from the twine with loops of cloth or panty hose.

Old-Time Wisdom

Keep an eye on those clockwise plants. The hop vine will start twining with the sun, as the hands of a watch travel. Though this would seem the more natural, the majority of twining vines twine in the opposite direction, from left to right. The common morning glory is one of them, the bean another.

William C. McCollom
Vines and How to Grow Them, 1911

Stash Your Trash behind a Vine

Set two posts firmly in the ground, one on each side of the can and close to the fence. Let their tops be slightly higher than the top of the can. Make the soil at the base of one of these posts deep and rich. With the can in place between these posts, fasten some common galvanized poultry netting (chicken wire), whose width is equal to the height of the can, to one post. When securely fastened, bend the netting around the front of the can until the second post is reached, and cut off the surplus netting at this point.

In the second post, screw three or four hooks and over these loop the meshes of the netting. At the base of the first post set a good plant of Hall's honeysuckle (*Lonicera japonica* 'Halliana'). Within a season the barrel can be completely screened by training the strongest shoots horizontally on the netting.

The Garden Magazine, 1907

Editor's Note: This screen idea is a good one as long as you use a less aggressive plant. Hall's honeysuckle grows so vigorously that it's become a nuisance in many areas. Try hiding your trash behind a clematis vine or a less vigorous honeysuckle like *Lonicera japonica* var. *chinensis* (also known as *repens*).

With a wire panel for support, a flowering vine can hide your trash cans and almost anything else in sight.

Weeping Trees Make Graceful Trellises

Instead of trusting to wire and ugly posts or the many artificial ways for supporting climbers, why should we not do as many Italians and people of South Europe do, and use living trees to carry the vine or climber? Weeping trees of graceful leaf and form might be used in this way with fine effect—the weeping cherry, weeping aspen, some willows even, and any light-leaved weeping tree would be charming for its own sake as well as for what it might carry.

William Robinson
The English Flower Garden, 1883

Editor's Note: The weeping cherry Robinson refers to is probably the weeping Higan cherry (*Prunus subhirtella* var. *pendula*), and the weeping aspen is most likely *Populus tremuloides* var. *pendula*.

Bring a Dead Shrub Back to Life

For the lover of something very frail and delicate (but still not at the expense of beauty), I recommend the Allegheny vine (*Adlumia fungosa*). It is a great favorite of mine, especially for planting beside a dead shrub over which it will quickly clamber, covering the eyesore with its delicate foliage, which is similar to that of the florists'

maidenhair fern. Its pretty pale pink flowers are produced freely, giving a tone and effect hard to reproduce. Though the Allegheny vine is a twiner, it is a weakling and requires a little attention at all times to keep it properly trained on any object. Give a good, sunny location and light (yet well-enriched) soil, and this vine will grow to a height of fifteen feet, forming perfectly fairylike festoons of flowers and foliage.

William C. McCollom
The Garden Magazine, 1907

Editor's Note: This vine may self-sow from year to year if it's happy with its location. Semi-shade is a better bet than the full sun that McCollom recommends. Commercial sources are hard to find, but the Allegheny vine is still available. See "Sources" on page 316 for ordering information.

In the wild, you'll find Allegheny vines cloaking bushes, and you can use them in the same way to decorate your yard. The pale pink flowers show a family resemblance to bleeding hearts.

Deck the House with Wild Grape Vine

I have found this to be the most practical, inexpensive, and effective way of decorating a frame house. The vine can be led anywhere over the house by means of small staples. It does not lift the boards, and as the leaves fold over each other in such a way as to exclude moisture, the house remains dry instead of becoming damp. The only care a wild grape requires is being cut back and trained whenever the growth becomes too dense.

Galen B. Royer
The Garden Magazine, 1909

Editor's Note: Lead the wild grape vine about by fastening it to your house with large electrician's staples. These staples are sturdy and are made for hammering into wood.

Vines Give Grace to Old Trees

Give every old tree a vine to comfort its old age.

Barbara
The Garden, You, and I, 1910

Editor's Note: As old trees decline, vines can fill in the gaps where branches are missing. Try decorating an old apple tree with a rambling rose, or train a clematis vine up an aging sugar maple. Avoid vines like oriental bittersweet (*Celastrus orbicalatus*), which is so vigorous it could smother a tree.

Crowning Glory

Nothing adds more to the beauty of an occasional tree than the tall canopy of verdure with which it is often crowned by the wild grape vine. They often completely overhang the head of the tree, falling like ample drapery around on every side, until they sweep the ground. We have seen very beautiful effects produced in this way by the grape in its wild state, and it may be easily imitated.

Andrew Jackson Downing
Landscape Gardening, 1859

Caring for Vines

Set Vines a Little Low

Most vines should be planted a trifle deeper than they were in the nursery, as this induces them to throw up from the roots suckers which are usually more promising than the wood the plants have when you get them. The only exception to this rule of deep planting is in the case of grafted stock.

William C. McCollom
Vines and How to Grow Them, 1911

Quick and Slow Vines Make Perfect Partners

Since all permanent vines require two years or more to make a tall growth, I should intersperse some annual vines.

Evelyn Prince Cahoon
The Garden Magazine, 1908

Editor's Note: Annual vines such as nasturtiums and black-eyed Susan vines (*Thunbergia alata*) make good temporary fillers while slower-growing perennial vines like climbing hydrangeas (*Hydrangea anomala* subsp. *petiolaris*) get established.

Give Climbing Vines a Boost

Some vines seem reluctant to climb, even when planted alongside a suitable place to ascend. What they need is encouragement; they must be tacked or tied up closely to the object. Such lack of encouragement will often result in dwarfed growth; the plants will sprawl around helplessly till they feel something erect upon which they may have support. Therefore, give the vines support immediately after they are planted, even though they appear too small to need it.

Meehans' Monthly, 1902

Put Off House Painting until Fall

If there are vines growing on the house and it needs painting, you will take the risk of killing them if painting is done in the spring. The best time for this operation is in early November, when vines may be laid down and returned to their old location after paint has dried.

Loring Underwood
A Garden Diary and Country Home Guide, 1908

Do-It-Yourself Wisteria Tree

The wisteria can be made to assume a tree form and be self supporting where it is not wanted upon a building. Set out a thrifty plant, and the next year cut it back to four buds. Each of these will make a thrifty growth, which can be twined around each other and tied to a stake four feet high the following spring. Keep the top pinched into shape for two or three years, when the stake can be removed.

Farm Journal, 1885

Editor's Note: A thrifty plant is one that's growing vigorously.

The wisteria vine needs strong support unless you train it into a tree form.

Pinch Buds to Spare Time

I save a good deal of pruning in autumn by nipping off superfluous buds and tender shoots during the summer from vines and bushes.

Abner Hollingsworth
Farm Journal, 1885

Take Tender Vines Underground

Some people take down their vines in autumn, wrap them in burlap, and then put them back against the building. Very tender vines, such as the Indian jessamine or a climbing La France rose, had better be taken down and buried.

W. C. McCollom
The Garden Magazine, 1908

Editor's Note: McCollom's Indian jessamine is most likely *Jasminum sambac* (Arabian jasmine). This climbing shrub comes from India and has fragrant flowers used for making jasmine tea. It cannot stand frost and is hardy only in southern Florida and Texas. 'La France' rose is an old, pale pink hybrid tea that is very fragrant. It is hardy to Zone 5.

Grow Jasmine for Winter Flowers

The winter jasmine, *Jasminum nudiflorum*, is very easy to propagate by laying some of the branches along the ground and

covering them with earth. In six or seven months they will have made good root, and can be taken up and planted where desired.

Marie Theresa Villiers Earle
More Pot-Pourri from a Surrey Garden, 1899

Editor's Note: This spreading shrub puts out bright yellow, scentless flowers as early as January in warm climates. It is hardy to Zone 5.

Tree, Shrub, and Vine Crafts

Sugar Maple Spring Preview

The blossoms of the sugar maple (*Acer saccharum*) provide one of the earliest wild scents of the year. A few twigs brought into a warm room fill it with a keen springlike fragrance. (It is only at a certain moment of their development that the small crimson blossoms are gifted with fragrance; as they age they give off a rather stale odor.)

Louise Beebe Wilder
The Fragrant Path, 1932

Branch Bouquets

A new idea in house decoration: six-foot branches laden with

flowers. In February in a city flat, when one is weary of winter and spring seems drearily far off, a bunch of glowing red maples in full bloom is a pleasant, comforting, and reassuring sight. For those who love old-fashioned, common things, nothing will give more pleasure than the flowering currant (*Ribes odoratum*) with its spicy yellow flowers. Even the garden currants—especially the black—are interesting. Forsythia is the earliest and easiest. Magnolia buds are fascinating in their gray-green calyx, even if never more than a glimpse of pink is seen.

In cutting twigs from fruit trees, select the full, round buds. They are the flower buds; the slender, more pointed ones being leaf buds.

Laura French Mordaunt
The Gardener's Magazine, 1906

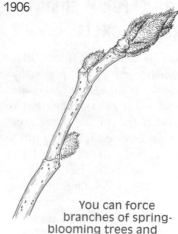

You can force branches of spring-blooming trees and shrubs from mid-January on. Cut branches on a mild day, choosing limbs with fat buds since those are the flower buds. Crush the bottom ends of the branches and place them in water immediately. The buds should open up within two to six weeks.

Long-Lasting Hardwood Bouquets

Flowers of trees and shrubs and everything hardwooded, such as lilacs, guelder roses (*Viburnum opulus* 'Roseum'), spireas, and cluster roses, should always have the cut end so treated as to enable it to take up the water more readily. This is best done by slitting up the stem for some distance, or by the easier though rather less effective means of slicing one side, or tearing up a ribbon of the bark for an inch or two, but not removing it.

Gertrude Jekyll
Home and Garden, 1900

Editor's Note: By cluster roses, Jekyll probably means any roses that produce sprays of flowers, such as floribundas.

Turn Shrub Prunings into Bouquets

Because forsythia, spirea, lilac, bush honeysuckle, *Philadelphus* (mock orange), weigela, and viburnum all flower on the wood of the previous year, great care should be taken to prune them only after they have bloomed. The best way to prune (for a double result) is to use as many flowering branches as possible while the shrub is in full beauty with flowers. Thus, wholesome cutting is accomplished and the pleasure joined to it of flowers for your rooms, or of giving them to others.

Louisa King
The Little Garden, 1921

Boil Bayberries for Sweet-Scented Candles

Candles of bayberry wax impart a delightful odor to the room in which they are burned and are particularly fragrant after being extinguished. The greenish-colored wax from which they are made is collected from the drupes or berries of the bayberry or wax myrtle (*Myrica cerifera*) by boiling them, the wax rising to the top of the water where it can be skimmed off. The berries may be gathered any time after September first. A bushel of berries will yield between four and five pounds of wax.

To make the candles, suspend the wicks from an iron ring over a large basin containing the liquid wax, and ladle the wax over the wicks. The candles are taken down when the proper thickness has been acquired and rolled out on a table, or slab of marble, and are then cut and trimmed in the regulation way. When making these candles by hand, the wax is kept in hot water and applied to the hanging wick by successive ladlings.

An easier way to make these is to use candle molds. The wick is suspended in the center of the mold and the wax is poured in until the mold is filled.

Phineas Nolte
The Garden Magazine, 1908

Editor's Note: The wax myrtle (*Myrica cerifera*) is hardy only from Zones 7 to 9, but that doesn't mean you can't make candles farther north. Grow the northern bayberry (*M. pensylvanica*) in Zones 2 to 6 for berries with the same wonderful fragrance as the wax myrtle. Even if you don't make use of the berries from these shrubs, the birds will. Birds usually feed on the berries late in the year, which gives you time to enjoy the fruit display before it's gobbled up.

A Pinecone Pet

Take a saucer and fill it with fresh green moss. Place in the center a pine cone, large size, having first wet it thoroughly. Then sprinkle it thoroughly with grass seed. The moisture will close the cone partially, and in a day or two the tiny grass spires will appear in the interstices, and in a week you will have a perfect cone of beautiful verdure. Keep secure from the frost, and give it plenty of water, and you will have a "thing of beauty" all the winter.

C. H. Fowler, D.D., LL.D., and W. H. De Puy, A.M., D.D.
Home and Health and Home Economics, 1879

Editor's Note: Did you think Chia pets were a modern invention? Here's proof that there's nothing really new under the sun. Place your pinecone pet in a sunny window, and let the grass grow until it flowers for a long-lasting and easy-care decoration. If you'd like to know what this grassy cone looks like, see the illustration on page 264.

Rocky Ground Grows Good Walking Sticks

Ash walking sticks are specially grown with a natural handle in this way. Beneath the soil of the plantation lies an immense bed of slate. The young saplings encounter this on their downward growth and, being arrested in their development, turn off in a new direction at right angles. The roots are turned into handles; the tops become the bottoms.

Pall Mall Gazette and Globe, 1897

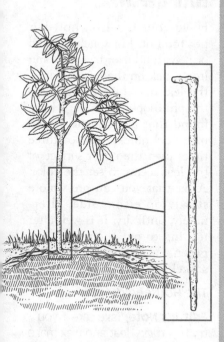

There are other ways to get walking sticks than growing them above a bed of rock. Check nearby woods for branches with nearly right angles. It may take a while to find the perfect stick, but you'll have some enjoyable walks while you're hunting.

Straighten Out a Walking Stick

Straightening sticks is done by tying a heavy weight to the lower end, and a rope or strong cord to the head, and lowering the stick in a well or pool of water deep enough to cover it. When perfectly straight, lay them to dry, when the final polishing with sandpaper, linseed oil applied with a woolen cloth, and last of all, a coat of shellac, will bring out the natural beauty of the wood. Undressed sticks are brought across the ocean tied to the rear and lower parts of vessels. They drag or trail in the saltwater and are made hard and as straight as an arrow by the continued resistance against the water.

Vick's Family Magazine, 1902

Editor's Note: Unless you're making walking sticks for a living, you can probably find all you need in the woods. Ash and oak sticks are sturdy and attractive, but you'll get plenty of use from any hardwood stick.

Grow an Oak Tree above the Fireplace

A very pretty mantel ornament may be obtained by suspending an acorn, by a piece of thread tied around it, within half an inch of the surface of some water contained in a vase, tumbler, or saucer, and allowing it to remain undisturbed for several weeks. It will soon burst open, and small roots will seek the water; a straight and tapering stem with beautiful, glossy green leaves, will shoot upward, and present a very pleasing appearance.

C. H. Fowler, D.D., LL.D., and W. H. De Puy, A.M., D.D. *Home and Health and Home Economics*, 1879

Flat Fungus Makes a Natural Shelf

Tree fringe, or "bracket toadstool," as they are sometimes called, make very pretty wall ornaments. They are usually a soft, velvety brown, with a flat surface which makes a good shelf, but should only hold appropriate ornaments—"woodsy" things, such as a mossy branch with one or two butterflies on it, or some twigs with red berries, or some fine lacy ferns, and not too much of anything.

Farm Journal, 1885

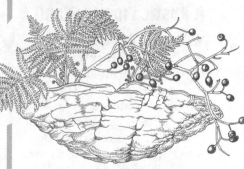

You can use a shelf fungus as a small display shelf. Drive small nails through the corky base to anchor it to a stud in the wall.

Plant a Turnip "Pot" with Flowering Vines

Take a large turnip and scrape out the inside, leaving a thick wall all around. Fill the cavity with earth, and plant in it some clinging vine or morning-glory. Suspend the turnip with cords, and in a little time the vines twine around the strings, and the turnip, sprouting from below, will put forth leaves and stems that will turn upward and gracefully curl around the base.

C. H. Fowler, D.D., LL.D., and W. H. De Puy, A.M., D.D.
Home and Health and Home Economics, 1879

Magnolia Messages

The beautiful broad white petals give a snowy surface for messages or valentines, which are written with a pin, when the letters turn dark brown.

Alice Morse Earle
Old-Time Gardens, 1901

A Rustic Flower Stand

Walks of children in the woods can be made interesting by their bringing home material for rustic work (crafts). Different-colored twigs and sprays of tree, such as the bright scarlet of the red-osier dogwood, the yellow of the willow, the black of the birch, and the silvery gray of the poplar, may be combined in a fanciful network. For this sort of work no other investment is needed than a hammer and an assortment of different-sized tacks (nails), and beautiful results will be produced. Here is a stand for flowers, made of roots, scraped and varnished.

Catherine E. Beecher and Harriet Beecher Stowe
The American Woman's Home, 1869

Editor's Note: If you'll be leaving the bark on the branches you use for crafts, gather them when the trees are dormant—that is, when the leaves are off in winter. Otherwise, the bark will be more likely to peel away.

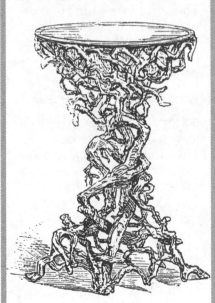

You can build rustic furniture like this by joining interesting branches together with small nails. Bend over any protruding nail points with light blows of a hammer until they're flush with the surface.

Dogwood Skewers for Cookouts

Dogwood makes the best skewers, because it does not taint the flesh.

John Evelyn
Silva, 1777

Editor's Note: For an impromptu cookout, cut skewers from a red-osier dogwood (*Cornus sericea*). The branches are straight as arrows and won't flavor your hot dogs.

Preserving Leaves with Beeswax

Have your flat-iron hot, but not too hot. Just touch the end of it with a bit of beeswax, and iron quick on the bright side of the leaf first. I cannot tell you the philosophy of it, but I have found that passing the waxed iron very quickly two or three times over the upper surface of the leaf seems to set the color. After that you can press more slowly on either side, alternately, until dry. It is well after ironing to put them away between papers under pressure for a week or two.

The Household, 1887

Editor's Note: Take care if you try this trick. Heat and wax make a dangerous mix. Start with medium heat, and turn the temperature up slowly, if necessary. For a safer method, dip your leaves in wax as described in the tip on the opposite page.

Wax Dip Keeps Leaf Colors Bright

Autumn leaves may be easily preserved and retain their natural tints, or nearly so, by either of the following methods: As they are gathered they may be laid between the leaves of a magazine until the book is full, and left with a light weight upon them until the moisture of the leaves has been absorbed; two or three thicknesses of paper should intervene between the leaves. If the leaves are large or in clusters, take newspapers, lay them on a shelf and use in the same manner as above.

Then dip the leaves into melted wax (such as is used for molding fruits, etc.), into which you will have to put a few drops of turpentine and lay upon newspapers to harden perfectly. This will make the leaves pliable and natural, and give sufficient gloss. Great care should be taken that the wax is of the right temperature. This can be ascertained by the first leaf which is dipped in. Draw out gently over the pan both sides of the leaf and hold it up by the stem. If the wax is too hot, the leaf will shrivel—if too cool, it will harden in lumps on the leaf.

Another method is to iron each leaf with a middling hot iron until the moisture is all out of them. These are best without varnish.

The Successful HouseKeeper, 1882

A Frieze of Leaves

The prettiest and most effective part of my work was arranging various colored leaves about the room. I had a very nice collection of them. In each corner of the room, about a foot down from the ceiling, I secured with small tacks a row of rich-hued leaves, fastened together with pins. The pins will not show, being up so high.

Nellie W.
The Household, 1882

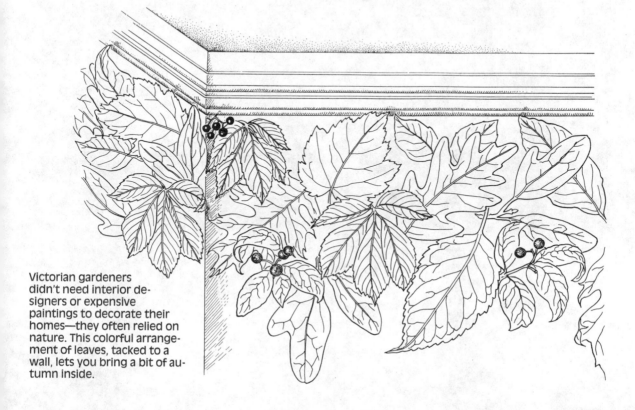

Victorian gardeners didn't need interior designers or expensive paintings to decorate their homes—they often relied on nature. This colorful arrangement of leaves, tacked to a wall, lets you bring a bit of autumn inside.

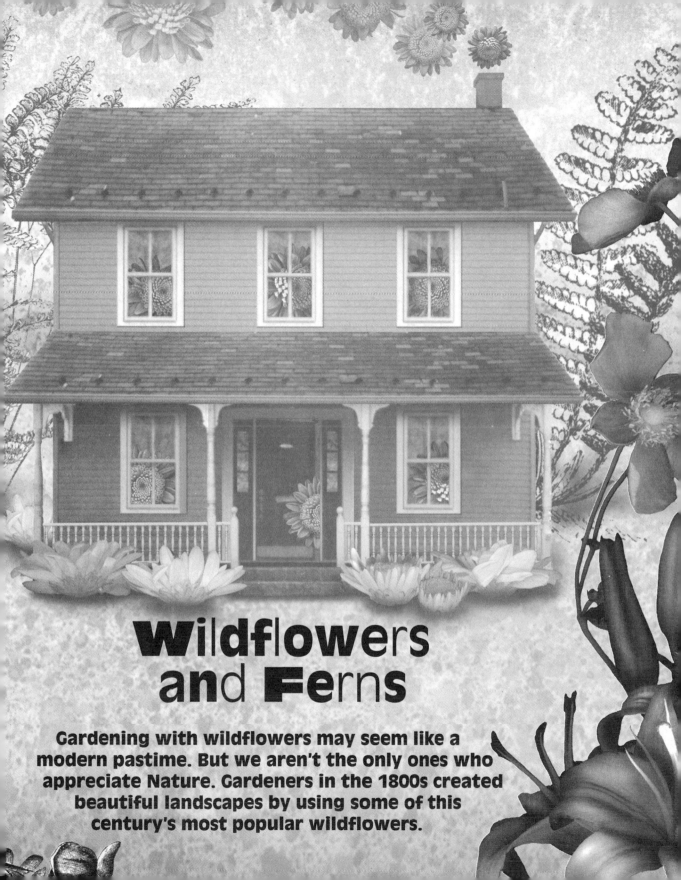

Wildflowers and Ferns

Gardening with wildflowers may seem like a modern pastime. But we aren't the only ones who appreciate Nature. Gardeners in the 1800s created beautiful landscapes by using some of this century's most popular wildflowers.

Wildflowers and Ferns

Wildflower Gardening

Put Wild Plants in Tame Sites

It is a common but mistaken impression that wild plants are inherently scraggly and unattractive in form. The fact is that if they are relieved of the intense competition that prevails in the wild and given room to develop in a congenial location, they quickly make luxurious growth, become compact and shapely, and produce larger and better flowers in greater profusion.

Herbert Durand
Wild Flowers and Ferns, 1925

Wildflowers by the Dozen

Wild gardening deals only with colonies, not single plants. Never plant less than a dozen of a kind.

Thomas McAdam
The Garden Magazine, 1908

Born Free

Not all wild flowers seem to me appropriate for garden decoration. I cannot bear to see the cardinal flower in captivity and feel that all its wild soul must be reaching out and yearning for the seclusion of the shaded stream sides, and the freedom of the wild world. No one, I believe, has yet been able to take the free spirit of the fringed gentian.

Louise Beebe Wilder
Colour in My Garden, 1918

Editor's Note: Twentieth-century gardeners tend to look at wildflowers as invited guests rather than captives. Cardinal flowers (*Lobelia cardinalis*) in particular have become extremely popular. There's even a variety available called 'Royal Robe', which has ruby red flowers. (See "Sources" on page 316 for ordering information.) The fringed gentian (*Gentianopsis crinita*) is another story. It's a biennial that's likely to die if moved from the moist, acidic meadow soils where it grows wild.

Asters for American Gardens

We seldom prize that which we can get easily. There are few more beautiful flowers than are comprised in our troop of native asters, and yet how rarely do we find them admitted to our gardens? In the Old World, it is getting quite common to have what are known as aster gardens, mostly made up from forms common and well known in our country.

One objection would be that the aster garden presents but little attraction until after midsummer, as none of them bloom at all until after that date. But the skill of the good gardener can be called in, and so arrange that there would be something especially attractive during every month of the year.

Meehans' Monthly, 1897

Editor's Note: You can stretch an aster garden's bloom season by adding white wood aster (*Aster divaricatus*) to it. Its star-like white flowers appear in early summer and continue into fall.

A "Wild" Planting Scheme

Many plants cannot be grown in our climate when exposed to cold, dry winds. If these plants were set in the borders of blackberry patches, or among similar wild bushes, they would do well. The chrysanthemum, which is often killed outright in our open borders, would live out safely in such wild clumps as these.

The Gardener's Monthly, 1876

Be Kind to Bloodroot

Why does one so seldom see good patches of *Sanguinaria canadensis* (bloodroot)? It seems to ask nothing more than planting and leaving alone, but I rather expect suffers from being lifted and stored, as is almost necessary for purposes of sale, and so is difficult to obtain in robust health. I have found it good-tempered enough if divided when in full growth, and it is one of the plants I am over

generous with, as I do so enjoy lifting a piece and seeing the realistic imitation of bleeding given by a broken root.

E. A. Bowles
My Garden in Spring, 1914

Editor's Note: Plant bloodroot in moist, humus-rich soil beneath deciduous trees where spring sun encourages flowering and summer shade protects its delicate leaves.

Bloodroot makes an attractive ground-cover in a shady woodland garden. A small planting will increase gradually via thick, creeping rhizomes and self-sown seedlings.

A High Place for Chicory

I am bound to say that when not in flower, chicory has the appearance of the commonest weed. If so placed that its quick-growing branches can mix with those of other subjects in a trellis, its coarser parts will not only be partially hidden, but the rich-colored flowers will show to advantage. I may mention that mine is mixed with Virginia creeper on wire, and the effect may easily be imagined.

John Wood
Hardy Perennials and Old-Fashioned Garden Flowers, 1884

Editor's Note: Virginia creeper sets off chicory's bright blue flowers with star-shaped green leaves in summer and red foliage in fall.

Best Garden Goldenrod

When the vote comes in on the question of the prettiest goldenrod for the flower garden, mine will be recorded for the *nemoralis* (gray goldenrod, *Solidago nemoralis*). Out of some half-dozen species I have been growing, this is by far the handsomest. I can imagine none more truly grand.

Meehans' Monthly, 1897

Editor's Note: Gray goldenrod thrives in sites with poor soil. In sun or light shade, its arching, two-foot-tall stems are topped with lemon yellow flowers from late summer into fall.

Join the Search for a Better Hepatica

A remarkable beautiful blue variety of our native hepatica or liverwort is figured in the *Belgian Horticultural Review*. Our lovers of herbaceous plants should examine our woods for new forms—for there are generally as good varieties from seeds sown by nature as by the gardener.

The Gardener's Monthly, 1877

Editor's Note: Responsible gardeners no longer collect plants from the wild, but there are other places to look for new forms of familiar natives, like seed exchanges.

The shade-loving hepatica is an early-spring wildflower with a leaf shape that reminded early herbalists of the human liver, giving the plant its common name, liverwort. Hepatica blooms in shades of white to blue and sometimes pink; the plants are low growing with evergreen foliage.

Musk Mallow Makes an Easy Wildflower

As I like profusion in the flower world, I confess to a fondness for *Malva moshata*, the musk mallow. It is such a happy, contented plant, and not at all particular whether it grows in sunshine or shade, but quite satisfied if you will only let it alone. Root it from the garden bed, and it will spring up in the path. Cut it down with the hoe, and it will creep in amongst the gooseberry bushes, and, defended by their prickly stems, it will bloom there abundantly.

Almon Dexter
And the Wilderness Bloomed, 1901

The musk mallow grows wild in fields over much of the eastern United States and Canada. Its large saucer-shaped flowers bloom in white or lavender pink and make a fine accent for a flower border.

Mayapples in Containers

Grow mayapple in pots, when exactly the required kind of compost can easily be given—peat and chopped sphagnum. Thus potted, plunged in wet sand, and placed in a northern aspect, it will be found not only to thrive well, as several specimens have done with me, but also to be worth all the trouble.

John Wood
Hardy Perennials and Old-Fashioned Garden Flowers, 1884

Editor's Note: In your garden, plant mayapples in moist to damp, humus-rich soil and light to full shade.

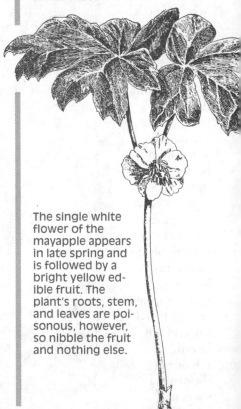

The single white flower of the mayapple appears in late spring and is followed by a bright yellow edible fruit. The plant's roots, stem, and leaves are poisonous, however, so nibble the fruit and nothing else.

Meadow Rue: A Summer Star

The wildflower that is the glory of my garden in early summer is meadow rue. It stands three or four feet high, and is a mass of foamy white when in bloom. Growing with pale pink peonies, no combination could be more attractive. It banks in behind the blue English delphiniums and bachelor's buttons. Wherever white is wanted in early summer, the meadow rue adapts itself. After the flowers are gone the tall stalks can be cut down to make way for other plants.

Flora Lewis Marble
The Garden Magazine, 1908

A Citrus-Scented Wildflower

The dull-white flowers of life-everlasting, which grow in pastures and on the edge of woodlands, make excellent filling for sofa pillows, and one may enjoy through the winter the sweet, wholesome fragrance that recalls the summer fields.

Farm Journal, 1905

Editor's Note: The crushed leaves of this wildflower (now called pearly everlasting, *Anaphalis margaritacea*) smell something like lemon and lime and have been used in sachets. Pearly everlasting has attractive woolly gray leaves and grows from two to four feet tall. It thrives in sun or partial shade.

Strange But True

Mr. Frank Seaman, at his summer home in the mountains not far from Ellenville, New York, has planted several thousand lady slippers collected by the farmers and their children, who were glad enough to gather them for three cents a plant.

The Garden Magazine, 1908

Editor's Note: Today we recognize mass plant collecting as eco-vandalism, but wild collecting was viewed much differently in 1908. The article in *The Garden Magazine* goes on to say that wildflowers tucked into a garden will be safe from the thoughtless bouquet picking of picnickers!

Spikenard for a Shady Spot

There is one native plant of such extraordinary decorative beauty that we have made it a characteristic feature of our wild garden. This is the spikenard (*Aralia racemosa*). It grows from three to five feet high. During the latter part of July and early in August the greenish white flowers are borne on long, slightly drooping spikes. Later these same racemes are densely packed with red berries which ultimately change to purple. The plant is easily grown from seed or from root cuttings taken in the fall.

William P. Longland
The Garden Magazine, 1907

Editor's Note: Spikenard likes a partially shaded spot, moderate moisture, and rich soil.

Large flower clusters and colorful berries aren't spikenard's only good features. This perennial herb also has attractive twice-compound leaves and aromatic roots that have been used medicinally.

Bargain Bulbs for a June Show

The best cheap June-blooming bulb for wild gardening that I know is the common star of Bethlehem (*Ornithogalum umbellatum*) which has run wild in this country. It is a starry white flower with a green back. I have seen it carpeting several acres of woods with fine effect on Long Island.

T. McAdam
The Garden Magazine, 1908

Editor's Note: Bulb catalogs sell star of Bethlehem bulbs by the hundreds. (See "Sources" on page 316 for ordering information.) But before you buy, look closely around you; this small wildflower may be growing in a nearby patch of long grass.

Once planted, stars of Bethlehem will spread rapidly. Their one- to two-inch-wide white star-shaped flowers add a cheery note to the garden in spring and summer.

Making More Violets

At the end of March or early April, I divide up and plant little bits of violets everywhere, and they grow and flourish and increase under gooseberry bushes and currant bushes, along the palings covered with blackberries, under shrubs—anywhere, in fact—and there they remain, hidden and shaded and undisturbed all the summer. When seedlings appear, they are let alone all the summer and autumn till after flowering time in spring.

Marie Theresa Villiers Earle
More Pot-Pourri from a Surrey Garden, 1899

Touch-Me-Not "Hedge"

A touch-me-not (jewelweed) hedge is one of the annual events in my garden. The seed of the yellow and spotted varieties (*Impatiens pallida* and *I. capensis*) was originally gathered from a brookside. Now it is thoroughly established in cultivation. It sows its own seed every fall and comes up early every spring. A lawnmower keeps the edge of the hedge straight. The plants grow to a uniform height, and bloom from July to frost.

Flora Lewis Marble
The Garden Magazine, 1908

Editor's Note: Touch-me-not puts on a fascinating seed show after it flowers. The ripe seed-pods eject their contents at the slightest touch, with remarkable force, which is how the plant got its name.

Thrifty Gardeners Sow Showy Tick Trefoil

Tick trefoil is among the many of our native plants that, when introduced into the garden, will compare favorably with the exotics of the season. It is another illustration of the fact that we have for these many years endeavored to impress upon our readers—that no lover of flowers need to be without a flower garden because of the expense of plants to stock it.

American Agriculturist, 1879

The showy tick trefoil (*Desmodium canadense*) really is the showiest of the trefoils, with its pink pealike blossoms. It grows wild from Canada south to the Mason-Dixon Line.

How to Handle Bird's-Foot Violet

Of our native violets, unquestionably the finest is the subject of our illustration, *Viola pedata* or the bird's-foot violet. It is one of the most elegant of our native plants. The general opinion that it cannot be cultivated is a great mistake. We grow it plentifully in the garden, where it comes up year after year, and increases. The only care is to transplant it, when in bloom, with a ball of earth; of hundreds moved in this way we have never lost a plant.

Edward Sprague Rand
Seventy-Five Popular Flowers and How to Cultivate Them, 1872

Editor's Note: Rand's advice to flaunt general gardening wisdom in this case is sound. Many plants have mistakenly been labeled difficult or impossible over the years.

Bird's-foot violets aren't as easy to grow as other violets, but they will thrive if you plant them in well-drained soil and partial shade.

Virginia Bluebell Disappearing Act

The Virginia bluebell (*Mertensia virginica*) is a charming plant, and as it is worthy of cultivation in groups, it often becomes a question where to place it so that the bare ground it leaves behind is not an eyesore. I grow it under large bushes of forsythia. Both bloom at the same time and the pink buds and open blue bells of the *Mertensia*, when seen through the fleecy mass of the golden bells of the forsythia, make a charming picture. After flowering, the forsythia hides the disrobing Mertensia with its heavy sheet of foliage.

W. C. Egan
Making a Garden of Perennials, 1912

Search Out Virginia Bluebell Seeds

About the middle of June the Virginia cowslip (another name for the Virginia bluebell, *Mertensia virginica*) begins to turn yellow before dying down. Now is the time to look out for the seeds. A few ripen on the plant, but most of them fall while green, and then ripen in a few days while lying on the ground. I shake the seeds carefully out, and leave them lying round the parent plant; a week later, when they will be ripe, they are lightly scratched into the ground. Some young plants of last year's growth I mark with a bit of stick, in case of wanting some later to plant elsewhere, or to send away; the plant dies away completely, leaving no trace above ground, so that if not marked it would be difficult to find what is wanted.

Gertrude Jekyll
Wood and Garden, 1904

Virginia bluebells thrive in evenly moist but well-drained, humus-rich soil in sun or shade. The plants go dormant after blooming in spring, so planting them beside shrubs or long-lasting perennials helps mark their location. That way you won't accidentally dig into these sleeping beauties when you're weeding or planting in summer and fall.

Ferns for Beautiful Gardens

Ferns for Small Yards

Flowering plants of all kinds require more sunlight than some of the small yards afford. In such localities ferns usually find their choicest homes. A few rocks or stones in an elevated position, in some neglected corner, can be arranged, and the hardy ferns planted among them. Here they will continue for many years without any special care, and indeed they usually throw up stronger and more luxuriant fronds after being in that place for a few years.

Meehans' Monthly, 1897

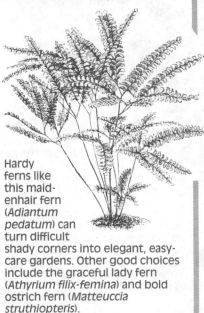

Hardy ferns like this maidenhair fern (*Adiantum pedatum*) can turn difficult shady corners into elegant, easy-care gardens. Other good choices include the graceful lady fern (*Athyrium filix-femina*) and bold ostrich fern (*Matteuccia struthiopteris*).

Include Flowers in the Fern Border

Where there is room for a break in the fern bed, a choice selection of woodland flowers may be utilized. *Thalictrum* (meadow rue), spirea, columbine, Solomon's seal, bleeding heart, anemone, May apple, tradescantia (spiderwort), trillium, *Polemonium* (Jacob's ladder), lily-of-the-valley, spring beauty, bird's foot violet, etc., can be introduced to make the border very attractive.

Meehans' Monthly, 1898

Lily-of-the-valley makes a perfect partner for ferns. Its bold dark green leaves set off the ferns' delicate pale foliage, and white bell-shaped flowers contribute a perfumey fragrance. Red berries add color to an otherwise green garden in summer.

An Ideal Location for Ferns

With ferns the best effect can be usually had in a spot shaded from the sun when at its height—say on the northeast side of a house—for there is to be found the most moisture. If the front of the house is toward the desired exposure, so much the better, as there is likely to be a porch along which these moisture-loving ferns will grow easily.

Meehans' Monthly, 1898

Editor's Note: Ferns favor a site along a porch because the soil there tends to catch more rain than beds along the foundation of the house.

Transplanting Tip

My method of handling ferns taken from the woods is to lift the roots carefully, wash off the soil in the nearest brook or pool, and wrap them, first with a layer of thin sheet moss, taken from some fallen log or the sloping sides of a boulder, then with two thicknesses of newspaper. The moss is dipped in water and squeezed until it is barely moist.

Herbert Durand
Wild Flowers and Ferns, 1925

Editor's Note: While collecting ferns from the wild is no longer recommended, Durand was on the right track. If a neighbor or gardening friend offers you a division of a fern, it's still a good idea to wrap the roots in something damp, like moistened newspaper or paper towels.

To Make Fern Prints, Start with a Drink

Dip ferns well in common porter, and then lay them flat between white sheets of paper, with slight pressure, and let them dry out.

William Dick
Encyclopedia of Practical Receipts and Processes, 1872

Editor's Note: Porter is a British-style dark beer that makes a good "ink" for leaf prints. You can also try using stout for a pleasant sepia-toned printing ink.

Fern-leaf prints are a beautiful way to decorate stationery or wrapping paper. Other fine-leaved plants such as columbine and yarrow make good print materials, too.

Roots Count When Transplanting Ferns

Don't bother about the tops of ferns, for new ones will grow, but look to the roots, and do not let them be exposed to the air or become dry in travel. Examine the quality of soil from which you have taken the ferns, and if you have none like it nearer home, take some with you for a starter.

Barbara
The Garden, You, and I, 1910

Editor's Note: Early spring and late fall are the best times to move ferns since you're least likely to disturb their roots then.

Raising Young Ferns from Spores

It is not generally known that our native ferns can be readily raised from the spores—those little dustlike products that are found in great abundance on the undersurface of many fronds. A good method is to fill a pot with any good garden soil, three-quarters the depth, the remaining one-quarter to be filled with brick broken to about the size of peas or beans. The pot can be sunk in a vessel of water to about one-half the depth of the pot. On the broken brick, the spores can then be sown, and the vessel placed in a comparatively shady spot. The brick will absorb enough water to be continually moist, while at the same time permitting the air to circulate through the vessel.

Meehan's Monthly, 1897

Editor's Note: A number of native ferns are easy to grow from spores. You'll have good luck with the Christmas fern (*Polystichum acrostichoides*), hay-scented fern (*Dennstaedtia punctilobula*), lady fern (*Athyrium filix-femina*), and the male fern (*Dryopteris fIlIx-mas*) shown here. All of these ferns are hardy to Zone 3. They range from 18 to 24 inches in height.

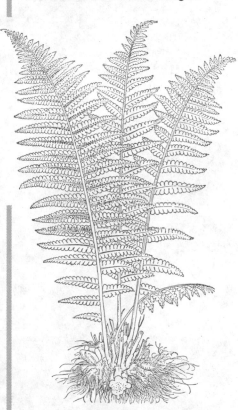

Gather spores from ferns when the sori (groups of spore sacks on the underside of leaves) are ripe—they'll turn from light green to very dark green, dark brown, or black. (Use a magnifying glass to check the color.) Lay a leaf, sori side down, on a sheet of white paper and cover it with newspaper. After two days, remove the newspaper and leaf and check for spores. Tilt the white paper and tap it lightly to remove the chaff, leaving the spores.

Houseplants and Flower Crafts

When it comes to growing plants indoors, no generation set a better example or had greener thumbs than the Victorians. Their growing secrets will have your home literally bursting with blooms and foliage.

Houseplants and Flower Crafts

Designing Indoor Gardens

Grow Living Curtains

Dispense with curtains. Let your plants beautify their window, and put your pretty curtains in some room where there are no plants to use the light.

American Agriculturist, 1894

To the devoted indoor gardener, every sunny window has all the possibilities of a newly tilled garden. Don't stop with the windowsill—there's an entire glass pane to fill.

Give Your Room a Victorian Touch

We present a plain kind of window, ornamented with a variety of rural economical adornings. In the center is a Ward's case. On one side is a pot of fuchsia. On the other side is a calla lily. In the hanging baskets and on the brackets are the ferns and flowers that flourish in the deep woods, and around the window is the ivy, running from two boxes; and, in case the window has some sun, a nasturtium may spread its bright blossoms among the leaves.

Catherine E. Beecher and Harriet Beecher Stowe
The American Woman's Home, 1869

Editor's Note: A Ward's case, or Wardian case, is a glass container for growing houseplants that thrive on humidity—it's the Victorian forerunner of the terrarium. You can make your own Wardian case by putting a clear, tight-fitting top on a bowl, aquarium, or other glass container. You won't need to water your plants very often since the lid holds the moisture inside. Keep the case out of direct sun though, or you'll cook the contents.

The authors of *The American Woman's Home* suggested adding striped spiderwort and strawberry geraniums (*Saxifraga stolonifera* or *S. sarmentosa*) to this setting in winter months. You can add forced bulbs, azaleas, lilies, and poinsettias to the mix throughout the year for a splash of seasonal color.

Strange But True

The Assistant Medical Inspector of the Philadelphia Board of Health says, "Growing plants should not be used as permanent school room decorations; many have medicinal odors to which some children are quite susceptible, and they may serve to harbor disease germs in the dust that many accumulate about them." Unfortunately, local boards of health are usually held as sacred as the oracles of the pagans; and the beautiful window flowers, for which so many of the public schools are famous, will probably have to go.

Meehans' Monthly, 1898

Editor's Note: This excerpt is remarkable for a couple of reasons: that a medical inspector of a major city would make such a statement and that our schools were once famous for windowsill gardening. In the 1880s, the popular *Vick's Illustrated Catalogue* offered free collections of seed to the first five schools in every county in the United States and Canada that asked for them.

You Need Houseplants Year-Round

What a natural mistake it is to feel that houseplants are unnecessary in summer! But palms and other decorative plants are needed to make a house look cool, comfortable, and homelike.

The Garden Magazine, 1908

Victorians tended to like the cluttered look in home decorating, and they created indoor forests with houseplants.

Do-It-Yourself Indoor Windowboxes

There is a very pretty way of fitting up a window which is but little practiced; it is, in fact, making the window a flower garden. Build from your window into the room a rounding wooden shelf—say, if the window is large, three feet in diameter from window to outer edge, but at any rate proportioned to the size of the window. On this, place a large box—wood, made to conform to the shelf—and in this put your plants, the taller at the back, and on each side a climber to run over the top of the window, on a neat wire trellis or on strings. It is desirable to have holes in the bottom of the box to allow superfluous water to escape, and to permit this, the shelf should be covered with zinc, and have a low rim all around it.

Edward Sprague Rand
The Window Gardener, 1873

Editor's Note: If you want an authentic zinc-lined window shelf, purchase zinc-plated steel at a building-supply store—it's sold as roof flashing. You could also cover the shelf with copper flashing. Copper is especially attractive, and it's easy to cut with metal shears and bend by hand. If you're interested in a more modern option, cover the shelf with a sheet of plastic or use plastic saucers under all of your plants to prevent drips, spills, and floods.

Caring for House- plants

The Best Window for Houseplants

The first morning ray is worth a dozen of the evening. The best aspect for room plants is the southeast. They seem like animals in their affection for the morning sun.

The Gardener's Monthly, 1871

Bright Plants Like Bright Windows

Plants with brightly colored flowers, such as *Compositae* and most succulent plants, enjoy the most ardent sunshine.

Nils Jonsson-Rose
Window and Parlor Gardening, 1895

Editor's Note: Plants in the family Compositae produce flower heads that are made up of many small ray or disc flowers or a combination of both. These types of common flowers include asters, calendulas, daisies, and mums.

Houseplants Enjoy a Spring Shower

Set your houseplants out in each of the warm, misty February rains that come. They will be so refreshed and cleansed that they will gladden you to see them.

Farm Journal, 1911

Editor's Note: Just don't forget to bring the plants back inside.

A Handy Little Watering Can

A small toy watering pot such as are sold for children's use is of the greatest assistance; it will sprinkle the surface of tiny pots without wetting either stands or window glass.

Henry T. Williams
Window Gardening, 1881

Lock In the Humidity

To keep the air about the plants moist is one of the secrets of window culture. Some who have windows well stocked with fine plants make glazed cases with folding doors on them, by which, when the room is highly heated and very dry, they can be enclosed in an atmosphere of their own. In such cases, ferns and mosses can be grown to perfection.

The Gardener's Monthly, 1876

Editor's Note: If your home has deep windowsills, you might try attaching glazed kitchen cabinet doors to the inside window frame to create this greenhouse space. Otherwise, a terrarium near the window is the best bet for ferns and mosses.

Cover Cuttings in the Window Garden

Those who try to raise plants from cuttings in their window gardens fail more frequently than they succeed. A cutting is a small branch, or short piece of stem, and usually with its leaves. These leaves are constantly evaporating water, which, so long as the cuttings remain attached to the plant, is supplied by the root. If cuttings are set in a pot of soil, the dry air takes up moisture from their leaves, more rapidly than it can be supplied from the soil, and the slips soon fail. Small cuttings may have a tumbler, goblet, or other glass turned over them. Preventing evaporation in this manner is often called by gardeners "keeping close."

American Agriculturist, 1884

Rummage around in your collection of planting pots and then in your glassware, and you should find pairs that will match up as little windowsill greenhouses.

Less Heat for Healthier Houseplants

The cause of so many window plants showing long, white, leafless stalks, with a tuft of leaves on the end, is too great heat and too little light. Proportion the two, and you obtain a short, stocky, healthy growth. In rooms, this proportion is always unequal.

Edward Sprague Rand
The Window Gardener, 1873

As central heating became more common in the late 1800s, gardening experts warned that the change in indoor climate might mean the end of houseplants. We continue to garden on our windowsills, of course, but it still is a challenge to compensate for heat and dryness. You can place your plants on a shallow tray filled with pebbles and a little water to keep them moist and cool. Use lights if your windows aren't bright enough.

Top-Dress Plants between Repottings

Top dressing is productive of good effects, particularly with old plants in heavy pots and tubs. It is simply removing the top soil as far down as the upper roots, and refilling the pot with fresh, light, rich soil.

Edward Sprague Rand
The Window Gardener, 1873

Editor's Note: A layer of finished compost makes a good top-dressing, too—each time you water, your plants get a drink of compost "tea."

Use a Potting Stick for a Tight Fit

The best way to work the soil in among the roots is to hold the plant with the left hand, put a little soil around the roots, and work the plant up and down a little. Tamp down with a potting stick. A potting stick is usually made from a piece of pine about a foot long, an inch wide, and an inch thick with the corners and ends rounded off. A piece of broom handle is sometimes used.

Parker Thayer Barnes
The Garden Magazine, 1907

Editor's Note: A potting stick is nothing more than a scrap of wood that fits comfortably in the hand and is the right size to tamp down earth in a pot. Use a smaller stick for little pots.

Poke Plants out of Their Pots

Prod gently with a pencil the piece of crockery covering the outlet of the flower pot; this loosens the earth on all sides, and the plant, a solid mass of roots and soil, may be easily slipped out and repotted in the necessary size.

M. K. Farrand
The Garden Magazine, 1906

Sand Scrub Cleans Off the Green

If the pots are old and green with algae, clean by scrubbing with sand and water, for the "green" makes them less porous and old earth dried on the inside surface interferes with the new root growth.

Parker Thayer Barnes
The Gardener's Monthly, 1878

Plant in Wet Pots

Be sure to soak clay pots in a pail of water before filling them with earth for plants. If this is not done, the plants will dry out quickly after being watered.

Loring Underwood
A Garden Diary and Country Home Guide, 1908

Editor's Note: Dry clay wicks water away from the soil in a pot and leaves plant roots high and dry. An hour or two of soaking puts a damper on clay pots' moisture-stealing ways.

Strange But True

It happens almost every winter that there are two or three nights so severely cold that the ordinary heating appliances will not keep the room warm enough to prevent freezing, at least at the window. At such times the plants should be placed in the middle of the room and covered with a sheet, or even with newspapers.

American Agriculturist, 1878

Editor's Note: Tips for reviving frozen houseplants were common in the nineteenth century. That gives you an idea of the lack of human comfort in the days before central heat. This tip is still handy if you heat with wood and temperatures drop drastically at night. You can also take another tip from the 1800s and grow native ferns as houseplants—they aren't easily killed by freezing temperatures.

place for them, a mere frame of boards set in a layer of sand. Set the pots, allowing room between them to fill in with sand. This will not only prevent drying out so rapidly, but also will avoid the injury often caused to the roots by the sun falling directly upon the pots, an unsuspected cause of much damage.

Farm Journal, 1884

Save Parlor Plants from Frost

Be prudent before hand, or some frosty night will cut every tender plant left out. Everyone who pretends to keep parlor plants should own a thermometer. If at sundown or at nine o'clock it stands anywhere near 40°F, your plants are in danger.

Henry Ward Beecher
Fruits, Flowers and Farming, 1859

Fight Off the Effects of Frost

Should any of our fair readers find her plants, by some unlucky calculation, frozen in the morning, do not remove them at once to a warm place, but dip them in cold water, and set them in a dark spot where they will barely escape freezing. Sunlight will only help the frost's destructive powers.

The Gardener's Monthly, 1871

Downsizing Pots

Most amateurs make a mistake in the size of the pot, using one a size or two too large. It is very easy, indeed, to overpot a plant, strange as it may seem, and really nothing in the plant's life can be more disastrous than an over-large pot. Nine times out of ten the plants will be over-watered and the soil become sour.

Parker Thayer Barnes
The Gardener's Monthly, 1878

Editor's Note: Before you repot plants, wait until the roots start growing out of the drainage hole. Of course, you don't want to let them go so long that they become rootbound. Move plants up one pot size at a time so you don't give them too much space to fill.

Protect Plants on Cleaning Day

If plants are kept in the living room in winter, it is a good plan to cover them with a thin cloth while sweeping. The dust clogs the pores of the leaves and keeps the plants from thriving. Dusty plants are not attractive to the eye.

Fannie M. Wood
Farm Journal, 1906

Editor's Note: Dust reduces the amount of light plants get, so dusting or rinsing leaves is a good idea.

Give Houseplants a Summer Home

Winter-blooming plants set out of doors for the summer are apt to suffer from neglect. Prepare a

Reblooming Easter Azaleas

The process of keeping azalea plants from year to year is very simple. After it has ceased blooming, we keep it in a light (but not sunny) window in a cool room, and when all danger of frost is past, we plunge it, pot and all, in the ground at the north side of the house, where it will have only a little eastern and western sun. One month of complete rest in the fall, in a cellar or other dark place, has often been advised for the azalea, but we always prefer to have ours in bloom as early as possible. Therefore, in the early fall we bring the plant into the house, putting it at once in a sunny window where it will have a temperature of about 60°F. We water judiciously and when buds appear the plant is placed in any ordinary room having a southern exposure. Each year our plant is in full bloom—a solid sheet of large flowers—by February 15.

Marian Williams
The Garden Magazine, 1908

Editor's Note: Azaleas prefer cool weather and do best in rooms set at 45° to 60°F. The high temperatures in modern homes mean your flowers may not last 2 to 4 weeks as they should. Since high temperatures are stressful, plants may also develop pest problems. Move plants to a cool or unheated room at night and mist daily to keep them happy.

Hot Foot Makes Callas Bloom Quicker

Calla buds that just show their creamy tips may be hastened into bloom by setting the pots containing them in deep saucers of steaming hot water.

The Household, 1893

Editor's Note: Ouch! Don't make it too hot or you'll sizzle your calla lilies (*Zantedeschia* spp.). The idea is to give the plants warm, steamy conditions. Move them into the bathroom when you take a shower, and they'll get steamed but not boiled. Calla blooms open into large, waxy white, yellow, or pink flowers.

Getting Cyclamens through the Winter

After cyclamens have done blooming, it is usual to dry them off; but we do best with them by keeping them growing till spring, then turning them out in the open border, and re-pot in August for winter flowering.

The Gardener's Monthly, 1876

Windowsill Geraniums

Quite frequently, an attempt is made to flower geraniums out of doors all summer and then pot them in the fall, expecting an abundance of bloom in the winter as well. The plants are weakened by blooming and potting, and do not respond to the care given. Plants intended for winter blooming should not be permitted to flower during the summer at will, but encouraged to make healthy, vigorous, compact plants. Pot them up in ample time for the roots to become active again before transferring to the house.

Meehans' Monthly, 1900

Editor's Note: Keep these indoor-bound geraniums from flowering by pinching back flower buds as they form.

Prepare Proper Soil for Heaths

The erica (heath family) will not thrive unless the soil is adapted to its peculiar nature; this is often difficult to learn. Heaths, like the azalea and rhododendron, make very small, hairlike roots; and where these latter are growing naturally will be found a good locality to collect soil for the artificial cultivation of the former.

Edward Sprague Rand
The Window Gardener, 1873

Editor's Note: Robbing soil from azaleas or rhododendrons isn't a great idea, but you can make your own mix based on what these plants thrive on in the wild. A well-drained, moist, humus-rich soil is best. You'll get good results if you mix two parts commercial potting soil or good garden soil with two parts builder's sand, two parts peat moss, and one part compost.

Prepping Mums for the Parlor

The best way to obtain a fine mum specimen is to set out in the garden in the early spring a small plant; give it constant attention during the summer, and pinch out the shoots so as to make lateral branches. About the first of September let it set for bloom, and on the approach of frost, pot it and remove it to the parlor. It will bloom for two months or more. Then dry it off for the winter in the cellar, and by the spring it will furnish you with plenty of young plants. The small-flowered pompon varieties are very desirable; the larger flowers are best seen in the garden.

Edward Sprague Rand
The Window Gardener, 1873

Pompon flowers may be flattened and buttonlike or compact with a globular shape like this one. Pinch the tips of the plants off once or twice for bushy growth. Make your pinches before July 15 in the North and before August 15 in the South so the plants have time to set flower buds.

Poinsettias Reborn

It is impractical to keep the poinsettia over from one Christmas to another without a greenhouse, as the best plants can be raised only by making cuttings every year. After the plant has ceased to flower it should be rested until late spring. Put it away in the cellar and give it very little water. In late spring it will give a liberal supply of cuttings if furnished with heat and moisture. These cuttings should be placed on a shelf for several days until the milky juice has run away; otherwise they will not root easily. During the summer the plants can be put into pots and plunged outdoors in the garden.

The Garden Magazine, 1908

Make Roses Feel at Home

Roses, when they are forced, do much better when the pots are plunged in some damp material. They may be set inside of a large pot, with moss between the two pots.

The Gardener's Monthly, 1876

Editor's Note: Roses that have been forced to bloom out of season are stressed and need extra care. A sphagnum moss liner keeps rose roots from drying out, so your plant has an easier time growing.

Old-Time House-plants

Give a Gift of Arbutus

A sweeter gift from country friends than the gem of the grand old family of *Ericacaea* (heath family) would be hard to find—trailing arbutus (*Epigaea repens*). Perhaps no wild thing travels so far by mail or express, and if properly packaged, arrives less travel worn. Arbutus gathered in the afternoon, properly trimmed, and placed in shallow bowls of water in a cool cellar overnight, is much better equipped for long journeys than if the transfer from field to box were made on the spot. The stems fill up with water in a few hours, and should then be arranged in dainty bouquets—tacked to the bottom and sides of a cardboard box; a ball of twine or cotton yarn will serve to prevent shaking about, which is so detrimental to cut flowers in general.

G. A. Woolson
American Agriculturist, 1894

Editor's Note: Gardeners in Woolson's day collected this fragrant-flowered, trailing evergreen from the wild. Today we know better than to pick or transplant this finicky wildflower and instead order nursery-grown plants.

Start a Daphne Revival

Winter daphne never receives the care and attention its beauty merits. It is one of the few old-fashioned plants which the modern rage for novelties has not driven entirely out of cultivation. As a window plant it is unsurpassed, flourishing and blooming in situations where most plants would dwindle and die.

Edward Sprague Rand
The Window Gardener, 1873

Editor's Note: Winter daphne (**Daphne odora**) is a wonderfully fragrant shrub that takes cool temperatures (50°F) and grows well in containers. More than a century after Rand called it "old-fashioned," varieties with pink or white blossoms are still popular.

Fuchsia for the Summer

As a pot plant for summer blooming, fuchsia is unsurpassed, being very floriferous, of brilliant foliage, and of symmetrical habit. Train up a leading shoot, and if the plant is supplied with pot room and plenty of light, and has not heat enough to draw it out weak, it will form side shoots in sufficient abundance to produce a handsome outline, the branches being allowed to take their own pendant form.

Edward Sprague Rand
The Window Gardener, 1873

Strange But True

A sponge, kept wet by daily immersion, can be filled with flaxseed and suspended by a cord, when it will ere long be covered with verdure and afterward with flowers.

Catherine E. Beecher and Harriet Beecher Stowe
The American Woman's Home, 1869

Editor's Note: Victorians were particularly fond of flaxes (*Linum* spp.), so seed catalogs offered many varieties. Flax makes a good garden flower too, with electric blue flowers and needlelike leaves. Most flaxes are perennials that are hardy in Zones 4 to 9.

Fuchsia's pendulous flowers come in bright solid colors or combinations of red, pink, purple, and white. Give this plant an eastern or western exposure and keep it evenly moist. Fuchsias actually prefer to be a little pot-bound, so don't be as generous with pot space as Rand was.

Sweet-Scented Geraniums

Now what, I wonder, has become of the many varieties of sweet-leaved geraniums that were once the pride of every plant fancier? Early in the nineteenth century, it is said, there were over two hundred varieties to be had in England, and I dare say as many in this country. Today no notice is taken of them at all.

A few pots of sweet-leaved geraniums ranged along the window ledges of the living rooms will give pleasure. And if the taste is set down as Victorian, so is a good deal else that is comfortable and agreeable.

Louise Beebe Wilder
The Fragrant Path, 1932

Editor's Note: Why scented geraniums aren't as popular as they used to be is a mystery—one sniff of their leaves and you'll be hooked.

Try Lantana in a Sunny Window

Why is it we do not see more lantanas in window collections? We have few freer-flowering plants. The white and pale yellow varieties are especially fine. Frequent cutting back will induce the production of new branches, and with new branches always come new flowers. They are most tractable plants, and can be trained in any form. Plants a year or two old are preferable to young plants, as they will have a greater amount of flowering surface.

American Agriculturist, 1894

Editor's Note: The reason you don't see many lantanas (*Lantana camara*) indoors is that they need bright light—at least three hours of direct sun daily—for best flowering. If you can't supply that much light, use lantanas in window-boxes and hanging baskets outside. Their flat-topped flowers are butterfly favorites.

Ornamental Onions

One does not look for desirable flowering plants among the onions, and yet there are several species in the genus *Allium* that are very interesting as ornamental plants. Perhaps the most beautiful of the cultivated species is *Allium neapolitanum*. Its flowers are white and are produced in large, loosely spreading umbels. This bulb is excellent for the window garden. The best treatment for it is to put three bulbs in a five-inch pot in the fall. They will immediately commence to grow and will be in flower in January. A succession can easily be kept up by planting at intervals.

American Agriculturist, 1891

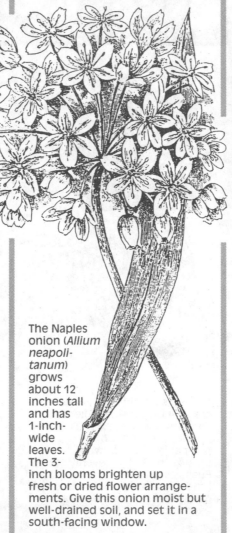

The Naples onion (*Allium neapolitanum*) grows about 12 inches tall and has 1-inch-wide leaves. The 3-inch blooms brighten up fresh or dried flower arrangements. Give this onion moist but well-drained soil, and set it in a south-facing window.

Put an Orange in the Parlor

The lemon does not bloom and fruit as easily as the orange, and is of taller growth and less fitted for the parlor.

Edward Sprague Rand
The Window Gardener, 1873

If you're buying citrus plants for houseplants, make sure you get varieties that grow well indoors. The sour orange, shown here, is a good choice, as are the calamondin orange and Meyer lemon. Citrus plants need plenty of light, so set them in a south-facing window and keep them evenly moist (except in winter when you should water only when plants are dry to the touch). Mist citrus plants daily to keep the humidity high.

A Windowsill Pitcher (Plant)

I put the plant in a mixture of about half sand and half bog (sphagnum) moss, pressed in as tight as possible about the roots. Then I get a vessel that will hold water, and put a stone or piece of brick in, and stand the pot with the plant on it, so that about a quarter or even half the pot is under the water. So you can see, all the water the plant gets is what comes up through the hole at the bottom of the pot. The plant itself is never watered, but I find it is always damp. I know of nothing that grows so easily, or gives more pleasure.

The Gardener's Monthly, 1876

Editor's Note: Do try growing this insectivorous wildflower, but do not collect pitcher plants (*Sarracenia* spp.) from the wild—some species are endangered.

Insects attracted to pitcher plants' nectar enter the unusual tubular-shaped leaves and are trapped inside. Whether you grow pitcher plants inside or outdoors (they're hardy to Zone 3), you don't need to "feed" them meat or insects. They'll do just fine in moist soil and full sun.

Strange But True

The tuberose, hyacinth, and jessamine, etc., are too sweet to be allowed to remain in a bedroom at night, and should not be patronized for this purpose by invalids.

Henry T. Williams
Window Gardening, 1881

Editor's Note: Houseplants were the rage in the Victorian era and took over windows and tabletops. The overpowering scent of elaborate displays may help to explain the misguided but popular idea that plants could use up all the oxygen in a tightly sealed room.

Pittosporum Is Perfect for the Parlor

This is an old-fashioned plant, a favorite for its fragrant flowers rather than for any beauty of foliage or blossom; the former is dull green, the latter dirty white. As a parlor plant it blooms from February to May. This plant will thrive with very little sun.

Edward Sprague Rand
The Window Gardener, 1873

Editor's Note: Pittosporums (*Pittosporum* spp.) are evergreen shrubs or small trees used as hedge plants in the South. In cooler climates, they're grown as houseplants for the orange blossom scent of their flowers. Pittosporums prefer bright light, despite Rand's claims, and they like good air circulation and daily misting. Move them outside for the summer.

Try a Pocketbook Plant

Probably no greenhouse flower is as little known or repays acquaintance as royally as the Calceolaria (pocketbook plant). Of infinite variety, its showy purse-shaped flowers range from a rare pure white through all the shades of pale lemon, orange, and scarlet to a deep, rich, velvety cardinal. It is one of the most easily cultivated houseplants. The seed germinates in eight or ten days.

Ida D. Bennett
The Flower Garden, 1904

Editor's Note: The annual pocketbook plant can take the moderate to low light of a north- or east-facing window. Keep the soil evenly moist and mist the leaves once or twice a day to keep this plant happy. The spotted flowers make a great conversation piece. Just keep any water off the blooms or you'll spoil their effect.

Roses for Your Windows

The China rose and its hybrids are the common rose of window gardening, and are known as "monthly roses." There will seldom be a day when it will not have a flower or bud upon it. It will survive almost any treatment, and will live if but a ray of sunlight can reach it. It is the poor man's friend, and clings to him in every vicissitude.

Edward Sprague Rand
The Window Gardener, 1873

Editor's Note: Your best choices for window gardens today are the miniature roses. They may have China rose (*Rosa chinensis*) in their background, but no one is really sure. The miniatures have small flowers and leaves on plants that range from 4 to 30 inches tall. Give them plenty of sun, cool temperatures, and high humidity for best results. Better yet, grow miniature roses outside in summer, and bring them in to decorate your windows when the plants are flowering.

Bring Salvia Indoors

The chief salvia variety cultivated is the Scarlet Mexican Sage, or red salvia, *Salvia splendens*. It is a rank-growing herb, with long, jointed stalks, crowned with scarlet flowers. The best way to grow it is to set the plant in rich soil in the garden in spring. It will grow vigorously. About the last of September pot it (it transplants easily), shade it for a few days, then remove it to a sunny window, where it will delight you with its brilliant blossoms for two months. Then keep it cool until spring, and repeat the operation until the plant becomes so large as to be unmanageable; then spring cuttings must be taken off and rooted.

Edward Sprague Rand
The Window Gardener, 1873

Editor's Note: Scarlet sage is a tender perennial that's usually grown as an annual. Break off old blooms as they fade to keep plants from setting seed, and they'll keep flowering and flowering. The stems are very brittle, so it's easier and quicker to break off old blooms than cut them off. For window-size plants, try dwarf varieties like 'St. John's Fire', which tops out at just 12 inches tall.

Underrated Winter Bloomer

It is pleasing to notice the interest some florists take in popularizing comparatively unknown plants. One of these particularly impressed the writer. This plant, the scarlet plume, is by no means new, but it has had its wave of popularity years ago, and is not now generally grown. Its flowers or bracts are small but numerous, of an orange-scarlet color, and are produced continuously throughout the winter. For winter flowering, it is scarcely excelled. It likes plenty of heat and little root disturbance.

Meehan's Monthly, 1899

Editor's Note: In spite of this enthusiastic recommendation, scarlet plume (*Euphorbia fulgens*) is still hard to find. (See "Sources" on page 316 for ordering information.) Its brightly colored bracts and graceful, drooping, two- to four-foot-long branches make it a plant worth looking for.

Sensitive Plant Thrills Curious Children

Plants for the pleasure and instruction of children are often sought for. The sensitive plant, *Mimosa pudica*, is an excellent one for this purpose. It is easily raised from seeds sown in spring. The habit is rather sprawling for a pot plant, but by a little pinching-in management, pretty and compact specimens may be obtained. Few plants give more interest to children in watching the leaves close or fall on being touched.

Meehans' Monthly, 1901

Editor's Note: The sensitive plant's name comes from its habit of folding up its feathery leaves when touched. Give it plenty of humidity indoors, or grow it outside as an annual. The sensitive plant is hardy only in Zone 10, where it has become a roadside weed.

Growing Ferns Indoors

Best Native Ferns for Pots

The fern species we have found to succeed best in parlor culture are: *Adiantum pedatum*, our native maidenhair fern; *Nephrolepis*; our pretty wild *Polypodium*, an evergreen species; and *Lygodium*, a beautiful genus of climbing ferns, of which one species, *L. palmatum* (climbing fern), is not uncommon in New England.

Edward Sprague Rand
The Window Gardener, 1873

Editor's Note: Rand's favorite ferns are still available to decorate your living room windows. ***Polypodium vulagare*** is the common polypody fern, which has leathery, evergreen fronds. The climbing or Hartford fern (***Lygodium palmatum***) has delicate vinelike stems and fronds with five to seven lobes arranged palmately or finger-fashion. See "Sources" on page 316 for ordering information.

There are several species of *Nephrolepis*, including this Java sword fern (*N. acuminata*). The Boston fern (*N. exaltata* 'Bostoniensis') is one of the best known and widely used species because it has longer and more graceful fronds.

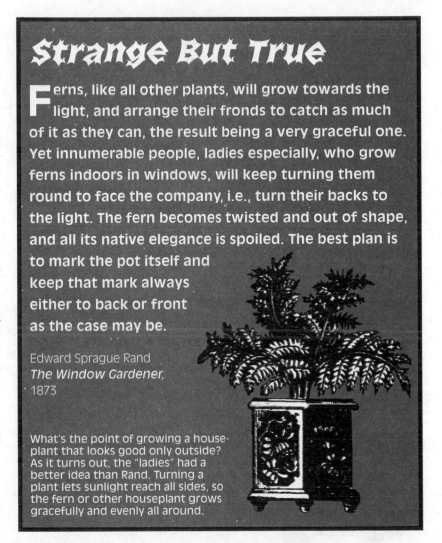

Strange But True

Ferns, like all other plants, will grow towards the light, and arrange their fronds to catch as much of it as they can, the result being a very graceful one. Yet innumerable people, ladies especially, who grow ferns indoors in windows, will keep turning them round to face the company, i.e., turn their backs to the light. The fern becomes twisted and out of shape, and all its native elegance is spoiled. The best plan is to mark the pot itself and keep that mark always either to back or front as the case may be.

Edward Sprague Rand
The Window Gardener,
1873

What's the point of growing a houseplant that looks good only outside? As it turns out, the "ladies" had a better idea than Rand. Turning a plant lets sunlight reach all sides, so the fern or other houseplant grows gracefully and evenly all around.

Air Your Ferns

It should not be forgotten that the glass case in which ferns are enclosed is not to keep out the air, but to keep in the moisture, as ferns will not thrive in the dry atmosphere of heated rooms. A few minutes' airing every day will, therefore, be of great benefit to them.

The Gardener's Monthly, 1871

Ferns for Winter Greenery

Our own native forest ferns have a period in the winter months when they cease to grow. They are very particular in asserting their right to this yearly nap, and will not, on any consideration, grow for you out of their appointed season. Nevertheless, if you make a Ward's case in the spring, your ferns will grow beautifully in it all summer; and in the autumn, though they stop growing, and cease to throw out leaves, yet the old leaves will remain fresh and green till the time for starting the new ones in the spring.

Catherine E. Beecher and Harriet Beecher Stowe
The American Woman's Home, 1869

Glass enclosures were made in the 1800s expressly for ferns. They were often called Ward's cases or Wardian cases after their inventor, Nathaniel B. Ward.

Indoor Vines and Hanging Baskets

A Climber for West Windows

One of the best vines for this purpose is the *Cobaea scandens*. It will thrive where there is but little light, is a rampant grower, and will flower the whole winter.

American Agriculturist, 1893

Editor's Note: The cup-and-saucer vine (*Cobaea scandens*) has purple bell-shaped flowers that bloom over a 6-month period. This climber can grow 10 to 25 feet tall in a single season, and its tendrils will attach to curtain cords, brackets, bookshelves, or anything else in their path. Make sure you give this plant plenty of space.

Color Explosion for Cool Windows

The manettia vine is one of the most satisfactory vines for winter blooming, requiring only a small pot and a place in a sunny window, and blooming better when pot bound. It does not require a warm atmosphere, blooming freely in a temperature of about 50°F, and giving an unfailing succession of its bright little flowers every day during the winter. It is that rare thing—a plant which the florists have not overpraised.

Ida D. Bennett
The Flower Garden, 1904

Editor's Note: The red and yellow flowers of the firecracker vine (*Manettia cordifolia*) are cylinder shaped and look like tiny firecrackers.

Carrot "Fern" from the Compost Bucket

A large carrot, with the smallest half cut off, scooped out to hold water and then suspended with cords, will send out graceful shoots in rich profusion.

Catherine E. Beecher and Harriet Beecher Stowe
The American Woman's Home, 1869

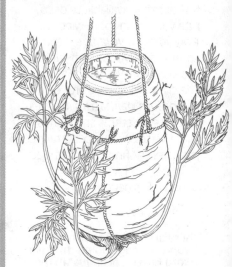

The common garden-variety carrot can be surprisingly elegant given a chance to display its ferny foliage.

Bring Home the Sweet Scent of the South

This plant, botanically *Gelsemium sempervirens*, is a native of our southern states. The foliage is dark, shining green; and the flowers, which are freely produced, are bright yellow and delightfully fragrant. This is a charming window plant, and easily grown. It is a half climber, and needs the support of a stake or trellis. We have seen a single plant, which, grown in a large tub, occupied the whole of a large bay window, and was a marked example of what success may be attained in window gardening.

Edward Sprague Rand
The Window Gardener, 1873

Editor's Note: Carolina jessamine (*Gelsemium sempervirens*) is not a true jasmine (*Jasminum* spp.), but it does have a sweet scent. This vine can grow 10 to 20 feet tall with support, or you can use it outdoors as a groundcover from Zone 7 south. Prune Carolina jessamine back to maintain a manageable size. Be aware that all parts of this vine are toxic—keep it away from children.

Windowbanks of Bloom

A box, as long as the window and rather deep, is fastened under a window where the sun shines in. A network of cord is fastened so that when the vines grow large enough they will begin to climb upon it, growing upward and toward the center of the room. The cords are fastened to the edge of the box inside, and when the plants are old enough to remain where they are trained, the net can be dropped to the floor, leaving an overflowing bank starred with bright blossoms of pink, blue purple, and white intermingled.

Mrs. E. M. Lucas
American Agriculturist, 1894

You'll need a south-facing window to pull off this unusual indoor floral arrangement. When you're not in the room, return your cascade of morning glories to their upright position so they'll get enough sunlight to keep flowering.

A Kinder, Gentler Smilax Vine

Smilax, this beautiful winter climber—the graceful queen of decorative vines—is adapted to the greenhouse and conservatory. With very little care it can be grown successfully as a houseplant. The seed should be sown in pots in the house and kept moist till the young plant appears. The seed being rather slow to germinate, you must not think it bad if it does not make its appearance in two weeks. The young plants should be potted off into three-inch pots as soon as they are three or four inches high. Once a year the bulbs should be allowed to dry off and rest; they will start into growth again in six weeks. The vine does not require the full sun, but will grow in a partially shaded situation. It can be trained on a small thread across the window or around pictures.

The Household, 1879

Editor's Note: The author is describing smilax asparagus (*Asparagus asparagoides*), not the prickly weed known as catbrier (*Smilax rotundifolia*). Dainty "leaves" (actually expanded branchlets that look like oval inch-long leaves) and fragrant white flowers made smilax asparagus a popular plant for florists' bouquets years ago. This plant also produces small purple berries. See "Sources" on page 316 for ordering information.

Garden-Variety Vine

The vine of the sweet potato is very graceful. Quite a good many who have admired a basket covered with its leaves have felt a little chagrined to find it was nothing after all but a sweet potato vine. The tubers can be set into a glass small enough to keep the root three or four inches from the bottom. Fill the glass with water, and place it in a warm room; give it two or three hours of sunshine each day, and in two or three weeks it will begin to grow. All through the winter it will continue to develop its glossy green leaves in profusion.

Henry T. Williams
Window Gardening,
1881

Decorating with a Passionflower

The blue passionflower is very desirable for parlor ornament. It thrives best in light, rich soil, and needs much sunlight to bloom in profusion. *Passiflora caerulea* has flowers of a sky blue color and remarkable character, grows finely, and is quite ornamental.

Henry T. Williams
Window Gardening, 1881

Strange But True

On either side of an arch stand my English ivy. Now it has several main stalks, the longest of which is ten yards long; these send out numerous shoots, and we think the vine with all its branches would measure over sixty yards. Every other morning, I give it clear, warm coffee, and in November I placed down in the earth a piece of raw beefsteak. Now that's absurd, I know, to give an ivy beefsteak and coffee, but if you could see the amount it has grown this winter, and the size of its leaves, you would think it liked its fare.

"E. Ivy"
The Household, 1882

You'll need to provide some support for the thin, wiry stems of blue passionflower. This vine can grow 20 feet long, but you can prune it back in early spring if it gets too big.

Try a Little Ivy— Everywhere

Ivies are grown in hanging baskets, around windows, made to trail around picture frames and looking glasses. If you have ivy growing out-of-doors, a pretty effect may be produced by cutting large branches, and keeping them indoors in vases of rain water; they will grow well all winter.

Edward Sprague Rand
The Window Gardener, 1873

Editor's Note: There are so many varieties of English ivy (*Hedera helix*) that you can grow a different kind around every window, picture, and mirror in your house. Some popular varieties include 'Ivalace' with fluted leaf edges and the variegated forms 'Glacier' and 'Gold Heart'.

Picture This

A beautiful ornament for a room with pictures is German ivy. Slips of this will start without roots in bottles of water. Slide the bottle behind the picture, and the ivy will seem to come from fairyland, and hang its verdure in all manner of pretty curves around the picture. It may then be trained to travel toward other ivy, and thus aid in forming green cornices along the ceiling.

Catherine E. Beecher and
Harriet Beecher Stowe
The American Woman's Home, 1869

Editor's Note: German ivy (*Senecio mikanioides*) is also sold as *Delairea odorata*. The yellow-green leaves look similar to English ivy, plus this plant has small, yellow daisylike flowers.

Frame a picture or mirror with a wreath of ivy. Tuck cuttings into a small bottle of water attached to the back of the frame with duct tape.

A Mini-Trellis for Indoor Vines

A very novel style of ornament is shown here. This is a box of a length varying from three to six feet, and one to two feet wide, mounted on castors. A number of laths of wood are nailed crossways, and fastened upright at the back of the box. Usually the height is about four to four and a half feet. The entire box and latticework should be painted green.

Henry T. Williams
Window Gardening, 1881

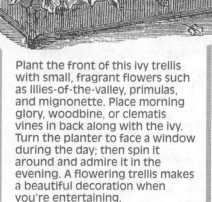

Plant the front of this ivy trellis with small, fragrant flowers such as lilies-of-the-valley, primulas, and mignonette. Place morning glory, woodbine, or clematis vines in back along with the ivy. Turn the planter to face a window during the day; then spin it around and admire it in the evening. A flowering trellis makes a beautiful decoration when you're entertaining.

A Portable Ivy Screen

A plant box, with rollers to allow it to be moved, has a wire trellis at the back. Two iron rods are firmly fixed at the corners, and wires stretched between them. Several small plants set in light, rich soil will soon form a dense screen for the front of the fireplace in summer and as a window screen in winter.

American Agriculturist, 1883

Editor's Note: The beauty of this box is that you can quickly move it wherever you need a decorative screen. See the preceding tip for building details.

If Space Is Short, Grow an Ivy Bush

A small ivy plant had its terminal bud pinched off, which caused two branches to start from the axils of the upper leaves; these when a few inches long were pinched, and as other branches grew they were treated in the same manner.

American Agriculturist, 1883

Editor's Note: Ivy will take on a different personality if you pinch it back to form a bush. Each time you remove a bud at the end of a vine, two new branches will appear, creating a fuller form.

Strange But True

Almost anything will do for a basket—anything that will hold earth. Even turnips and carrots can be hollowed out and made to hold pretty little plants.

Henry T. Williams
Window Gardening, 1881

Dependable Dripless Pots

A coarse sponge might be put in, if the vessel is deep, to drink up the surplus moisture, and yet keep the soil moist by giving it out again when dry. Hanging baskets provided with charcoal and the sponge in the bottom need not have a hole for drainage.

Henry T. Williams
Window Gardening, 1881

Editor's Note: A sponge is a good way to soak up excess water from potted plants, but it's no substitute for a drain hole. Your plants will be healthier if extra water can drain away from the roots instead of soaking them.

Put Parrot Tulips on Display

The parrot tulip is especially adapted for basket culture. The weak stems and heavy flower heads make it a difficult variety to grow effectively under ordinary conditions, but a wire basket lined with moss and filled with good earth, so planted that parrot tulips grow out from it in different directions, is one of the few ways in which both this plant and this form of decoration may be made really effective.

Amelia Leavitt Hill
Garden Portraits, 1923

Editor's Note: Parrot tulips have fancy ruffled petals. Like other tulips, they need a cold period in order to bloom. So plant them in baskets in fall using a well-drained soil mix; then place them in a cold frame or under a blanket of mulch. Check the soil occasionally to make sure it's moist. When the bulb tips grow one inch tall, bring the baskets inside to a window in a cool room. Once the plants start blooming, you can move them wherever you need some color.

Bluets in a Basket

For those who cultivate wildflowers, the *Houstonia caerulea* is one of the best of our early flowers for baskets. When set in a basket of leaf mould, they branch freely, spreading over the sides of the basket, and bloom profusely long after their companions have disappeared from the meadows. Their roots are so diminutive that they will thrive in a very small vessel. I once saw a clump growing in the inverted lid of a tea pot. Give them sunlight, keep the soil moist, and they will grow in a cup scarcely larger than an eggshell.

Margaret Donaldson
American Agriculturist, 1884

Editor's Note: Bluets or Quaker ladies (*Houstonia caerulea*, now known as *Hedyotis caerulea*) have tiny blue or white flowers in spring. Their little leaves are evergreen.

Bluets grow only two to four inches tall, which makes these little wildflowers suitable for your smallest containers—even a teapot lid will do!

Pretty Seashell Planter

Large seashells (nautilus or conch) will hold soil enough to support trailers (trailing plants), and are usually very tasteful window ornaments. One of the prettiest baskets was made from a single seashell, quite large. Holes were bored through the edge to fasten cords to hang it by; the interior of the shell was filled with light, rich soil, and *Lycopodiums* and lobelias were planted in it.

Henry T. Williams
Window Gardening, 1881

Editor's Note: Club mosses (*Lycopodium* spp.) are endangered plants, so leave them out of your seashell baskets. Annual lobelias and other cascading flowers like sweet alyssum, sedums, and ajuga are good plant choices. For shadier windows, fill your planters with creeping Jenny (*Lysimachia nummularia*), violets, or strawberry geraniums (*Saxifraga stolonifera*, also sold as *S. sarmentosa*).

A New Houseplant— Oaks!?

If an acorn be suspended by a bit of thread tied around it within half an inch of the surface of water contained in a small vase or tumbler, and allowed to remain undisturbed for one or two weeks in a warm place, it will burst its shell and throw a root into the water and shoot upwards, its straight and tapering stem covered with glossy green leaves. A young oak tree growing in this way is an elegant object. The water should be kept clean with bits of charcoal, and if the leaves turn yellow, add a little ammonia to it.

Henry T. Williams
Window Gardening, 1881

Thunbergia for Baskets

The thunbergias are excellent for baskets and all house decoration, for which they should be much more generally used in preference to many poor weedy things entirely worthless, that strangely seem to be received with more favor.

Vick's Illustrated Catalogue and Floral Guide, 1872

Editor's Note: *Thunbergia alata* is the black-eyed Susan vine, which has orange, yellow, or white one- to two-inch-wide blooms with dark centers. This vine can grow to six feet long and looks attractive in a hanging basket.

Turn Salad Bowls into Flower Bowls

Homemade baskets of wooden bowls, such as we use in our kitchens, are very common and desirable. Four or five holes should be bored in the bottom or sides, and there must be several holes bored around the edge in which to fasten the cords it is supported by—three are enough.

To ornament the outside of the bowl, choose the gray and white lichens of the woods, fasten them on with glue, or nail on with small brads. Such a basket, if planted with nothing more than the *Tradescantia zebrina*, and the green-leaved variety of the same plant, mingled with soft hanging grasses or the bright green of the moneywort, would be very pleasing.

Henry T. Williams
Window Gardening, 1881

Editor's Note: Leave the lichens in the woods, and let hanging plants decorate your wooden "baskets." One or two wandering Jews (*Tradescantia zebrina*, now known as *Zebrina pendula*) mixed with the rounded leaves and yellow flowers of moneywort or creeping Jenny (*Lysimachia nummularia*) will be plenty to fill, and overflow, your bowl.

OLD-TIME WISDOM

A water-saving hint from grandma. Most old-fashioned lady gardeners (and may we ever bless them for the many lessons they have taught us!) take every opportunity to set their window plants out of doors when a warm shower happens to occur.

The Gardener's Monthly, 1876

Wake Up to Morning Glories

This is a highly ornamental plant, of drooping, half shrubby character, slender habit, with a profusion of elegant light blue blossoms, forming an admirable plant for suspended vases or baskets. Flowers appear every morning.

Henry T. Williams
Window Gardening, 1881

Plant morning glory seeds in a hanging pot in late winter, and you'll have a basketful of blossoms all summer. These flowers also come in white and lavender.

Hanging Wire Basket

Here is a pretty wire basket, filled with ivy and ferns; branches of the partridge vine hang over the sides; the interior is filled with moss, and over them all peep out clusters of exquisite ferns. The stems of the ivy, ferns, and partridge vine are all stuck into bottles filled with water, and hid away here and there in the moss.

Henry T. Williams
Window Gardening, 1881

Editor's Note: The partridge vine is actually the groundcover called partridgeberry. This little woodland plant grows just one to two inches tall and has leathery evergreen leaves and bright red berries.

For an instant lightweight hanging basket that won't drip, place cuttings from your houseplants in small bottles and set them in a wire basket cushioned with moss. Remember to water your cuttings every few days.

Forcing Flowers

Bulbs That Guarantee Blooms

Whatever may have been the disappointment attending the cultivation of other plants, for winter blooming there are three that can be relied upon: hyacinth, crocus, and tulips.

E. B. Davis and B. G. Jefferis
The Household Guide, 1891

Editor's Note: You can buy prechilled bulbs that are ready to bloom from nurseries and mail-order catalogs. Put them in hyacinth jars, add water, and watch them grow—it's easier than trying to chill bulbs yourself. Hyacinth jars have wide mouths and narrow necks so they hold bulbs above the water and let the roots dangle down.

There Is Life after Forcing

The following plants that are forced into bloom for Easter time are perfectly hardy, and it is well worthwhile to save them for planting outdoors: spirea, lilacs, wisteria, lilies, and rambler roses. Plant outdoors when danger of frost is past. Do not throw away the single-flowering azaleas that may have been given to you in the holiday season. If given care, they will form new buds for the following winter. (Those with double flowers will not always form buds.)

Loring Underwood
A Garden Diary and Country Home Guide, 1908

Editor's Note: Forcing plants to bloom out of season stresses them—some recover after a rest, others don't. A summer outside is a good way to revive your Easter presents.

Strange But True

Many will doubtless be ready to exclaim, "Who would cut holes in one's dinner table or tablecloth for such a purpose?" Imagine the striking effect which young tree ferns or palms have in such a position, their elevated fronds shading the smaller arrangements of flower and fruit laid here and there.

A spare table leaf should be cut in two, and a half-circular piece cut out of each piece, which will leave a circular hole in the center. A wooden box should be placed as a stand for the plant. The plant should be placed on it and carefully raised to a proper height, keeping the surface of the pot just below the level of the table.

The Gardener's Monthly, 1874

Victorian gardeners enjoyed filling their parlors (and sometimes their dining rooms) with houseplants. If you'd like to recreate this extravagant table setting, all you need is a keyhole saw, a saber saw, an old table, and a good sense of humor.

Grow Hyacinths in Glasses

A healthy root growth is of the first importance. To secure this it is an excellent plan, about November first, to place the bulbs in a box of wet sand, say two inches in depth. The bulbs should not be pressed into the sand more than half an inch. Put the box where it is cool and dark, and the roots will start in a few days; when they are half an inch in length, the bulbs may be put in the glasses where they are to grow. Place the glasses, after they are filled with water enough to just touch the bulb, in a dark closet until the roots touch the bottoms of the glasses, then bring to the light.

C. L. Allen
Bulbs and Tuberous-Rooted Plants, 1893

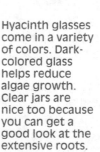

Hyacinth glasses come in a variety of colors. Dark-colored glass helps reduce algae growth. Clear jars are nice too because you can get a good look at the extensive roots.

Chill Lilies-of-the-Valley Outdoors

Lilies-of-the-valley may be started and flowered in pots very successfully. Twenty-five pips can be grown in a seven-inch pot. The top of the pip should be a little below the surface. Water thoroughly. Place in a cold frame or shed, where they can have a little frost, but not severe freezing. Some mulching should be thrown over the tops, to prevent freezing, as well as to keep the air from them. They should remain in this condition at least four weeks, when they may be forced.

C. L. Allen
Bulbs and Tuberous-Rooted Plants, 1893

Potting Soil for Keeping Daffodils

The ideal potting soil for daffodils is prepared six months or more before using. It should be sod taken from rich, loamy land. Make your "mold pile" by first putting down a layer of inverted sod, and then covering this with a layer of old manure—cow manure, thoroughly rotted, is the best. Over this spread a layer of leaf mold. Proceed in that way with another layer of inverted sod, etc., until the required quantity is stacked. This should be in the proportion of 50 percent loam sod, 25 percent manure, 25 percent leaf mold. Compost this by turning the pile three or four times during the season. Before using, add about four quarts of sand and two quarts of fine bonemeal to a bushel of the mold.

A. M. Kirby
Daffodils, Narcissus and How to Grow Them, 1907

Editor's Note: You can force bulbs and then throw them away, in which case you don't have to worry about potting soil. Crowd bulbs close together in a shallow container filled with gravel. Fill the container with water, just up to the bottoms of the bulbs, and they'll grow.

If you'd like to save your bulbs, start them out in a good potting mix like the one above. You can substitute potting soil for the loam sod and compost for the manure and leaf mold. Make sure your container has drain holes.

The fragrant poet's narcissus (*Narcissus poeticus*) will spread if you plant it outside. It's a good choice if you're looking for a bulb to force and keep.

Flowers from Christmas to Easter

The six pots of bulbs that gave us uninterrupted bloom were all started during the month of October, for house and table decoration (see the chart below.) The succession was managed by bringing the pots into the light at different times according to the needs of the case.

I. M. Angell
The Garden Magazine, 1906

Editor's Note: Here's how to start your own succession of blooms. Pot up healthy bulbs, place them in a cold frame, and cover the pots with mulch.

Bulbs require a cold period with temperatures of 33° to 50°F to develop roots. Tulips need 14 to 20 weeks of cold, daffodils need 16 to 22 weeks, and hyacinths need 10 to 14 weeks (they can take warmer temperatures). Crocuses and other small bulbs must have 12 weeks of cold. Make sure the bulbs are moist, and bring them inside when their tips have grown 1 inch tall. Keep the bulbs cool (50° to 55°F) until they bloom.

Don't bother trying to track down these same plants; hundreds of other varieties will do as well. But the 'Grand Soleil d'Or' narcissus deserves special mention. It is a yellow daffodil with many small, fragrant flowers on a stem. It remains a top choice for forcing.

Potted	Brought to Light	Blooming Period
Chinese lilies	10/30–11/13	2/23–1/12
'Double Roman' narcissus	10/19–12/19	1/13–1/25
'Grand Soleil d'Or' narcissus	10/5–12/7	1/22–2/13
Crocus	10/31–12/26	2/7–3/12
'Van Sion' narcissus	10/31–2/12	3/7–3/25
'Princess Marianne' tulip	10/31–3/1	3/23–4/12

Forcing Branches into Bloom

An interesting occupation is to force, into leaf and flower, twigs of many of the ornamental trees and shrubs. In March, cut branches two to three feet long, and place them in a vase of warm water in a sunny window. The following will respond quickly to the treatment: apples, pears, peaches, cherries, lilacs, flowering dogwood, and forsythia. Change the water every few days, and be content with small flowers.

Loring Underwood
A Garden Diary and Country Home Guide, 1908

Floral Arrangements

Keep Evergreens Fresh for Christmas

A great many people use holly and evergreens at Christmas time to stick about the room in empty vases, round pictures, etc. But they hardly ever take the trouble to peel their stalks and put them in water, though—especially with holly—this makes all the difference as regards the retaining of its freshness; and if arranged in a glass, not too thickly, it looks much more beautiful, and does not acquire a dusty, de-graded appearance before New Year's Day. I cannot bear to see the poor evergreens shrivelling in the hot rooms.

Marie Theresa Villiers Earle
More Pot-Pourri from a Surrey Garden, 1899

Decorate with Mountain Ash

I go in heavily for mountain ash. Its fruit is not a bright scarlet, but like everything which has a dash of orange it is more brilliant than a true red under artificial light. A few bunches make a magnificent decorative material.

Jabez Tompkins
The Garden Magazine, 1908

Editor's Note: The European mountain ash (**Sorbus aucuparia**) is a medium-size tree that grows from Zones 3 to 7. This tree has gorgeous fruit but is plagued by many insect pests and diseases and can't stand high temperatures. The Korean mountain ash (**S. alnifolia**) also has beautiful fruit, but it suffers from many of the same problems as the European mountain ash. Try to keep these trees healthy by givng them good, well-drained soil and as much water as they need.

Decorations from Acorns and Oak Galls

Acorns and oak puffballs (oak galls) can be used for decorating fancy baskets, brackets, or small tables. Provide each acorn with a stem of green crewel silk, about two inches long. Remove the cup, and run the silk through it with a large needle, and knot it inside the cup. The acorn can then be firmly glued into its place again. A bunch of these look very pretty hanging from a ribbon bow, or with a handful of oats or grasses, and can be used similarly by merely running a thread through each of the "balls" and knotting one end.

American Agriculturist, 1893

Editor's Note: A century ago, frugal gardeners would use almost anything to make an arrangement—even acorns and oak puffballs or galls. Puffballs are formed by the tree in reaction to insects living inside. Apparently, the oaks aren't harmed.

OLD-TIME WISDOM

A never-ending debate: Does music affect houseplants? Some fancyist has written about the benefits of music on the health of plants. Of course it is but a seasonable joke, but many of "the papers" are passing it around as the best of sense.

The Gardener's Monthly, 1876

Underwater Bouquet

I generally take sweet alyssum, fuschsias, rose geranium leaves, and perhaps a pink or two, arrange them in a small bouquet, wind the stems closely together with thread, then leave about a finger length of thread to which fasten a small pebble; also fasten tin foil around the stems. Get a pail of water, a glass tumbler, and a small plate, put the plate in the bottom of the pail, your bouquet in the glass with the stems upward, lower your glass in the pail upside down upon the plate, raise up your plate, and if all the air is out of the glass, you will have a beautiful bouquet to adorn parlor or schoolroom.

The Household, 1882

Editor's Note: This is a novel idea—a tiny bouquet inside an upside-down glass, full of water. You'll have to experiment to find a glass and plate that meet flush, without leaks.

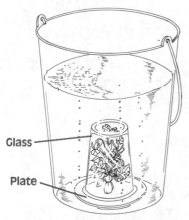

Glass

Plate

Assemble an underwater bouquet in a water-filled pail. If all goes according to plan, the water will stay in the overturned glass. But keep a sponge handy.

Forget-Me-Not Wreath

The common forget-me-not (*Myosotis sylvatica*), if gathered in bud and made into wreaths, and placed in water on a common dinner plate, will grow and flower for a long period, making a perfect mass of blue.

Nils Jonsson-Rose
Window and Parlor Gardening, 1895

Look to Trees for Bouquet Greens

In the late spring and early summer months, make use of the young shoots of the hornbeam. Their pleasing reddish-brown hue and beautifully crimped leaves have a fine effect in bouquets.

The Gardener's Monthly, 1873

Editor's Note: The American hornbeam (*Carpinus caroliniana*) is a small tree that likes partially shaded sites. Its leaves look similar to those of beech trees, and they turn bright orange to red in fall. The American hornbeam grows from Zones 3 to 9.

Pinecone Planters

Far prettier than many a pretentious and costly ornament is a simple bowl of grasses planted in pinecones, set in sand, in moss, or common soil. If grown in cones—procure them from the woods, and sprinkle in as much soil as their scales will re-

tain; then scatter the grass seed over it, and sprinkle with water; place the cones in sand or moss—and be sure that they do not become dry—but water them sparingly at first, once a day, and set in a moderately warm place. Soon the seeds will sprout, and the tiny spears protrude in every direction. Children can derive much pleasure from raising a grass garden.

Henry T. Williams
Window Gardening, 1881

A few pinecones, some soil, and a handful of leftover grass seed are all you need to make a Victorian "Chia pet." You can also use ornamental grass seed for an even showier arrangement. Try annual hare's-tail grass (*Lagurus ovatus*), which has woolly seedheads, or blue fescue (*Festuca cinerea*), with its silvery blue foliage.

Drying Grasses Naturally

When you cut grasses to dry for winter decoration, do not tie and hang them up, or they will dry in an upright, stiff position. Put them untied in an old pitcher, or even a bit of upright stove pipe in the attic, so that they fall and dry in graceful, natural shapes.

Farm Journal, 1887

Preserving Pampas Grass

Cut the pampas grass stems before the spikes are half out of the sheath, store them in a very dry place, and leave them undisturbed till entirely dried, then remove the leaf which partly envelops the spikes; the latter will appear perfectly bright, and with a silken gloss on them, only they are rather stiff. Then submit them to goodly heat, either in a well-heated oven, or, better still, before a brisk fire, when each floret will expand and give the spikes the featherlike appearance so much appreciated.

The Gardener's Monthly, 1877

Editor's Note: Pampas grass (**Cortaderia selloana**) is hardy from Zones 8 to 10, but you can grow it in colder areas if you let the leaves stand all winter and mulch plants well. Cut back the dead foliage in spring before new leaves emerge.

You've probably seen pampas grass decorating neighbors' yards. This 8- to 12-foot-tall South American grass produces large, feathery flower heads that look just as dramatic in bouquets as they do in the landscape. Mix these showy blooms with bold flowers like sunflowers for spectacular flower arrangements.

Make Pompoms out of Thistles

Select a large, half-blown (partly open) thistle and cut off all the green part at the base of the blossom, just above the stem. Hang the thistle in the open air, exposed to the sun and wind, and in the course of a day or two the inside downy part will expand into a full, rounded pompom, or puff ball. Then pull out the purple petals which had developed into blooms when you had selected the half-open thistle. Hang up the pompom again in an airy place, and in the course of a week it will have bleached a cream white. These pompoms are as feathery and delicately pretty as swan's down. They are a great addition to a bouquet, or a basket of grasses.

Yankee Blade, 1889

Making Milkweed Pompoms

Milkweed pompoms are more silky and nearer pure white than thistles. Have some very fine wire, such as is used for beadwork, and cut it into pieces four inches long. Dip the pod in water, and then open it. It will be found filled with many bundles of weblike white fibers. Pull off several of these and wrap the wire around the ends which were attached to the center stem. Brush off the black seeds adhering to the other ends. Wire a number of the bundles, as just described, then with another piece of wire, to wind round and round, put them together as you would a bouquet of flowers, thus making a rounded pompom.

Yankee Blade, 1889

Pest, Disease, and Weed Control

Bunnies and birds, slugs and snails,
mildew, thistles, and more caused just
as many problems for old-time gardeners
as they do for us today. In this chapter,
you'll find great organic controls
from the past that are both
effective and safe.

Pest, Disease, and Weed Control

Attract Garden Allies

Birds Year-Round

Observe that it is quite important to keep insect-eating birds with us, and at work all winter. A supply of winter food should include mountain ash, viburnum, pokeberry, barberry, hackberry, and dogwood.

Amelia Leavitt Hill
Garden Portraits, 1923

Gardener's Best Friend

Many insects are preyed upon by native birds, and it is strange that so few of our gardeners are familiar with this fact. While they are in the garden battling with the destructive insects, their sons, with air gun and sling, are destroying their best friends. Birds should be protected against the ruthless onslaught of cruel and thoughtless boys.

E. B. Davis and B. G. Jefferis,
The Household Guide, 1891

The Protection of Birds means the Destruction of Insects.

Birds are efficient insect eaters that belong in and around your garden. Provide them with water and with trees and shrubs for berries and shelter, and they'll repay your kindness by providing pest control.

A Modest Bird Sanctuary

Even one elderberry bush or a single dogwood tree can constitute a bird sanctuary and, if near a window, may afford greater pleasure to the observer inside than a woodland preserve covering acres would to its owner if he took no interest in birds. I have a handsome dogwood tree just off my sun porch which is visited by birds every day in the year.

Herbert Durand
Wild Flowers and Ferns, 1925

Briars Save Birds from Cats

Belling a cat will prevent it from capturing old birds, but will not keep it from pouncing upon and devouring fledglings. A conveniently located tangle of catbriers and blackberry brambles will prove much more effective, by providing a refuge into which cats and other predatory animals cannot easily penetrate.

Herbert Durand
Wild Flowers and Ferns, 1925

Cat-Proof Birdhouse Posts

I tried the simple and effective remedy of wrapping tightly about the birdhouse pole, six feet from the ground, a section of old stove pipe, about two feet long, and securely fastening it with nails. A coat of paint made it hardly distinguishable from the pole itself. Before the paint was dry, one of the cats that had been making frequent dashes up the pole, to the great annoyance of the birds, made a rush and went up the pole as far as the tin, when her claws failed to hold and she fell back to the ground, surprised and no doubt wondering what had happened.

A. C. Hall
The Garden Magazine, 1908

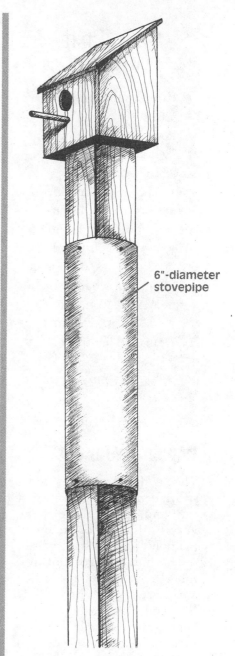

6"-diameter stovepipe

By covering part of a birdhouse post with a section of stovepipe, you can keep cats from troubling nesting birds. Use six-inch-diameter pipe for a standard four-inch-square post. Because pipe usually comes with an open side seam, you can slip a section around a post that's already in place.

OLD-TIME WISDOM

Share your bounty with the birds. Birds are sometimes harmful, but on the whole they do more good than harm in a garden, and I am inclined to agree with an old gardener, who, when having caught a blackbird among the gooseberries, was asked by his master what he had done with it. "Oh," he replied, "I just gave 'im a warning and let 'im go."

Harry Roberts
The Book of Old-Fashioned Flowers, 1904

Impound Your Cat

The family cat succeeds in destroying nine birds' nests out of ten; and, unfortunately, the very birds we most need to multiply—such as the catbirds, indigo bird (indigo bunting), robin, and song sparrow. I like a cat, but cannot allow all my best-laid plans to be circumvented by an unscrupulous carnivora. I strongly suggest you furnish your grimalkin with summer quarters, where he can have good shade, with shelter from showers, a back yard and a front yard; and all securely under netting. Feed him well, and talk with him once in a while; but don't let him loose until the birds' nests are empty of fledglings—sometime in September.

E. P. Powell
The Orchard and Fruit Garden, 1914

Editor's Note: An easier option than building an elaborate outdoor shelter for your cat is just to keep it indoors. If neighboring cats are bothering your birds, lay chicken wire on the ground under the birds' nesting areas and the cats will stay away.

The Helpful White-Faced Hornet

During the last few years the pear psylla has made havoc. Bear in mind that the little white-faced hornet is of immense value from the fact that it destroys millions of such insects in the larval state. Their nests of paper will follow very closely after the appearance of the psylla, and should never be destroyed. This little hornet rarely troubles man or beast.

E. P. Powell
The Orchard and Fruit Garden, 1914

Editor's Note: Pear psyllas look like little 1/10-inch-long cicadas. Their young are tiny nymphs that suck juices from pear leaves and fruit.

The adult white-faced hornet is valued as a beneficial insect because it feeds pest insects to its larvae. Its papery nests are roundish and hang from branches.

Strange But True

When I was young, I was told if I killed toads the cows would give bloody milk; being fond of milk, the fear of such catastrophe saved the toads.

Boston Cultivator, 1868

Editor's Note: Killing toads might not affect your milk, but it sure can affect your harvest. One toad can eat 10,000 to 20,000 insects in a growing season. Rather than squash toads, try to attract these pest eaters by providing them with water in a shallow saucer and with a moist, shady shelter.

Invite Toads In to Keep Insects Out

There is no better insect destroyer than the toad. He will eat one hundred rose bugs or slugs in one night. If you haven't plenty of these sturdy little hoppers in your garden, go on a hunt to collect some and bring them home in a bag.

Loring Underwood
A Garden Diary and Country Home Guide, 1908

Attract toads rather than kidnapping them, and they're more likely to stick around. Build toads a shelter by chipping a piece out of the rim of an old flowerpot for a doorway. Turn the pot upside down, and presto—you've got a toad house.

Pit Toads against Pea Aphids

My garden peas were badly infested with the pea aphid. I put several toads in the garden, and in a very short time the aphids had disappeared. It was amusing to watch the toads at work; they would jump as high as they could on the vines, shake down the aphids, and then feast on the result of their labors.

L. C. Porter
The Garden Magazine, 1909

Controlling Insect Pests

Save Your Soapsuds

It is not perhaps generally known that soap suds form one of the most valuable applications to a great number of vegetables, and that by allowing them to be thrown away, a serious loss to the garden and fruit orchard is sustained. Applied to melons, squashes, and cucumbers, it materially aids their growth, besides having a good effect in helping to banish the multitude of worms, bugs, and flies that harbor near them, and feed upon them. It is one of the best remedies for plants attacked by the plant louse

(aphid), and would annually save large numbers of turnips, cabbages, etc., from falling a prey to this minute but formidable insect, were it thrown over them instead of being thrown away.

Genesee Farmer, 1838

Editor's Note: Soap isn't what it used to be—now it's apt to contain all sorts of perfumes, colorings, and additives to increase performance. Garden centers and mail-order catalogs sell soaps especially formulated for ridding plants of bugs.

Parboil Insect Pests

The hot-water bath will, in nearly every case, take the place of insecticides and give better results, as it thoroughly cleanses the foliage and leaves no bad effects, if not too hot. Heat to 140°F if for spraying, and use before it cools; or 136°F if the plants are to be dipped.

Ida D. Bennett
The Flower Garden, 1904

Editor's Note: A hot-water spray or dip that lasts one to three seconds can kill pests. Don't let the exposure to hot temperatures last any longer than that or you may kill or injure plants. Wear rubber gloves, safety glasses, a long-sleeved shirt, and pants when you turn up the heat on pests, and take care that you don't get burned.

Dunk Rose Pests

There are no less than thirty-two different enemies among insects known to science which prey on the rose. Of late, a new mode of catching these in many forms has been made by hanging up wide-necked glass jars half filled with a sweetened substance, as molasses water, or a weak solution of fruit syrup, into which the insects dive for a drink and so get caught, and they cannot escape.

Meehans' Monthly, 1897

Editor's Note: Other old-time control methods that are still effective today are handpicking and spraying plants with water. Handpick Japanese beetles, rose chafers, rose curculios, and sawflies. Spray water vigorously on the tops and bottoms of rose leaves to keep aphids and spider mites from becoming big problems.

Gooey Molasses Trap

To keep off flies, ants, and other insects from houseplants and outdoor plants, take dry branches of the same size and quality of the molested plants, and grease them over with molasses, add flour to make it thick and so as not to run off when warmed by the sun. The luxurious ant or fly will soon try to taste, and entangle its feet or wings, and is catched. Repeat greasing when necessary.

The Household, 1878

Insect Pests A to Z

Ants

Milk Traps Lure Ants

Place small gallipots (small dishes) about half full of milk and a little sugar on the ants' "high road," into which they will soon find their way, congregating in hundreds around the edges of the milk, when by constantly tapping the gallipot the ants are shaken into the mixture and drowned.

Meehans' Monthly, 1891

Beetles

Attack Asparagus Beetles

If there are only a few asparagus beetles, they may be crushed between the finger and the thumb. They must especially be looked for during bright sunshine, which is the time they generally make their appearance. If they are too many to be destroyed in this way, we must take a bowl or other vessel full of water, and holding it under the asparagus, tap the stems lightly, so as to shake off the insects into the water. As soon as they feel the blow their instinct teaches them to imitate death and drop off the shoot. When all have been caught the water may be thrown on the ground and the insects crushed to death with the foot.

James Barnes and William Robinson
Asparagus Culture, 1881

Asparagus beetles gnaw the tips of their favorite plant in spring and its leaves in summer. They have ¼-inch-long bluish black bodies. You'll usually see them with their wings folded over their backs. The wing covers have 4 white spots and a red border.

Look Out for Larvae

The gardener often observes his cucumber vines withering at the root. It soon extends to the head until they die, when he remarks, "The dry weather is killing my vines." On examination, however, the bark will be found entirely removed or perforated with innumerable small surface pits, but the cucumber beetle larvae have by this time disappeared, having entered the ground while yet the vine appeared healthy.

Boston Cultivator, 1865

Editor's Note: Two types of beetles attack your cucumber vines: the striped cucumber beetle and the spotted cucumber beetle. You can keep both pests off your crop by covering seeds or transplants with cheesecloth or a floating row cover immediately after planting.

Strange But True

The oak apples being broken in sunder about the time of their withering, so foreshow the sequel of the year, as the expert Kentish husbandmen have observed by the living things found in them: as if they find an ant, they foretell plenty of grain to insue; if a white worm, then prognosticate sickness of beasts and cattle; if a spider, then (say they) we shall have a pestilence of some such like sickness to follow amongst men.

John Gerard
The Herball, 1633

Gardeners have always been interested in telling the future, especially when it relates to harvests or the weather. If you have an oak tree with "oak apples," you can try the method Gerard describes. Oak apples are galls or growths that form on oak trees when they are injured by insects. Slice the galls open and see what's inside. You're likely to find the larva of the wasp that formed the gall. It looks like a white worm, so watch your beasts!

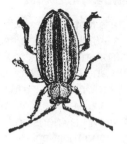

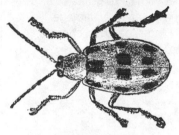

Striped cucumber beetles (*left*) are yellow or orange with 3 black stripes and a black head. Spotted cucumber beetles (*right*) are greenish yellow with 11 black spots on their backs and a small black head. Both beetles are ¼ inch long.

Try Onions against Cucumber Beetles

To keep striped cucumber beetles off cucumbers, try planting an onion in each hill.

Farm Journal, 1895

Tents Taunt Cucumber Beetles

Place over each cucumber hill a thin piece of cheesecloth about two feet square, and fasten the edges down by loose earth. A little twig may be bent in the form of a curve and stuck into the ground to keep the cloth from the plants.

E. B. Davis and B. G. Jefferis
The Household Guide, 1891

By arching a twig over a young cucumber, melon, or squash plant, you can support a square of cheesecloth to form a barrier against cucumber beetles. For large cucumber patches, cover your plants with a floating row cover or floating insect barrier, and remove the material when the plants start to flower.

Block Out Cucumber Beetles

The best way to raise vines which cucumber beetles feed upon is to get eight-inch tile, cut them in two in the middle, and set into the earth several inches, plant the seeds inside the tile and keep it covered with a window glass until the vines are beyond the reach of the bugs. The glass draws the heat and makes the growth thrifty and rapid.

E. B. Davis and B. G. Jefferis
The Household Guide, 1891

Editor's Note: Vinyl tiles would work as well as ceramic ones. You can cut them easily by scoring them with a utility knife and then snapping the tiles over a straight-edge. Set the tile walls in a square surrounding each seed; then add a glass or plastic roof to create a mini-greenhouse.

Cure for Plum Curculio

We tested the plan of strewing tomato vines under plum trees, as a preventative of the curculio; and on a tree that we have invariably lost all, or nearly every plum, we had a nice quantity of most-beautiful fruit.

Shaker and Shakeress Monthly, 1878

Editor's Note: Plum curculios are ¼-inch-long, dark brown snout beetles (weevils) that feed on leaves, flower petals, and fruit. They also lay eggs in young fruit that hatch into grubs. These pests seriously damage apples, plums, peaches, cherries, apricots, and nectarines.

Borers

Snag Currant Borers

The currant borer is a great pest, eating out the pith of the young shoots, and causing them to grow poorly and bear but small fruit next year. Gummy "flypaper" is, we think, the best thing to catch them.

The Gardener's Monthly, 1877

Editor's Note: Flypaper is used to snare the adult form of the currant borer, a small, slender moth that is active during the day. With its clear wings, the moth looks something like a wasp. To check for the borers, look for holes the larvae make at the base of currant canes. Cut out and burn infested canes.

Stop Strawberry Borers

Strawberry plants may be wrapped in wire fly screening (window screening) when set; the roots grow through the netting, but the grubs cannot get to the crown.

S. W. Fletcher
Strawberry-Growing, 1917

Editor's Note: Two kinds of grubs attack strawberries: the larvae of strawberry crown moths and the larvae of strawberry crown borers (adult borers are weevils). The moths and weevils lay eggs on the plants, and their larvae or grubs hatch out and burrow into the strawberry crowns. Destroy infected plants since there is no cure.

Give Grubs the Heave-Ho

If a strawberry plant collapses, dig it up and kill the white grubs on the roots.

The Garden Magazine, 1906

Editor's Note: The white grubs of root weevils bore into the roots and crowns of strawberry plants, stunting and sometimes killing them. The adult weevils clip half-circles from the leaf edges and cut off flower stems. If plants are infested, kill the brown-headed larvae as recommended above, or drench the soil with insect-parasitic nematodes when the larvae are present, in early May (when the soil warms) and in August.

Carry Coal Ashes against Borers

About small trees use a peck of ashes, and about old trees pile a bushel or more. That is the true remedy for all borers that work around the base or crown of trees.

E. P. Powell
The Orchard and Fruit Garden, 1914

Editor's Note: It's easy to try this remedy if you live in a coal-burning area. If you don't, keep the soil at the base of the tree trunks clear of mulch. Probe inside borer holes with a piece of wire to kill the pests. Scrape away damaged wood, and paint the area with a one-to-one mix of lime sulfur and white latex paint.

Bugs

Squash Bugs: Off with Their Heads

The large black squash bug which infests squashes and pumpkins is a formidable insect, often destroying the whole plant. It very rarely attempts to fly away, and may be caught without difficulty. We never crush them, but decapitate them with the thumbnail.

Genesee Farmer, 1838

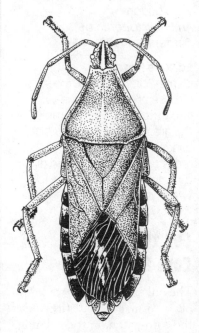

The squash bug preys on melons and cucumbers in addition to squash and pumpkins. Why should you behead them instead of crushing them? Because squash bug juice stinks. You can avoid the whole messy procedure if you cover young plants with floating row covers. Remove the covers when the plants flower.

It's a Cinch to Catch Chinch Bugs

In order to prevent corn plants from lodging (falling over), let the interstices of the leaf blade and stalk be filled with sand or loose dirt, flatten the earth at the root, by clapping it with the hoe, and then shake the insects off. By this means they will all fall on the hill, where they can be beaten with the hoe, and covered over with dirt so as to prevent their recovery. The hill must be clapped smooth with the hoe each morning, and left in that way, so as the better to get at the bugs the next morning.

Farmers' Cabinet, 1837

Editor's Note: If you don't have time to smash chinch bugs each morning, interplant your corn with soybeans or bush beans—the bugs don't like the shade and so tend to stay away.

OLD-TIME WISDOM

Enlist in the war on bugs. In your generation and mine, men must shoulder their squirt guns as our ancestors shouldered their muskets.

L. H. Bailey
American Garden, 1890

Harlequin Bug Trap

Sow mustard early as a catch crop and destroy the bugs thereon with kerosene, or resort to hand picking.

Ida D. Bennett
The Vegetable Garden, 1908

Editor's Note: Kerosene doesn't really have a place in the garden anymore, but knocking the bugs into a jar of soapy water will kill them just as effectively. Planting wild mustard can have a beneficial effect beyond serving as a trap crop. The red and black, shield-shaped harlequin bug has enemies, namely, parasitic wasps. These wasps are attracted by small-flowered plants like mustard that provide them with pollen and nectar. Other good plant choices include dill, parsley, catnip, and goldenrod.

Caterpillars and Moths

Catch That Caterpillar

Catching the adult caterpillar (usually a moth) is undoubtedly the most certain plan for preventing a renewal of the same injury the following year, for the death of one female will cut off a generation of many hundred larvae; but from the difficulty that attends its general adoption, the time that is requisite to become expert in the use of the insect net, and the uncertainty of capturing that particular moth which does the injury (all moths flying only at night), it does not appear likely to be of much practical utility. It is obvious that if the caterpillars are numerous, twenty may be picked in the same time that two moths might be caught, and thus the advantage of one operation over the other is as two to twenty.

J. C. Loudon
An Encyclopedia of Gardening, 1850

Editor's Note: Just be sure to identify caterpillars before you dispose of them—some turn into butterflies. For example, the green caterpillar with black bands and yellow dots that feeds on your parsley and dill turns into the beautiful black swallowtail butterfly.

Con the Corn Earworm

The only remedy that we know of, is to make small fires near the corn-patch, in the evening, to attract the moths, and in this way destroy them before laying their eggs.

P. T. Quinn
Money in the Garden, 1871

Editor's Note: This pest also goes by the name of tomato fruitworm. The adults are light tan moths with 1½- to 2½-inch wingspans. Their larvae are light green, pink, yellow, or brown with white and dark stripes on their sides. Corn earworm larvae eat corn silks and kernels. They also gnaw holes in tomato leaves and burrow into the fruits.

Boil the Corn Rootworm

Get a supply of old gourds or squashes; cut an inch hole in each, and after removing half of the old pulp, set them about in infested places. It is astonishing what a liking the beetle has for the old gourds, which form good hiding places. By stopping the hole with a corncob I disposed of the catch with boiling water.

M. F. Berry
American Agriculturist, 1894

Editor's Note: Corn rootworms are white, slender, ½- to ¾-inch-long larvae with brown heads. They feed on corn roots and spread bacterial wilt disease. The adults are beetles that feed on pollen, leaves, and corn silk. There are different types of rootworms in various parts of the country. Western rootworm adults are ¼-inch-long yellow beetles with 3 black stripes. Northern rootworm adults are yellow to pale green beetles, and southern rootworm adults are yellow-green with 11 black spots—they're also known as spotted cucumber beetles.

Trap Cutworms with Clover

The thought occurred to me that the worms might be baited and taken so as to clear the land of cutworms before the tomato plants were set. Accordingly, I mowed some clover and applied it fresh in little compact wads about the size of a large apple; the result was, that on the next morning I found the worms had collected about the clover in great numbers. I have this day destroyed with my own hands over 15,000 cutworms. I did it by pouring boiling water over and about these wads of clover.

D. Boynton
The Gardener's Monthly, 1872

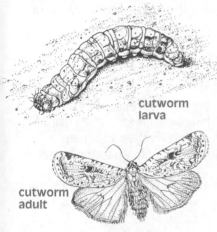

cutworm larva

cutworm adult

Cutworms are the larvae of a gray or brown night-flying moth with a 1- to 1½-inch wingspan. The larvae grow 1 to 2 inches long, are gray or brown, and curl up when you bother them. If your cutworm troubles start after you've already planted your vegetables, place cardboard collars around the stem of each seedling or transplant to keep the worms away.

Use Skunk Cabbage against Cutworms

The Shaker gathered the skunk cabbage. He dropped the leaves from six to seven feet apart between the rows, and found it to succeed to admiration; as on an examination a few days afterward, he found the corn untouched, but under each leaf of weed he had dropped he found from twenty-three to forty-seven cutworms. The worms being thus collected were easily destroyed.

Farmer's Monthly Visitor, 1839

Editor's Note: The Shaker refers to a member of a religious community. Skunk cabbage was probably handy for this farmer, but any large leaf should do the trick.

Lure Cutworm Moths with a Light (and Milk)

A great enemy of garden plants is the larva of the dark-colored miller or moth. This worm will cut off the plant close to the ground. Place a lighted lamp or torch in the garden in the early part of the evening and a pan of water well whitened with milk nearby, and many of the moths will fall victims.

E. B. Davis and B. G. Jefferis
The Household Guide, 1891

Recipe
Moth Destroyer

½ pound dried rosemary
½ pound dried mint
¼ pound dried tansy
¼ pound dried thyme
2 tablespoonfuls fresh ground cloves

Mix well together and store in a well-closed box. Scatter lavishly among fur, blankets, and clothing as they are stored and no moth will go near them.

Mrs. Marian Cran
The Garden of Ignorance, 1913

Spread Coal Ashes to Check Cutworms

Insects that work on the surface of the ground, like cutworms, may be held in check by spreading fine coal ashes around the roots of plants.

Loring Underwood
A Garden Diary and Country Home Guide, 1908

Editor's Note: In coal-burning areas, coal ashes are easy to come by. In other areas, you can try wood ashes or diatomaceous earth, a fine powder made from the fossilized shells of algae known as diatoms.

Mow Down the Strawberry Leafroller

Mow the strawberry plants close to the ground while the worm is among the leaves. Let them dry a short time and pile them up with a little straw and burn them. It is also recommended to burn them right over the roots of the plants. This can be done without much injury to the strawberry plants.

E. B. Davis and B. G. Jefferis
The Household Guide, 1891

Editor's Note: The author is probably referring to the strawberry leafroller. These green or brown, ½-inch-long caterpillars are the larvae of a small moth. They form webs and roll themselves up in strawberry leaves as they feed.

Codling Moth Potion

The codling moth is fond of the bottle. Fill some with vinegar and molasses, and they will drink—drowning sorrow and life at the same time.

The Household, 1879

Editor's Note: Adult codling moths are gray-brown moths with a ¾-inch wingspan. They lay eggs in fruit trees in early spring, which is when you should offer them this potion.

Trap Bugs in a Rug

Bands of carpet, fastened around the trunks of apple trees with a single long tack, will catch many appleworms (the 1-inch-long larvae of codling moths). Examine weekly and kill.

American Agriculturist, 1884

Earwigs

Beans Keep Currants Clean

As currants are very liable to be devoured by earwigs, which take shelter under their leaves and branches, bundles of beanstalks should be hung up some time before the bushes are covered with mats or nets to protect the fruits from birds. After the bushes are covered, take the mats off once in three or four days, and kill the earwigs that have got into the beanstalks, which it will be necessary still to keep up. As there is a sweetness in the inside of beanstalks which attracts the earwigs, they very readily take shelter in them from the rain.

J. C. Loudon
An Encyclopedia of Gardening, 1850

Editor's Note: Earwigs are beetlelike insects with a pair of pincers on their abdomen. (There's no truth to the rumor that they crawl inside people's ears.) Earwigs are omnivorous: They'll eat nearly anything, including fruit, vegetable, and animal matter. They usually don't harm plants and often get the blame for damage done by other night-feeding pests. Earwigs can even be good guys, feeding on aphids and other small insects. Before you trap them, make sure they're the pests that are eating your currants.

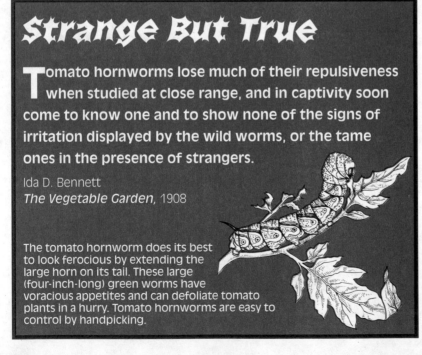

Strange But True

Tomato hornworms lose much of their repulsiveness when studied at close range, and in captivity soon come to know one and to show none of the signs of irritation displayed by the wild worms, or the tame ones in the presence of strangers.

Ida D. Bennett
The Vegetable Garden, 1908

The tomato hornworm does its best to look ferocious by extending the large horn on its tail. These large (four-inch-long) green worms have voracious appetites and can defoliate tomato plants in a hurry. Tomato hornworms are easy to control by handpicking.

Flies

Flies Flee Loosestrife

Lysimachia vulgaris (garden loosestrife) is a somewhat downy herb with yellow flowers in showy branching clusters in summer. The peculiar odor of the plant is said to keep away flies, and the Romans are reported to have put the leaves under the yokes of their oxen in the belief that if they were kept free of flies they would be less quarrelsome.

Louise Beebe Wilder
The Fragrant Path, 1932

Editor's Note: This wildflower is a garden escapee, and you can see it along roadsides from maritime Canada through the northeastern United States. You probably won't find it in garden catalogs because it's been replaced by more ornamental loosestrifes like yellow loosestrife (**Lysimachia punctata**). You can see if other loosestrifes have the same fly-shooing effect. If not, you'll still have a pretty perennial for moist spots in Zones 3 to 8.

Chase Flies with Wild Indigo

The wild indigo, *Baptisia tinctoria*, or false indigo, has pretty yellow, pea-shaped blossoms, and small oval leaves, thick and simple, with a disagreeable smell when bruised. The most use I have ever seen made with the plant is placing them beneath the bridle head-stall on

the horses' heads, to keep the carnivorous flies from plaguing the horses.

F. K. Steele
Meehans' Monthly, 1898

Flies Will Rue the Day

A few sprigs of rue hung in a room will keep flies from the apartment.

M. Grieve
Culinary Herbs and Condiments, 1934

Rue has a curious scent that not everyone likes. Even insects tend to stay away from it. Handle rue with gloves since it may irritate your skin.

Roll Over Cabbage Maggots

Nothing protects young turnips, cabbages, and other cruciferous plants so effectually from the depredations of the fly, as the operation of rolling. For when the surface of the ground is thus rendered smooth, the insects are deprived of a lodging place under the clods of earth, and disperse.

Genesee Farmer, 1838

Editor's Note: The fly is the adult stage of the cabbage maggot. Females lay their eggs in the soil beside plant roots. The larvae or maggots hatch, tunnel in the roots for three or four weeks, then pupate in the soil.

Packing the soil tight makes it harder for these pests to find shelter and discourages them from making a home near your crops. You can keep female flies from laying eggs by covering plants with floating row covers or mounding wood ashes, diatomaceous earth, powdered ginger, or powdered hot pepper around the plant stems.

Onion Maggot Mulch Cure

A Westminster, Massachusetts, farmer prescribes white pine sawdust broadcast to save onions from the ravages of the worms. It should be sown as soon as the onions are up.

Boston Cultivator, 1865

Editor's Note: Onion maggots are ¼-inch-long, white wormlike pests that burrow into onions, killing young plants and hollowing out or stunting older plants. The adult form of the onion maggot is a ¼-inch-long gray fly.

Sawflies

Cows Make Gooseberry Pests Cringe

The plan of pouring cow urine around the stem of the gooseberry bush may be useful at particular seasons, when certain insects may be lodged in the ground in their chrysalis state.

J. C. Loudon
An Encyclopedia of Gardening, 1850

Editor's Note: Loudon was probably trying to eradicate the imported currant-worm with this novel approach. The adult sawfly lays its eggs on gooseberry bushes. The larvae feed on the leaves and then drop to the ground to pupate. They overwinter in cocoons, not chrysalis cases, which are

the homes of pupating butterfly larvae.

The imported currantworms lift both ends of their body when they're disturbed—it's a good way to recognize these 1-inch-long green worms with black spots. The adult form is a sawfly, just ⅕ inch long, that lays shiny white, flattened eggs on the undersides of leaves.

OLD-TIME WISDOM

Little hands versus imported currantworms. Employ children to collect the egg-bearing leaves at a certain rate per hundred: these are to be burned or scalded.

J. C. Loudon
An Encyclopedia of Gardening, 1850

Editor's Note: Of course, it's the leaves, not the children, that are to be burned or scalded. Gardening books of the 1800s often recommended hiring children for pest control.

Make Pear Slugs Bite the Dust

Dark slimy slugs on the leaves of the pear or cherry trees? Dry road dust, thrown in the trees, will kill every slug it covers.

Farm Journal, 1906

Pear slug adult

Pear slug larva

Adult pear slugs are black and yellow sawflies that are just a little larger than houseflies. Their ½-inch-long larvae aren't really slugs—they just look like them and are covered with slime. Pear slug larvae are dark green to orange. They gnaw on the upper surface of leaves until the foliage looks skeletonized and scorched.

Dust is an effective way to kill these pests, but if you have a hose handy, you can also wash them off trees with a hard spray of water.

Not for the Squeamish

The larvae of the rose fly, in the form of small green caterpillars, which skeletonize the leaves, are easily kept down by *pinching them*. If the job is too severe for delicate nerves, there are plenty of boys who will clear one's whole rose patch of them in an hour for 25 cents.

The Gardener's Monthly, 1871

Editor's Note: The rose fly is a sawfly whose velvety green larvae look somewhat sluglike. The larvae grow to ½ inch long by munching on the soft parts of rose leaves. Handpicking is an effective control, but at today's prices, you'll be paying a lot more than a quarter to de-slug your rose patch.

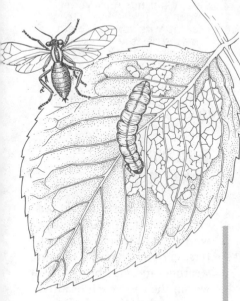

Sawfly larvae (*right*) skeletonize rose leaves by eating the upper surface and leaving just the veins and lower leaf intact. The adult rose slug (*left*) is a typical sawfly with clear wings.

Slugs and Snails

Leafy Slug Snare

The most effectual way of destroying slugs is to place cabbage leaves near those plants that appear to have suffered from their attacks: on examining this bait early in the morning, the slugs will be found upon it; and, by repeating this for several days, great numbers may be captured and destroyed.

J. C. Loudon
An Encyclopedia of Gardening, 1850

Electric Collar Shocks Slugs!

The only thing I have found really efficacious in warding off slug attacks is a ring of zinc around the plant. It is not ornamental, but can be removed as soon as the plant has made its growth, when the slugs can do but comparatively little damage, the crucial time being when growth is just commencing. These zinc rings are simple to make. Get a sheet of zinc and cut into strips about 1¼ inch wide, and long enough to go round the plant, and fasten the ends together with copper wire. The theory is that as zinc and copper in contact create a certain amount of electricity, the marauding slug gets a shock on touching this

barrier. Whether this is the case or not I cannot say, but the fact remains that they will not cross the zinc.

Lewis B. Meredith
Rock Gardens, 1914

All-copper collars repel slugs just as well as zinc and copper ones and are available through garden-supply catalogs.

Enlist Citrus against Snails

Set traps by scattering pieces of orange peel over the ground. Snails are so fond of this delicacy that they will remain clinging to the peel rather than go back to their hiding places at the break of day. Examine the traps every morning, and destroy the marauders.

Jacob Biggle
Biggle Garden Book, 1912

Spider Mites

Hot Water Wilts Mites

The hollyhock is subject to attack very early in the season by a variety of red spider which feeds on out-of-door plants. The plants may simply be showered with hot water at about 145°F.

Ida D. Bennett
The Flower Garden, 1904

Editor's Note: A one- to three-second shower is long enough to kill insect pests. Longer doses may injure your plants.

Scent Spider Mites Away

The exhalation given out by bruised laurel leaves, will more effectually destroy the red spider than simply syringing the plants.

J. C. Loudon
An Encyclopedia of Gardening, 1850

Springtails

Dung Does Pests In

Take the dung of horses and put that upon the field, and the springtails or ground fleas will no longer do you any harm.

John George Hohman
The Long-Lost Friend, 1819

Editor's Note: Garden springtails are tiny insects, ⅕ inch long, that can jump like fleas. They can chew holes in thin-leaved plants like spinach, and they may munch on the cotyledons, or seed leaves, of beans and cucumbers. Normally springtails won't cause you any trouble. If they do, try Hohman's advice.

Wireworms

Potato Shish Kebab Traps Wireworms

Hand-picking is effected by placing in the pests' way, as a trap, more-tempting food than that afforded by the plant from which it is desired to remove them. For the wireworm, and other insects that feed upon the roots of vegetables, let slices of potatoes be stuck through with skewers, and then buried near the seeds or plants; the grubs will collect upon these slices during the night; and by examining them in the morning, vast numbers may be captured.

J. C. Loudon
An Encyclopedia of Gardening, 1850

Editor's Note: The adult wireworm is the click beetle, named for the sound it makes when it flips onto its feet. The adult beetle feeds on leaves and flowers but typically doesn't do much damage.

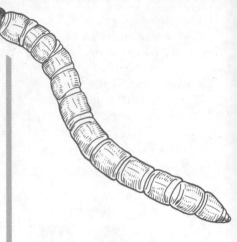

Wireworms are the larvae of click beetles. These 1½-inch-long, yellow to brown, leathery, jointed, wormlike insects bore into the seeds, crowns, and roots of vegetables as well as some flowers like gladiolus. Affected plants may be stunted or killed. Delay plantings until your garden soil is very warm to prevent wireworm problems. Once the pests are present, lure them to pieces of raw potato or carrot buried several inches deep near your root crops. Destroy all of the wireworms that collect there.

Turn Wireworms out of Bed

Late fall plowing is doubly beneficial, as it turns the wireworms out of their winter quarters, exposes them to freezing weather, and also brings them within the easy reach of insect-eating birds.

American Agriculturist, 1883

Aggravating Animal Pests

Birds Bypass Pie Cherries

The sweet cherry is usually devoured by the birds—the robin, among its many virtues, having especially this great sin to answer for. But not even the ruthless English sparrow cares to take the pie or sour cherry for dessert.

Meehans' Monthly, 1901

Sour or pie cherries (*Prunus cerasus*) are easier to grow than sweet cherries. They're great for baking and taste sweet enough to eat off the tree if you let them get very ripe.

Feed the Birds

Professor Beal of Michigan advises planting the native shadberry and the Russian mulberry to protect cherries; and the elderberry and the choke-cherry to protect raspberries and blackberries in July and August. In September and October those birds which meddle with peaches and grapes are fond of the fruit of the Virginia creeper, which may be easily grown over old stumps and stone fences.

E. P. Powell
The Orchard and Fruit Garden, 1914

Editor's Note: Plant birds' favorite foods and they'll leave your favorite fruits alone. The shadberry is also known as the downy serviceberry or juneberry (*Amelanchier arborea*). It's a multistemmed shrub or small tree with fruits that taste somewhat like blueberries.

Protect Cherries with More Cherries

Some cherry growers plant early sweet varieties to feed the birds, which, getting their fill, give less attention to the main crop.

L. H. Bailey
The Horticulturist's Rule-Book, 1895

Make the Most of Mulberries

The Russian mulberry is wonderfully productive, and a single tree of this fruit we find very tempting to the birds, as they prefer mulberries to almost any other fruit, and it affords plenty of fruit each season to keep quite a flock of birds out of mischief. It will pay to plant a few mulberry trees to protect your fruit and feed the birds.

Meehans' Monthly, 1897

Editor's Note: The Russian mulberry is a variety of the white or common mulberry (*Morus alba* var. *tatarica*). If you can't find it, don't worry. Birds love the fruits of any mulberry. The fruits of the white mulberry can be white, pinkish, or purple. The droppings of birds that have gorged on mulberries are very messy, so plant your mulberry trees away from the house, car, and sidewalk.

Lure Robins Away from Cherries

Don't shoot robins to save your cherries. Plant Juneberries and the robins will eat them instead.

The Garden Magazine, 1907

Editor's Note: Robins and wrens, orioles, and swallows all eat insects in your garden. Provide birds with water and their favorite berries, and your cherry harvests will be safe. Juneberries (*Amelanchier arborea*) make a tasty snack for you or the birds. These multistemmed shrubs or small trees grow 25 feet tall in Zones 4 through 9 in full sun or partial shade. Purplish black berries ripen in June and make great pies and cobblers, if you can get any before the birds do.

Boys Make the Best Scarecrows

The most-certain expedients for keeping birds away are setting boys to watch, or carry about a wooden clapper during seedtime.

J. C. Loudon
An Encyclopedia of Gardening, 1850

Distract Crows from Seedlings

Scatter soaked corn to attract attention from the young plants.

L. H. Bailey
Farm and Garden Rule-Book, 1911

Crows are clever creatures that like to eat seed corn and yank out corn seedlings. They catch on to scarecrows fast, but you can save your corn patch from crows' antics by bribing the birds with scattered corn kernels.

Amazing Mechanical Scarecrow

The best scare is one in which there is constant change of motion, which confuses the memory and bewilders the intelligence of the crow. This scare consists of a frame mounted upon a post and attached to a small windmill, by which it is kept rotating. The frame has four bars, from one to another of which wires are strung, and to the wires are fastened many pieces of bright tin, glass, both plain and colored, broken crockery, and colored feathers or rags. The rotating frame is mounted in a stationary one, and as it revolves, the bright pieces flutter and change positions at every moment, jangling when the wind blows. The effectiveness may be increased by hanging a few small bells upon the top bar of the outer frame, so that the clapper may be moved by the edges of the inner rotating frame as they turn. The builder will never be humiliated by finding a crow perching contemptuously upon the top of it, as is sometimes seen upon the simulated gun of the usual dummy in the cornfield.

American Agriculturist, 1876

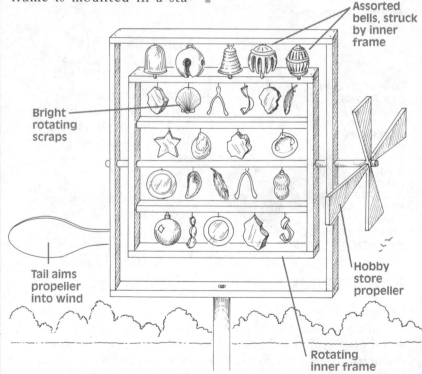

Assorted bells, struck by inner frame

Bright rotating scraps

Tail aims propeller into wind

Hobby store propeller

Rotating inner frame

Crows aren't easily fooled or scared. This elaborate device keeps them guessing with a variety of constantly changing sights and sounds. The propeller is the engine that rotates the inner frame.

Strange But True

Birds are scared away by means of lengths of string on which are fastened old tins containing several loose stones, bells, pieces of glass, etc. The string is kept several feet above the ground by means of strong forked sticks. A boy is stationed at one end, and is sometimes armed with a noisy rattle, and it is his duty to keep the birds at a distance by scaring them with his rattle, by emitting such vocal sounds of a hideous nature as he is capable of making, and by frequently pulling the string bearing the other noise-making instruments. So that when he is simultaneously hallooing, using his rattle, and pulling the string he creates a noise that only a bird stone-deaf could bear without fright.

John Weathers
Commercial Gardening, 1913

Easy Protection for Espaliered Fruit

Lines of black worsted wool yarn, fastened to projecting nails fixed in the walls, have a very good effect in protecting wall fruits. The birds, taking these lines for twigs, light upon them; and the worsted turning round by the grasp, as well as sinking by the weight, the bird falls; and, if he attempts it a second time, falling in the like manner, he is deterred for the future.

J. C. Loudon
An Encyclopedia of Gardening, 1850

Editor's Note: Espalier is a method of training fruit trees flat against a wall or trellis. This technique saves space and promotes early, abundant fruit production.

Trample Snow to Make Mice Go

Trample the snow around young trees to prevent mice from working at them.

American Agriculturist, 1878

Gardener's Mousetrap

A very effective mouse trap is formed by burying an empty flowerpot with the bottom uppermost, and the hole covered with a handful of straw, as shown.

J. C. Loudon
An Encyclopedia of Gardening, 1850

If mice are a problem in the garden, you can snare them in a simple trap made by burying a large flowerpot. Getting them out of the trap is the tricky part.

Fend Off Field Mice with Mulch

After the first heavy frost has sent the field mice to their winter quarters, mulch every newly planted tree, i.e., cover the ground about it two to four inches deep with strawy manure, last year's autumn leaves, or other litter.

The Garden Magazine, 1907

Make sure you wait until after a heavy frost to spread leaves or straw around your trees, or the mice may decide to make your mulch their cozy winter home.

Let Wildlife Nibble on Leftovers

An experienced orchardist says that it is an excellent plan to leave the clippings under the trees in the winter when pruning an orchard, so that mice and rabbits will eat such tender twigs instead of gnawing at the tree trunk itself.

Farm Journal, 1906

Fight Moles with Molasses

Try opening mole's holes and pouring in a little cheap molasses. It gums their fur and they leave for different quarters. One molasses application will do wonders.

Farm Journal, 1904

Underground Fences Make Good Mole Defenses

The moles seem to have an especial liking for the roots of the Japanese iris, and have caused me much loss. The only preventive is to shut the moles out of the bed by sinking a close-wire netting around it to a depth of eighteen inches.

Ida D. Bennett
The Flower Garden, 1904

Editor's Note: For a sturdy barrier, try burying hardware cloth (a heavy metal screening with a grid of approximately ¼ inch) around your plantings. It's available at hardware and building-supply stores.

De-Mole-ition

The best method of getting rid of moles is by digging up their nests in spring, the heaps of earth over these nests being easily distinguished from the common molehills by their size.

J. C. Loudon
An Encyclopedia of Gardening, 1850

Moles Are Good for Gardens

The injury the mole does is immediate and apparent; the benefits derived from his work are not so immediate or apparent. Hence, he is not receiving full credit. It is not probable that the mole eats vegetable matter in any form. I have kept numbers of moles confined where they could not get any food except what I gave them—potatoes, bulbs, tender roots—and although ravenously hungry and dying of starvation they would not eat such food. I have starved them to death in these experiments. It was cruel but I wanted to know if they would eat vegetable matter. I have offered to some of them grubs (larvae of the May beetle) and immediately had them lie in my hand and eat thirteen large grubs at one meal.

Their runs extending in various direction are their traps. Insects working through the soil fall into them. The mole travels along these runs five to six times per day and eats the insects. The mole does not like to have his larder interfered with, so if you tramp it shut two or three times soon after he has opened it, he will come out of the ground and seek more congenial regions in which to work.

If the mole heaves up choice plants in beds, the roots are still in the soil in natural position, and if watered no injury will result to the plant. It is quite likely the mole, by destroying insects, has really benefited the plant.

Theo Longenecker
American Agriculturist, 1895

Editor's Note: Grubs really are what moles are after, and not your plants. You can send moles on their way by using Longenecker's method, or by using beneficial nematodes to kill the grubs.

Moles Don't Like This Short-Order Meal

Salt pork or bacon rinds buried in mole runs will sometimes drive them away for a time.

Ida D. Bennett
The Flower Garden, 1904

Dual-Purpose Beans

Last year I planted only a few beans to keep moles at bay, and not one has been seen. Castor beans form beautiful and stately plants. They thrive in sunshine or shade. Four varieties are especially handsome, and when grouped together are very effective. *Ricinus sanguineus* has fresh green foliage, veined with dark red stalks and stems, and very brilliant red seed pods. *R. cambodiensis* has dark bronzelike leaves and seed pods. *R. macrocarpus* has almost white leaves, with dark stalks and pods. *R. gibsoni* is of dwarf habit, and has very dark, purplish-red stalks and leaves.

E. M. Lucas
American Agriculturist, 1895

Seed catalogs once gave a lot of attention to the castor bean as an ornamental. You'll have trouble finding all of these castor beans today (the names listed above are actually varieties of *Ricinus communis*, not separate species), but it doesn't take a fancy variety to repel moles. Be aware that all parts of the castor bean plant are poisonous, particularly the seeds.

Ruin a Rabbit's Appetite

Hares and rabbits are both very destructive to plants in general, but are particularly injurious to plantations (orchards), from their habit of barking trees; from this, however, they may be deterred by smearing the stem with cow-dung.

J. C. Loudon
An Encyclopedia of Gardening, 1850

Editor's Note: Rabbits are particularly bad about barking, or chewing the bark off fruit trees, in winter when there aren't many other foods available. If you want to test this smelly remedy, that's the time to try it.

Rabbits Won't Eat These

The following plants are not favorite food for the rabbit—azalea, rhododendron, spurge laurel (*Daphne laureola*), juniper, furze (*Ulex europaeus*), forsythia, winter jasmine (*Jasminum nudiflorum*), tree peonies, snowberry (*Symphori-carpos albus*), European spindle tree (*Euonymus europaea*), privet, yuccas, bigleaf hydrangea (*Hydrangea macrophylla*), American smoke tree (*Cotinus obovatus*), boxwood, rose-of-sharon, iris, winter aconite, daffodil, solomon's seal, lily-of-the-valley, periwinkle, columbine, scilla, delphinium, primrose, anemones, violets, Canterbury bells, foxglove, poppy, grape hyacinth.

E. T. Cook
Gardening for Beginners, 1901

Sooty Milk Mix Sends Rabbits Running

A spray made of buttermilk and common stove soot has proven quite satisfactory here. Buttermilk, 1 gallon; common stove soot, ½ pound. Boil for 20 minutes. Keep well stirred to prevent clogging the pump.

Kansas Agricultural Station, 1911

Editor's Note: Stove soot is that black stuff you get when you clean your stovepipe or chimney. If you burn wood, you won't have any trouble coming up with ½ pound of the stuff. Save this spray for your ornamental plants, since soot isn't something you'd want to soak your vegetables with.

Gory Repellent Grosses Rabbits Out

Smear the tree trunks with blood, or rub them with bloody flesh, to keep off rabbits.

American Agriculturist, 1878

Rabbits Avoid Trunk Gunk

Mix a teaspoon of tincture of asafoetida in a half pailful of liquid clay, mud, or muck of any kind. Apply with a brush to the stem and branches of young trees. Use two or three applications during winter.

L. H. Bailey
Farm and Garden Rule-Book, 1911

Editor's Note: Asafoetida is a pungent exotic spice. Bricks of the resin are sold in East Indian grocery stores. You could pulverize some resin with a nutmeg grater, dissolve it in hot water, and experiment with the resulting tea.

Arm the Dog Alarm

The concealed alarm is a system of wires spread over a garden or orchard, and terminating in a bell or gong alarm. In addition to setting off an alarm, the same wire may let loose a watchdog.

J. C. Loudon
An Encyclopedia of Gardening, 1850

Editor's Note: A radio signal dog fence is a modern alternative.

Aloe Aggravates Bunnies

Commercial aloes, 1 pound to 4 gallons of water, both sprinkled on leaves and painted on the bark, gives a bitter taste which repels rabbits.

L. H. Bailey
Farm and Garden Rule-Book, 1911

Editor's Note: Aloes (*Aloe* spp.) are succulent plants that are often grown as houseplants. *A. vera*, now called *A. barbadensis*, is particularly popular because its gelatinous sap soothes burns. It's not often that you'll find a pest repellent that works as a hand lotion!

Gardeners long ago discovered that rabbits are not fond of plants that have been swabbed with a potion containing manure. One old-time recipe calls for a mixture of lime, water, and cow manure, applied generously with a brush. Blood meal makes bunnies unhappy, too, but the most effective method to keep rabbits from chewing your trees is a fence.

Controlling Plant Diseases

Prevention Is Better Than a Cure

Diseases in the vegetable kingdom are rather to be prevented than cured. A good soil on a dry subsoil is the grand foundation of health; and the judicious use of the knife, to thin out superfluous, diseased, or injured branches, shoots, or leaves, is all that can be done to be depended on.

J. C. Loudon
An Encyclopedia of Gardening, 1850

New Soil Cures Sick Seed Beds

In infected seed beds, use new or sterilized soil. Do not add to the seed bed soil from a field in which diseased crops of the given kind have grown.

L. H. Bailey
The Principles of Vegetable Gardening, 1901

Keep Compost Disease-Free

In the control of insects and diseases that infest garden crops it is often possible to accomplish a great amount of good by careful sanitary management. Dead vines or leaves of plants are frequently covered with spores of diseases that affect those crops during the growing season, and these should be burned, as they possess very little fertilizing value.

The Vegetable Garden, 1917

Editor's Note: It's a good idea to burn or bag diseased vines and leaves, but save your healthy plant waste for the compost heap. Compost may not have a high fertilizer content, but it's a rich source of organic matter. Living organisms in the soil transform organic matter into nutrients that your plants need to thrive. Compost also has some disease-suppressing qualities, so it's an ideal way to dispose of healthy plant matter.

Tidiness Tames Diseases

Let no crop of fruit or herbaceous vegetables, or any part thereof, go to waste on the spot. Instantly remove it, when decay or any symptom of disease appears, to the compost-yard, or to be consumed by pigs or cattle.

J. C. Loudon
An Encyclopedia of Gardening, 1850

Editor's Note: It takes really hot compost to kill pathogens, and that means turning the materials in your pile every time the temperature starts to cool, which can be every three days. If you need exercise or want to save on your trash bill, making hot compost is a good project.

Unfortunately, most of us don't have pigs or cattle to feed our fading fruits and vegetables to anymore. If your plants are diseased, it's better to burn them or throw them in the trash rather than on the compost heap.

Apply Plant Juice for Mildew Prevention

The best preventative against mildew is to keep the plant subject to it occasionally syringed with a decoction of elder leaves, which will prevent the fungus growing on them.

William Dick
Encyclopedia of Practical Receipts and Processes, 1872

Editor's Note: Another home remedy for mildew prevention is a baking soda spray. Mix one teaspoon baking soda in one quart warm water. Add one teaspoon liquid dishwashing soap if you like, to help the solution stick to the leaves. Spray the mix on the tops and bottoms of leaves every two weeks.

Healthy Plants Resist Mildew

My view is that mildew being a fungus growth, its seeds or spores are ever present in the atmosphere; and when a relaxed condition of the plant ensues, the minute germs find a suitable place for their development in the enfeebled leaf. Therefore I believe that anything that impedes the flow of the sap places the plant in the condition fitted to develop mildew. All care should be taken to avoid great variation of temperature.

Peter Henderson
Practical Floriculture, 1913

Editor's Note: You may not have much control over temperatures, but evenly moist soil will also help keep plants from becoming "relaxed" or wilted.

Mulch Mildew Away

Prevent the mildew by placing large and heavy mulches under the gooseberry bushes. The high temperature of the earth seems to injure the resisting power of the plant. Where the soil is cool the plants are usually free from mildew.

Meehans' Monthly, 1892

Editor's Note: Several inches of a straw or wood chip mulch should do the trick. A mulch that's three to four inches deep will keep roots cool enough to resist mildew.

Beating Weeds

Mow Thistles by the Moon

I have a certain way to kill Canada thistles. In the new moon of June or the full moon of August, mow them with a scythe and they will die to the last root. Try it.

Lester H. Morris
American Agriculturist, 1895

Throttle Thistles

The only effectual remedy for thistles in all cases is, never to allow them to breathe. Plants must have light and air, or they can live but a short time.

The leaves are their lungs, and if the stalks or the leaves is never allowed to form, the root must perish. Any method of treatment, then, which secures this object of never letting a plant show its head above the surface will destroy the thistle, whether it be ploughings repeated as often as the roots spring, or cutting them off beneath the surface of the earth as often as they show themselves.

Genesee Farmer, 1836

Even the most troublesome weeds, thistles included, will eventually die if you continually cut away the young leaves as they appear in spring. The key here is persistence. Miss one opportunity, and you've allowed the weed to reestablish itself.

Weeds Weakest in Hot Weather

Weeds kill easiest when the sun shines hot.

Jacob Biggle
Biggle Garden Book, 1912

Hot Weeding Tip

A hot, windy day is a good time to hoe between your plants, because the wind and sun kill the uprooted weeds in a short time. They dry up, and there is but little to remove.

W. C. Egan
Making a Garden of Perennials, 1912

Wait Out the Weeds

It is said that if no seeds were brought into the land by wind or manure, or growth, the stock of weeds might be eradicated in eight years.

Henry Ward Beecher
Fruits, Flowers and Farming, 1859

Strange But True

The number of people susceptible to the poisoning influences of poison ivy must be extremely scarce. The writer of this paragraph knows of a tract of land on which the plant grows profusely, and on which many scores of laborers are employed. These laborers are frequently set to weeding and pulling out the plant by the naked hand, and, so far as the writer knows, none of these men were even poisoned by it.

Meehans' Monthly, 1897

Gardeners of the 1800s disagreed over which plants were poisonous to the touch. While poison ivy often was described as relatively harmless, one magazine warned that turnip greens were intensely toxic to the skin.

has touched you. If you are by a roadside or in a field, take a handful of dust or fresh earth and rub the spot of contact thoroughly. Water will avail little in removing such a persistent oil. This is an invention of my own for absorbing the oil, that I use with great success.

Amanda B. Morris
Wildflowers and Where They Grow, 1882

Editor's Note: There are many home remedies for dealing with poison ivy. The best is to wash with soap and water as soon as possible after contact. Other "cures" include applying the sap of jewelweed or spotted touch-me-not (*Impatiens capensis*) to the affected area and rubbing plantain leaves on the skin.

Break Down Briars

If you have to clear a field and mow a lot of old berry canes, throw a heavy pole against them to break them down, then cut them off, and avoid scratches and hard words.

Farm Journal, 1910

Pyre of Poison Ivy

A friend of ours puts straw along the stone fences, etc., infested with poison ivy, and then sets fire to the straw, repeating the operation at intervals until the plants give up trying to grow. This is easy, yet effective. By wearing gloves and approaching the vines on the windward (upwind) side, no one should have trouble in carrying out this treatment.

Farm Journal, 1909

Editor's Note: Even the fumes of burning poison ivy can set off a reaction in people who are sensitive to the plant. Don't try this if you're one of the sensitive ones.

Poison Ivy Rx

Try to rid the skin as quickly as possible of the oil when once it

OLD-TIME WISDOM

Weeds don't have magic powers! It is really strange that there should be in these days any intelligent people who could bring themselves to believe that a plant could develop from a piece of dirt, without the agency of any seeds; yet we read it over and over again in papers which claim to have a considerable degree of intelligence.

Meehans' Monthly, 1882

Garden Projects

Would you like a Victorian plant stand?
How about a hotbed, coldframe, walk,
fence, or wall? Take a tip from 19th- and
early 20th-century gardeners and make
them yourself. You'll find that
homemade garden structures
are the best match for
home landscapes.

Garden Projects

Structures and Yard Art

Harvest Your Own Garden Poles

Grow plants especially for poles. A waste piece of ground may be set with willows, paulownias (empress trees), ailanthus (tree-of-heaven), or any fast-growing trees which can be cut every second year.

The Gardener's Monthly, 1874

Editor's Note: Bamboos make wonderful plant poles, too. When you grow them, choose clumping types, like clump bamboo (*Fargesia nitida*), that won't take over your garden. Or put running bamboos inside a pot or basin before you set them in the ground to contain their growth.

Grow a Children's Playhouse

Children like some place which they can call theirs, where they can have their playthings, and where they can invite their young friends. Pine leaves make a capital carpet. A very pretty house may be made by putting up a roof supported by posts, and then plant vines all around to serve for the sides. Morning glories, beans—especially scarlet runners—cypress vines, and others, can be trained upon strings to make a nice shady arbor. Then boxes, kegs, and other articles can be turned into furniture. Youngsters do not need to be told what to do with such a house. The school keeping, the tea parties, the going a'visiting will all come of themselves.

American Agriculturist, 1876

Rely on Rustic Recycling

What to do with the clippings of trees need never be a question. The rough twisted and gnarled pieces make excellent rustic work, which always gives a garden much interest. The worst of this kind of mechanism is, that if exposed to all weather it soon rots, and it does not seem worth the labor it takes to put it together. So only that should be made up with the bark on, which can be placed under cover in winter. Where rustic work is to be left out at all seasons, it should be built of pieces with the bark removed.

Meehans' Monthly, 1888

Editor's Note: What is rustic work? Any yard or garden object you can build from branches and twigs, such as a bench, swing, table, chair, trellis, birdhouse, or bird feeder.

"Plant" a Bench

If, instead of taxing his brain to find flowers that will grow under a tree, the gardener should abandon the problem and plant instead a comfortable garden bench, many a visitor would be glad of the chance to sit down and call him blessed.

Frances Duncan
The Joyous Art of Gardening, 1917

End Unsightly Clothes Poles

There are dozens of arrangements whereby a little ingenuity can circumvent the insistence of the clothes posts. If tall enough, the fence posts may lend themselves to that use; a tree could serve as one of them.

Frances Duncan
The Joyous Art of Gardening, 1917

Create a Rustic Plant Stand

Stumps of good old trees that have lived their usefulness and been relegated to the wood pile are not uncommonly seen upon our lawns. The stump is first sawed off perfectly level and then fitted with a top of thick boards of the desired dimensions. Four rustic supports are placed underneath at the four corners. These should be as much as possible in their natural state, with any little crookednesses or knots allowed to show, as they add much to the pretty effect of the whole. The edges, too, of the top board may be given a rustic tone by tacking to them strips of wood with the bark on them. All summer long it will be a charming abiding place for the choicest houseplants.

American Agriculturist, 1895

Turn a liability—a stump in the middle of your lawn—into an asset. By nailing crooked branches to the stump as supports for a top, you can make a table that looks completely intentional.

Green Grows the Clothes Pole

The clothes pole need not be ugly. Pole beans will profitably drape one arranged like this; nasturtiums, dolichos hyacinth bean, or morning-glories will make it even more beautiful.

E. L. D. Seymour
Garden Profits, 1911

Editor's Note: Climbing vines can beautify any number of backyard structures, from toolsheds to your compost bin. In addition to the annual vines listed above, you can use sweet peas, scarlet runner beans, black-eyed Susan vines, and moon vines. For more permanent coverings, plant perennial vines like clematis or ivy, or decorate a structure with a climbing rose.

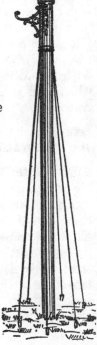

The clothesline was a backyard necessity before the advent of the clothes dryer, and even today people continue to prefer the fresh smell that only sun drying gives clothes and linens. To turn the poles into a landscape asset, plant climbing annuals at the base.

To Cure Garden Ills, Look to Lattice

One of the most valuable accomplishments for the amateur gardener is skill in the making of a lattice. Lattice work, like charity, covers a multitude of sins. It is the most convenient of defenses against ugliness. And there is a very real satisfaction to its author in having done the work herself.

Frances Duncan
The Joyous Art of Gardening, 1917

We tend to think of lattice as made up of diagonal strips, as shown above. But you can create a less busy effect by nailing up a pattern of vertical and horizontal wood pieces for your lattice.

Best Color for Garden Structures

For little gardens, like yours and mine, I think deep green paint the best color for pergola, pillars, seats, plant tubs, and the like. White paint is clean and cheerful, but stains easily.

Barbara
The Garden, You, and I, 1910

Another Vote for Green

In England I saw a circular rose arbor painted very light apple green. Upon it grew white and pale lemon colored roses with now and then a great splash of purple clematis. It was most unusually fresh and pretty.

Louise Beebe Wilder
Colour in My Garden, 1918

Apple Green Seating

I have been delighted with the effects obtained in various gardens where I have had the seats painted an apple green. The real apple green as it comes from the can is usually too strong and high-keyed for the garden, but a tiny bit of lamp black mixed with it gives it a soft tone.

Elsa Rehman
Garden-Making, 1926

Editor's Note: If you buy your paint at a store that will do custom mixing, you can ask to have a shocking chartreuse tamed with a very small amount of black pigment.

OLD-TIME WISDOM

A proper timepiece for gardeners. A sundial is calm time, old time, beautiful spacious time in a garden; it is slow waltz time—time that flows like a shining twist of honey, sweet and slow. A sundial prods nobody, a sundial can trance and forget; it lets the green hours glide.

J. H. Yoxall
The Villa for Coelebs, 1914

Getting Serious about Sundials

Of course, the ordinary sundial is not accurate, within a half-hour or so, everyday in the year. If it is your habit to garden until train time, you can buy a dial with an adjustable gnomon which will give you absolutely correct time.

Henry H. Saylor
The Garden Magazine, 1907

Editor's Note: The gnomon is the pin or fin of a sundial that shows the time with the shadow that it casts. If you're interested in accurate time-keeping, start by making the base for your sundial absolutely level. Then adjust the face of the sundial so the gnomon shows the correct time (not daylight savings time).

Leave Lawn Art Behind

A tyro (novice) in gardening will be more apt to render himself ridiculous by the use of decorations than by any other point of practice. Wooden lions, sheep in stucco, or any other figures of men or animals, intended to pass for realities, though still used in Holland and France, may be pronounced as too puerile (childish) for the present age.

J. C. Loudon
An Encyclopedia of Gardening, 1850

Editor's Note: These decorations appeared childish to Loudon, but they seem like fun to today's gardeners—and we can all use more of that.

Start with Season Extenders

Cold Frame on Your Cellar Steps

You can use an outside cellar stairway, when this is on the sunny side of the house, in starting plants in spring for later transplanting into the garden. A sash is fitted into the opening, which can be covered by the outside door at night, to prevent too rapid cooling.

American Agriculturist, 1895

Collapsible Cold Frame

If one expects to use coldframes or hotbeds every year, it is advisable to make the frames of 2-inch stuff, well painted, and to join the parts with mortise and tenon joints, so that they may be taken apart and stored until needed for the next year's work.

L. H. Bailey
The Principles of Vegetable Gardening, 1901

Removeable wedge

Mortise

A cold frame doesn't have to be a permanent fixture of the yard. If you build a frame with mortise-and-tenon joints, it can be knocked down when warm weather comes. Then use the spot as a flower bed until fall brings cool temperatures.

Bottomless Cold Frame

An excellent type of forcing-hill is made by the use of the hand-box. This is a rectangular box, without top or bottom, and a pane of glass is slipped into a groove at the top. The earth is banked slightly about the box, in order to hold it against winds and to prevent the water from running into it. If these boxes are made of good lumber and painted, they will last for many years.

L. H. Bailey
The Principles of Vegetable Gardening, 1901

Tenon

Earth-Sided Cold Frames

The cold frame mold is a box with flaring sides and no top or bottom, and provided with a handle. This frame is placed with the small end down at the point where the seeds are to be planted, and the earth is hilled up about it and firmly packed with the feet. The mold is then withdrawn, and a pane of glass is laid on the top of the

mound to concentrate the sun's rays.

L. H. Bailey
The Principles of Vegetable Gardening, 1901

Editor's Note: This ingenious idea for a cold frame made of soil lets you quickly create all the seed-starting spaces you need. It's a great option for gardeners who don't have enough space for permanent structures.

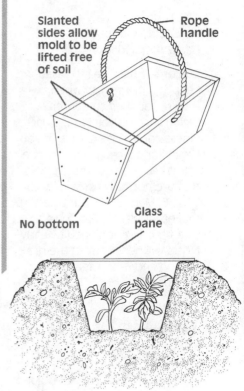

Slanted sides allow mold to be lifted free of soil

Rope handle

No bottom

Glass pane

With a simple wooden box, you can make any number of temporary cold frames. Simply pile soil around the box, and tamp it down firmly to form the walls. Then remove the box, and plant seeds or seedlings inside. Place a pane of glass on top of the cold frame to keep your plants toasty. When the weather warms and the plants are well on their way, you can hoe away the earthen walls.

Plant beside Walls for Warmth

The mean temperature of a south wall, or within a few inches of one, is equal to the mean temperature in the open plain of 7 degrees farther south. Hence it is, that grapes which ripen in the open air at Bordeaux, require a south wall in the neighborhood of London, which is 7 degrees farther north.

J. C. Loudon
An Encyclopedia of Gardening, 1850

Editor's Note: The increased heat that plants gain when they're set close to a south-facing wall lets you jump a hardiness zone. For example, if you live in Zone 5 and plant beside a warm wall, you can grow plants that are normally hardy only to Zone 6. Magnolias, fruit trees, and other plants with flowers that tend to get nipped by early frosts will benefit from the protection and heat a south wall provides.

Build a Hotbed That Lasts

A properly made hotbed is good for six or seven or sometimes eight weeks; the heat gradually declines.

Jacob Biggle
Biggle Garden Book, 1912

Editor's Note: How is a hotbed different from a cold frame? Both are structures that provide protected areas for starting seeds. But a hotbed has bottom heat (from decomposing manure or a heating cable) and a cold frame doesn't. By starting seeds in a hotbed, you can get an even faster jump on the growing season than with a cold frame.

Does a Hotbed Pay?

Perhaps not, if you charge up your time, cost of the manure, the old boards you pick up around the place, doctor's bills in case you catch cold, etc. But it's fun. And you get better varieties.

The Garden Magazine, 1906

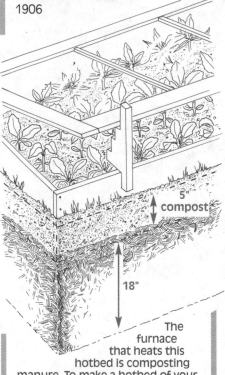

5" compost

18"

The furnace that heats this hotbed is composting manure. To make a hotbed of your own, dig a pit 2½ feet deep and fill it with 18 inches of fresh manure. Water the manure well, and cover it with 5 inches of compost or good topsoil to make a seedbed. As the manure decomposes, it will give off heat and warm the soil.

Who Needs a Hotbed?

"I do not use a hotbed," says H. E. Haydock, a successful New York State gardener. "I find that a number of shallow boxes in a sunny room answer every purpose in starting the tomatoes, cucumbers, melons, etc., that I intend to raise."

Jacob Biggle
Biggle Garden Book, 1912

Editor's Note: Millions of gardeners would agree. You need a sunny window—and a tolerant disposition toward spilled soil.

Creating Walkways and Borders

Front Yard Illusion

When the door of the house is twenty or more feet from the entrance gate, curves may usually be introduced by having the gate not directly in front of the door, but a little to one side. Such an arrangement tends to keep the area in front of the house larger, when the walk is set to one side.

Elias A. Long
Ornamental Gardening for Americans, 1884

Give Curves a Cause

In the laying out of walks or drives in the garden or pleasure ground, there should never be any deviation from a straight line unless for some real or apparent cause. So, if curved lines are desired, trees, rocks, buildings, or mounds must be placed at the bend or curve, as a reason for going around.

Peter Henderson
Henderson's Handbook of Plants, 1890

Easy Wooden Edging

For a curving margin, a strip of board—an inch wide and twelve or fifteen feet long, with pegs attached by screws or nails at various distances along its length, so that it can be made fast in the ground to correspond with the design—may be used instead of a line.

Joseph Breck
The Flower-Garden, 1860

Editor's Note: Inch-wide boards are thicker than you'll need. Instead, buy one or more lengths of 1 × 3 lumber, a commonly available size. It measures

roughly ¾ inch thick and should be supple enough to allow you to make curves. You can use a half-dozen 5-inch-long nails to anchor each strip, instead of the wooden pegs described above. Drill ¼-inch-diameter holes for the nails, as shown, every 3 feet or so along each strip. To lay out curves in the yard, anchor the strips by tapping the nails through the holes as you press the wood into the desired shape.

Strange But True

A coating of gravel upon common soil will not make a permanent walk. The earth should be thrown out for the depth of at least two feet, and the excavation filled with stones; the larger at the bottom, smaller above, with gravel at the top.

American Agriculturist, 1883

Editor's Note: This is a walk for people who like to shovel! You can make a perfectly serviceable gravel walk by spreading one inch of gravel on smoothed and leveled ground. You will have to add more gravel every few years, but that's a small maintenance fee for a quick-made path that's easy to walk on. If you add more than an inch of gravel, as described in the tip above, you'll be wading through rock when you walk, and that's not easy!

Nix Narrow Walks

Very narrow walks, unless the grass is frequently clipped, often look like ditches.

Peter Henderson
Practical Floriculture, 1913

Editor's Note: Narrow walks have some other drawbacks too. It takes lots of maintenance to keep plants clipped away from the edges, and there isn't much room for working or walking. Most pathways should be at least two or three feet wide (four or five feet wide if you want two people to be able to walk side by side). When you design new walks, check the width of your garden equipment such as carts and mowers first; then make sure your path is wide enough to maneuver.

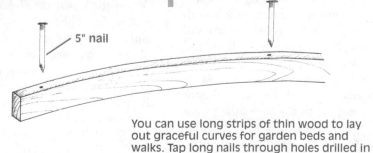

5" nail

You can use long strips of thin wood to lay out graceful curves for garden beds and walks. Tap long nails through holes drilled in the wood to make the strips stay in place.

Stake Out a Curved Walk

In getting the curves, the practiced gardener trusts much to his eye, but a person of no experience finds this is not easy. The curve rod is a useful implement in this work. It consists of a six-foot rod with a wire hook on one end, and a crosspiece with holes in it at the other, with a notch at the center. To use it, we start with a stake at the hook (or large screw eye) at A, and one in the notch at B, a third one is then put through one of the holes of the crosspiece. Then the rod is lifted, leaving the stakes to stand, and is moved forward into position BD, setting a fourth stake at D. After this we bring into position CE with a stake at E, and so on. Such a course leaves the stakes on a good curve.

Elias A. Long
Ornamental Gardening for Americans, 1884

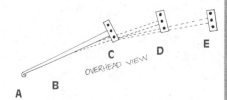

OVERHEAD VIEW

A B C D E

A curve rod can be used to lay out long, sweeping curves. You determine the direction and tightness of the curve by where in the crosspiece you place a stake. The rod is shown here in three positions; the first is drawn with solid lines, and the second and third with dotted lines. Stakes are set at A, B, C, D, and E; they establish the beginning of what will be a graceful curve.

A Walk in the Woods

Just as wild gardening should never look like garden gardening, so wood paths should never look like garden paths. There must be no hard edges, no conscious boundaries. The wood path is merely an easy way that the eye just perceives and the foot follows.

Gertrude Jekyll
Colour in the Flower Garden, 1908

Drive a Design across Your Lawn

On large grounds a carriage driven rapidly and skillfully over the surface will make very regular and graceful curves. The bicycle also may be brought into use for this work.

Elias A. Long
Ornamental Gardening for Americans, 1884

Sometimes the Direct Approach Is Best

There is a danger, when curves are used, of making them ungraceful or indirect, in a way to serve neither beauty or convenience. Tortuous walks like these prove worse than useless in one sense, for there will be a constant inclination, if not very frequent practice, to cut across the lot, as indicated by the dotted lines, instead of using walks. People when they are in hurry, and especially children, have little respect

for long, winding inconvenient curves, introduced for beauty but in such cases sadly lacking it, because they lack utility.

Elias A. Long
Ornamental Gardening for Americans, 1884

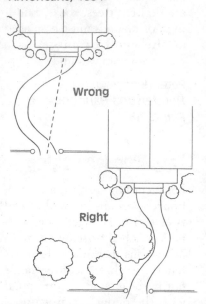

Wrong

Right

When curves make walks inconvenient (*top*), walkers are apt to make a beeline across the lawn. Make sure your walks curve for a reason (*bottom*), and walkers won't stray from the path.

Gravel Walks for City Gardens

One of the minor details which makes for charm in a city garden is the matter of paths. If it is a possible thing, let these be of gravel, for concrete or flagstone bring a reminiscence of the pavement into the garden which one would fain keep out.

Frances Duncan
The Joyous Art of Gardening, 1917

I Took the One Less Traveled By...

When two walks diverge from each other, they should not appear as if intended to join again, as shown below (version B); but rather as if each leads to points apart, as shown here (version A).

Thomas H. Mawson
The Art and Craft of Garden Making, 1907

A

For a decisive fork in a path, curve the two branches away from one another to create a sense of mystery.

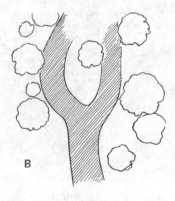

B

A fork in the road should offer visitors a choice of *different* directions. A path like this one, where the branches appear to join together, isn't very exciting or interesting. It doesn't matter which way you go. If there's no reason for a fork, create one or use a simple curve instead.

Let Toadflax Decorate Your Walk

The alpine toadflax (*Linaria alpina*) is never more beautiful than when self-sown in a gravel walk.

William Robinson
The English Flower Garden, 1883

Editor's Note: Start this matlike perennial from seed in spring; then move it to your walkway when the plants are large enough to handle. The purple and yellow flowers look somewhat like snapdragons and appear on short spikes above the narrow gray-green leaves. Alpine toadflax is hardy to Zone 4.

Shrub Strategy for Circular Driveways

Never put flower beds in a turnaround—too trifling. Shrubs are better.

J. T. Scott
The Garden Magazine, 1907

Hoed Walks Invite a Fall

Walks, of whatever kind, should never be hoed, and the weeds must be removed from them by hand. Hardness and smoothness are the requisites of a good walk.

Ida D. Bennett
The Flower Garden, 1904

Editor's Note: Hoeing not only scuffs up your walk so it's lumpy to walk on, it also gives weed seeds a place to grow. Use a hand trowel to remove weeds from walks, and pack these areas firmly once the weeds are removed.

Collect Coal for the Neatest Walks in Town

It is often said that I have the best walks in town. Where the edge of my walk comes to the grass, I cut out the earth, as shown in the engraving, and place in sifted hard coal ashes. This stops the grass roots at the edge. My walk is over a hundred feet long, and for the last five years it has not taken three hours of labor to keep the edges neat and clean.

John Barker
American Agriculturist, 1883

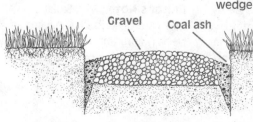

Gravel   Coal ash

In time, grass will invade most gravel walks. You can make an effective barrier by cutting a wedge-shaped section along the edge of the walk and filling it with coal ash. If you don't heat with coal, use screenings (a very fine gravel) instead of coal ash.

Fill Flagstone Walks with Flowers

Better than the customary American way of handling "hit-or-miss" walks of broken flagging is the English method of planting the spaces between the stones with tiny flowering plants.

Amelia Leavitt Hill
Garden Portraits, 1923

Editor's Note: Try filling in the spaces in a flagstone path with one of the many varieties of creeping thyme. This low-growing, fragrant herb doesn't mind being treated like a carpet.

Perennial Stairway Stars

Steps allow great opportunities for the growth of such rock plants as thymes, lithospermum (hoary puccoon), cerastiums (snow-in-summer), drabas (whitlow grass), toadflax, aubretias (rock cresses), dianthuses (pinks), and veronicas.

Thomas H. Mawson
The Art and Craft of Garden Making, 1907

Edge a Bed with Ornamental Grass

The hare's-tail grass (*Lagurus ovatus*) is such a delightfully pretty little plant that I am sure, if you grow it, you will always want it in the future. The tuft of leaves grows only about eight inches high, and the leaves are densely covered with soft, whitish down. They bend downward, and the plant is ideal for use as an edging to the flower bed, or along the walks.

Parker T. Barnes
The Garden Magazine, 1906

Editor's Note: This fuzzy-headed annual grass is available from several mail-order nurseries. See "Sources" on page 316 for ordering information.

Depend on Dianthus for Edging Paths

A hard, cold-looking edging will spoil the prettiest garden. Tile, slates, and wood are abominations. One of the prettiest edgings is that composed of the ordinary white Pink and 'Mrs. Sinkins', or any other variety. I also admire the fringed Pink of the cottage garden. One thoroughly enjoys the perfumed flowers in early summer, and the silvery tufted growth at all times.

Harry Roberts
The Book of Old-Fashioned Flowers, 1904

Editor's Note: 'Mrs. Sinkins' pinks are described as having especially fragrant, white double blossoms. See "Sources" on page 316 for ordering information.

Essential Edgings

Edgings to walks are essential to the beauty and completeness of a kitchen garden. Box (boxwood) is superior to everything else. Parsley may be sown for an edging; or slips of thyme, winter savory, hyssop, and other aromatic herbs may be planted.

J. C. Loudon
An Encyclopedia of Gardening, 1850

Editor's Note: Be creative when you think about edging materials for your kitchen garden. A colorful mesclun mix puts on a show and provides good eating.

Cottage pinks (*Dianthus plumarius*) are cheerful, clove-scented perennials that are easy to grow from seed. They work especially well as a low, trim edging along walks.

Building Fences That Last

Living Fence Posts

Where timber is expensive and difficult to obtain, live or green posts can be grown in a few years. In setting out trees for this purpose, however, only those species that are known to flourish in that locality should be used, and if they be fruit or nut bearing, so much the better. When they attain six inches in diameter, either prune heavily every year or cut off the trunk at the top of the fence and the stubs will serve as posts for from three to four years longer. Only wire fence should be used with live posts. Use long staples, letting them project at least one inch. Pull them out half their length before the bark of the tree grows out to the wires.

S. P. Welles
American Agriculturist, 1894

Charred Posts Stop Rot

A great objection to the common board or picket fence is the certainty of the rotting of the lower parts of the posts in the ground. There is one very effectual remedy for preventing this, which should be more frequently noticed and practiced. This consists in charring the bottoms of the posts. The preservative qualities of charcoal are well known. It is not affected by moisture, and hence the extremities of posts properly charred will not decompose. Most of the houses in Venice stand upon piles of wood, which have all been previously charred for their preservation.

All that is necessary is to build a smart (hot-burning) fire on the ground, and pile on as many posts as can be easily managed. After posts have been in the flames long enough to be well coated with charcoal, they should be removed from the flames and water thrown upon them to extinguish the fire. They are then ready for use.

The People's Journal, 1854

Strange But True

Since the inquiry relative to the proper time to cut timber for fence posts and the best means to preserve it from premature decay, the general opinion appears to settle upon the month of August, within one day of the time when the moon is full, as the best time to cut all kinds of oak.

Farmers' Cabinet, 1837

Because charred wood is less susceptible to decay, fence posts were often set afire, just long enough to build up a protective layer of charcoal on the end that was put into the ground.

Upside-Down Posts Last Longer

Some farmers have a notion that setting the posts small end downwards in the ground, contrarywise to the direction in which the sap rises in the tree, will tend to preserve the post several years longer than otherwise.

The People's Journal, 1854

Faster Fence Posts

We were much pleased with the very easy mode of setting posts for a board fence by driving them. The small end of the post is sharpened. A hole is then made in the ground with a crowbar three or four inches in diameter at the top, by working the bar backward and forward. The post is inserted and driven the necessary depth with a heavy maul. In soil that is rather loose and free from large stones, they may be driven two feet or more with great ease. One man can set them faster than two men can nail on the boards, and they are firmer in the ground than posts set the usual way by digging. The proper time to drive them is when the ground is moist and yielding.

Genesee Farmer, 1838

Editor's Note: If swinging a heavy maul isn't your idea of a good time, you can rent a post hole digger to speed up the process.

Strange But True

I would say that in taking up old fences I have always found that where the posts stood in wet ground, they remained sound and hard, when those on dry ground were completely rotten. Observing this, I thought it would be a good plan to turn a small stream of water along all of my post fences whenever I could conveniently do so; I am led to think it would be advantageous to farmers generally, whenever the location would admit of it, to turn a stream of water along their fences, sufficiently large to keep the bottom of the posts always wet.

William Dripps
The Progressive Farmer, 1855

Making Well-Built Walls

Plan Your Wall to Catch Rainfall

The faces of the rocks should not as a rule overhang so as to prevent the rain reaching the ground at their foot, for this would prove fatal to many kinds of plants. It is very important to make sure that the under rock projects beyond the upper, otherwise rain falling on the sloping face of the rock above will miss the fissure altogether, and whatever is planted in it will in all probability soon die; for if no moisture reaches the roots from the front, they will have to extend 12 inches or more to the back of the rock before they obtain any.

Lewis B. Meredith
Rock Gardens, 1914

When building a stone wall, make sure that rain will be able to reach all the plants. Stagger the rocks, as shown here, to allow rain to water plant roots at each layer of stone.

Building a Wall for Plants

A wall garden is usually a wall built without mortar. Each row of stones recedes an inch from the lower, and the bed of the stones should tip towards the back. To ensure strength, build in with each yard of wall a large through or bonding stone to tie it.

Thomas H. Mawson
The Art and Craft of Garden Making, 1907

Editor's Note: A wall garden is built without mortar, so there's room for soil and plant roots between the rocks.

Wall Gardens Mean Low Maintenance

One charm of this kind of garden is that little attention is required afterwards. Even in the best rock gardens things get overrun by others, and weeds come in; but in a well-planted wall we may leave plants for years untouched beyond pulling out any interloping plant or weed that may happen to get in. If the stones were stuffed with much earth, weeds would get in, and it is best to have the merest dusting of soil with the roots, so as not to separate the stones, but let each one rest firmly on the one beneath it.

William Robinson
The English Flower Garden, 1883

Editor's Note: Lots of plants thrive in the warm, well-drained

conditions wall gardens offer. Some favorites include sedums (*Sedum* spp.), basket-of-gold (*Aurinia saxatilis*), creeping phlox (*Phlox subulata*), pinks (*Dianthus* spp.), and snow-in-summer (*Cerastium tomentosum*).

Moss Softens Stones

In our country (the United States), where time is slow to bestow its softening touch of moss and lichen, stonework in the garden is apt to have an alien, unconnected look. But by encouraging suitable plant life in the chinks and joints and, where it is possible, building the walls and steps with this end in view, a more harmonious ensemble is created of the widely differing elements that go to make up the garden.

Louise Beebe Wilder
Colour in My Garden, 1918

Editor's Note: You can soften the look of a new wall by planting rock cresses (*Arabis* spp. and *Aubrieta deltoidea*), basket-of-gold (*Aurinia saxatilis*), and candytuft (*Iberis* spp.) in crevices. Or encourage mosses to grow by blending moss, buttermilk, and water together, and pouring the mix over the wall. The proportions of this moss mix don't matter much, so feel free to experiment.

Try a Double-Sided Wall

In Devonshire they build two walls with their stones, setting two edgeways, and then one between; and so it rises. Fill the interval with earth, continuing the stonework and filling; and as you work, beating in the stones flat to the sides. This is absolutely the neatest, most saving, and profitable fencing imaginable, where slaty stones are in any abundance. Upon these banks they plant not only quicksets (cuttings), but even timber trees, which exceedingly thrive, being out of all danger.

John Evelyn
Silva, 1777

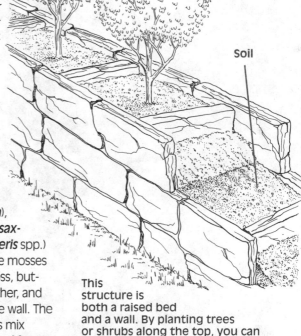

Soil

This structure is both a raised bed and a wall. By planting trees or shrubs along the top, you can raise the effective height of the wall by several feet.

Tools and Gadgets

When it's time to transplant your tomatoes or harvest your cabbage, get out your bricklayer's trowel. It's just one of the inventive devices early gardeners discovered to make weeding, watering, and labeling gardens easier. Read on for more ingenious ideas.

Tools and Gadgets

Choosing and Using Tools

A Place for Every Tool

There is no more maddening aphorism than "A place for everything and everything in its place." To an unsystematic gardener like myself, it is sheer torture, after hours of hard work, to scrape and clean my trowel or hoe and put it exactly where it belongs. But I know from sad experience what are the results of neglect upon the keenness and effectiveness of those implements, and how much time is lost in looking for them.

Julia H. Cummins
My Garden Comes of Age,
1926

Women's Tools Work As Well for Men

Those three-piece sets of garden tools—rake, hoe, and spade—known as ladies' sizes are not only constantly in my own hand, but are evidently regarded with some favor by those members of the sterner sex whose business it is to keep the garden trim. These tools have small heads, but han-dles of the regulation length, and far be it from me to find fault if the little neatness of the garden can be best maintained by the use of these ladies' sizes.

Louisa King
The Well-Considered Garden,
1915

OLD-TIME WISDOM

Develop a passion for hoeing. To cut down a weed is, therefore, to do a moral action. My hoe becomes an instrument of retributive justice. Hoeing becomes, not a pastime, but a duty. Nevertheless, what a man needs in gardening is a cast-iron back, with a hinge in it. The hoe is an ingenious instrument, calculated to call out a great deal of strength at a great disadvantage.

Charles Dudley Warner
My Summer in a Garden, 1872

Tool Decorum

Do not throw down your hoe blade upwards, or across the rows, and run off the nearest way to the walk the moment the breakfast or dinner hour strikes. Lay your implement down parallel to the rows, with its face or blade to the ground.

J. C. Loudon
An Encyclopedia of Gardening, 1850

Look Sharp

Sharp hoes make sharp work. Carry a file and apply it often. Learn to use a hoe so as to leave the ground *smooth*.

Jacob Biggle
Biggle Garden Book, 1912

Sharpen Hoes at Home

Time spent in sharpening garden hoes is not lost. Fasten hoes in a vise and use a large flat file. This is done quicker than sharpening on a grindstone.

Abner Hollingsworth
Farm Journal, 1887

Customize a Weed Hoe

One trial will prove my assertion that a shallow-bladed hoe, set at an angle that will give it a good draw, will loosen and pulverize the soil in one-half to one-quarter the time required with a hilling hoe. Notwithstanding that the hilling hoe is a very popular type, it nevertheless wastes more labor than any hoe I ever used. It has no place in the home garden.

Buy a square-top hoe with as shallow a blade as possible and cut this to two inches in depth. It can then easily be cut to any width desired and set at the proper angle, 63 degrees. The angle gives it such a draw cut that when pressed into the soil and drawn forward quickly, the soil passes over the shallow blade and falls behind it in a crumbled condition nearly as level as it was before hoeing. The shallow blade permits the use of the hoe under such low-growing plants as lettuce and cabbage without injuring them.

J. L. Kayan
The Garden Magazine,
1908

Make your hoe more efficient by cutting the blade down to size and then bending it to a 63-degree angle.

Save Steps with a Scuffle Hoe

One trouble with most hoes is that the operator walks over the ground he has already worked, and treads the weeds which have just been cut off back into the earth, where they take root again. With a scuffle hoe it is different. The best way to use this is for the operator to walk backward, so that the newly stirred ground shall not be walked on.

Ida D. Bennett
The Vegetable Garden,
1908

The scuffle hoe works on a different principle than the standard garden hoe does. Instead of chopping the soil, this hoe scuffles the earth as you push the handle away from you and pull it back towards you.

Planting with a Tool-Handle Ruler

It is convenient to mark the handles of hoes and rakes with feet and half-feet.

American Agriculturist, 1884

Editor's Note: Lay your marked hoe or rake down beside a row or furrow at planting time. Use the marks to get just the right spacing for seeds or transplants.

Bricklayer's Trowel

The bricklayer's pointing trowel is, of course, not even listed as a garden tool, but I have found it indispensable as it answers the purpose of both knife and trowel for cutting apart and lifting tomato, pepper and other plants from the flats when setting them out; for gathering and trimming lettuce, cabbage, etc., it is just the tool. The blade is thin and sharp on both edges.

J. L. Kayan
The Garden Magazine, 1908

Look for a bricklayer's pointing trowel at hardware stores or home centers. It makes a nimble tool for transplanting or harvesting vegetables.

Remodel Your Hoe for Tight Spots

Buy an extra hand hoe and cut it with a file into the shape shown by the dotted lines; this kind of hoe is very useful at times, especially in the strawberry patch.

Jacob Biggle
Biggle Garden Book, 1912

Customize a hoe by removing the shaded areas as shown, and you'll be able to do precise weeding, even around small or intertwined plants.

A Life-Changing Hoe

Somebody has sent me a new sort of hoe, with the wish that I should speak favorably of it, if I can consistently. As to this hoe, I do not mind saying that it has changed my view of the desirableness and value of the human life. It has in fact, made life a holiday to me. It is made on the principle that man is an upright, sensible, reasonable being, and not a grovelling wretch. It does away with the necessity of the hinge in the back. The handle is seven and a half feet long.

There are two narrow blades, sharp on both edges, which come together at an obtuse angle in front; and as you walk along with this hoe before you, pushing and pulling with a gentle motion, the weeds fall at every thrust and withdrawal, and the slaughter is immediate and wide-spread.

Charles Warner
My Summer in a Garden,
1872

This ferocious version of a scuffle hoe will make mincemeat of your weeds. Draw it back and forth through the surface of the soil when weeds are small to get the best results.

Fit Your Cultivator to Your Garden

The adjustable cultivator is one of the most useful hand garden tools on the market. It will put out the weeds and pulverize the ground thoroughly, leaving it level. It will work between the rows, or the center shovel can be removed to straddle the rows if desired.

The Garden Magazine, 1908

The adjustable cultivator was once a common tool. You can adjust the little shovels to suit your needs. See "Sources" on page 316 for ordering information.

Discover the Wheel Hoe

While the rake and hand hoe are well adapted to the tillage of a small garden, the real pleasures of gardening remain unknown to the person who has never used a wheel hoe. This modern invention stimulates good gardening.

John W. Lloyd
Productive Vegetable Gardening, 1914

Choosing a Wheel Hoe

I prefer the one with double wheels, for it can be used in most places to better advantage than the single-wheel hoe. It is an extremely handy tool to have late in May and early in June, when the weeds are growing fast. It is made to straddle the row.

Ida D. Bennett
The Vegetable Garden, 1908

Water the Garden with This "Hired Man"

The "hired man" is the garden fork, which can hold the hose and does not talk back or trample down the seedlings. In this respect it is the best labor saver I have ever found.

H. Howard Pepper
The Garden Magazine, 1908

Firmly jab a traditional garden fork into the soil, and use the D-shaped handle to support your water hose. You can go on to other tasks while the fork pitches in to help you water.

You can clear weeds out of large vegetable gardens with ease using a wheel hoe. There's no bending or stooping—just push the tool between the rows. Try a wheel hoe with double wheels for extra easy weeding. Just straddle the rows with the wheels.

Use the Wheel Hoe instead of Water

Keep the wheel hoe working hard all through the summer drought. This is as good as the hose and an excellent substitute. The garden that is cultivated continuously does not suffer from absence of water.

The Garden Magazine, 1908

Strange But True

From our own recent observations and experiments, we have come to set a high value upon the oil of the common woodchuck or "ground hog" for leather. An old pair of heavy boots, so stiff as to hurt the feet unbearably, received a good coating of this oil August first, and they soon became almost as soft and easy to the feet as moccasins.

Woodchucks are common in many hilly parts of almost the entire country, and it is easy to kill a few for their oil, as well as to get rid of them, for they are a nuisance. We have taken fully two quarts of oil from a full grown, fat fourteen-pound "chuck."

American Agriculturist, 1883

Editor's Note: Some do-it-yourself projects are more trouble than they're worth. Groundhog oil may keep your garden boots in good shape, but neat's-foot oil from the shoe store will do as well—and it's a lot easier to come by.

Features to Look for in a Fork or Shovel

A first-quality spading fork or shovel of any kind is made with a strap ferrule as shown below. The ferrule is continued in one piece part way up the handle in the form of two straps, which are riveted through it. As can be readily seen, this adds much strength to the handle. If constructed with a short ferrule, the handle is very liable to break at the top of the ferrule.

J. L. Kayan
The Garden Magazine, 1908

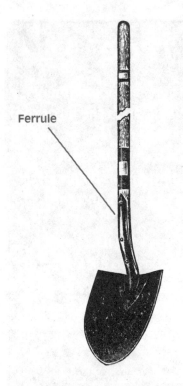

Ferrule

If you want your digging tools to last, look for handles that have a long strap ferrule or a long solid socket for reinforcement.

Mark Your Rows with a Gap-Toothed Rake

A wide, iron garden rake and three or four pieces of corncob make an easily constructed garden marker. Wide or narrow spaces may be marked at will, by changing the cobs.

Jacob Biggle
Biggle Garden Book,
1912

To mark garden rows without stooping, place corncobs over the tines of a metal rake to suit the spacing you need. Then draw the rake lightly over the prepared beds.

Rake Early and Often

The efficiency of a rake as a tillage tool depends on the frequency of its use. If a crust is allowed to form, or the weeds to start, the rake is rendered useless, and the only resort is the hoe.

John W. Lloyd
Productive Vegetable Growing,
1914

Gadgets and Labels

Border Bridge

To reach the back part of the border without walking all over the front of it and yet be in a comfortable enough position to allow me to pull weeds, cultivate, and set plants in the spring was a hard problem until I had built this bridge. By its use the work is made much easier. It is long enough to reach to the back of the border, is high enough not to injure the young plants, and is made broad enough not to sink into the soil or tip over.

Jno. K. Allen
The Garden Magazine, 1906

Editor's Note: Allen's plant bridge is clever but heavy. For an easier, lighter-weight version, check out the plastic step stools and benches at your local building-supply store.

Foot

You can build this garden bridge with nails and scrap wood. Use 1-inch-thick lumber for the top and 2 × 4 timbers for the legs. Make the legs high enough to clear seedlings, and add a foot on the front leg to take pressure off the bed so the bridge won't compact the soil. The back leg rests between rows.

A Tiskit, a Tasket, a Cut Flower Basket

For carrying flowers, I often cut double sheets of heavy wrapping paper into a roughly graceful shape of some picturesque arching basket which is in my memory, leaving two strips at top for a handle. These strips are fastened together by pins at their ends, the sides of the papers are joined in the same manner, and the whole pressed gently open from within, when a practical and satisfactory receptacle is created for holding and keeping cool the stems.

Louisa King
The Well-Considered Garden, 1915

When you gather flowers from the garden or take them to a friend, transport them in this simple paper basket. Use heavy wrapping paper you have on hand, or buy large rolls of inexpensive white drawing paper from art-supply stores. Tape the seams and handle together as shown.

Long-Handled Scissors Extend Your Reach

There is the fascinating tool known as cueille-fleurs. A rod about a yard in length has at its farther end small scissors which cut and hold a flower, and these are opened and closed by a small arrangement in the handle of the rod. Designed for reaching into a wide border or up above one's head, this is a useful addition to gardening aids.

Louisa King
The Well-Considered Garden, 1915

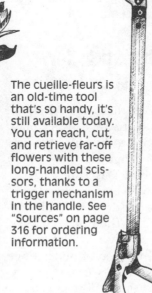

The cueille-fleurs is an old-time tool that's so handy, it's still available today. You can reach, cut, and retrieve far-off flowers with these long-handled scissors, thanks to a trigger mechanism in the handle. See "Sources" on page 316 for ordering information.

Homemade Planting Cards

I cut cards of strong white pasteboard, measuring eight by twelve inches, and in the middle of the narrow side of these I put a loop of string for hanging. The back of the card is left blank so that garden notes and memoranda may be written there, and on the face of the card I paste the names of the vegetables to be planted and their cultural directions. These I obtain from the catalogs of the seedsmen from whom I order my seeds. Toward the right I leave a margin on which to note the dates of sowings.

Louisa King
The Well-Considered Garden, 1915

With these handy planting cards, you can keep garden records wherever you store your gardening tools—in the basement, garage, or toolshed.

A Compass for Laying Out Beds

A rough form of compass is very useful. This may be made of three pieces of lath, sharpening two of the ends for points. Drive a nail through the other two ends so that the points can be moved to any distance you wish. Nail the other lath in the middle of either one of the others. This is the guide.

J. T. Scott
The Garden Magazine, 1907

Editor's Note: Lath is 1 × 3 lumber that is widely available at building-supply stores.

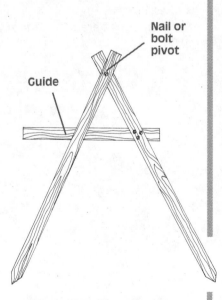

Guide

Nail or bolt pivot

A jumbo compass is handy for laying out garden beds. Once you decide on the size bed you want, note the position of the compass leg against the guide. Then tie or nail the compass leg to the guide to hold it in place while you outline your bed.

Pad Your Knees with a Kneeling Mat

It is an oblong mat, dark crimson in color, and is made of nothing more nor less than two thicknesses of woolenplush covering from an old Shaker chair. This mat might in one way be better. Its color might be a bit brighter, so that it should be more easily discernible on the grass. I would suggest a bright blue or a yellow.

Louisa King
The Well-Considered Garden, 1915

Editor's Note: Garden suppliers eventually heeded King's suggestion, and now you can buy kneeling mats in a variety of bright colors. Modern mats are made of cushy foam instead of chair coverings and are available at garden centers.

Number Sticks for Long-Lasting Labels

Wherever there is a variety of plants cultivated, it becomes necessary to be able to mark and distinguish them. The number stick is a slip of lath, nine or twelve inches long, sharpened at one end and squared at the other. Seton's botanic tally is a highly improved method of numbering. The ten ciphers are denoted by as many single, distinct cuts, of easy and expeditious execution; and any number, however high, requiring no more marks than it would require figures written with a pen.

J. C. Loudon
An Encyclopedia of Gardening, 1850

Editor's Note: A numbering system makes it easy to track down individual plants in large plantings. Start by mapping the plants in your yard and assigning each one a number. Then cut numbers on your plant labels that match the numbers on your planting plan. You can use Seton's botanic tally system shown here or create your own system.

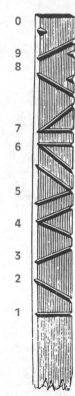

To record numbers that can't wash away, you can try this trusty numbering system, using lines and notches cut with a knife or saw.

A Weatherproof Label

The label is a wooden one, and consists in fastening, with a small screw, a short piece of wood or metal over the name.

Thomas Firminger
Firminger's Manual of Gardening for India, 1918

Here's an attractive, durable label, made of 1 × 3 wood. The cover protects the written information and is attached with a screw so you can push it aside to reveal the name underneath. Note that the point of the label is tapered on all four sides so you can easily insert it into the soil.

Emergency Plant Label

If you made no labels this year, split a clothes pin in two. This makes a fair emergency label.

Ellen Eddy Shaw
The Garden Magazine, 1909

Plant Bulbs with a Broomstick Dibble

To "naturalize" crocuses, scillas, and snowdrops, make a dibble by pointing a broomstick. Make about a hundred little holes irregularly over your lawn, each four inches deep. Drop into each a good teaspoonful of sand, then set in, root side down, the little bulbs. Rake the ground over them. Scatter grass seed over the holes, and step on the seed.

Evelyn Prince Cahoon
The Garden Magazine, 1908

Editor's Note: You can easily turn an old broomstick into a dibble by sharpening one end. Place the broomstick in a vise, and shape it with a file.

Dependable Depth Dibble

In order that seeds may be planted to a uniform depth I always use a marker, which may be made as follows: to a piece of one-inch board, 4 inches wide, and as long as the hot or coldframe is wide, tack down the middle a 1/4-inch-square strip. This marker is pressed into the soil until the board touches the surface of the soil, and then carefully removed. This leaves a clean drill 1/4 inch wide and deep, in which to drop the seeds.

W. Clark
The Garden Magazine, 1906

Spare Your Back with a Seed Tube

The illustration is a tube permanently fastened to a two-quart tin cup, for sowing small seeds, the sower standing nearly erect and dropping the seed where wanted, regardless of wind or weather. It is a simple and cheap affair, but the gardener who once uses it will ever after consider it indispensable.

F. Grundy
American Agriculturist, 1884

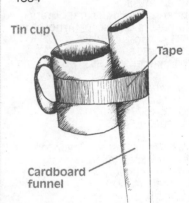

Tin cup

Tape

Cardboard funnel

This device saves you the effort of getting on your hands and knees to plant seeds. Form the funnel from a sheet of thin cardboard left over from a dress or shirt box. Use strong duct tape to fasten the funnel and cup together. When you're ready to plant, place seeds in the cup and drop pinches of them through the funnel as you walk down the rows.

SOURCES

It's not easy finding old-time plant varieties and gardening supplies. So we've compiled sources here for some of the more unusual items mentioned in this book—they're listed by chapter. If you're trying to find other plants and products, here are some good source lists.

Andersen Horticultural Library's Source List of Plants & Seeds,
4th ed., 1996
Andersen Horticultural Library
Minnesota Landscape Arboretum
3675 Arboretum Drive
P.O. Box 39
Chanhassen, MN 55317-0039

Combined Rose List
Peter Schneider
P.O. Box 677
Mantua, OH 44255

Fruit, Berry, and Nut Inventory
Seed Savers Exchange
3076 N. Winn Road
Decorah, IA 52101

The Garden Seed Inventory
Seed Savers Exchange
3076 N. Winn Road
Decorah, IA 52101

RHS Plant Finder
The Plant Press
10 Market Street
Lewes
BN7 2NB, England

Planning Your Yard and Garden

Brent & Becky's Bulbs
7900 Daffodil Lane
Gloucester, VA 23061
877-661-2852 (phone)
804-693-9436 (fax)
autumn-blooming crocus

Carroll Gardens, Inc.
444 E. Main Street
Westminster, MD 21157
800-638-6334 (phone)
410-857-4112 (fax)
plume poppy

Corn Hill Nursery
2700 Route 890
Corn Hill, New Brunswick
E4Z 1M2, Canada
506-756-3635 (phone)
506-756-1087 (fax)
wichuraiana rose

Forestfarm
990 Tetherow Road
Williams, OR 97544-9599
541-846-7269 (phone)
541-846-6963 (fax)
**'Klehm's' flowering crab;
wichuraiana rose**

Fragrant Path
P.O. Box 328
Fort Calhoun, NE 68023
sweet vernal grass

Greer Gardens
1280 Goodpasture Island Road
Eugene, OR 97401-1794
800-548-0111 (phone)
541-686-0910 (fax)
'Klehm's Improved' flowering crab

Henry Field's Seed & Nursery Co.
P.O. Box 397
Aurora, IN 47001
513-354-1494 (phone)
513-354-1496 (fax)
cut-leaved birch

Mellinger's, Inc.
2310 W. South Range Road
P.O. Box 157
North Lima, OH 44452-9731
330-549-9861 (phone)
330-549-3716 (fax)
Bechtel's double flowering crab

Rose Acres
6641 Crystal Boulevard
El Dorado, CA 95623-4804
530-626-1722
wichuraiana rose

Planting and Caring for Gardens

Gardens Alive!
5100 Schenley Place
Lawrenceburg, IN 47025
812-537-8650 (phone)
812-537-5108 (fax)
gardenhelp@gardensalive.com (e-mail)
green manure crops

Harmony Farm Supply
3244 Highway 116 North
Sebastopol, CA 95472
707-823-9125 (phone)
707-823-1734 (fax)
info@harmonyfarm.com (e-mail)
green manure crops

Irish Eyes–Garden City Seeds
P.O. Box 307
Thorp, WA 98946
877-733-3001 (phone)
800-964-9210 (fax)
cover crops

Peaceful Valley Farm Supply
P.O. Box 2209
Grass Valley, CA 95945
530-272-4769 (phone)
530-272-4794 (fax)
green manure crops

Territorial Seed Co.
P.O. Box 158
Cottage Grove, OR 97424-0061
541-942-9547 (phone)
888-657-3131 (fax)
green manure crops

Vegetables

Baker Creek Heirloom Seeds
2278 Baker Creek Road
Mansfield, MO 65704
417-924-8917 (phone/fax)
Queen Anne's pocket melon

The Cook's Garden
P.O. Box 535
Londonderry, VT 05148
800-457-9703 (phone)
800-457-9705 (fax)
**beans: heirloom varieties;
cardoon; celeriac; chicory;
greens: cress, dandelions;
'Rouge d'Hiver' lettuce;
tomatoes: heirloom varieties**

Edible Landscaping
P.O. Box 77
Afton, VA 22920-0077
434-361-9134 (phone)
434-361-1916 (fax)
www.eat-it.com (Internet)
citron

Field & Forest Products, Inc.
N. 3296 Kozuzek Road
Peshtigo, WI 54157
800-792-6220 (phone)
715-582-0181 (fax)
shiitake mushroom spawn

Forestfarm
990 Tetherow Road
Williams, OR 97544-9599
541-846-7269 (phone)
541-846-6963 (fax)
hops

Fungi Perfecti
P.O. Box 7634
Olympia, WA 98507
360-426-9292 (phone)
360-426-9377 (fax)
mycomedia@aol.com (e-mail)
mushroom spawn

The Gourmet Gardener
12287 117th Drive
Live Oak, FL 32060
888-404-4769 (phone)
407-650-2691 (fax)
**cardoon; celeriac; chicory;
greens: corn salad (mache),
cress, dandelion, 'Rouge d'Hiver'
lettuce, purslane**

Heirloom Garden Seeds
P.O. Box 138
Guerneville, CA 95446
**angelica; greens:
shepherd's purse**

Heirloom Seeds
P.O. Box 245
West Elizabeth, PA
15088-0245
412-384-0852 (phone/fax)
**tomatoes: heirloom
seedlings**

Henry Field's Seed & Nursery Co.
P.O. Box 397
Aurora, IN 47001
513-354-1494 (phone)
513-354-1496 (fax)
hops

Irish Eyes–Garden City Seeds
P.O. Box 307
Thorp, WA 98946
877-733-3001 (phone)
800-964-9210 (fax)
heirloom bean seed

J. L. Hudson, Seedsman
Star Route 2, Box 337
La Honda, CA 94020
'Little Gem' squash

Johnny's Selected Seeds
955 Benton Avenue
Winslow, ME 04901
207-861-3900 (phone)
207-861-8363 (fax)
**beans: scarlet runner, 'Midnight'
black turtle soup; black corn;
'Blue Ballet' squash; celeriac;
chicory; crimson clover; greens:
corn salad (mache), cresses,
dandelions, purslane, 'Rouge
d'Hiver' lettuce; radishes: 'Nero
Tondo' (black Spanish type);
salsify; scorzonera; tomatoes:
heirloom varieties**

Louisiana Nursery
5853 Highway 182
Opelousas, LA 70570
337-948-3696 (phone)
337-942-6404 (fax)
dedurio@yahoo.com (e-mail)
citron melon

Mushroompeople
560 Farm Road
P.O. Box 220
Summertown, TN 38483-0220
931-964-2200 (phone/fax)
mushroom@thefarm.org (e-mail)
mushroom spawn

Native Seeds/SEARCH
526 N. 4th Avenue
Tucson, AZ 85705
520-622-5561 (phone)
520-622-5591 (fax)
scarlet runner beans

Nichols Garden Nursery
1190 Old Salem Road NE
Albany, OR 97321-4580
541-928-9280 (phone)
541-967-8406 (fax)
customersupport@nichols
gardennursery.com (e-mail)
**cardoon; greens: corn salad
(mache), cresses; crimson
clover; salsify; scorzonera;
tomatoes: early**

Orchid Gardens
2232 139th Avenue NW
Andover, MN 55304-3908
763-755-0205
silverweed

Peaceful Valley Farm Supply
P.O. Box 2209
Grass Valley, CA 95945
530-272-4769 (phone)
530-272-4794 (fax)
**black corn; buckwheat; crimson
clover**

Pinetree Garden Seeds
P.O. Box 300
New Gloucester, ME 04260
207-926-3400 (phone)
888-527-3337 (fax)
**'Black Spanish' radish; citron
melon; greens: orach**

Richters
357 Highway 47
Goodwood, Ontario
L0C 1A0, Canada
905-640-6677 (phone)
905-640-6641 (fax)
orderdesk@richters.com (e-mail)
**angelica; greens: curled dock,
hops, orach, shepherd's purse**

Ronniger's Seed Potatoes
Star Route, Road 73
Moyie Springs, ID 83845
208-267-7938 (phone)
208-267-3265 (fax)
heirloom seed potatoes

Seeds of Change
P.O. Box 15700
Santa Fe, NM 87506-5700
888-762-7333 (phone)
505-438-7052 (fax)
gardener@seedsofchange.com
(e-mail)
**beans: heirloom varieties,
scarlet runner; black corn**

Shepherd's Garden Seeds
30 Irene Street
Torrington, CT 06790
860-482-3638 (phone)
860-496-1418 (fax)
**beans: heirloom varieties;
celeriac; greens: corn salad
(mache), cresses, dandelions,
purslane; 'Rouge d'Hiver' lettuce**

Smith & Hawken
P.O. Box 8690
Pueblo, CO 81008-9998
800-776-3336
cloches

Territorial Seed Co.
P.O. Box 158
Cottage Grove, OR 97424-0061
541-942-9547 (phone)
888-657-3131 (fax)
**angelica; buckwheat; celeriac;
chicory; crimson clover; greens:
corn salad, cresses, purslane;
mushroom kits; tomatoes: early
and heirloom varieties**

Tomato Growers Supply Co.
P.O. Box 2237
Fort Myers, FL 33902
239-768-1119 (phone)
888-768-3476 (fax)
**tomatoes: early and heirloom
varieties, including 'Amana
Orange', 'Black Krim', 'Garden
Peach', and 'Great White'**

Totally Tomatoes
P.O. Box 1626
Augusta, GA 30903
803-663-0016 (phone)
888-477-7333 (fax)
**tomatoes: early and heirloom
varieties**

Vermont Bean Seed Co.
334 W. Stroud Street
Randolph, WI 53956
800-349-1071 (phone)
888-500-7333 (fax)
**beans: heirloom varieties,
scarlet runner bean; celeriac;
greens: corn salad (mache)**

Herbs and Home Remedies

Baker Creek Heirloom Seeds
2278 Baker Creek Road
Mansfield, MO 65704
417-924-8917 (phone/fax)
heirloom herbs

Caprilands Herb Farm
534 Silver Street
P.O. Box 190
Coventry, CT 06238
860-742-7244
**angelica; lady's bedstraw;
mugwort; scented geraniums;
southernwood**

Carroll Gardens, Inc.
444 E. Main Street
Westminster, MD 21157
800-638-6334 (phone)
410-857-4112 (fax)
**chaste tree; lady's bedstraw;
milk weed**

Dabney Herbs
P.O. Box 22061
Louisville, KY 40252
502-893-5198 (phone/fax)
dabneyherb@win.net (e-mail)
**lady's bedstraw; valerian; white
or lettuce poppy**

Forestfarm
990 Tetherow Road
Williams, OR 97544-9599
541-846-7269 (phone)
541-846-6963 (fax)
**balsam fir; chaste tree; Chinese
quince; Japanese quince; rugosa
rose; sweet fern; valerian**

J. L. Hudson, Seedsman
Star Route 2, Box 337
La Honda, CA 94020
**chaste tree; lady's bedstraw;
rugosa rose**

Johnny's Selected Seeds
955 Benton Avenue
Winslow, ME 04901
207-861-3900 (phone)
207-861-8363 (fax)
purslane

Joy Creek Nursery
20300 N.W. Watson Road
Scappoose, OR 97056
503-543-7474 (phone)
503-543-6933 (fax)
chaste tree

Kurt Bluemel, Inc.
2740 Greene Lane
Baldwin, MD 21013-9523
800-498-1560 (phone)
410-557-9785 (fax)
marsh marigold

Las Pilitas Nursery
3232 Las Pilitas Road
Santa Margarita, CA 93453
805-438-5992 (phone)
805-438-5993 (fax)
field mint

**Meadowbrook Nursery–
We-Du Natives**
2055 Polly Spout Road
Marion, NC 28752-9338
828-738-8300 (phone)
828-287-9348 (fax)
**boneset; mullein; New Jersey
tea; sweet or fragrant
goldenrod**

Mellinger's, Inc.
2310 W. South Range Road
P.O. Box 157
North Lima, OH 44452-9731
330-549-9861 (phone)
330-549-3716 (fax)
balsam fir; rugosa rose

Nichols Garden Nursery
1190 Old Salem Road NE
Albany, OR 97321-4580
541-928-9280 (phone)
541-967-8406 (fax)
customersupport@nichols
gardennursery.com (e-mail)
**angelica; elecampane; hops;
mugwort; saffron crocus;
valerian**

Orchid Gardens
2232 139th Avenue NW
Andover, MN 55304-3908
763-755-0205
**corn or field mint; marsh
marigold**

Richters
357 Highway 47
Goodwood, Ontario
L0C 1A0, Canada
905-640-6677 (phone)
905-640-6641 (fax)
orderdesk@richters.com (e-mail)
**chaste tree; curled dock;
damask rose; hops; mugwort;
New Jersey tea; saffron crocus;
southernwood; speedwell;
valerian; verbena**

Roses of Yesterday and Today
803 Brown's Valley Road
Watsonville, CA 95076-0398
831-728-1901
damask rose; rugosa rose

Sandy Mush Herb Nursery
316 Surrett Cove Road
Leicester, NC 28748-5517
828-683-2014
angelica; boneset; hops; licorice; mallow; mother-of-thyme or creeping white moss; mullein; scented geraniums; verbena

Seeds of Change
P.O. Box 15700
Santa Fe, NM 87506-5700
888-762-7333 (phone)
505-438-7052 (fax)
gardener@seedsofchange.com
(e-mail)
chaste tree; elecampane; heirloom herbs; mugwort; white or lettuce poppy

Shady Acres Herb Farm
7815 Highway 212
Chaska, MN 55318
952-466-3391 (phone)
952-466-4739 (fax)
elecampane

Shepherd's Garden Seeds
30 Irene Street
Torrington, CT 06790
860-482-3638 (phone)
860-496-1418 (fax)
scented geraniums; white or lettuce poppy

Thompson & Morgan
P.O. Box 1308
Jackson, NJ 08527-0308
800-274-7333 (phone)
888-466-4769 (fax)
heirloom herbs

Well-Sweep Herb Farm
205 Mt. Bethel Road
Port Murray, NJ 07865
908-852-5390 (phone)
908-852-1649 (fax)
mallow; mother-of-thyme or creeping white moss; mullein; southernwood; speedwell; verbena; water mint

Woodlanders, Inc.
1128 Colleton Avenue
Aiken, SC 29801
803-648-7522 (phone/fax)
Chinese quince

Flowers

Arena Rose Company
P.O. Box 3096
525 Pine Street
Paso Robles, CA 93447
888-466-7434 (phone)
888-347-5580 (fax)
antique roses; rugosa roses

Baker Creek Heirloom Seeds
2278 Baker Creek Road
Mansfield, MO 65704
417-924-8917 (phone/fax)
sweet peas; love-in-a-mist; hollyhocks; sunflowers

Brent & Becky's Bulbs
7900 Daffodil Lane
Gloucester, VA 23061
877-661-2852 (phone)
804-693-9436 (fax)
Cuban lily; goldband lily; *Tulipa aucheriana*; *T. celsiana* var. *persica*; wild daffodils; wild tulips

W. Atlee Burpee & Co.
300 Park Avenue
Warminster, PA 18974-0001
800-333-5808 (phone)
800-487-5530 (fax)
goldband lily; heliotrope; mignonette

Busse Gardens
17160 245th Avenue
Big Lake, MN 55309
800-544-3192 (phone)
763-263-1473 (fax)
***Delphinium* x *belladonna*; plantain lily**

Corn Hill Nursery
2700 Route 890
Corn Hill, New Brunswick
E4Z 1M2, Canada
506-756-3635 (phone)
506-756-1087 (fax)
cinnamon rose; 'Madam Plantier' rose; wichuraiana rose

Dabney Herbs
P.O. Box 22061
Louisville, KY 40252
502-893-5198
(phone/fax)
dabneyherb@win.net
(e-mail)
blackberry lily; false Solomon's seal

Davidson Greenhouse and Nursery, Inc.
3147 E. Ladoga Road
Crawfordsville, IN 47933
877-723-6834 (phone)
800-276-3691 (fax)
'Prince of Orange' pelargonium

Forestfarm
990 Tetherow Road
Williams, OR 97544-9599
541-846-7269 (phone)
541-846-6963 (fax)
broom; burnet or Scotch rose; echeverias; *Phlox paniculata*; wichuraiana rose

Freshwater Farms
5851 Myrtle Avenue
Eureka, CA 95503-9510
800-200-8969 (phone)
707-442-2490 (fax)
info@freshwaterfarms.com
(e-mail)
white Japanese iris

Goodwin Creek Gardens
P.O. Box 83
Williams, OR 97544
800-846-7359 (phone)
541-846-7357 (fax)
plume poppy

Greenmantle Nursery
3010 Ettersburg Road
Garberville, CA 95442
707-986-7504
green rose; heirloom roses, including 'Autumn Damask', 'Gruss an Teplitz', and 'Marie Pavie'

Greer Gardens
1280 Goodpasture Road
Eugene, OR 97401-1794
800-548-0111 (phone)
541-686-0910 (fax)
spurge

Heirloom Garden Seeds
P.O. Box 138
Guerneville, CA 95446
cup-and-saucer vine; peach-leaved bell-flower; tufted pansies

**Honeywood [Dr. A. J. Porter]
Heritage Nursery**
Box 48
Parkside, Saskatchewan
S0J 2A0, Canada
306-747-3522 (phone)
306-747-3395 (fax)
lemon daylily; siberian squill

Inter-State Nurseries
1800 Hamilton Road
Bloomington, IL 61704
309-663-9551
'Persian Yellow' rose

J. L. Hudson, Seedsman
Star Route 2, Box 337
La Honda, CA 94020
**China rose; false hellebore;
rugosa rose**

Johnny's Selected Seeds
955 Benton Avenue
Winslow, ME 04901
207-861-3900 (phone)
207-861-8363 (fax)
amaranth; love-in-a-mist

Joy Creek Nursery
20300 N.W. Watson Road
Scappoose, OR 97056
503-543-7474 (phone)
503-543-6933 (fax)
heirloom roses; penstemons

Lilypons Water Gardens
6800 Lilypons Road
P.O. Box 10
Buckeystown, MD 21717-0010
800-999-5459 (phone)
800-879-5459 (fax)
waterlilies; white Japanese iris

Logee's Greenhouses
141 North Street
Danielson, CT 06239-1939
888-330-8038 (phone)
888-774-9932 (fax)
**'Prince of Orange' pelargonium;
scarlet plume**

Lowe's Roses
6 Sheffield Road
Nashua, NH 03062
603-888-2214 (phone)
603-888-6112 (fax)
**roses: 'American Pillar', 'Dorothy
Perkins', and 'General
Washington'**

McClure & Zimmerman
108 W. Winnebago Street
P.O. Box 368
Friesland, WI 53935-0368
800-883-6998
British tulip; Cuban lily; *T.
aucheriana*; *T. celsiana* var. *persica*; **wild daffodils; wild tulips**

**Meadowbrook Nursery–
We-Du Natives**
2055 Polly Spout Road
Marion, NC 28752-9338
828-738-8300 (phone)
828-287-9348 (fax)
common beardtongue; *Phlox
paniculata*; **rabbit-ear iris**

Mellinger's, Inc.
2310 W. South Range Road
P.O. Box 157
North Lima, OH 44452-9731
330-549-9861 (phone)
330-549-3716 (fax)
Boston ivy

Messelaar Bulb Co., Inc.
160 County Road, Route 1A
P.O. Box 269
Ipswich, MA 01938
978-356-3737 (phone)
978-356-8850 (fax)
lemon daylily

Niche Gardens
1111 Dawson Road
Chapel Hill, NC 27516
919-967-0078 (phone)
919-967-4026 (fax)
orders@nichegardens.com
(e-mail)
plaintain lily

Nichols Garden Nursery
1190 Old Salem Road NE
Albany, OR 97321-4580
541-928-9280 (phone)
541-967-8406 (fax)
customersupport@nichols
gardennursery.com (e-mail)
night-scented stock; wallflower

Orchid Gardens
2232 139th Avenue NW
Andover, MN 55304-3908
763-755-0205
brake or bracken

Paradise Water Gardens
14 May Street
Whitman, MA 02382-1841
800-955-0161 (phone)
781-447-4591 (fax)
**rabbit-ear iris; waterlilies; white
Japanese iris**

Park Seed
1 Parkton Avenue
Greenwood, SC 29647-0001
800-213-0076 (phone)
864-941-4206 (fax)
**Canterbury bells; Dutch crocus;
heliotrope**

Pickering Nurseries
670 Kingston Road
Pickering, Ontario
L1V 1A6, Canada
905-839-2111 (phone)
905-839-4807 (fax)
**burnet or Scotch rose; 'General
Washington' rose; Heirloom
roses, including 'Gruss an
Teplitz' and 'Marie Pavie'**

Plants of the Southwest
3095 Agua Fria Road
Santa Fe, NM 87507
800-788-7333 (phone)
505-438-8800 (fax)
common beardtongue

Prairie Nursery, Inc.
P.O. Box 306
Westfield, WI 53964
800-476-9453 (phone)
608-296-2741 (fax)
thin-leaved coneflower

Richters
357 Highway 47
Goodwood, Ontario
L0C 1A0, Canada
905-640-6677 (phone)
905-640-6641 (fax)
orderdesk@richters.com (e-mail)
**blackberry lily; blood-
root; damask rose; love-
in-a-mist; orris**

**Ron's Rare Plants &
Seeds**
415 Chappel
Calumet City, IL
60409
708-862-1993
**Canterbury bells;
moonflower; night-
scented stock;
obedient plant**

Roses of Yesterday and Today
803 Brown's Valley Road
Watsonville, CA 95076-0398
831-728-1901
'American Pillar' rose; Austrian rose; damask rose; heirloom roses, including 'Gruss an Teplitz' and 'Marie Pavie'

Seeds of Change
P.O. Box 15700
Santa Fe, NM 87506-5700
888-762-7333 (phone)
505-438-7052 (fax)
gardener@seedsofchange.com (e-mail)
bloodroot

Select Seeds Antique Flowers
180 Stickney Hill Road
Union, CT 06076-4617
860-684-9310 (phone)
800-653-3304 (fax)
Delphinium elatum; **moonflower**

Slocum Water Gardens
1101 Cypress Gardens Boulevard
Winter Haven, FL 33884-1932
863-293-7151 (phone)
800-322-1896 (fax)
waterlilies

Stokes Seeds
Box 548
Buffalo, NY 14240-0548
800-396-9238 (phone)
888-834-3334 (fax)
cup-and-saucer vine; obedient plant

Sutton's Iris Gardens
16592 Road 208
Porterville, CA 93257-9011
888-558-5107 (phone)
559-784-5107 (local phone)
559-784-6701 (fax)
irises

Thompson & Morgan
P.O. Box 1308
Jackson, NJ 08527-0308
800-274-7333 (phone)
888-466-4769 (fax)
echeverias; maurandya; Spanish poppy; wallflower

Van Ness Water Gardens
2460 N. Euclid Avenue
Upland, CA 91784-1199
800-205-2425 (phone)
909-949-7217 (fax)
waterlilies

Wayside Gardens
1 Garden Lane
Hodges, SC 29695
800-213-0379 (phone)
800-817-1124 (fax)
spurge

White Flower Farm
167 Litchfield Road
Morris, CT 06763
800-255-2852 (phone)
860-576-3507 (fax)
broom; *Delphinium x belladonna*; **Dutch crocus; foxglove penstemon; siberian squill; tree peony**

Wildseed Farms
425 Wildflower Hills
P.O. Box 3000
Fredericksburg, TX 78624-3000
800-848-0078 (phone)
830-990-8090 (fax)
wildflower mixes; sunflowers

Woodlanders, Inc.
1128 Colleton Avenue
Aiken, SC 29801
803-648-7522 (phone/fax)
thin-leaved coneflower

Fruits and Nuts

Applesource
1716 Apples Road
Chapin, IL 62628
800-588-3854 (phone)
217-245-7844 (fax)
heirloom apples (sells fruit only, no trees)

Classical Fruits
8831 AL Highway 157
Moulton, AL 35650
256-974-8813 (phone)
256-974-4060 (fax)
apples: 'Early Joe', 'Rambo', 'Rhode Island Greening', 'Roxbury Russet'

Corn Hill Nursery
2700 Route 890
Corn Hill, New Brunswick
E4Z 1M2, Canada
506-756-3635 (phone)
506-756-1087 (fax)
Missouri currant

Forestfarm
990 Tetherow Road
Williams, OR 97544-9599
541-846-7269 (phone)
541-846-6963 (fax)
medlar; Missouri currant; quince; siberian crabapple; swamp azalea

Louisiana Nursery
5853 Highway 182
Opelousas, LA 70570
337-948-3696 (phone)
337-942-6404 (fax)
dedurio@yahoo.com (e-mail)
Japanese flowering quince; quince

Miller Nurseries
5060 W. Lake Road
Canandaigua, NY 14424-8904
800-836-9630 (phone)
585-396-2154 (fax)
apples: 'Duchess of Oldenburg' 'Baldwin', 'Roxbury Russet', 'Twenty-Ounce Pippin'

National Virus-Tested Fruit Tree Collection
WSU, IAREC
24106 N. Bunn Road
Prosser, WA 99350-8694
509-786-9251 (phone)
509-786-9370 (fax)
'Damson' plum; 'English Morello' cherry; 'Flemish Beauty' pear

Raintree Nursery
391 Butts Road
Morton, WA 98356
360-496-6400 (phone)
888-770-8358 (fax)
alpine strawberry; Japanese flowering quince; medlar; miniature peach; 'White Imperial' currant

Richters
357 Highway 47
Goodwood, Ontario
L0C 1A0, Canada
905-640-6677 (phone)
905-640-6641 (fax)
orderdesk@richters.com (e-mail)
alpine strawberry

Southmeadow Fruit Gardens
P.O. Box 211
10603 Cleveland Avenue
Baroda, MI 49101
616-422-2411 (phone)
616-422-1464 (fax)
'English Morello' cherry; 'Flemish Beauty' pear; pears: old varieties

Stark Bro's Nurseries
Highway 59 West
Louisiana, MO 63353
800-478-2759 (phone)
573-754-3701 (fax)
'Damson' plum; miniature peach

Trees of Antiquity
20 Wellsona Road
Paso Robles, CA 93446
805-467-9909 (phone/fax)
tom@treesofantiquity.com (e-mail)
heirloom apples; pears: old varieties

Twombly Nursery
163 Barn Hill Road
Monroe, CT 06468
203-261-2133 (phone)
203-261-9230 (fax)
siberian crabapple; swamp azalea

Trees, Shrubs, and Vines

Check local nurseries for trees, shrubs, and vines first—it's nice to see these plants before you buy. If you can't find what you're looking for, there are many mail-order companies you can order from, such as those listed below.

A. M. Leonard, Inc.
241 Fox Drive
Piqua, OH 45356
800-543-8955 (phone)
800-433-0633 (fax)
burlap tree wrap

Arborvillage
P.O. Box 227
Holt, MO 64048
816-264-3911 (phone)
816-264-3760 (fax)
American mountain ash; laurel-leaf willow; Scotch elm; smooth-leaved elm

Banana Tree, Inc.
715 Northampton Street
Easton, PA 18042
610-253-9589 (phone)
610-253-4864 (fax)
passionflower

Forestfarm
990 Tetherow Road
Williams, OR 97544-9599
541-846-7269 (phone)
541-846-6963 (fax)
Dutch woodbine; sea buckthorn; staghorn sumac; teas weeping mulberry; woad wax

Freshwater Farms
5851 Myrtle Avenue
Eureka, CA 95503-9510
800-200-8969 (phone)
707-442-2490 (fax)
info@freshwaterfarms.com (e-mail)
balsam poplar

Greenmantle Nursery
3010 Ettersburg Road
Garberville, CA 95542
707-986-7504
Rosa **'La France'**

Greer Gardens
1280 Goodpasture Island Road
Eugene, OR 97401-1794
800-548-0111 (phone)
541-686-0910 (fax)
Irish (or English) yew

Heronswood Nursery Ltd.
7530 N.E. 288th Street
Kingston, WA 98346
360-297-4172 (phone)
360-297-8321 (fax)
Dutch woodbine; white-stemmed bramble

Hidden Springs Nursery
170 Hidden Springs Lane
Cookeville, TN 38501
931-268-2592
sea buckthorn

Mellinger's, Inc.
2310 W. South Range Road
P.O. Box 157
North Lima, OH 44452-9731
330-549-9861 (phone)
330-549-3716 (fax)
Irish or English yew; Japanese creeper; Japanese honeysuckle; quaking aspen

Midwest Groundcovers
P.O. Box 748
St. Charles, IL 60174
847-742-1790 (phone)
847-742-2655 (fax)
Japanese creeper

Milaeger's Gardens
4838 Douglas Avenue
Racine, WI 53402-2498
800-669-9956 (phone)
262-639-1855 (fax)
Japanese honeysuckle

Niche Gardens
1111 Dawson Road
Chapel Hill, NC 27516
919-967-0078 (phone)
919-967-4026 (fax)
orders@nichegardens.com (e-mail)
groundsel shrub

Raintree Nursery
391 Butts Road
Morton, WA 98356
360-496-6400 (phone)
888-770-8358 (fax)
medlar

Richters
357 Highway 47
Goodwood, Ontario
L0C 1A0, Canada
905-640-6677 (phone)
905-640-6641 (fax)
orderdesk@richters.com (e-mail)
matrimony vine

Roses of Yesterday and Today
803 Brown's Valley Road
Watsonville, CA 95076-0398
831-728-1901
rambling roses

Southmeadow Fruit Gardens
P.O. Box 211
10603 Cleveland Avenue
Baroda, MI 49101
616-422-2411 (phone)
616-422-1464 (fax)
Japanese rose

Thompson & Morgan
P.O. Box 1308
Jackson, NJ 08527-0308
800-274-7333 (phone)
888-466-4769 (fax)
passionflower

Twombly Nursery
163 Barn Hill Road
Monroe, CT 06468
203-261-2133 (phone)
203-261-9230 (fax)
box elder; Irish or English yew

Valley Nursery
P.O. Box 4845
Helena, MT 59604
406-458-3992
**laurel-leaf willow; staghorn
sumac**

Wayside Gardens
1 Garden Lane
Hodges, SC 29695
800-213-0379 (phone)
800-817-1124 (fax)
laurel or mountain laurel

Wildflowers and Ferns

Carroll Gardens, Inc.
444 E. Main Street
Westminster, MD 21157
800-638-6334 (phone)
410-857-4112 (fax)
**cardinal flower; Christmas fern;
hepatica; lady fern; musk
mallow**

Fancy Fronds
P.O. Box 1090
Gold Bar, WA 98251
360-793-1472 (phone)
360-793-4243 (fax)
**lady fern; maidenhair fern; male
fern; ostrich fern**

Ion Exchange
1878 Old Mission Drive
Harpers Ferry, IA 52146-7533
800-291-2143 (phone)
563-535-7362 (fax)
**bird's-foot violet; spotted
touch-me-not; yellow touch-
me-not or jewelweed**

Kurt Bluemel, Inc.
2740 Greene Lane
Baldwin, MD 21013-9523
800-498-1560 (phone)
410-557-9785 (fax)
spikenard

Louisiana Nursery
5853 Highway 182
Opelousas, LA 70570
337-948-3696 (phone)
337-942-6404 (fax)
dedurio@yahoo.com (e-mail)
**Christmas fern; lady fern;
maidenhair fern; male fern;
ostrich fern**

Meadowbrook Nursery–
We-Du Natives
2055 Polly Spout Road
Marion, NC 28752-9338
828-738-8300 (phone)
828-287-9348 (fax)
**bird's-foot violet; Christmas
fern; hepatica; maidenhair fern;
male fern; ostrich fern;
spikenard**

Niche Gardens
1111 Dawson Road
Chapel Hill, NC 27516
919-967-0078 (phone)
919-967-4026 (fax)
orders@nichegardens.com
(e-mail)
wildflowers

Prairie Nursery, Inc.
P.O. Box 306
Westfield, WI 53964
800-476-9453 (phone)
608-296-2741 (fax)
**gray goldenrod; showy (Canada)
tick trefoil**

Wayside Gardens
1 Garden Lane
Hodges, SC 29695
800-213-0379 (phone)
800-817-1124 (fax)
hay-scented fern

Wildseed Farms
425 Wildflower Hills
P.O. Box 3000
Fredericksburg, TX 78624-3000
800-848-0078 (phone)
830-990-8090 (fax)
wildflower mixes; sunflowers

Houseplants and Flower Crafts

Bovees Nursery
1737 S.W. Coronado Street
Portland, OR 97219
800-435-9250
trailing arbutus

Brent & Becky's Bulbs
7900 Daffodil Lane
Gloucester, VA 23061
877-661-2852 (phone)
804-693-9436 (fax)
'Grand Soleil d'Or' narcissus

Carroll Gardens, Inc.
444 E. Main Street
Westminster, MD 21157
800-638-6334 (phone)
410-857-4112 (fax)
bluets or Quaker ladies; heath

Corn Hill Nursery
2700 Route 890
Corn Hill, New Brunswick
E4Z 1M2, Canada
506-756-3635 (phone)
506-756-1087 (fax)
**European mountain ash;
maidenhair fern**

Davidson Greenhouse
and Nursery, Inc.
3147 E. Ladoga Road
Crawfordsville, IN 47933
877-723-6834 (phone)
800-276-3691 (fax)
**blue passionflower; German ivy;
Mimosa pudica; wandering Jew**

Forestfarm
990 Tetherow Road
Williams, OR 97544-9599
541-846-7269 (phone)
541-846-6963 (fax)
**Carolina jessamine; Korean
mountain ash; pocketbook
plant; winter daphne**

Heaths and Heathers
502 E. Haskell Hill Road
Shelton, WA 98584-8429
800-294-3284 (phone/fax)
heaths

Joy Creek Nursery
20300 N.W. Watson Road
Scappoose, OR 97056
503-543-7474 (phone)
503-543-6933 (fax)
spiderwort

Logee's Greenhouses
141 North Street
Danielson, CT 06239-1939
888-330-8038 (phone)
888-774-9932 (fax)
**Boston fern; 'Meyer' lemon;
native ferns; scarlet plume;
smilax asparagus**

Louisiana Nursery
5853 Highway 182
Opelousas, LA 70570
337-948-3696 (phone)
337-942-6404 (fax)
dedurio@yahoo.com (e-mail)
Carolina jessamine; firecracker vine; pittosporums; winter daphne

Plant Delights Nursery
9241 Sauls Road
Raleigh, NC 27603
919-772-4794 (phone)
919-662-0370 (fax)
native ferns; pitcher plant

Ron's Rare Plants & Seeds
415 Chappel
Calumet City, IL 60409
708-862-1993
black-eyed Susan vine; European mountain ash

White Flower Farm
167 Litchfield Road
Morris, CT 06763
800-255-2852 (phone)
860-576-3507 (fax)
calla lily; cyclamens

Woodlanders, Inc.
1128 Colleton Avenue
Aiken, SC 29801
803-648-7522 (phone/fax)
Carolina jessamine; firecracker vine

Pest, Disease, and Weed Control

Arborvillage
P.O. Box 227
Holt, MO 64048
816-264-3911 (phone)
816-264-3760 (fax)
American smoke tree; common mulberry

Carroll Gardens, Inc.
444 E. Main Street
Westminster, MD 21157
800-638-6334 (phone)
410-857-4112 (fax)
bigleaf hydrangea; juneberry or serviceberry; snowberry; winter jasmine

Gardens Alive!
5100 Schenley Place
Lawrenceburg, IN 47025
812-537-8650 (phone)
812-537-5108 (fax)
gardenhelp@gardensalive.com (e-mail)
floating row covers; insecticidal soap

Harmony Farm Supply
3244 Highway 116 North
Sebastopol, CA 95472
707-823-9125 (phone)
707-823-1734 (fax)
info@harmonyfarm.com (e-mail)
bird netting; copper collars; diatomaceous earth; insecticidal soap; lime sulfur

Heronswood Nursery Ltd.
7530 N.E. 288th Street
Kingston, WA 98346
360-297-4172 (phone)
360-297-8321 (fax)
garden loosestrife

Louisiana Nursery
5853 Highway 182
Opelousas, LA 70570
337-948-3696 (phone)
337-942-6404 (fax)
dedurio@yahoo.com (e-mail)
aloe **spp.; downy serviceberry; winter jasmine**

Peaceful Valley Farm Supply
P.O. Box 2209
Grass Valley, CA 95945
530-272-4769 (phone)
530-272-4794 (fax)
bird netting; diatomaceous earth; insecticidal soap; lime sulfur

Richters
357 Highway 47
Goodwood, Ontario
L0C 1A0, Canada
905-640-6677 (phone)
905-640-6641 (fax)
orderdesk@richters.com (e-mail)
aloe **spp.; castor bean; wild mustard**

Ron's Rare Plants & Seeds
415 Chappel
Calumet City, IL 60409
708-862-1993
wild indigo

Territorial Seed Co.
P.O. Box 158
Cottage Grove, OR 97424-0061
541-942-9547 (phone)
888-657-3131 (fax)
floating row covers; insecticidal soap

Thompson & Morgan
P.O. Box 1308
Jackson, NJ 08527-0308
800-274-7333 (phone)
888-466-4769 (fax)
furze

Walt Nicke Co.
36 McLeod Lane
P.O. Box 433
Topsfield, MA 01983
800-822-4114 (phone)
978-887-9853 (fax)
copper collars

Garden Projects

Arborvillage
P.O. Box 227
Holt, MO 64048
816-264-3911 (phone)
816-264-3760 (fax)
tree-of-heaven

Baker Creek Heirloom Seeds
2278 Baker Creek Road
Mansfield, MO 65704
417-924-8917 (phone/fax)
hyacinth bean

Carroll Gardens, Inc.
444 E. Main Street
Westminster, MD 21157
800-638-6334 (phone)
410-857-4112 (fax)
empress tree; 'Mrs. Sinkins' dianthus

Thompson & Morgan
P.O. Box 1308
Jackson, NJ 08527-0308
800-274-7333 (phone)
888-466-4769 (fax)
alpine toadflax; dolichos hyacinth bean; hare's tail grass

Tools and Gadgets

A. M. Leonard, Inc.
241 Fox Drive
Piqua, OH 45356
800-543-8955 (phone)
800-433-0633 (fax)
garden tools; scuffle hoe

Gardener's Supply Co.
128 Intervale Road
Burlington, VT 05401
888-833-1412 (phone)
800-551-6712 (fax)
garden tools

Harmony Farm Supply
3244 Highway 116 North
Sebastopol, CA 95472
707-823-9125 (phone)
707-823-1734 (fax)
info@harmonyfarm.com (e-mail)
adjustable cultivator; winged weeder

Johnny's Selected Seeds
955 Benton Avenue
Winslow, ME 04901
207-861-3900 (phone)
207-861-8363 (fax)
wheel hoe

The Kinsman Company, Inc.
P.O. Box 428
Pipersville, PA 18947
800-733-4129 (phone)
215-766-5624 (fax)
garden tools

Peaceful Valley Farm Supply
P.O. Box 2209
Grass Valley, CA 95945
530-272-4769 (phone)
530-272-4794 (fax)
garden tools; wheel hoe

Smith & Hawken
P.O. Box 8690
Pueblo, CO 81008-9998
800-776-3336
ladies' size garden tools

Territorial Seed Co.
P.O. Box 158
Cottage Grove, OR 97424-0061
541-942-9547 (phone)
888-657-3131 (fax)
winged weeder

Walt Nicke Co.
36 McLeod Lane
P.O. Box 433
Topsfield, MA 01983
800-822-4114 (phone)
978-887-9853 (fax)
cueille-fleurs (cut-and-hold flower gatherer)

Womanswork
P.O. Box 65
Sharon, CT 06069
800-639-2709 (phone)
860-364-9356 (fax)
ladies' size garden tools

Recommended Reading

The books and magazines in this list are the sources of the quotes in *1,001 Old-Time Garden Tips*. If you'd like to find more great gardening ideas from the past, these publications are a good place to start.

Books

Abercrombie, John. *Abercrombie's Practical Gardener*. London, England: Clerk Abel, 1818.

Adams, Hester Ann. *Memorandum Book*. Canterbury, NH: N.p., 1839.

Agar, Madeline. *Garden Design*. Philadelphia, PA: J. B. Lippincott, 1912.

Agricultural Service Co. *The Vegetable Garden*. New York, NY: Doubleday, Page, 1912.

Albaugh, Benjamin F. *The Gardenette*. Cincinnati, OH: Stewart and Kidd, 1915.

Allen, C. L. *Bulbs and Tuberous-Rooted Plants*. New York, NY: Orange Judd, 1893.

Askham, Anthony. *Herbal*. 1550. Reprint, as *A Little Herball of the Properties of the Herbes*. Norwood, NJ: Walter J. Johnson, 1977.

Bacon, Francis. *Utopian Garden*. N.p., n.d.

Bailey, L. H. *American Garden*. New York, NY: Macmillan, 1890.

—. *Farm and Garden Rule-Book*. New York, NY: Macmillan, 1911.

—. *The Horticulturalist's Rule-Book*. New York, NY: Macmillan, 1895.

—. *The Principles of Vegetable Gardening*. New York, NY: Macmillan, 1901.

Banckes, Richard. *Bancke's Herbal*. London, England: W. Powell, 1550.

Barbara. *The Garden, You, and I*. New York, NY: Macmillan, 1910.

Barnes, James, and William Robinson. *Asparagus Culture*. London, England: George Routledge and Sons, 1881.

Barton, William P. C. *Barton's Florae*. 2 vols. Philadelphia, PA: M. Carey and Son, 1818.

Beach, S. A. *The Apples of New York*. Albany, NY: New York Agricultural Experiment Station, 1906.

Beale, Galen, and Mary Rose Boswell. *The Earth Shall Blossom: Shaker Herbs and Gardening*. Woodstock, VT: The Countryman Press, 1991.

Beecher, Catherine E., and Harriet Beecher Stowe. *The American Woman's Home*. New York, NY: J. B. Ford, 1869.

Beecher, Henry Ward. *Fruits, Flowers and Farming*. New York, NY: Derby & Jackson, 1859.

Beeton, Mrs. Isabella. *Mrs. Beeton's Book of Household Management*. New York, NY: Exeter Books, 1986. Originally published in 1859–61 in monthly supplements to S. O. Beeton's *The Englishwoman's Domestic Magazine*. First published by S. O. Beeton in 1861 as one volume entitled *The Book of Household Management*.

Bennett, Ida D. *The Flower Garden*. New York, NY: McClure, Phillips and Co., 1904.

—. *The Vegetable Garden*. New York, NY: McClure, 1908.

Biggle, Jacob. *Biggle Garden Book*. Philadelphia, PA: Wilmer Atkinson, 1912.

Bisset, Peter. *The Book of Water Gardening*. New York, NY: A. T. De La Mare Publishing Co., 1905.

Blanchan, Neltje. *Nature's Garden*. Toronto, Canada: William Briggs, 1900.

Blomfield, Reginald, and F. Inigo Thomas. *The Formal Garden in England*. London, England: Macmillan, 1892.

Bowles, E. A. *My Garden in Autumn and Winter*. New York, NY: Dodge Publishing Co., 1915.

—. *My Garden in Spring*. New York, NY: Dodge Publishing Co., 1914.

—. *My Garden in Summer*. New York, NY: Dodge Publishing Co., 1914.

Breck, Joseph. *The Flower-Garden*. New York, NY: C. M. Saxton, Barker & Co., 1860.

Briggs, Richard. *The New Art of Cookery*. Philadelphia, PA: Printed for W. Spotswood, R. Campbell, and E. Johnson, 1792.

Burbidge, F. W. *Cultivated Plants: Their Propagation and Improvement*. Edinburgh, Scotland: William Blackwood and Sons, 1877.

Burr, Fearing. *Garden Vegetables and How to Cultivate Them*. Boston, MA: J. E. Tilton, 1866.

Cecil, Alicia M. *Children's Gardens*. London, England: Macmillan, 1902.

Chaptal, John Antony. *Chymistry Applied to Agriculture*. Boston, MA: Hilliard, Gray, 1836.

Cleland, Elizabeth. *The Receipt Book of Elizabeth Cleland*. N.p., 1759.

Clutton-Brock, A. *Studies in Gardening*. New York, NY: Charles Scribner's Sons, 1916.

Cook, E. T. *Gardening for Beginners*. London, England: Country Life, 1901.

Cornelius, Mrs. *The Young Housekeeper's Friend*. Boston, MA: Brown, Taggard, and Chase, 1859.

Cran, Mrs. Marian. *The Garden of Ignorance*. New York, NY: Brentano's, 1913.

Culpeper, Nicholas. *Culpeper's Complete Herbal: Consisting of a Comprehensive Description of Nearly All Herbs with Their Medicinal Properties and Directions for Compounding the Medicines Extracted from Them*. London, England: W. Foulsham & Co., 1652.

Cummins, Julia H. *My Garden Comes of Age*. New York, NY: Macmillan, 1926.

Davis, E. B., and B. G. Jefferis. *The Household Guide*. Naperville, IL: J. L. Nichols, 1891.

Dexter, Almon. *And the Wilderness Bloomed*. Philadelphia, PA: H. W. Fisher and Co., 1901.

Dick, William. *Encyclopedia of Practical Receipts and Processes*. New York, NY: Dick & Fitzgerald, 1872.

Digbie, Sir Kenelme. *The Closet of the Emminently Learned Sir Kenelme Digbie, K.T., Opened*. London, England: Printed by E.C. for H. Brome, 1669.

Downing, Andrew Jackson. *The Architecture of Country Houses*. New York, NY: D. Appleton and Co., 1850.

—-. *Landscape Gardening*. New York, NY: Orange Judd, 1859.

Duncan, Frances. *The Joyous Art of Gardening*. New York, NY: Charles Scribner's Sons, 1917.

Durand, Herbert. *Wild Flowers and Ferns*. New York, NY: G. P. Putnam's Sons, 1925.

Earle, Alice Morse. *Customs and Fashions in Old New England*. New York, NY: Charles E. Tuttle Company, 1973. First edition published in 1893 by Charles Scribner's Sons, New York, NY.

—-. *Home Life in Colonial Days*. New York, NY: Macmillan, 1898.

—-. *Old-Time Gardens*. New York, NY: Macmillan, 1901.

Earle, Marie Theresa Villiers. *More Pot-Pourri from a Surrey Garden*. New York, NY: Macmillan, 1899.

Egan, W. C. *Making a Garden of Perennials*. New York, NY: McBride, Nast & Co., 1912.

Ely, Helena Rutherfurd. *The Practical Flower Garden*. New York, NY: Macmillan, 1911.

Evelyn, John. *Silva*. York, England: Printed by A. Ward, for J. Dodsley, etc., 1777.

Firminger, Thomas. *Firminger's Manual of Gardening for India*. Calcutta, India: Thacker, Spink, and Co., 1918.

Fletcher, S. W. *Strawberry-Growing*. New York, NY: Macmillan, 1917.

Flint, Martha Bockée. *A Garden of Simples*. New York, NY: Charles Scribner's Sons, 1900.

Gerard, John. *The Herball*. London, England: Adam Islip Joice Norton and Richard Whitakers, 1633.

Good, Peter Peyto. *Good's Family Flora*. Cambridge, England: Peter Peyto Good, 1854.

Grieve, M. *Culinary Herbs and Condiments*. New York, NY: Harcourt, Brace and Co., 1934.

Hawthorne, Nathaniel. *The American Notebooks*. 1868. Reprint. Columbus, OH: Ohio State University Press, 1972.

Henderson, Peter. *Henderson's Handbook of Plants*. New York, NY: Peter Henderson and Co., 1890.

—-. *Practical Floriculture*. New York, NY: Orange Judd, 1913.

Hill, Amelia Leavitt. *Garden Portraits*. New York, NY: Robert M. McBride, 1923.

Hill, Mary Ann. *Recipe Book*. Canterbury, NH: 1857. Collection of the United Society of Believers, Sabbathday Lake, ME.

Hohman, John George. *The Long-Lost Friend*. 1819. Reprint. State College, PA: Yardbird Books, 1992.

Holt, Emily. *The Complete Housekeeper*. Garden City, NY: Doubleday, Page, 1912.

Howe, Walter, ed. *The Garden*. New York, NY: G. P. Putnam's Sons, 1890.

Hubbard, Henry Vincent, and Theodora Kimball. *An Introduction to the Study of Landscape Design*. New York, NY: Macmillan, 1929.

Hughes, John Arthur. *Garden Architecture and Landscape Gardening*. London, England: Longmans, Green, 1866.

Jekyll, Gertrude. *Colour in the Flower Garden*. London, England: George Newnes, 1908.

—- and Lawrence Weaver. *Gardens for Small Country Houses*. London, England: George Newnes, 1913.

—-. *Home and Garden*. New York, NY: Longmans, Green, 1900.

—-. *Wood and Garden*. London, England: Longmans, Green, 1904.

Johnson, C. Pierpoint. *The Useful Plants of Great Britain*. London, England: Robert Hardwicke, 1862.

Jonsson-Rose, Nils. *Window and Parlor Gardening*. New York, NY: Charles Scribner's Sons, 1895.

Kellaway, Herbert J. *How to Lay Out Suburban Home Grounds*. New York, NY: John Wiley & Sons, 1915.

King, Louisa. *The Little Garden*. Boston, MA: Atlantic Monthly Press, 1921.

—-. *The Well-Considered Garden*. New York, NY: Charles Scribner's Sons, 1915.

Kirby, A. M. *Daffodils, Narcissus and How to Grow Them*. New York, NY: Doubleday, Page, 1907.

Langham, William. *The Garden of Health*. 2nd ed. London, England: Printed by T. Harper, 1633.

Lightfoot, John. *Flora Scotica*. 2nd ed. London, England: Printed for J. Dickson, 1792.

Lloyd, John W. *Productive Vegetable Growing*. Philadelphia, PA: J. B. Lippincott, 1914.

Long, Elias A. *Ornamental Gardening for Americans*. New York, NY: Orange Judd, 1884.

Loudon, J. C. *An Encyclopedia of Gardening*. London, England: Longmans, Green, 1850.

McCollom, William C. *Vines and How to Grow Them*. New York, NY: Doubleday, Page, 1911.

MacFarland, Charles. *The Rose in America*. New York, NY: Macmillan, 1923.

McFarland, J. Horace. *My Growing Garden*. New York, NY: Macmillan, 1915.

Magnus, Albertus. *The Book of Secrets of Albertus Magnus of the Virtues of Herbs, Stones and Certain Beasts, Also a Book of the Marvels of the World*. 1560. Edited by Michael R. Best and Frank H. Brightman. Reprint, Oxford, England: Clarendon Press, 1973.

Marshall, Rev. Charles. *An Introduction to the Knowledge and Practice of Gardening*. London, England: Printed for the author by John Rider, 1796.

Mawson, Thomas H. *The Art and Craft of Garden Making*. London, England: B. T. Batsford, 1907.

Maynard, Samuel T. *Landscape Gardening as Applied to Home Decoration*. New York, NY: John Wiley & Sons, 1899.

Meredith, Lewis B. *Rock Gardens*. London, England: Williams & Norgate, 1914.

Miller, Phillip. *The Gardener's Dictionary*. 2 vols. London, England: Printed for the author, 1754.

Miller, Thomas. *Common Wayside Flowers*. London, England: Routledge, Warne, and Routledge, 1860.

Morewood, Samuel. *A Philosophical and Statistical History of the Inventions and Customs of Ancient and Modern Nations in the Manufacture and Use of Inebriating Liquors*. Dublin, Ireland: William Curry, Jr., and Co., and William Carson, 1838.

Morris, Amanda B. *Wildflowers and Where They Grow*. Boston, MA: B. Lothrop, 1882.

Newhall, Charles S. *The Vines of Eastern North America*. New York, NY: G. P. Putnam's Sons, 1897.

Newington, Thomas. *Book of Receipts*. Manuscript. N.p., 1719.

Nott, John. *The Receipt Book of John Nott*. Manuscript, N.p., 1723.

Parkinson, John. *Paradisi in Sole Paradisus Terrestris*. London, England: Humfrey Lownes and Robert Young, 1629.

—. *A Garden of Pleasant Flowers*. New York, NY: Dover Publications, 1976. This is an unabridged republication of the work *Paradisi in Sole Paradisus Terrestris*, originally printed by Humphrey Lownes and Robert Young in 1629.

—. *Theatricum Botanicum*. London, England: Printed by T. Cotes, 1640.

Phillpotts, Eden. *My Garden*. London, England: Country Life, 1906.

Powell, E. P. *The Orchard and Fruit Garden*. New York, NY: Doubleday, Page, 1914.

Quinn, P. T. *Money in the Garden*. New York, NY: Tribune Association, 1871.

Rand, Edward Sprague. *Seventy-Five Popular Flowers and How to Cultivate Them*. Boston, MA: Shepard and Gill, 1872.

—. *The Window Gardener*. Boston, MA: Shepard and Gill, 1873.

Rayne, Mrs. M. L. *What Can a Woman Do*. St. Louis. MO: F. B. Dickerson, 1885.

Receipts of Material Medica. Groveland, NY: N.p., 1842.

Recipe Book. Hancock, MA: N.p., 1859.

Rehman, Elsa. *Garden-Making*. Boston, MA: Houghton Mifflin, 1926.

Rexford, Eben E. *Amateur Gardencraft, A Book for the Home-maker and Garden Lover*. Philadelphia, PA: Lipincott, 1912.

—. *The Making of a Home*. Philadelphia, PA: G. W. Jacobs and Co., 1916.

Ridley, Henry N. *Spices*. London, England: Macmillan, 1912.

Ripley, George, and Charles A. Dana, eds. *The New American Cyclopedia*. New York, NY: D. Appleton, 1858–1863.

Roberts, Harry. *The Book of Old-Fashioned Flowers*. London, England: John Lane, 1904.

Robinson, William. *The English Flower Garden*. First edition, 1883; subsequent editions were revised and updated by the author. Information for *1,001 Old-Time Garden Tips* was from a reprint of the 15th edition, 1933 original. Sagaponack, NY: Sagapress, 1995.

Roe, E. P. *Success with Small Fruits*. N.p., 1881.

Rose, Giles. *A Perfect School of Instructions for the Officers of the Mouth: Shewing the Whole Art of a Master of the Household....* London, England: Printed for R. Bentley and M. Magnes, 1682.

Royal Caledonian Horticulture Society. *Journal of a Horticultural Tour*. Edinburgh, Scotland: N.p., 1832.

Schneider, George. *Choice Ferns for Amateurs*. New York, NY: Charles Scribner's Sons, 1905.

Scott, Frank Jessup. *The Art of Beautifying Suburban Home Grounds*. New York, NY: D. Appleton, 1870.

Sevey, Glenn. *Bean Culture*. New York, NY: Orange Judd, 1914.

Seymour, E. L. D. *Garden Profits*. Garden City, NY: Doubleday, Page, 1911.

Smith, Charles H. J. *Parks and Pleasure Grounds*. Philadelphia, PA: Henry Carey Baird, 1852.

The Successful HouseKeeper, A Manual of Universal Application, Especially Adapted to the Everyday Wants of American Housewives. Harrisburg, PA: Pennsylvania Publishing Co., 1887.

Ten Acres Enough. New York, NY: James Miller, 1864.

Thomas, Rose Fay. *Our Mountain Garden*. New York, NY: Macmillan, 1904.

Thoreau, Henry David. *Journal IX, 1857*. Reprint of 1906 edition. New York, NY: Dover, 1975.

Treueris, Peter. *The Grete Herball*. London, England: P. Treueris, 1526.

Turner, William. *Herbal of William Turner*. Collen, England: Arnold Birckman, 1568.

Underwood, Loring. *A Garden Diary and Country Home Guide*. New York, NY: Frederick A. Stokes, 1908.

Van Rensselaer, Mariana. *Art Out-of-Doors*. New York, NY: Charles Scribner's Sons, 1893.

The Vegetable Garden. A compilation of information from *Farmer's Cyclopedia*. Garden City, NY: Doubleday, Page, 1917.

Vilmorin-Andrieux, Mme. *The Vegetable Garden*. 1885. Reprint. Berkeley, CA: Ten Speed Press, 1981.

Wagner, Abraham. *Specimen Book of Remedies*. Manuscript. Pennsburg, PA: Schwenkfelder Library, 1740.

Walker, Dr. Emma E. *Every Woman's Library*. N.p., 1910.

Waring, William G. *The Fruit Grower's Handbook*. Boalsburg, PA: N.p., 1851.

Warner, Charles Dudley. *My Summer in a Garden*. Boston, MA: James R. Osgood and Co., 1872.

Waterfield, Margaret. *Garden Colour*. New York, NY: E. P. Dutton, 1905.

Weathers, John, ed. *Commercial Gardening*. 4 vols. London, England: Gresham Publishing, 1913.

Weed, Clarence Moores. *Insects and Insecticides*. Hanover, NH: Published by the author, 1891.

Wilder, Louise Beebe. *Colour in My Garden*. New York, NY: Doubleday, Page, 1918.

—. *The Fragrant Path*. New York, NY: Collier Books, 1932.

Williams, Henry T., ed. *Window Gardening*. New York, NY: Henry T. Williams, 1881.

The Woman's Book, Dealing Practically with the Modern Conditions of Home-Life, Self-Support, Education, Opportunities, and Every-Day Problems. 2 vols. New York, NY: Charles Scribner's Sons, 1894.

Wood, John. *Hardy Perennials and Old-Fashioned Garden Flowers*. London, England: L. U. Gill, 1884.

Wright, Walter P. *The Garden Week by Week*. New York, NY: Doubleday, Page, 1909.

Yoxall, J. H. *The Villa for Coelebs*. London, England: Smith, Elder, 1914.

Periodicals

The dates listed for these magazines are not the publication dates. They refer to the issues used as sources for tips in *1,001 Old-Time Garden Tips*.

American Agriculturist. New York, NY: Geo. A. Peters. 1876–1895.

Boston Cultivator. Boston, MA: Otis Brewer. 1855–1872.

Boston Globe. Boston, MA: Globe Pub. Co. 1903.

Cornell Experiment Station, *Bulletin 32*. Ithaca, NY: Cornell University Agricultural Experiment Station. 1891.

Country Gentleman. Albany, NY: Luther Tucker. 1854.

David Landreth Seed Company Catalog. 1914.

Detroit Post and Tribune. Detroit, MI: Post and Tribune Co. 1878.

Farm and Home. Springfield, MA: Phelps Pub. Co. 1889–1899.

Farm Journal. Philadelphia, PA: Farm Journal, Inc. 1905–1906.

Farmers' Cabinet. Philadelphia, PA: Kimber & Sharpless. 1837.

Farmer's Monthly Visitor. Concord, NH: Wm. P. Foster. 1839.

The Gardener's Monthly and Horticultural Advertiser. Philadelphia, PA: Charles H. Marot. 1871–1888.

The Garden Magazine. New York, NY: Doubleday, Page. 1905–1909.

Genesee Farmer. Rochester, NY: B. F. Smith & Co. 1836–1850.

Green's Fruit Grower. Willoughby, OH: Meister Pub. Co. 1902.

The Horticulturist and Journal of Rural Art and Rural Taste. Albany, NY: Luther Tucker. 1847–1852.

The Household. Brattleboro, VT: Geo. E. Crowell. 1878–1893.

Kansas Agricultural Station publication. Manhattan, KS: Kansas Agricultural Experimental Station. 1911.

Lyon-Horticole. Lyon, France: L'Association Horticole Lyonnaise. 1897.

Meehans' Monthly. Philadelphia, PA: Thomas Meehan & Sons. 1884–1902.

Monthly Genesee Farmer. Rochester, NY: Luther Tucker. 1836.

New York World. New York, NY: World. 1878.

Pall Mall Gazette and Globe. London, England: Richard Lambert. 1897.

Park's Floral Magazine. LaPark, PA: Geo. W. Park. 1902.

The Pennsylvania Farm Journal. West Chester, PA: Bowan, Meredith, etc. 1855.

The People's Journal. New York, NY: Scientific American. 1854.

Portland Oregonian. Portland, OR. 1899.

Practical Farmer. Philadelphia, PA: Walker Pub. Co. 1902–1904.

The Progressive Farmer. Philadelphia, PA: James H. Bryson. 1855.

Retail Druggist. Detroit, MI: Hayes Pub. Co. 1902.

Rural Advertiser. Philadelphia, PA: Paschall Morris. 1865.

Shaker and Shakeress Monthly. Mt. Lebanon, NY: United Society. 1878.

Spectator. London, England: Printed for Sam Buckley. 1712.

Transactions of the Horticultural Society of London. London, England: Horticultural Society of London. 1830.

Utica Herald. Utica, NY: Charles Hoyt. 1865.

Vick's Family Magazine. Rochester, NY: Vick Pub. Co. 1902.

Vick's Illustrated Catalogue and Floral Guide. Rochester, NY: The Firm. 1872.

Vick's Illustrated Catalogue and Floral Guide. Rochester, NY: James Vick's Sons. 1884.

Yankee Blade. Waterville, ME: Wm. Mathews. 1889.

The Yankee Farmer. Cornish, ME. 1838.

Index

Note: Page references in **boldface** indicate illustrations.

USDA Plant Hardiness Zone Map

This map was revised in 1990 to reflect changes in climate since the original USDA map, done in 1965. It is now recognized as the best estimator of minimum temperatures available. Look at the map to find your area, then match its pattern to the key on the right. When you've found your pattern, the key will tell you what hardiness zone you live in. Remember that the map is a general guide; your particular conditions may vary.

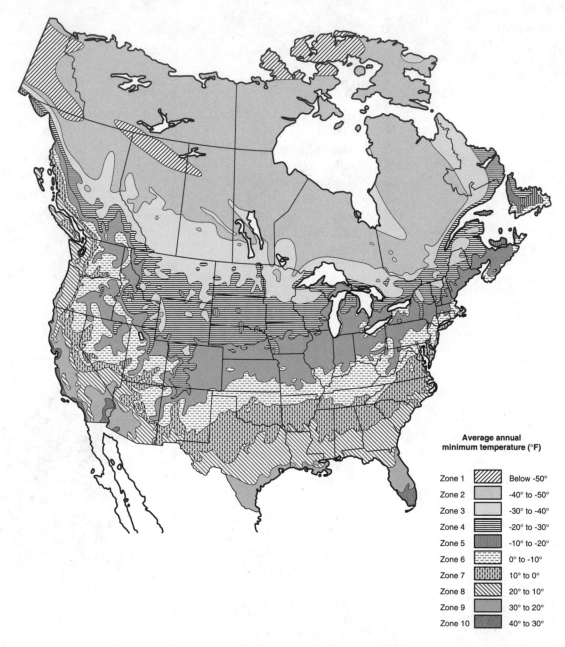

Average annual minimum temperature (°F)

Zone 1		Below -50°
Zone 2		-40° to -50°
Zone 3		-30° to -40°
Zone 4		-20° to -30°
Zone 5		-10° to -20°
Zone 6		0° to -10°
Zone 7		10° to 0°
Zone 8		20° to 10°
Zone 9		30° to 20°
Zone 10		40° to 30°